THE LAW WARS:

CAN MEN CHOOSE THEIR OWN LAWS?

Jim Johnson

dawsonrebel@hotmail.com

© 2023

Cover: pixabay.com

TABLE OF CONTENTS

INTRODUCTION

If you watch old western movies, one theme is repeated over and over: bringing Law and Order to the Wild West. That order was almost always imposed by the use of guns. Often, the town council would vote to restrict certain activities, but that did not bring order. They would then let it be known that a certain town was looking for a 'hired gun' to enforce the laws that a certain class of 'outlaw' refused to obey. This hired gun would shoot a few people and at the end of the movie, everyone is shown shopping and walking about in peace. In American history, Guns and Laws are considered synonymous. Even, as I write, President Biden warned the people who resist the new laws or seek to protest such laws to remember one thing: The President has F-16s and the people protesting the laws do not. In the eyes of the rulers, Wild America has replaced the Wild West. The solution remains the same.

Apparently, laws have no meaning beyond the methods used to enforce those laws. In the West, the town folks required the person hired to have a quicker draw than those resisting the law. In early America, as illustrated in the First Amendment, the people and the government were to be equal in the ownership of 'guns.' It was considered obvious that if one side had a monopoly on guns or who had the superior means to kill people, then that side could produce a totalitarian order: there was nothing anyone could do to resist it. No one can ever vote a tyrant out of office: a law requiring him to leave office is meaningless if he has bigger guns or a monopoly on guns. In fact, as I write, the government is producing killer drones that can seek out any person that it has been instructed to search out and destroy. No gun can counter a killer bot.

The above view is the American historic view about law and order. And yet, at times, law and order appeared to be achieved without the use of guns. There have been short periods in American history when everyone agreed that Western Civilization was the law and people just assumed there was no other option. No one rocks the boat when they have money in their pocket. However, that is the

4

exception in history. Even God's Laws needed some kind of 'gun' to obtain law and order. When God gave the Ten Commandments to His people, the people had weapons and God's prophets did not have any. Many prophets who proclaimed the laws of God found that it was very dangerous to proclaim laws without a weapon. In fact, it was a common occurrence for those who proclaimed the Laws of God to meet their Maker a lot sooner than anticipated. The masses do not like laws, any laws, even if they are said to come from the God of this earthly Order. Just because someone says a law comes from God does not impress everyone—not even a majority.

Now, the prophets warned the people that disobeying God's laws did have its consequences: Hell. For most people, the pleasures of today are certain, but the afterlife is questionable. The general rule of the masses: pleasure now feels good, but there is no pleasure in delayed gratification: especially if you have to wait years or until after you. Anyone seeking to teach obedience to God's laws to the masses will never win an election. Politicians get elected by promising laws that will facilitate the desire of the masses for a life of immediate gratification or for easier means to attain that gratification. If the people of a nation are evil, the politician has to promises evil things to get elected. Democracy can only work when the masses are willing to accept the laws of God over the laws passed by the majority. The rarely happens.

In a democracy, it is amazing the people have any just laws at all. Actually, there is a reason for this. People discover that, just like the small Western town, there are evil people who desire to attain wealth without having to work for it: lawbreakers or those who operate outside the law, outlaws. Evil people know how to manipulate the votes of the gullible masses to obtain or to keep themselves in power. And in modern times, there are no guns for hire to keep an evil government in check. [Evil governments can only be brought down by an act of God. The early Christians did not defeat the Roman Empire, God did. That is why every book about Rome appears to have a different reason for Rome's fall. No one wants to include an act of God in their equation. In reality, God is modern man's 'hired' gun, the only one.] **When God's absolute laws are considered 'unconstitutional', then absolute power will replace absolute laws every time.**

Most people discover that as much as they would like to live without any laws, no one can live in a lawless world, i.e. the law of the jungle, or the Wild West. The same problem occurred in the Old Testament when God handed down His laws. The first thing the people did was look for a god who had fewer laws than the God of Abraham, Isaac, and Jacob. The god Baal immediately came to mind; and he also offered people the promise that they could worship him through a variety of prostitutes available at the local temple. The God of Israel required one mate for life: in sickness and in health, and for better or worse, till death do you part. For the masses, that was one bad law. Satan's gods offer the opportunity to break God's Laws and worship Satan at the same time. What a deal. After all, 'false' gods are merely a matter of opinion. Gods, like men, must compete in a free market and sexual prostitutes certainly are a 'best seller.' Give Baal a try, you'll like his ways.

You see, so-called religious wars are really law wars. What kind of laws do a people want ruling over them, and what kind of ruler do the people want who can promise the right kind of laws. This is the promise of Democracy: the voice of the people is the voice of God. Every man wants to be his own king. This is how the Bible describes such a time:

Judges 21:25. In those days *there was* no king in Israel: every man did *that which was* right in his own eyes.

In this scenario, the lack of a king represented a time when there was no one to proclaim the Laws of God throughout the nation of Israel. There was anarchy in the sense that there was no common civilization in which everyone agreed to submit. A good nation is when everyone obeys the laws of the land because they are the right thing to do. Even those who may not agree with all of the laws obey them out of necessity: breaking the laws has social consequences. The social criminal becomes typecast in a society as someone that cannot be trusted. Such people end up living on the outskirts of civilization—like the old hermits in the deserts or mountains. Actually, a sign of when a civilization is dying is this: most of the laws have to be enforced by some court or police action. And ultimately, criminals are allowed to run free because there are just too many of them. Such is the age in which we live, and I want to discuss the history of laws and how civilizations have operated in the past without security cameras and police in swat gear.

There is also the Communization of Law which discounts all laws as being illegitimate. All laws represent one group, one religion, one class, one race, or one corporate worldview. There are no such things as true laws because there is no truth. Truth is Evolutionary and laws are transitory. Every law represents one power expecting other powers to submit to its rule. For example, Western Civilization is condemned because it was founded by dead White Men; therefore, that Civilizations stands condemned because dead White men have no right to rule over anyone, not even live White men. The bottom line is this: all legitimate laws come from God and in order to escape from God, all laws must be tossed out. If not, God and His followers will sneak His Laws in through some back door. Better to have anarchy than to have just one law taught to man from God: As the mob cried out at the crucifixion of Jesus: We will not have this man rule over us. If there is only one legitimate law—from an absolute source--in the universe, then man stands condemned for not obeying that law. **Men assert a war upon God by declaring war upon the visible aspect of the God they despise-, i.e. His Laws.**

Chapter One: There is no escape from laws. God created man to be a keeper of laws. Ouch!

Don't you know that is against the Law? In an age of lawlessness, what is a law?

I am not a lawyer, or a judge, or a legislator, so why I am writing about Laws. My specialty is Biblical Laws. I have one advantage over the other specialists, Biblical Laws are natural to the created universe. They are absolute. And they are unchanging. Today, laws have become political and have no connection to any true reality. Laws represent Power, not righteousness. God's Laws are fair and just, unlike human laws. So where did God get His laws? He is the Law; they represent His very character and nature. His creation was designed to reflect the 'personality' that created them. No one can separate God from His Laws. When Men abandon God's laws, they are abandoning God. They are also abandoning REALITY.

We all live under Laws as listed below and followed by one example.

Scientific Laws—Gravity and technology

Civilizational Laws—An assumed reality of the universe

Constitutional Laws—Procedural Laws

Government Laws—Traffic Laws

Traditional Laws—Marriage Laws

Common Laws—Who owns property

Corporate Laws—Legal rights of incorporation

Free Market Laws—Money supply

Environmental Laws—Wetland Laws

Ethical Laws—child pornography

Biblical Laws—Salvation

Family Laws—Laws that families apply internally

Tax Laws—filing income tax forms.

And there are many other public guidelines: School Policies, Park regulations, Sporting game rules, and social public behavioral expectations. Laws regulate every aspect of our lives and yet we are told we are free. And yet, because most laws have become so much a part of our lives, we no longer think of them as laws. In this book, I want you to think about laws and how they determine our everyday reality more than you would think. Some refer to man as a tool maker, but it might be more important to think of man as a law keeper. Nations and Civilizations can be known by the laws they enforce. Study all of the laws that are enforced within a given area, and you will know what the masses are taught to be true.

When raising a child, much of that involves teaching the laws of community and national life. An immigrant arriving to a new land is expected to adapt to the laws of the land. Community life is not possible without most of the above law systems operating. Even a person living alone in the woods has to obey a few of the natural laws—you plant your garden in the spring. There is no escaping the fact that men are enclosed by laws just as men are enclosed by the air they breathe. Civil Wars are times when social laws are no longer recognized or obeyed. During the 1960s, the flouting of social laws and governmental laws became ritualized. Without really thinking about it, there are so many more rules that we just ignore: those long banking rules; the rules when you download software—everyone just checks 'I agree'—the internet rules on web sites everyone also checks the same. Ever read your car insurance policy or life insurance policies? I don't think so. Most people just accept those rules as normal and move on as if they were not there.

Not only are there multiple laws and multiple lawmakers in modern cultures, but **the idea that laws should reflect reality has been lost**. Under the control of evolutionary thought, even the laws of reality are evolving and changing as men evolve also. That is why ancient laws, such as in the Bible, represent early evolutionary thought. Modern liberation requires that Men reject early beliefs if men are to keep in touch with Evolutionary progress. Absolute laws cannot exist in a world of change and progress. When laws are separated from God, they are also being separated from the nature of man which was created to image the laws of God's nature. In a sense, to reject God's Laws is to declare war upon the divine nature of Man. Man is left to find another source of divinity in place of the God that had been killed. Men have attempted to divinize themselves, but they lack the power to defend that proclamation. Secular Divinity can only be enforced through Power. The most powerful institution of any society is the God of that social order. That is why, when God died, the modern Nation-State has taken over the status of divine power.

Evolution is, in reality, an obituary for God. Now you understand why Evolution, Material Progress, and the Centralized Nation-State all need each other. That is a major reason why the schools demand that every student be indoctrinated into the theories of Evolution. **If reality is evolving, then no one has any ground upon which they can oppose the expansion of governmental power.** Also, Evolution authorizes an open future. There is nothing that man cannot do. Because Man has lived in a Fallen, i.e. corrupted, condition since the Garden of Eden, there is nothing man will not do. That is why the Reformation did more to destroy Biblical Christianity than any other modern movement. When the Church rejected the Biblical Laws of the Middle Ages, there was nothing to replace them. The Reformation considered the Vatican's insistence on good works as a detriment to salvation by grace alone.

When the emphasis upon good works was eliminated, people now were expected to produce another kind good works replacing the Vatican's laws and expectations. People now owed their allegiance and service to the Nation-State. "I pledge **allegiance** to the Flag...." Or, to refuse to be drafted into the State's military is often considered an act of treason. To oppose the State's drive for empire is to be unpatriotic. A modern Christian is supposed to be an obedient servant to his government. That is why they call the military a 'service'. Someone might ask, 'How long have you been in the service?' No one asks that kind of question of a person joining a Church. The only service there is the Sunday morning Church 'Service.'

You see, as shown above, there is no escape from living under a system of laws, and serving those who make those laws. **The new religion replacing Catholicism was not Protestantism, but Patriotism or Nationalism.** Whoever makes the laws of the land is the controller of that land. Under the Vatican, people served in all kinds of charities and the people created a welfare system better than any State mandated one—before or since. Supposedly, the Reformation was to liberate the people from the Vatican's laws, and from the necessity of performing good works. Luther maintained that Christians were under grace not laws. The reality is this: Biblical Christians are under Grace and Biblical Laws. After Luther, the governing laws of the Bible were replaced by the secular laws of the State. Yes, the King had the divine right to make the laws of the land.

The secularization of law started after and because of the Reformation. When the Reformation revolted against Vatican's Laws and traditions, a previously unified church was transformed into a thousand bickering sects. Not only that, every prince wanted to become a King over all the land and people he could gather together. Not only were Christians liberated from the Vatican's Laws, so were the many and assorted forms of government. Despite the corruption in Rome, the Catholic Church, outside of Rome, provided a unified religious system of laws that all were expected to honor—for fear of excommunication. That especially kept the ruling elites in check as the people were freed from obeying or paying taxes to any leader who had been excommunicated. Even kings were expected to obey the laws of God and the Church.

Individuals were expected to accept the laws of God as representing the ultimate goal of perfection. One of the faults of man is that when he no longer finds perfection in the atoning death of Jesus Christ, he will seek to achieve perfection in other areas of life: the perfect Constitution, the perfect wife, or the perfect form of government. It ain't gonna happen. Americans are chasing after a 'more perfect union', in order to achieve equality and equity in all areas of life.

It ain't gonna happen. When the Order of God is rejection, men seek to attain a New World Order based upon the laws of men, or better yet, the laws of some men. Each Church, after the Reformation, sought to sell to the masses its own form of perfect worship or perfect form of church government. In the same way, the nations of the world have been at war offering their own vision of a better world through their own ideas and laws. The destruction of Christendom and its 1000 year reign of the Catholic World Order, has never come close to achieving heaven upon this earth.

*

After the Reformation, the Catholic universal culture and law system was abolished within the newly formed nations that chose Protestantism to be their national faith. What happened is this: Protestantism was weaponized to aid in the establishment of the new Nation-States. The masses naturally have a loyalty to some form of religion. For the previous thousand years, religion and small nations were under one order under Christendom and the Vatican. Religion and politics were united in each locality. The separation of Church and State was not even considered: A house divided against itself cannot stand, and so with nations. The new power hungry princes after the Reformation understood this principle. In order to attain the consent of the masses, you have to pretend to be a 'Defender of the Faith.' The prince is one with the people in their belief system: support your prince and he will support your faith. This aspect of history is usually totally neglected. This is what made the American Constitution so revolutionary: it was the first attempt to create a totally secular nation—a nation that did not need to support a God as the State was declaring itself to be the new god. George Washington may have been considered the 'Father of his country', but he was not the Defender of the Faith.

After the Reformation, a new religious faith appeared: secularism was created. This appeared to catch the Protestant leaders off guard. "Protestant Christians were unable to withstand the onrush of the new secular humanist conceptions of law, politics and state which emerged in the writings of political thinkers such as Thomas Hobbes and John Locke in England, Johannes Althusius and Hugo Grotius in Holland, and Benjamin Franklin and Thomas Jefferson in the

United States...."[1] These thinkers had one major goal—to build a new social order that was totally cut off from any political or philosophical thinking of that 1000 year period [450-1450 A.D.] based upon Biblical Law. One of the first substitutes for Biblical Law was Natural Law. Taylor cites Paul Hazard in *The European Mind*: "Natural Law was the off-spring of a philosophy which rejected the supernatural and the divine God an immanent Order of Nature."[2] This is the god that Jefferson invoked in the Declaration of Independence, i.e. Nature's God. It is amazing how many think Jefferson was talking about the God of the Bible. He was invoking a pagan deity to bless the efforts of the Revolutionaries. This and other gods and goddesses have been in charge of the United States ever since. The Statue of Liberty depicts a pagan, demonic goddess. The liberty celebrated is the liberty **from** God and His Laws.

The failure of the American Church to recognize and fight these demonic gods has resulted in a church that is only allowed to operate within the legal confines as outlined by Satan's servants. "Lacking a carefully worked-out Reformed doctrine of law, politics and the state, it is hardly surprising that Protestant Christians have been powerless to meet the needs and challenges of modern society and to provide it with Christian answers to all its pressing problems."[3] Rather than openly confront the principalities and powers of the America's Satanic leaders, the church hid inside the little church in the wildwood. When the government took education away from the church, was there a major outcry? Somehow, you can convince people to do anything if you tell them it is 'free.' No one stopped to think where the government obtained that 'free' money to make the school free of charge. In reality, it is a form of theft: the government taxes your neighbor so you do not have to pay to educate your children or take the time to educate them yourself. Larceny has always been popular under America's form of government.

*

---

[1] E. L. Hebden Taylor. Christian Philosophy of Law, Politics and the State. P. 4.
[2] Taylor. P. 4.
[3] Taylor. P. 5.

The post-Reformation era re-introduced ancient paganism into the modern civilization. Taylor cites James Hastings' book *The History of Christinaity1650-1950.* "Modern Western culture, whatever its positive meaning, may be distinguished from that of earlier phases by the emancipation from explicit Christian direction. In their domestic policies ... modern Western states have no longer recognized Christian criteria for policy. Most of them, to be sure, at least in the early modern period, thought of themselves as 'Christian states' and maintained established churches. But the emergence and prevalence of the theory of 'sovereignty' show that in fact the modern state has insisted on its independence of and superiority to Christian direction. The actual criterion has been the military, commercial and general economic welfare of the state. The modern state has generally declined to serve as the 'secular arm' of a Christian society, and the political influence of the Christian has been confined to secondary and indirect manifestations. Modern political thought has found the governing sanctions for political association in the nature of man in general, without benefit of biblical revelation or ecclesiastical authorities."[4]

Christians have generally accepted the political environment as being normal and acceptable for a Bible believer. The State is envisioned as the most powerful entity in any society. There is no power greater than the government, and no ideas or ethical standards can stand in judgment over any actions by the State. Whatever the State declares to be true is true. All modern nation-states exist under the same umbrella of total sovereignty. The Bible must be relegated to a secondary source of information and any contradictions from the public culture must be ignored by the Christian. No Christian in his right mind would ever defend the Biblical view of slavery: that is totally un-American.

Humans are wonderful at adapting to whatever environment in which they happen to find themselves. Even prisoners of war describe how routines of life are invented in which to navigate through the strange situation in which the prisoners find themselves. In time, prison life becomes normalized. That is what happened after the American Revolution. God was written out of American life by the Constitution. In the early 1800s, there were massive attempts to place

---

[4] Taylor. P. 5.

some Christian amendment within the Bill of Rights. Those efforts failed and church people soon accepted the new secular nation as being both real and normal. The ability of men to normalize any situation helps them survive adverse conditions or human tragedies. Men are able to impose some kind of order even in chaotic situations. Our Brains need an acceptable working order: continual chaos is insanity. Evil governments and evil men understand and use this human principle.

One of the understated topics is that mankind hates the Ten Commandments and by killing God man can be liberated from the Laws of God. "The sovereign God of the Scriptures was dethroned and apostate man enthroned upon the vacant seat. It is the will of unbelievers, humanists and apostate Christians henceforth decides political issues. All power and authority on this earth is now proclaimed to proceed from the sovereign will of the state or of the will of the majority or of whoever seizes power."[5] Under the secular State, everyone is expected to become secular. There is no such thing as a Christian policeman, or a Christian bureaucrat. There are administrative rules everyone is expected to conform to and one's beliefs about God should not interfere with a person's chosen vocation. A person is to always obey the laws of the State: right or wrong no longer apply, only legal and illegal.

The very idea of secularism is based upon the theory that there is a neutral no-God zone in which God's Laws do not apply. The reasoning mind is said to be able to solve every problem without any reference to either God or His Laws. In a static culture where everyone lives in the same town from birth until death, it needs the laws of marriage in order to insure a stable community. In an impersonal and mobile society, men are free to choose marriage for a night, or a year or five years. That is what secular freedom means. Biblical marriage laws— no way. No God equals no laws. The corollary of this is this: **when the people are freed from the Laws of God, so is their government.** The masses have given up Biblical Laws in exchange for sexual freedom, but the government is now freed to set up its own lawless regime. **The people get adultery and the government gets total control.**

---

[5] Taylor. P. 6.

There is another aspect with total moral freedom for everyone. The government is also freed from the Constitution. If the people are not accountable to God, neither is the government of the people. Constitutions are supposed to be a law system that is greater than the government. Secular Democracies have been reduced to a mere majority vote on any issue—and a majority can be attained by propaganda, by force, or by fraud. After all, the majority rules regardless of how that majority was attained. Of course, since 2020, America has been under the 'majority by any means' form of government. A Canadian, John Farthing this about Canada in his book *Freedom Wears a Crown*:

"Deny the ideal of [true] democracy and with it goes the sense of loyalty; the sense of constitutional authority enshrining an ideal; the sense of tradition and of history which nourishes respect for such authority. Thus having destroyed our Constitution, we destroy all truth and principle belonging to the fabric of our national life. We are left with nothing to revere but the idol of power based on appeal to mere opinion or will. So long as it is this will or opinion of the great number, it is sacred, no matter what it may be. [Or who creates the greatest number.] Power is freed from respect for authority; opinion from concern for truth; will from principle; and the life of a people in the present from all that comes from the past to inspire and guide it to the future. Propaganda in the service of power leads all opinion to a national worship of the new golden calf: the greatest possible number."[6] [No matter how that number is attained.]

*

There is another aspect of Christians and their beliefs about Laws: they are from God and God holds people accountable for a person's choices. The true primary form of government is self-government. Unless people voluntarily obey the laws of the land, it becomes almost impossible for a nation to preserve any kind of order. It has been stated that if only five per cent of a population become rebels against the laws of a nation, the nation is in danger of disintegration. Even families and other organizations are held together by people voluntarily obeying moral and legal laws. As Americans have been totally liberated from all personal and social responsibility, the nation is running straight into moral anarchy. When

---

[6] Taylor. P. 14.

that happens, the government is unable to gain control. There is just not enough police or troops to restore any kind of order. When Laws become meaningless, life becomes meaningless. The result is always national and personal death. This happened several times in the Old Testament to the nations of Israel and Judah.

William Penn wrote: "Men must choose to be governed by God or they condemn themselves to be ruled by tyrants." In other words, men will either serve God or they will end up serving a man. God's Laws are essential for a working civilization. In fact, to ignore God's Laws is very dangerous. This has been shown throughout history, and yet men keep repeating the same suicidal acts over and over. This is probably the best illustration of Satanic power to deceive Mankind, and destroy that which is good. Men keep hoping that men can make better laws than God's laws. That is the promise of Democracy that a 'million' men are wiser than God, i.e. the herd mentality. This is the ultimate act of faith that a million sinners can discover wisdom and ethical standards. This belief in the power of the crowd is seen in TV game shows where the audience often knows the correct answer to a quiz show question. However, those quiz shows questions are only about factual data, not about ethical and moral issues. If you asked an audience if abortion is the right choice for an unexpected pregnancy, the answer would reflect the values of the audience, not the values of God. The group mind can be very dangerous when it is allowed to be manipulated by Satan and his followers for political gain. A new law that comes recommended by Satan's followers is 'probably' not in the best interests of a person or a nation.

*

God created the earth according to His own nature: true laws describe God. Because His nature is unchangeable, the universe operates according to the character of God: we call them physical laws. The word *law* and derivatives of that word are found 593 times in the Bible. When men pass laws, they are expected to build upon the already revealed laws of God. No man can pass original laws without violating the laws of creation. The ancient nation of Israel was the first nation in history to be built upon the laws of God. Other nations had law systems based upon lawful practices to preserve the social order under the

17

ruler: the Code of Hammurabi or the laws of Ur-Namma. The United States developed its own law code based upon Evolution. Just as plants and animals have evolved, so laws must evolve to meet the needs of each age. Laws are not absolute which also means words are not absolute. When the Constitution states that "...the right of the people to keep and bear Arms, shall not be infringed", it only applies to the time in which it was written. Ancient men cannot tell modern man what is best for the nation—'shall not be infringed' must evolve to the dictates of each generation of lawmakers. Evolutionary laws will always produce tyranny: yesterday's promise does not apply for today. To allow yesterday to determine today will negate all forms of evolutionary progress: social, political, and scientific.

This is what separates Biblical Law from all other law systems. The Ten Commandments cannot be abridged, or altered to fit the needs of the people. Satan introduced his view of God's Laws to Eve in the Garden:

Genesis 3:1.   Now the serpent was more subtil than any beast of the field which the LORD God had made. And he said unto the woman, Yea, hath God said, Ye shall not eat of every tree of the garden? **2** And the woman said unto the serpent, We may eat of the fruit of the trees of the garden: **3** But of the fruit of the tree which *is* in the midst of the garden [The tree of the knowledge of good and evil], God hath said, Ye shall not eat of it, neither shall ye touch it, lest ye die. **4** And the serpent said unto the woman, **Ye shall not surely die**: **5** For God doth know that in the day ye eat thereof, then your eyes shall be opened, and ye shall be as gods, knowing good and evil.

Satan introduced the idea that God's Laws are merely His way of controlling the people. As said today: God does not want people to have any fun. Therefore, His Laws need to be revised from time to times to allow the people to decide for themselves what is good and what is evil. Democracy is just an amplification of Satan's lie in the Garden. Satan tells modern man that God's Laws deny him the freedom to make his own laws. God wants men to be kept in bondage to His Kingdom and deny man the right to form his own ideas of right and wrong. God keeps man enclosed in a limited world, but through technology, man can create his own heaven here on earth without having to submit to God's moral reign of terror upon mankind.

The American Church also developed its own ideas about God's Laws. The Church adopted two heresies to accommodate the Bible to American culture: Free Will, and Antinomianism. Under free will, men make their own choices whether to serve God or themselves, i.e. serve Satan. This resulted in the church adopting the fire-and-brimstone revival service. The goal of the evangelist is to market God's message as a salesman for God. The message relates how God can be captured and used to fulfill one's American Dream: God is just waiting to bless you if you will but raise your hand 'while all heads are bowed and all eyes closed.' In fact, in order to get more people to raise their hands, the Gospel is placed on sale 'for this night only.' All a person has to do is raise their hand, say a simple prayer, and then attend one hour of church each week. That guarantees, for those who agree to the terms, a place reserved for them in heaven. You can't get a deal like that in any other church. So hurry, before this offer expires!

The other doctrine of antinomianism means that when Jesus died for your sins, he fulfilled the law for you. The Christian now lives under grace and not under law: he is dead to the law. Antinomianism is the doctrine of Democracy, or Christian Democracy as the Church would like to believe. Having been freed from the laws of the Old Testament, men are now free to create laws for the age of Finance Capitalism, and the Industrial Revolution. The new age of prosperity was built upon the negation of Biblical Laws. It was built upon the degrading of the family and its clan. Industry needed solitary individuals who would put their jobs above any family relationships. And in time, industry and government wanted women to join the workforce. Women were considered better at performing repetitive jobs. In my home town there is a business that provided pre-cracked eggs for restaurants. Two women were hired to crack eggs all day long. When they got good at it, they could take two eggs in each hand, crack them into a container and then repeat that process for eight hours, five days a week. Also, Governments wanted women in the workforce because the labor of a housewife was not taxable. But the labor in the factory provides taxable income for the government. No church dare oppose the new order of financial prosperity for fear of being ostracized by those who have enough money to support the church. Single-income families may not have enough money to truly support their church.

If you want to know why the American Church has never suffered official persecution this is why: it has always taught doctrines that would support he prevailing and popular culture. The theological excuse for neglecting the teaching of God's Law was based upon the books of Galatians and Romans where the Christian is said to be 'dead to the law.' "[This] has reference to the believer in relationship to the atoning work of Christ as the believer's representative and substitute; the believer is dead to the law as an indictment, a legal sentence of death against him, Christ having died for him, but the believer is alive to the law as the righteousness of God. … Man is restored to a position of law keeping."[7] Christians are freed from the law of death so that they might perform good works according to the laws of God.

James 2:1. My brethren, have not the faith of our Lord Jesus Christ, *the Lord* of glory, with respect of persons. **2** For if there come unto your assembly a man with a gold ring, in goodly apparel, and there come in also a poor man in vile raiment; **3** And ye have respect to him that weareth the gay clothing, and say unto him, Sit thou here in a good place; and say to the poor, Stand thou there, or sit here under my footstool: **4** Are ye not then partial in yourselves, and are become judges of evil thoughts? **5** Hearken, my beloved brethren, Hath not God chosen the poor of this world rich in faith, and heirs of the kingdom which he hath promised to them that love him? **6** But ye have despised the poor. Do not rich men oppress you, and draw you before the judgment seats? **7** Do not they blaspheme that worthy name by the which ye are called? **8** If ye **fulfil the** royal law **according to the scripture**, Thou shalt love thy neighbour as thyself, ye do well: **9** But if ye have respect to persons, ye commit sin, and are convinced of the law as transgressors. **10** For whosoever shall keep **the whole law,** and yet offend in one *point*, he is guilty of all. **11** For he that said, Do not commit adultery, said also, Do not kill. Now if thou commit no adultery, yet if thou kill, thou art **become a transgressor of the law. 12** So speak ye, and so do, as they that shall be judged by **the law of liberty. 13** For he shall have judgment without mercy, that hath shewed no mercy; and mercy rejoiceth against judgment. **14** What *doth it* profit, my brethren, though a man

---

[7] Rousas John Rushdoony. The Institutes of Biblical Law. The Craig Press. 1973. P. 3.

say he hath faith, and have not works? can faith save him? **15** If a brother or sister be naked, and destitute of daily food, **16** And one of you say unto them, Depart in peace, be *ye* warmed and filled; notwithstanding ye give them not those things which are needful to the body; what *doth it* profit? **17** Even so faith, if it hath not works, is dead, being alone. **18** Yea, a man may say, Thou hast faith, and I have works: shew me thy faith without thy works, and I will shew thee my faith by my works. **19** Thou believest that there is one God; thou doest well: the devils also believe, and tremble. **20** But wilt thou know, O vain man, that faith without works is dead?

The Christian while redeemed from the condemnation of the Law, is to exhibit his salvation from the law by keeping the law. The laws of God do not change and they remain the same both before and after conversion. The big difference is the Christian in his liberty is now free to fulfill the laws of God. Before the Law brought condemnation; now the law provides guidance for the Christian life. For the Christian, the Law provides the bullseye for which he is to aim.

I John 2:1. My little children, these things write I unto you, that ye sin not. **And if any man sin**, we have an advocate with the Father, Jesus Christ the righteous: **2** And he is the propitiation for our sins: and not for ours only, but also for *the sins of* the whole world.

As the Christian aims to follow the law, he will fail at times, but the relationship with God is not harmed. The non-Christian does not have a lawful target, and the law for him brings only condemnation. For the non-Christian, because he is not perfect, the Law condemns him. To break one part of the law makes him into a lawbreaker. While those who aim to keep the law through Christ and fail, they have a relationship that covers that failure. The non-Christian has no relationship to allow him to pick himself up and move on to try again. I am not talking about major crimes, but the sins that are the result of immaturity. Nevertheless, the law remains in place for the Christian as a guide and a goal, not as an instrument of condemnation. The Christian has the freedom to fail which the non-Christian does not have. The Christian has a God-given standard which the non-Christian does not have. The Christian also can look forward to a time when he will be perfect, which the non-Christian does not have.

*

During times of social unrest, every politician runs on the platform of restoring law and order. Generally, this means more government laws and more police-enforced order. However, that is not how the words have traditionally been interpreted. An ORDER is a Civilization which is the overall world view which most people believe, within a common location and time, agree is REALITY. During the Middle Ages, Christendom was assumed to be the true order for all those that lived under that umbrella of truth. Civilizations do not need laws in order to maintain their truths no more than a government can pass a law negating gravity. Christendom was the real world and no one thought any differently—except those pagans in other nations and those Muslims who sought to control the world through violence. No one has to pass laws to produce a civilization as civilizations are formed at the grass roots level, not by edict.

The role of government and its laws is to maintain public peace within the people's view of reality. Protecting the social order from criminals both foreign and domestic. That is the Biblical view of government and laws. Those laws protect the masses so that they can be free to work out their personal lives under the overall umbrella of the accepted civilization, i.e. order. What happened in 1776 is that the United States Constitution attempted to set up a rival ORDER to the traditional one of Western/English Civilization. Yes, if you read British history, you know that Western Civilization arose out people reading and believing the King James Bible and using that to confront the 'King's Civilization.' English history is filled with violent conflicts between the King's 'Church' and the people's grass roots church. Charles II and Queen Mary are famous for their persecution of Protestants/Puritans, and Henry VIII is famous for his war on Catholics and their charitable institutions. And yet, out of those conflicts Western Civilization was born.

I want to elaborate a bit to help you understand how modern Western Civilization came to be accepted by so many. Western Civilization was not developed by the King's Anglican Church that supported the government, but it was a civilization based upon how people behaved and what kind of world they wanted in which to live and raise their children. Eventually, laws were passed to

22

protect that civilization from those who would want to destroy the traditions of the people in favor of their own ideas about the real world. In the United States, before the Revolution, there were local traditions that differed from other localities, but most accepted the King James Bible as the real and accepted world order.

For the common folk, that Bible provided a common language and shared moral expectations which provided an environment of community trust. Even 'bad' people knew that in order to be accepted in any community, they had to abide by the laws of civilization—at least in public and in business. Even politicians had to appear to be honest: that is why Abraham Lincoln gave himself the handle of 'Honest Abe.' Being a highly successful big time lawyer did not endear him to the public, so he just made up the title and the press accepted it at face value. As one person noted, he was honest in the same way people call obese people, 'slim' or 'tiny'. When people no longer feel an obligations to abide by the principles of civilization, you know that civilization is on its way out. Even the genocidal killer, Dwight D. Eisenhower, had to pretend to be a 'Christian' and the wildly immoral John F. Kennedy had to pretend to be something he was not: Western Civilization demands that. And the very evil Lyndon Johnson used to invoke God in his speeches.

*

Up until the 1776, there were four major cities that propagated historical civilizations: Jerusalem, Athens, Rome, and London. Each developed different philosophies of government and the nature of a successful culture. Every culture must be founded upon an order that everyone accepts as being natural to some reality or given to man from a god. As I write, through corruption, the social order is breaking down. Men can burn down cities and be pardoned. This dissolves man's trust in justice and the belief that the government can be a neutral peacekeeper. Russell Kirk cites one's man's story as an example of the absolute need for a social order above all else:

"When the Bolsheviks seized power in St. Petersburg, he fled to Odessa, on the Black Sea, where he found a great city in anarchy. Bands of young men commandeered street cars and clattered wildly through the heart of Odessa, firing with rifles at any pedestrian, as though they were hunting pigeons. At any moment, one's apartment might be invaded by a casual criminal or fanatic, murdering for the sake of a loaf of bread. In this anarchy, justice and freedom were only words. 'Then I learned that before we can know justice and freedom, we must have order,' my friend said. 'Much though I hated the Communists, I saw then that even the grim order of Communism is better than no order at all. Many might survive under Communism, no one could survive in general disorder.'"[8] When people speak of Law and Order, you now know that without order, there can be no laws. Of course, there are only two different kinds of order: one imposed by God and His Word, and one imposed by Satan and his servants. That is why the Bible is more than a book about salvation, it provides the foundation upon which a social order can be built. **Also, Satan's servants know that by creating social and political unrest, Satan's order can be greeted with open arms—even Satan's order is better than no order at all.**

The above story about order has been the secret of the American secular order. Whether Christian or atheist, everyone accepted the American Way of Life as suitable for everyone. The Christian and the atheist could each pursue their private goals within in an order that allowed for both to prosper. Good men and evil men both found an environment where they could express their personal desires. In a sense, the Church accepted a culture in which it could privatize the Gospel message. The message was for inside the church and personal evangelism. However, the Church did not believe that Biblical rule of law should or even could stand in judgment over an inclusive society where everyone just wanted to pursue the same material dreams. After the Revolution, the American legal culture had separated itself from Western [English] Civilization and its tradition of Common Law, i.e. laws of tradition. Americans were free to start with a blank sheet and write laws that had no historical traditions. America was to establish laws that everyone could feel comfortable obeying as citizens of the nation: laws designed to protect personal peace and personal prosperity. [As I write, personal peace now means personal moral and sexual satisfaction in whatever way turns you on.]

---

[8] Russell Kirk. The Roots of American Order. 1974. P. 7.

*

Under Western Civilization, the general culture was based upon the King James Bible and its application to the problems of society. Most people felt comfortable with a nation publically honoring the Ten Commandments. Sinners were content to keep their lifestyles private. Behaving as a 'Christian' in public did not seem hypocritical, it was just the way life was. Similar to today where Christians keep their Biblical lifestyle private. After all, everybody has a private life but there was no need to live in a glass house. Public confessions were not necessary. In America, the common faith was not the Bible or Christian traditions. It was the American way of life. The United States actually developed a new religion to replace Christianity, and new laws that reflected that change. Russell Kirk wrote:

"All the aspects of any civilization arise out of a people's religion: its politics, its economics, its arts, its science, even its simple crafts are the by-products of religious insights and a religious cult. For until human beings are tied together by some common faith, and share certain moral principles, they prey upon one another. In the common worship of the cult, a community forms. At the heart of every culture is a body of ethics, of distinctions between good and evil; and in the beginning, at least, those distinctions are founded upon the authority of revealed religion. Not until a people have come to share religious beliefs are they able to work together satisfactorily, or even to make sense of the world in which they find themselves. Thus all order—even the ideological order of modern totalist states, professing atheism—could not have come into existence, had it not grown out of general belief in truths that are perceived by the moral imagination."[9] Without a common faith, nations die. America no longer has a common faith: it is every man to his own desires.

The American nation was founded by religious refugees from Europe. They brought with them their King James Bible and a devotion to the laws of God as being applicable to the whole of society. However, such beliefs were not accepted by those who followed in their footsteps. They saw America as a land of opportunity, not a place to build religious character. Obviously, there were two

---

[9] Kirk. P. 14.

basic Americas, depending one's worldview. When the American Revolution was fought only one third favored the War. One third wanted to remain loyal to England, and one third just wanted to ignore the whole affair. People clearing land and establishing new businesses had no time for such nonsense. The people of the United States before the war were not very united at all.

When it came to establishing a 'national' government, some form of unity had to be discovered which would unite the masses around the new nation. One of the purposes of the Declaration of Independence was to proclaim a new national faith which, it was hoped, everyone could unite around. Thomas Paine's great books sought to present to the general public what America's new religion should be. The age of reason allowed men to unite around their belief in the power of mankind to rule themselves. This belief would bring everyone together to serve their own personal, rational interests. He wrote *The Age of Reason, Common Sense,* and *The Laws of Man* which helped to create a common faith, a new religion for the new nation. The political trends of that time were Democracy, and the Enlightenment. Christianity was considered either too British or too ancient. Whatever, the new nation would not be built upon a Biblical culture, but upon the new rights of man and the laws that man's reasoning power could create. America would pursue the common sense teachings of Benjamin Franklin as something everyone found reasonable. He published a series of homilies which promoted the ideas of honesty, hard work, and personal success. Those homilies could be accepted by everyone. The ultimate goal of his homilies was the building of a personal character that would lead a person to success and prosperity. Franklin's faith in 'do what works for you' represented the true Bible for everyone. The King James Bible was replace by Franklin's *Poor Richard's Almanac.*

Chapter Two: When God's Laws are no longer recognized, Men end up debating what Laws are.

Laws are essential to every social order. That is why, the first thing God did when he formed the Nation of Israel, he revealed the Ten Commandments. Under Egyptian rule with the Pharaoh, he ruled by edict or an early form of Executive Order. Laws are considered separate from edicts in that laws are expected to be published, and to be enforced fairly. Laws apply to everyone the same: there are no special laws for different classes. You could say that a nation can be judged by whether it rules by Laws or by Edicts. Edicts reflect the personality of the ruler. Biblical Laws are based upon the personality and character of God. For those nations that reject such a definition of Law, then what is left? In 21st century United States, people have been debating what the laws of marriage should be. Not only that, but what constitutes a male or female. Today, Laws are viewed by many as merely the personal choices of the most powerful and dominant group in that society. And they must change with the times and the needs of the people.

Biblical Laws are based upon what could easily be called REALITY. Most rarely think about what that means. In the 1960s youth rebellion, reality was believed to be the right to 'do your own thing.' Everybody had some kind of 'King for a Day' vision of how they could make the world a better. I loved college dorm debates—bull sessions—where after taking a class or two in political science or economics, we became world-class experts. There is a reason, in times past, teenage kings could be dangerous for the same reason it would have been disastrous for my dorm mates to be put in charge of any government. We all knew what needed to be done and we saw no problem forcing the lower cast rabble to submit to our 'wisdom.' We had no conception of Law, but only of some utopian goal. And we believed that goal needed to be forced upon everyone because the hoi polloi did not know what was in their own best interest.

The above dorm-room scenario is actually closer to the American way of government than most would like to admit. Americans basically landed on a blank continent with no established government, laws, or boundaries. The early settlers knew that laws were needed; otherwise, the law of might makes right would prevail. As a result, many brought with them to America *Blackstone's Commentaries on the Laws of England.* After all, at that time, America was a

British colony, or actually, multiple colonies and business ventures. The British East India Company played a big part in establishing the business aspect of settling the continent—along with the Dutch East India Company. These companies actually operated as corporate nations. These corporations had their own armies and their own navies beside the usual cargo ships. As today, private corporations had their own system of laws which they brought with them in their travels and which they had the power to enforce their laws: they had their own battleships. This is important because 'Corporate Law' became a big part of America from the very beginning. [This aspect of law is rarely mentioned in any textbooks. Maybe for good reason as Corporate Law still plays a large part in the United States.]

For the most part, American Corporations today have ruled through lobbyists. In the 19th century, bribes were given openly and liberally to those who controlled the powers of government. Today, bribes still rule, but are no longer given openly. Also, bribes have been transferred to campaign donations, book deals, speaking engagements, insider information, favors to friends, and well-paying jobs for family members. Therefore, Laws in America are often the result of corporate influence. While the British East India Company no longer exists under that name, America is still a Corporate State. America's national flag, the stars and stripes, was borrowed from the British East India Company. The use of their flag signaled to the world that America was aligned with the interests of the global commercial powers. This has contributed to America's dual system of laws in the land: one for the masses and one for the elites. America was founded, despite the rhetoric, to aid the international business interests. That is why, from the very beginning, America wanted to form a world-wide commercial and banking empire. Of course, the masses were never told this. Nationalism and Patriotism are merely catch phrases to hide reality from the people.

The Constitution did not incorporate any legal philosophy into its document: it merely detailed the procedures for the making of laws. Many Christians felt betrayed because this opened the door to non-Christian Laws, or, in reality, the nature of laws could be sold to the highest bidder, or the group that was able to capture government through propaganda. If the mob can vote, those who control the mob control the laws of the land. So who has the power to control the America mobs? Obviously, the door was opened for powerful lobbies or corporate money to be the true law makers of the land. This is why the United States has actually been a dysfunctional government on the national level. If it were not for the power of local governments, America might have dissolved into multiple states long before the coming if a second Civil War in the 2020s.

Ancient laws were largely practical laws: laws of inheritance, the ownership of property and other laws that keep a city from dissolving into civil war. In the United States, laws also were practical with the additional need for self-defense. Early on, it was discovered communal laws did not work. People would not work for the good for the group, or for the good of the lazy or immoral. Laws of ownership and forms of money were needed. In other words, the needs of the moment dictated the types of laws that were needed. With the Declaration of Independence a new form of laws were introduced adopted from the Enlightenment thinkers: governments were to work for the happiness of the general community. Talk about a blank check. The singer Ted Lewis adopted the catch phrase: "Is everybody Happy?" as part of his act in the 1920s. That phrase represents the American philosophy from Thomas Jefferson up until 9/11.

Laws that guaranteed the continuation of happiness became essential to every political campaign. Rights and freedoms were just two of the elements in America's constant pursuit of happiness. This phrase from the Declaration totally subverted traditional ideas of culture, laws, and government. It also opened the door to making the government everyone's source of happiness. The masses, if they found themselves in a state of unhappiness, then it was the role of the government to change circumstances to make everybody happy. Once happiness was accepted as the goal of government, America slowly became a welfare state. Actually, the first acts of welfare were for corporations that were established to supply products for the Union troops. While the soldiers died by the hundreds of thousands, the corporations were making the real killing. The War established these War industries as essential to the American Way of Life. It was their role to provide happiness for the American masses. The government established business welfare to keep the business owners happy. Is every stockholder happy?

The welfare laws for business worked great until 1929. The American businesses, even with subsidies, failed to keep the American public happy. The government business partnership was perceived to be at fault. I regard the Civil War as the first American Revolution. The Depression of 1929 launched the second American Revolution. [The American Revolution of 1776 was actually a true Civil War as only one third of the people supported the Revolution and the new form of government was imposed upon the people by the winners of that war. The winners were labelled Founders, but they really were subversives. They were populists only their own ideas about themselves.] The Civil War, so called, was fought to divert attention away from its true nature, the establishment of totally centralization form of government. This centralized power was used to launch the United States into the pursuit of a global empire. Empires are good for business: why own a small general store when you can own a giant corporation with global markets protected by the American Navy and Army.

The Second American Revolution occurred to keep the people from overthrowing the government and establishing a government that served American traditional values—which did not include massive corporations. Something had to be done to avoid a true Revolution of the people. Basically, new laws were passed which allowed the people of the land to share in the wealth of the nation through a variety of bribes. Social Security and a whole list of personal subsidies became part of American life from the 1930s until today. The list of assorted transfer of payments has increased greatly with every election. The United States became a nation hooked upon the drug of 'free money.' No one ever stopped to ask, what is 'free money' and how is it created? All people know is that if government passes a spending bill, then it spends that amount of money. It is magic; just like the alchemists who sought to turn lead into gold through chemistry. Now governments could turn paper into gold with a printing press. Whenever the government needs more money, it just passes a spending law and then it spends that money. Much better than turning water into wine. The State really has the power of a god.

When people think of government and laws, it brings to mind modern spending laws and modern welfare laws. Modern man has come a long ways from the Laws of God in the Old Testament. God's Laws reflect the real world; Modern Laws reflect a fantasy or magical world. The laws of economics do not apply in the magical world of government spending and subsidies. Under the old laws the income had to match the outgo. If the government needed more money, it had to either raise taxes or conquer a nation that possessed some form of wealth. Raising taxes is never popular as it gives the people the idea that they have to pay for their own free money. Taxing corporations is one way to raise money invisibly—which the corporations then just pass onto the public with higher prices. That way the inflation can be blamed on the 'rich' corporations and not the government. Printing money is another way to raise money, but that leads to inflation. Of course, inflation can be blamed again on business owners and not the government's printing of worthless money. In reality, the best way to raise more money is through various forms of colonialism and the plundering of other nation's wealth. The final method is sold to the populace as a patriotic war against some slight by a foreign nation. Generally, wars are popular if sold to the public as the righting of some wrong. Again, illegitimate Laws are used to declare wars which further diminishes the nature of true laws which are designed to create a sound social order. Wars are actually designed to export America's financial debts to another nation, i.e. to spread democracy to the entire world. Huh? Laws do not have to make sense as long as they make money.

*

More and more, Laws are seen as a way to manipulate reality. Modern laws are, in fact, a war upon God and the Laws He imbedded within his creation. Laws have been weaponized in the war against God's reality. Because, on the surface, imaginary laws can appear to win the war against God's restrictions, they appear to be real laws. The Federal Reserve has been printing magical money for over a hundred years and it is only now becoming worthless. Because God's judgment is not immediate, people think they have either fooled God or defeated Him. A false heaven appears to have eliminated hell in man's perceptions of reality: Man's laws can be used to defeat God's Laws. Maybe Satan was right in the Garden of Eden: Satan's Laws are more powerful than God's Laws. The cosmic situation is actually a battle between two different ideas about laws. Laws are that important. A person's or nation's Laws cannot be separated from their god. If you want to know what a people worship, just check their laws.

Chapter Three: Law as a means of solution change.

The very idea of any law is to obtain obedience. If there are penalties involved in any law, people will obey most laws just to avoid the consequences. There are two forms of laws to produce cultural change: carrot and stick, or hammer and stick. Modern laws have become weaponized to achieve an anti-Christian agenda. Laws and force are one and the same. Every tyrant rules through laws, or edicts disguised as laws. Many talk a lot about 'brainwashing.' The hope is that the masses can be controlled through the manipulation of human perceptions. While brainwashing tends to work from behind the curtain, there is also something called 'Law-washing.' As I write in 2023, America has become a nation of social change through the hammer of 'justice.' More and more rights are being discovered or being invented which 'require' legal protection.

In the aftermath of 9/11, America has destroyed the very idea of self-government. America was founded by religious leaders who believed the primary form of government was the family and a civilization that expected people to behave in a 'civilized' way. Those days of control by culture or control by religion, or control by traditions have been replaced. The American people are now ruled by the Total Information Awareness about every person, and laws of control enforced by Total Surveillance. There used to be saying that a man's home is his castle. A man's home was off limits to government officials unless a very specific search warrant was issued by a judge who respected a man's right to privacy. A man was also promised in the Bill of Rights to be secure in his papers and the right not to not cooperate with hostile government officials. The income tax laws ended all that. A taxing agency cannot convict any person of breaking some tax law without first confiscating a man's private papers. Of course, that was the real purpose of the income tax laws—laws of personal confession before the government.

The problem with a centralized government is that its power over people becomes unlimited. Such a form of government attracts criminal and social psychopaths. Such people love to force people to do what they are told. If you have seen them in operation you understand that they love to pass laws that destroy people's lives. These people are demonic and carry out the agenda of

Satan and his fallen angels. How can they do this? Easy: they get together with other psychopaths and pass laws of control. I believe the decline of any nation can be gauged by the number of laws it passes. Nations that become Empires are operated as an army of bureaucrats. These armies are run by psychopathic generals, and they do not serve the people. The far reaching nature of any imperial rule requires a system of laws (Oppression) that can hold the empire together. Also, those merely happy with their home and family must be enlisted to serve the goals of the Empire also, i.e. either through force or propaganda. Psychopaths love controls and an Empire gives them the power to control the world. That is why the power that is needed to completely control a nation attracts the demons (criminal psychopaths) that want to control the world. And it all starts when the people become addicted to the 'free' money of a powerful state. Updating Patrick Henry: Give me free money or give me death.

Empires cannot be controlled by the military alone. However, Empires must be run as a military operation. Everyone within a nation must be enlisted in the pursuit of the Empire's goals. There are several ways this is accomplished: the tax base must be expanded, and the people must be persuaded that the sacrifices required by the empire are needed to protect the nation. Of course, taxes are never voluntary: governments do not raise money through telethons. Even tax laws can designed to encourage or discourage certain types of behavior. A government can tax those things it wants to restrict and not tax those things it wants to encourage. The same principle applies to 'anti-taxes', i.e. subsidies. When the government started subsidizing unwed mothers, the number of such children increased. The government taxed Biblical families to support non-Biblical families. Biblical families produce people who are strong and will resist the efforts of any government to impose taxes and restrictions upon the people. Better to have a nation of people dependent upon the government, i.e. those accepting government bribes, welfare.

Empires also need diversionary laws: laws that hide the true nature of the government's expanding powers. The Empire develops issues to disguise its grab for power and more power. A strong Empire is necessary to tackle global problems: Global warming; Climate change; illegal drugs; immigration issues; free trade issues; monetary problems; border issues; wars and rumor of wars; minority rights; and inflationary pressures. If the people do not submit to the laws of the Empire, the world will self-destruct—that is the lie. Of course, to deal with all these issues requires new laws and lots of them. There again, most laws benefit one class over another. Corporations are subsidized to work with the government to 'tackle' these global issues. To oppose these issues means one is opposing one's own government and placing oneself in opposition to those who wish to 'save' the world. A modern form of treason, i.e. an enemy of the people.

Understand, the masses never like paying taxes, especially if it is to support an Empire. No one likes the laws that are 'necessary' to support the actions of that Empire. In order to maintain control over any opposition that might oppose the laws of modern colonialism, the laws must be tied to 'legitimate' causes. Anyone opposing these laws is a traitor to the nation and all future generations. More laws are passed to control the opposition to any government action or some proclaimed agenda. Whatever cause is being promoted does not matter. Laws are merely an excuse to consolidate power and to keep the masses in their place: slaves to the global state and its order. As I write the government is proposing an internet security act. It sounds great, but it involves the power to delete anything from the internet contrary to government policies, and to punish anyone deemed by the government to have said or posted anything deemed objectionable. Basically a blank check to imprison, fine, or punish anyone in the United States. That is, anyone a threat to the American Empire State.

What is amazing about laws is that most people in a civilization readily obey the laws of the land, even bad laws. When people live under the umbrella of a civilization, it is very difficult for them to become lawbreakers. Normally, most people fear the unknown. Accepting a little chaos today from the government is better than learning to live under anarchy tomorrow. Tyrants rely upon this tendency in humans to accept restrictive laws: bad laws are better than no laws. Every nation has its criminal element, but most are able to find some satisfaction in their private lives. As long as most are able to establish some safe haven, they will tolerate a government that oversteps its bounds of a true law-abiding government. Any government that even pretends to be a good government will satisfy the masses. We were all created by God to affirm the laws of the land. One of the first acts in the Garden of Eden was for God to teach them the laws of the Garden. Men were created by God to be keepers of the Law. Evil men understand how to use this tendency to create a submissive population.

Chapter Four: Laws exclusively belong to God.

The neglected aspect of laws is one that is rarely mentioned. All laws have a religious aspect: they define reality. God created the Laws of reality. Those who oppose God attempt to create laws that define their idea of reality. Anyone who attempts to create laws is, in reality, claiming the powers of a god. That is why Democracy claims that the voice of the people is the voice of a god. In modern times, the executive order claims to have the power to make its own laws: the pen of the President is now the voice of a god. That is why Evolution and other scientific myths are so vital to the modern state. Whether it is in medicine, astronomy, geology, anthropology, psychology, sociology, history, and others, they all agree upon modern worldviews that do not need God or His Revelation in order to describe the laws of their field of study. In fact, if Biblical Laws are true, the foundations of the above studies would be undermined.

To be a successful nation, its law system and its god must be in agreement. In the past, a nation had a State Church to support the State Laws system. "...in any culture *the source of law is the god of that system.* If law has its source in man's reason, the reason is the god of that society. ... Modern humanism, the religion of the state, locates law in the state, or the people as they find expression in the state, the god of the system."[10] This is why the Declaration of Independence, and the United States Constitution were so revolutionary. A new law system was announced that had nothing to do with the founding system of the early immigrants. "... in any society, any change of law is an explicit or implicit change of religion. ... When the legal foundations shift from Biblical Law to humanism, it means that the society now draws its vitality and power from humanism, not from Christian theism."[11]

Every nation must have some form of religion which acts to support the laws of that nation. If a dictator rules over a nation by edict and commands, then he is, in fact, the god of that order. That is why, in ancient times, most rulers were considered divine or were connected to some divine power. All laws need divine sanction unless they are backed by brute force. That is why, as America becomes a godless nation, it is increasing relying upon brute force to make a legal

---

[10] Rushdoony. P. 5.
[11] Rushdoony. P. 5.

order. The Social Credit System is being designed as a system of brute force: Total Information Awareness combined with Total Surveillance. Every place you go and every thing you say on your phone or purchase anywhere is recorded and becomes part of your personal profile. This includes your medical records. No longer does any law have to be just or justified by some authority. Law is now strictly power. However, where does law come from? Where does power come from? There are only two sources of power and two sources of law upon the earth: God or Satan. That is why, those in charge of America in the 2020s are connected to demonic powers and demonic ceremonies. This is not by accident. Evil people are wiser than people realize. They know that the only way they can rule over America is by tapping into the dark side. These leaders are taking up the promise made to man in the Garden of Eden: Ye shall be as gods.

*

No nation can be ruled by two law systems. In early America, after the Revolution, many thought that Secularism and Christianity could rule together to support the laws of the Nation. The individual states were allowed great autonomy in establishing a 'state' church in the individual states. It became obvious to those who controlled the government in Washington, D.C., that their power to enforce their wishes upon the land were quite limited. Originally, the central government was concerned with maintaining the peace between the nations, regulating foreign trade, and defending the nation against foreign invaders. **There has never been a government or a leader of a government that was content with limited power.** The fallen man that came out of the Garden of Eden cannot be satisfied with anything less than being a god himself. When men reject the true God, they consider themselves next in line for the throne. Again, Adam and Eve took up the promise that they too could become gods. That has not changed in six thousand years.

Thus, between the Founders in Philadelphia and the Civil War, the United States were established upon the belief in legal tolerance. The people of one region tolerated the legal dissimilarities, eccentricities, of the other regions. In a sense, the different ideas about the law in each state signed a peace treaty under the U.S. Constitution. However, gods always hate signing any type of agreement with any other god. Even in paganism, there can really be only one god. In the United States, the South had a different God than the one serving in the North: Christianity versus Deism/Transcendentalism. Of course, no one wanted to directly attack America's belief in tolerance. Another issue had to be used to attack the Southern God. The issue was Big Cotton and the International Trade Cartel that controlled slavery and operated the large plantations in the South. Now, no one wanted to go to war against the powers that controlled global trade. That would do nothing to overthrow the God of the South. So a great switch was made: the Southern people now all became slave owners or the beneficiaries of slave labor. Nothing was said that the common folks in the South wanted slavery to end, as the small farmer could not compete with the giant plantations. Nothing was said that the North owned the ships that brought the slaves to America; nothing was said that the North financed the building of those ships; nothing was said that the crews of those ships were from the North; nothing was said that those ships flew under the American Flag; and nothing was said that the North financed the slave trade. It was those Southerners that had to be destroyed, i.e. the Southern God had to be destroyed.

The reason the North wanted to end toleration of a multiple system of local laws is this: no nation can have two legal systems if one of them desires to become the absolute sole determiner of Lawful and unlawful. Toleration is a very dangerous thing. You can see that in the gay rights movement. At first, all they wanted was to be treated as just another American citizen like everyone else. Then they wanted gay marriage to become equal with heterosexual marriage. Then they wanted protection from those who did not recognize their special rights and status. Then they wanted their beliefs to be taught in the government schools. Then they wanted be accepted into the military as openly a homosexual. That is how tolerance has always worked. When you tolerate a false god, that false god will always end up attacking the true god. That is why the North feared the South: their True God was a threat to their false gods of wealth and power. Today Washington, tomorrow the world. The building of Empires requires total unity—One god, one Law, and one leader.

There is an important concept about both religion and law: "Every law system must maintain its existence by hostility to every other law-system and to alien religious foundations or else it commits suicide."[12] The North recognized this before the Civil War. Another law system and another religion was allowed to exist in a large part of the nation. The same is true of the Christian. His beliefs that there is only one way to God and that is through Jesus Christ is a declaration of war against all other faiths and political beliefs. Open evangelism is an attack upon other cultures, other beliefs, and even other nations. That is why there is a war for a One World Order with a new religion to replace the one religion that stands in total opposition to global unity. In the days of Rome and early Christianity, the major reason Christians were persecuted was not because of what they believed, but because they refused to accept their status as one religion amongst many. To declare that only Jesus Christ was God was to declare every other Roman faith as being false. The unity of Rome was built around the Caesar and he tolerated no other gods before him. Any empire can have it no other way. That is why before America could become an empire, the Southern way of life and its God had to go.

*

Few realize that the words of Jesus are a declaration of War upon the entire earth:

Mathew 28:19. Go ye therefore, and **teach all nations**, baptizing them in the name of the Father, and of the Son, and of the Holy Ghost: **20 Teaching them** to **observe all things** whatsoever **I have commanded you:** and, lo, I am with you alway, *even* unto the end of the world. Amen.

Matthew 5:17. Think not that I am come to destroy the law, or the prophets: I am not come to destroy, but to fulfil. **18** For verily I say unto you, **Till heaven and earth pass, one jot or one tittle shall in no wise pass from the law**, till all be fulfilled. **19** Whosoever therefore **shall break one of these least commandments**, and shall teach men so, he shall be called the least in the kingdom of heaven: but

---

[12] Rushdoony. P. 5-6.

whosoever **shall do and teach *them***, the same shall be called great in the **kingdom of heaven**. 20 For I say unto you, That except your righteousness shall exceed *the righteousness* of the scribes and Pharisees, ye shall in no case enter into the kingdom of heaven.

The Gospel message is not just a simple raise-your-hand salvation, but the teaching the Laws of God, i.e. the Kingdom of God. The Kingdom of God is a civilization that is based upon the Laws of God as revealed in the Old Testament. Jesus did not come to abolish those laws but to have His people teach the whole world about those laws and the civilization which those laws produce. "In the law, *the total life of man* is ordered: 'there is no primary distinction between *the inner and the outer life;* the holy calling of the people must be realized in both.'"[13] Because there is only one God, His Law system applies to the whole world. The New World Order and God cannot exist on the same earth. That is why governments in nations that contained a large number of White people are attempting to neutralize Christianity. The White Race has been the number one race to evangelize the world for Jesus Christ and His Laws.

There is no such thing as a 'saved only' culture. Those who serve Jesus Christ automatically form a culture if there are enough of them. The Bible calls that culture the Kingdom of God. When missionaries go throughout the world teaching the doctrines of the Bible, they represent an invading culture. A Christian is automatically at war with any culture that leaves God and His Laws out of the national culture. There is a reason tyrants and other forms of paganism hate Christians: their teachings have and will destroy anti-Biblical Law people and their nations. Since the American Civil War, most church people have given up confronting the alien powers that control the nation. The result is the Church ceased teaching the Laws of God and found other messages to preach about.

The number one goal of the church became to create religious or emotional experiences. Books have been written instructing 'ministers' on the use of techniques to create such experiences. Religion is no longer about living a life of good works according to the laws of God, but creating experiences which make a person feel religious: **Americans no longer want to be religious, they want to**

---

[13] Rushdoony. P. 8.

feel religious. These feelings make a person think he is a Christian without having to live a life of service—outside of the church 'service.' That is why the Laws of God are so important: these laws tell us what a Christian Culture should look like. It is not about everyone enjoying the same music, but about everyone doing good works as a proof of their salvation. True Christians are not just saved from something, hell; they are saved to do something for the Kingdom of God.

Chapter Five: One God; One Law.

Exodus 20:1. And God spake all these words, saying, **2** I *am* the LORD thy God, which have brought thee out of the land of Egypt, out of the house of bondage. **3** Thou shalt have **no other gods before me**.

I keep reminding everyone of Satan's promise to man in the Garden: ye shall be as gods. Not only did Adam and Even desire to take up Satan on that promise, so have men ever since that Garden Affair. Every god desires to establish his own law system. Now, God's system of laws are absolute. Therefore there is no wiggle room for those who wish to create their own laws that are not absolute. Therefore, **the creation of non-absolute laws requires the death of the creator of absolute laws.** When it comes to laws, God and relativity cannot co-exist. Before man's laws can be introduced, God must die. Sorry God, but we really had no choice. Man wants to build a heaven upon the earth and God wants mankind to work for the heavenly city of God.

Just as God intervened to keep Nimrod from creating his view of heaven upon the earth, so God judges all man's attempts to steal God's heaven and build it here upon the earth. God says to Man: you are a fallen and corrupted person; heaven is beyond your reach during the time when Satan is still allowed to operate. The only way mankind knows how to build some kind of utopia is through a system of laws. If the government can merely get everyone to work together as one, there is nothing that men cannot do. The problem is fallen men do not like submitting to other fallen and corrupt men. "Even more, because an absolute law is denied, it means that the only universal law possible is an *imperialist law,* a law imposed by force and having no validity other than the coercive imposition."[14] Man can only create relativistic laws—laws for a day in time. That is why every government tends toward tyranny because man's laws can only last if maintained by force. The greater the goal, the more force is needed. As I write, the U.S. is attempting to push a new World Order upon the world. Because the goal is beyond man's reach, men think that with enough

---

[14] Rushdoony. P. 17.

power and control, the goal of Globalism can be reached. The more unrealistic the goal, the greater the power that is needed.

When men attempt to replace God, they need the power of a god in order to accomplish their plans. God's absolute power is then replaced by man's attempt to have absolute power. Only absolute power can rule the earth—either God's or Man's. That is why the Bible warns that men should never allow any other entity upon the earth to assume the power of a god. When the United States established a Democracy, it was felt that the people could become gods. Instead of one tyrannical god, America could have a hundred million or more tyrannical gods. Each man could be his own sovereign ruler over his own domain. And by working together, a nation could be created where a hundred million gods could select some form of overall god who would attempt to keep the peace so that everyone could operate free from outside interference. Each person would be endowed with godlike rights which no one could interfere with. Inalienable rights are really about allowing men to hold onto their god-like powers. [In reality, inalienable rights have been used as a weapon to destroy those who claim their right to express their Biblical beliefs. Christians are not allowed to oppose those people who have inalienable rights.]

There can be no separation between the laws of a nation and the gods of that nation. No nation can worship the God of the Bible and obey laws that are not connected to His Laws. That has been the problem in the United States ever since the Revolution. The nation was founded upon secular, and democratic laws. However, the people still wanted the God of the Bible around for good luck. The church leaders even attempted to convince the people that American Laws could be sanctified by God if men would just worship God on Sunday. After all, America was a nation of many Christians, so the laws that they approved or their representatives passed were Christian also. That was the first Grand Deception the Church agreed to after the Founding: Democratic Laws created by 'Christians' could supplant the Laws of God found in the Old Testament.

The whole idea of American Law was that there was a neutral ground upon which the people could agree upon were the best laws for a nation: it would be a law that would be totally inclusive which did not deny anyone their rights as a free citizen. Biblical Law is very exclusive and it was deemed too narrow for a nation that desired to welcome all that arrived on its shores. God's Laws were designed for only those that wanted to serve Him, but a secular nation cannot pass laws that offend those of other beliefs and traditions. A democratic nation should adopt laws that act as a peace treaty between the various religions and their dogmas. However, that is not the Biblical view of reality. "The opposite of true religion is never described in the Bible as atheism, secularism, agnosticism or neutralism…. Instead it is described as idolatry, apostasy, and rebellion. Unbelief is not thought of in the Bible as the absence of belief but as misdirected faith in a false god or idol."[15] The new inclusive god of America was the worship of the State, i.e. patriotism or nationalism. This is the America most church people have pledged to support and even offer their sons to fight to protect: an American idolatrous government where anyone can become rich. Living the American dream must be available to everyone, not just for Christians who follow their own moral values.

*

There is an important corollary to American Patriotism and the Nation-State. The Statist philosophy needed the support of the masses in order obtain their allegiance to a new god. The people were bribed with the promise that the State would grant each individual the rights to express his own desires. In a sense, the State decided to share some of its divine powers with each person—at least, that was the promises. The Sovereign State decided to create a society of sovereign individuals: each man could behave as one god among many gods. Thus, American Individualism became the great American religion: every man a god unto himself. Even the Churches adopted a theology where one's personal choice was more powerful than God's sovereignty: individual man chooses God— God does not choose man.

John 6:65. And he said, Therefore said I unto you, that **no man can come unto me, except** it were given unto him of my Father.

---

[15] Taylor. P. 17.

God's power takes precedence over the freedom of American Man. This concept negates the whole idea of the evangelist attempting to convince people by emotion or by logic to become a living sacrifice for Jesus Christ. Well, actually, the message had to be toned down a little. Not everyone was called to serve God and others, but only the special representatives of the Church: preachers and missionaries. The people serve God and others through their emotional and prayerful support of those who have specialized callings of service. Thus, the individual is free to serve the State and other institutions that expect forms of obedience: schools, jobs, and private associations. "The principle of the Revolution is the idolatrous cult of humanity; man recognizing no sovereign but himself, no light but his own reason, no law but his will, worshipping himself while dethroning God."[16] It is this selfish individualism which the State promises to protect in exchange for obedience to the laws of the Nation/State. The State could not have pulled this power grab off without the State itself submitting to the powers Satan.

The hidden agenda in rights promised to man is this: what the State hath given, it can also take away. The State also determines the hierarchy of rights, i.e. when does one person's right negate the rights of others. As I write, the rights of the LGBTQ crowd are greater than the rights of Christians and those who still support Western Civilization. A group's rights depend upon their usefulness to the agenda of the State. There is a corollary to the human rights issue. A Modern governments "Denies and abolishes all differences between the sexes, between the races, classes and nations on the grounds of a supposed common reason all share."[17] Any person claiming that there are real differences is perceived as one who is guilty of prejudicial discrimination. The role of the State then becomes the equalizer of everyone's rights, so that everyone experiences an equality of results. Statist equality is like this: If $2 + 3 = 5$, the State, in the name of equality must declare that $2 + 3 = 4$. If you disagree, you are a sexist, racist, or a homophobe. The bottom line is this: non-Christian groups are legally superior to Christian groups. However, Christians and their moral values must admit that they are equal to non-Christians. Evil does not have to be consistent or logical.

---

[16] Taylor. P. 35.
[17] Taylor. P. 47.

Most do not realize but the above game is an attack upon Christianity and Western Civilization. Both recognize multiple differences in all of the above listed categories of personal existence. Not only that, but every person in every group makes good and bad decisions. The result, each person is allowed to suffer the consequences of their life choices. Yes, some have more opportunities than others, and this leads to another problem: how does a state equalize the accidents of life, family, traditions, and the accidents of birth. The State has determined that a person who ancestor was a slave deserves reparations, while a family that lost its husband and father in war is not entitled to reparations—even those who were drafted, i.e. statist slavery, into war. A military slave does not qualify that family for reparations. Again, rights have become relativized and politicized by the god of the State. When God is replaced by the State as God, the problems become insurmountable. As I write, the people and their lawmakers cannot even determine what a man is and what a women is: $3 + 2 = 4$. [By executive order.]

*

The problem since 1776 has been a conflict between the God of Western Civilization and the god of the Nation/State. Christians were quite aware of this conflict and attempted to rectify this problem in the first half of the 19th century. This conflict eventually led to the Civil War. From 1865 and onward, the State became the one and only god of America. All those who served other 'gods' had to accept the fact that the god of the State was greater than all other gods. Statist laws controlled the churches and the public expressions of a person's religious beliefs. Throughout history, men have battled over the role of the State in the creation of man and his culture. Because governments have always been the most powerful agency of man's culture, the State has usually been looked to for the order of society. What is man is a question only the God/State could answer. And after that, what role should the State play in the 'private' affairs of men? Of course, the Statist god keeps expanding its powers into every area of a person's life. Just as a Christian has no private life from the God he serves, so the subject to the State has no private life separate from the total surveillance of the State.

Of course, the above jurisdictional questions are also answered in the Bible. The modern State offers the security and protection formerly supplied by the God of Christianity. Previously, man saw life in terms of one's soul and the protection of one's soul from an evil environment. He understood that this required only a limited form of government. The church was to direct the State into the proper channels in order to prevent attacks upon a person's physical existence. For example, sexual crimes were either restricted or kept to a certain part of a city. Also, children were to be protected from those who would lead the young into certain types of evil. With the general acceptance of Evolution and Darwinian man, the idea of man having an eternal soul was no longer possible. Evolution produces bodies, not spirits or souls. Therefore, the god of that order became more concerned with the bodily freedoms than man's spiritual freedoms. In a sense, the State controls the physical world, and each person is free only in the invisible world—whatever that entails. [That is only true because the State cannot as yet read your mind.]

There are two types of men: the physical man and the religious man. Because the State is the god over man's body, the protection of man's body and man's personality—his public expression of his thoughts--became the duty of the god of government. Basically, the individual is really defined by his bodily senses. The freedoms guaranteed are centered around the right of each person to have the freedom to satisfy those senses in whatever way that person chooses. Rights are sensual rights: the rights guaranteed by Nature's god. Western and Christian Civilizations were more concerned with the soul and the social institutions created by the Biblical Revelation. The Bible exalts communal institutions which are considered part of reality: family, church, and local communities. Biblical Man cannot be separated from his belonging to some form of community. The State exalts the individual and his rights over his personal community and familial obligations. The individual as 'god' does not need other people.

The senses are considered real; while the other realities outside of one's sensual world are said to be socially constructed. Anything that is constructed by man is temporary and not connected to the real world. For example, marriage is just a convenient way to have sex and to produce children. However, there is nothing 'wrong' with other ways to satisfy one's sexual urges or to produce children for the State. As with other Commandments, who says a person should honor his father and mother? Every isolated individual is free to honor or dishonor people of his choice. Biblical Dead White Males should have no power over that person's life or choices. Deconstructing reality is the right of every man born of Nature and Nature's Evolution. The role of any government is to protect the individual from unwanted intrusions from every socially constructed institution or manufactured moral constraint.

Chapter Six: Biblical Laws restrict the State's Power to Control the people under the state's jurisdiction.

When people think of Biblical Laws, the first law that comes to mind—or some other part of the body—is this: Thou shalt not commit adultery. Okay, we got that out of the way. However, there are multiple laws that few know about and are designed to prevent tyrannies and a totalitarian social order. One of the primary means of controlling the State is the tithe. Now, today, the tithe is used to support a church building and its professional staff, i.e. a religious bureaucracy. However, that is not how the tithe in the Bible is supposed to operate. Under Christendom "… broad governmental functions belonged to the world of the tithe. … Schools, hospitals, lazar-houses for lepers, charity to orphans, widows, strangers, and the poor, all this and more was the province of the tithe. … The Bible provides, as the foundation law of a godly social order, the law of the tithe. To understand the full implication of the tithe, it is important to know that Biblical law has *no property tax*; the right to tax real property is implicitly denied to the state, because the state has no earth to tax. 'The earth is the Lord's (Ex. 9:29; Deut. 10:14; Ps. 24:1; I Cor. 10:26, etc.); therefore, only God can tax the earth. For the state to claim the right to tax the earth is for the state to make itself the god and creator of the earth, whereas the state is instead God's ministry of justice (Rom. 13: 1-8). To the state to enter into God's realm is to invite judgment."[18]

Under Christendom, the land was covered with charities that operated outside the control of governments and outside of statist financing. These charities acted like a spiritual government in contrast to the secular government. The promise of a tyranny is that it can lower taxes and provide charity more efficiently. After the Reformation, those in power did everything they could to expand their powers and their tax base. Money given to charities is money that could have been taxed and used without regard to the exclusive use of religious people. The problem with religious charities is that they not only operate on a personal level, they operate on an ethical level. Churches do not subsidize immoral or lazy behavior. As a result, many had to adopt some sort of character and personal commitments in order to receive aid. Christian orphanages teach religious doctrines to the children in those homes. They also might teach trades

---

[18] Rushdoony. P. 56-57.

and expect the children also to perform charitable work. The big fear is that independent and ethical people can operate outside of the controls of the State. Every tyranny encourages behaviors that make people dependent upon the state and more importantly, independent of religious organizations. The people must worship and serve the State, not God.

*

The Bible forbids something that most might find surprising. The taxing of people was to be accomplished in an impersonal manner. For example, the head tax, the toll, and other taxes are legal if they remain anonymous taxes. To avoid the state using taxes to spy upon people, taxation was to be equal for rich and poor alike.

Exodus 30:14. Every one that passeth among them that are numbered, from twenty years old and above, shall give an offering unto the LORD. **15** The rich shall not give more, and the poor shall not give less than half a shekel....

This form of taxation not only protects a person's privacy, but it keeps the state from passing excessive taxes. The State is limited in how much it can tax or the poorer people might rebel against their leader. This also puts a restraint on the ability of the tyrant to spend excessively: he will be made to operate on a budget. America was founded upon impersonal taxes. Up until the Civil War, no one had mailing addresses. They were instituted in order to draft young men into the Northern Army. Before this time, the government in Washington had no idea where people lived: it was none of the government's business to keep track of the people. People received their mail by general delivery at a post office or general store. As I write in 2023, privacy has completely disappeared from the land: one, for purposes of taxation, and the other for control. You can run but you cannot hide. Wait, you can no longer run either.

*

Another vital Biblical Law was this:

Deuteronomy 19:14. Thou shalt **not remove thy neighbour's landmark**, which they of old time have set in **thine inheritance**, which thou shalt inherit in the land that the LORD thy God giveth thee to possess it.

One of the principles of interpretation in the Bible is this: God's revealed laws are absolute and they are meant to be applied by God's people to real life situations. One example is as follows:

I Timothy 5:18. For the scripture saith, Thou **shalt not muzzle the ox** that treadeth out the corn. And, **The labourer** *is* **worthy of his reward.**

Biblical Laws do not change, but circumstances do change over time. The purpose of Christian leaders is to faithfully apply the laws of God to the circumstances of life without changing the meaning of God's revealed laws. Laws are not to be manipulated for political, personal, or social reasons, or to gain any advantage. Jeremiah said this about man's ability to corrupt the laws of God:

Jeremiah 17:9. The heart *is* **deceitful above** all *things*, and **desperately wicked:** who can know it? **10** I the LORD search the heart, *I* try the reins, even to give every man according to his ways, *and* according to the fruit of his doings. **11** *As* the partridge sitteth *on eggs*, and hatcheth *them* not; *so* **he that getteth riches, and not by right,** shall leave them in the midst of his days, and at his end shall be a fool.

God knows human fallen nature and He reminds everyone that they will be held accountable for the mishandling of God's Word in order to gain personal advantage: they can expect to die before their time. That man shall have gained wealth and things through deceit and then he will be dead. Everyone will think: what a fool, he gained everything and lost his soul—what a fool. He laid eggs but was not around to see them hatch. That is why when men approach the Word of God, they must in all humility seek to apply them the way God intended and not for personal gain. Thus, the above listed law about landmarks means a lot more than a pile of stones that denotes where one person's property ends and his neighbor's begins. Cultures and nations also have boundaries, borders, and landmarks—even the human God-given personality should not be violated through manipulation and propaganda.

*

Every order requires boundaries in terms of business laws and laws that protect the family and local affairs. As I write, the sexual boundaries are being decimated by government financed propaganda in the school system. Even criminal has been so revised that legal and illegal boundaries have almost disappeared. Even most churches are abandoned theological boundaries. Religious and spiritual inclusiveness have caused churches to abandon doctrines which tend to divide people, especially into categories of 'saved' and 'lost.' The Law against theft is not just about property, but is part of the very nature of God's created order: "Theft is therefore more than an offense against another person; it is an offense against God. God requires us to respect the life, marriage, and property of our neighbor and enemy, not because our neighbor or enemy is not possibly evil, and not because our own needs are not great, but because His law-order takes priority over the conditions of man."[19] Circumstances do not change the laws of God.

One of the greatest violators of God's boundaries throughout history has always been governments. There is a reason for this: governments can legally steal money from people and transfer to others. Not only does theft become 'legal' but the government has the monopoly upon force within a nation. This means theft is both legal and will be defended by the military. "Theft as a short-cut to the possession of property seeks not only to by-pass *work,* as the means to wealth but also to deny the validity of God's law-order. In terms of Scripture, wealth can be acquired by labor, inheritance, or gift. A thieving order will oppose all three means of acquisition."[20] There is another important reason people support governments that authorizes legalized theft: After the fall of Man in the Garden of Eden, God told Adam that from now on, Man would have to work up a sweat to attain life from the earth. Corrupt governments are ways Man can achieve wealth outside of God's Laws; it is an act of defiance against the curses of God. 'See, God, I am stealing wealth and attaining it without a sweat.'

*

There are other areas of Biblical Law found in Western Civilization that are no longer found in American Civilization. I mentioned earlier that modern governments were created to transfer wealth—from those that work to those

---

[19] Rushdoony. P. 453.
[20] Rushdoony. P. 455.

that seek to reap the benefits from those that labor. This is a vital concept to grasp. Governments manufacture nothing. They are a protection racket very similar to the 'old days' of organized crime. Criminals who went to jail this time discovered one thing: before you steal from someone, make the act of stealing is legal. A Biblical government is based upon protecting the borders and protecting the people from those who would steal their life or their money. Again, the Commandments of God are to be applied to all situations. Thou shalt not steal applies to the multiple ways that people have devised to obtain money and wealth without having to work. Communism, Socialism, and Democracy are all based upon assorted ways for one group to take money from others without using a gun: those who make the laws also make the money.

When governments obtain power and money, everyone seeks to obtain subsidies for their particular business or to have laws passed which limit one's opponent's business ventures. This again is not a function of a Biblical government. Christian governments are not to be organized crime with its own enforcers. Good governments are to support a civilization of freedom to do good things. Government regulations are little more than the suppression of freedom in disguised form. During Christendom, private unions sought to regulate evil to protect the common good from being exploited. Free Markets were restricted because evil people knew how to manipulate markets so as to put others out of business. America's Robber Barons used their free market rights to gain a total monopoly over any business climate. These men aggressively, and legally, put their competition out of business.

A new form of wealth transfer was the invention of the 'limited liability' corporation. Businesses are allowed to make as much money as they could, but the same business was limited in how much it can lose. That is a very subtle way of transferring wealth from those who were exploited by the business to those who owned the corporation. Heads the corporate owners win; tails, those who did business with that corporation become the losers. Many Biblical Laws are revealed to protect the common folks from those who would take their wealth from them. Again and again, the prophets cry out against the exploitation of the common people. A righteous society is one in which the Laws of God were implemented in their fullest extent. The prophets spoke out to apply the laws against theft to every area of society and government.

"Although the ostensible purpose [of limited liability] is to protect the shareholders, the practical effect is to limit their responsibility and therefore encourage recklessness in investment. A limited liability economy is socialistic. By seeking to protect people, a limited liability economy merely transfers responsibility away from the people to the state, where 'planning' supposedly obviates responsibility. Limited liability encourages people to take chances with limited risks, and to sin economically without paying the price. Limited liability laws rest on the fallacy that payment for economic sins need not be made. In actuality, payment is simply transferred to others. Limited liability laws were unpopular in earlier, Christian eras but have flourished in the Darwinian world."[21]

This idea of limited liability came to permeate all of culture. The American Church adopted a theology based upon the limited liability Corporation. Mankind's spirituality was not killed in the Garden of Eden when Adam and Eve chose Satan's way of salvation over that of God's way. Mankind was only slightly wounded. After all, the whole situation was God's fault: he never should have placed that Tree in the garden to begin with. Fortunately, Man's spiritual condition was not as bad as God had promised: Adam and Even merely suffered a 'flesh' wound. With the proper treatment, Man could be restored to his original power and talent. A simple prayer could heal man's spiritual wound. Men could then use his repaired body and mind to bring the problems of the earth under his control. Yes, rejecting God only produced a limited liability.

The same principle applies to Communism, Socialism, and Democracy. Each form of government offers man a limited liability culture. When men fail, the government is there to pick that person up from his sinful lifestyle. After all, it was not totally the victim's fault, but was the result of living in a corrupt American culture. No man should be expected to live like the Bible teaches when everything in American life entices him into situations that are just too tempting to resist. Man should only be held to a limited liability for his sins. If a person were only to live in a better environment and without being surrounded by such

---

[21] Rushdoony. P. 664-665.

wicked people, everyone could live by the Biblical standards. "The curses and the blessings of the law stress man's unlimited liability to both curses and blessings as a result of disobedience or obedience to the law. ... Man cannot step outside of the world of God's consequence. At every moment and at every point man is overtaken, surrounded, and totally possessed by the unlimited liability of God's universe."[22] When Men reject God's reality, it distorts and destroys every aspect of man's life, government, and culture. Sin and rebellion are merely flesh wounds, and a little religious *Band-Aid* is all a person needs. An hour sitting in church each week should be enough penance for one's shortcomings.

Chapter Seven: The Family as the foundation of all Reality.

When people think of the family, they think of the TV family sitcoms: *Leave it to Beaver; Father Knows Best;* and *The Walton's.* From a Biblical point of view, that is a very limited concept of the family. While Adam and Eve formed the first family when Eve gave birth to the Twins Cain and Abel, which was merely the

---

[22] Rushdoony. P. 665.

beginning of God's revelation of the nature of the family. This ideal family did not last very long as Cain killed his brother Abel. As a result, Cain was expelled from the Garden of Eden. What was his first act upon no longer belonging to a family? He created a government, the very first city. The fact that the family and a government are introduced early in Genesis is important. God wants you to understand some important principles about His order and Satan's oppositional order. There are two basic foundations of creating order in a society: the family and the city, i.e. government. God works through the personal nature of the family, and Satan works through the impersonal nature of the city.

Since the time of the Enlightenment in the late 18th century, the family has been viewed as some leftover from the age of primitive man. It is also seen as a relic from the teachings of the Bible. The very idea of getting married for life; committing oneself to the raising of dependents, and the limiting oneself from enjoying the sensual pleasures of life goes totally against modern individualism. Evolution teaches that man is a product of nature and shares his sensual side with other animals. The only world that man can understand arrives through his senses. Every other reality is constructed by man for his pleasure and convenience. For example, marriage is a way a man can claim one person for his sexual enjoyment. Marriage restricts his wife from pursuing her own personal pleasures and opportunities in life. Marriage is a socially constructed prison and has no connection to Evolution or Nature. Family is seen by many as legalized exploitation of one person over another, of a man over a woman, and Man and a woman over their dependents. Evolution produces colonies, herds, mounds, or hives as ways to protect the living and to provide for food. Evolution is all about survival and man is no different from the animals in nature: everything else is mere cultural creations which have no connection to reality. They are only temporary cultural adaptations to the situations of the time. This is the freedom all men desire—to create his own world.

Biblically, the family is connected to God's created reality and is not an artificial construct. God not only created Men and Women, he created the environment in which His creations are to work out their calling upon this earth. The Ten Commandments represent God's foundation stones of His natural order.

When Men rebelled against God, Satan offered his laws of this world to man. Basically, the individual ego is all that exists. Each person is free to form his own laws and his own culture. Of course, men run into conflicts with other egos who also desire to form their own personal view of reality. This leads to the fundamental problem: all men are at war with all other men. Earth has a limited supply of everything and men desire an unlimited supply. There is just not enough of worldly pleasures to go around. In ancient times, the more powerful men were able to have multiple wives which left the weaker ones looking for sexual pleasures in multiple other ways: other men who were also without a mate, or even with animals.

This is where the Bible becomes an obstacle to many men: bestiality and homosexuality are considered capital crimes, and prostitution is considered a major offense. Intercourse is confined to one's wife. Biblically, restricting men to one wife is a partial solution to this sexual predicament. In fact, men and women seem to be born in equal numbers which works out pretty well. But marriage is more than a place where every man can have an opportunity to fulfill his sexual needs; the activities within the family are the foundation stones upon which the rest of reality are to be built. Not only does marriage teach commitment, based upon God's ideal of commitment, but it also teaches the personal character that God desires His people to have. Again, modern man considers 'character' and other traits such as honor and honesty to be merely useless tools in the modern, impersonal city life. If you live in a world of strangers, no one knows anything about one's life's moral choices. Total privacy is a product of the impersonal city.

The family also forms the basis of personal property. Biblically, property belongs to the family, not any one person. That is why the state cannot tax the property or the inheritance of the family. The legal rule is this: the inferior power can never tax the superior power. For example, a no state can tax the Federal Government. When some states have tried the courts have ruled such taxes illegal for a simple reason: "The power to tax is the power to destroy." If the states could tax the property of the federal government within that state, it could destroy the power of the government within that state. That is why God forbids any government from taxing a family's income, its property, or its inheritance.

Yes, in this sense, the family is superior to the State. Biblically, governments sit on the bottom of an inverted pyramid with the family on the top. Other institutions fall below the family. In fact, the family and a community of families are designed to be the creators of all that falls below. They are there to create an environment in which the family can thrive. Government is to be the servant of the family and not the other way around. Power and government start with the family and the clan, and proceeds down to less important forms of government.

This is why God created the family in the Garden as one of His first acts. That is why Cain, Satan's servant, created the State as the primary institution as Satan is at war with the family and all that it stands for. As I write, the World Economic Forum is at war with the family and the culture which it has created over the centuries. That is why the Forum has declared war upon personal property: You will own nothing and be happy. That is a declaration of war upon God and that is why Satan's legions are seeking to establish their New World Order. The other aspect of the family is that it promotes religious beliefs. It is the belief that God created the family institution that allows people to commit themselves to that structure. Men do not have to experiment with other living arrangements throughout their life to discover what is best for them. This allows men to devote themselves to invest their time in more profitable ventures.

Rushdoony exposes modern man's war upon the family: *"Religion, thus, is seen as a projection of the family, and the family must therefore be destroyed in order that religion may also be destroyed.* But this is not all. *Private property is similarly seen as an outgrowth of the family, and the abolition of private property requires the destruction of the family as a prerequisite."*[23] Knowing this, you can understand why the World Economic Forum is at war with both property and religion. It also reveals the Satanic nature of this organization. It is not just a group of men attempting to 'save the planet.' It is a Satanic religion that is attempting to expel God and His people from this earth.

There is a secondary nature to the family that is often ignored: The family is called to transform the earth into a garden and to spread the nature of God's culture throughout the earth. The Bible and its Laws of culture actually create

---

[23] Rushdoony. P. 161.

Cultural Intelligence. God commands His people to spread the nature of God's reality throughout all pagan cultures so that they can become both prosperous and intelligent. It is rarely mentioned, but in nations where people live by the law of immediate gratification, there is a lower IQ. There appears to be a connection with the farmer who is the picture of delayed gratification and those who are hunter/gatherers. The Bible is a Book designed for a rural lifestyle and for those who invest their time and energy into building up a community for the future. God's Laws and Commandments are tools for survival and culture formation.

In one sense, the family and their association with other families are to reflect the true nature of colonialism, i.e. a spiritual one of teaching the people of the earth what constitutes true reality. *"The meaning of the family is thus not to be sought in procreation but in a God-centered authority and responsibility in forms of man's calling to subdue the earth and to exercise dominion over it."*[24] Of course, Satan's form of government has adopted the roll of the family for itself. State is to have dominion over the earth. The United States claims dominion over the earth by supposedly spreading democracy—by force—upon every other nation. However, democracy is really a propaganda sham. If the voice of the people is the voice of God, then other nations should be able to form governments that reflect their own values. American Democracy means accepting America as a business partner, i.e. a subject.

The Nation/State knows that the true family is its primary enemy. The last thing it wants is for families to teach the nations the laws of God. The State promotes feminism (and other deviancies) as one of its tools to negate the effectiveness of God's family. In fact, this has been one of the State's most effective attacks upon Biblical teachings. "...the function of the woman in this aspect of God's law-order is to be a help-meet to man in the exercise of his dominion and authority. She provides companionship in his calling (Gen. 2:18), so that there is a community in authority, with the clear preeminence being the man's. Man's sin is to attempt to usurp God's authority, and woman's sin is to attempt to usurp man's authority, and both attempts are a deadly futility. ... But the authority of the woman as help-meet is no less real than that of a prime

---

[24] Rushdoony. P. 164.

60

minister to a king; the prime minster is not a slave because he is not king, nor is the woman a slave because she is not man."[25]

This is how the Bible describes the virtuous woman:

Proverbs 31:10.   Who can find a virtuous woman? for her price *is* far above rubies. **11** The heart of her husband doth safely trust in her, so that he shall have no need of spoil. **12** She will do him good and not evil all the days of her life. **13** She seeketh wool, and flax, and worketh willingly with her hands. **14** She is like the merchants' ships; she bringeth her food from afar. **15** She riseth also while it is yet night, and giveth meat to her household, and a portion to her maidens. **16** She considereth a field, and buyeth it: with the fruit of her hands she planteth a vineyard. **17** She girdeth her loins with strength, and strengtheneth her arms. **18** She perceiveth that her merchandise *is* good: her candle goeth not out by night. **19** She layeth her hands to the spindle, and her hands hold the distaff. **20** She stretcheth out her hand to the poor; yea, she reacheth forth her hands to the needy. **21** She is not afraid of the snow for her household: for all her household *are* clothed with scarlet. **22** She maketh herself coverings of tapestry; her clothing *is* silk and purple. **23** Her husband is known in the gates, when he sitteth among the elders of the land. **24** She maketh fine linen, and selleth *it*; and delivereth girdles unto the merchant. **25** Strength and honour *are* her clothing; and she shall rejoice in time to come. **26** She openeth her mouth with wisdom; and in her tongue *is* the law of kindness. **27** She looketh well to the ways of her household, and eateth not the bread of idleness. **28** Her children arise up, and call her blessed; her husband *also*, and he praiseth her. **29** Many daughters have done virtuously, but thou excellest them all. **30** Favour *is* deceitful, and beauty *is* vain: *but* a woman *that* feareth the LORD, she shall be praised. **31** Give her of the fruit of her hands; and let her own works praise her in the gates.

The wife "... is not a helpless slave nor of a pretty parasite, but rather of a very competent wife, manager, business-woman, and mother—a person of real authority."[26]

*

---

[25] Rushdoony. P. 164.
[26] Rushdoony. P. 164.

Another one of God's Laws that is vital for the formation of a culture is the idea of honoring one's parents. In the fundamentalist church of my upbringing, the term was used to tell a child to totally submit to the demands of one's parents. When I was twelve, my grandfather became 'disabled' and after school, I would walk to his farm and work until supper time. Eat, study, and then go to bed. Then, every Saturday morning I was expected to help my father, and then Saturday afternoon I was expected to do janitorial work in the church. Fair or not, that is what 'honoring one's parents' meant in my childhood. That was just part of rural living. However, 'honoring' in the Bible goes way beyond being a good boy. Consider the following verse:

Deuteronomy 5:16. Honour thy father and thy mother, as the LORD thy God hath commanded thee; that **thy days may be prolonged, and that it may go well with thee, in the land which the LORD thy God giveth thee.**

Growing up fundamentalist, I was told that if I wanted to live to an old age, I must submit to the demands of the needs of the family clan: family came before personal desires. However, the Bible is talking about much more than a personal retirement plan, it is talking about the health and longevity of a culture and a nation. While respect for one's parents is not negated in the Bible, it goes beyond that. **Men are to honor the traditions, values, and the land of the family.** Honoring one's parents means respecting the moral traditions of one's parents. 'Teenage' rebellion is nothing new. I grew up in the Revolutionary decade of the 1960s. My high school and college year went from 1960-1968. That decade was noted for the cultural wars between parents and their children.

For me as a Christian, I was torn between serving God and serving my parents. I was a Vietnam War protestor and a Conscientious Objector. I was never tempted to escape to Canada, but was determined to stand my ground. I won my appeal and spent two years performing 'community service' versus two years in a Federal Penitentiary. My stand did not set well with my parents, my patriotic church, and my relatives. But I discovered that I was honoring the values of my parents even though at the time it did not seem that way. I was taught to always take a stand against evil and I really believed that the War was evil—and eventually I was proven right.

The bigger picture in this Commandment involves the long-term health of a nation, it families, and its cultural traditions. America basically had a stable rural culture for most of its existence. [TV and National subsidies pretty well ended that. For example, local schools became nationalized and even the people in Cactus Flats had to submit to national agenda and textbooks.] This decentralized order is why the people of true character could point to their small town and rural up bringing for their love of hard work, and personal honor. In the Old South in the United States, one's honor and one's word were considered sacred. Even the poor tenant farmer understood the importance of being a respectable person. You see, being poor tenant farmer and not owning his own land did not determine who he was. Sometimes a man had no control over the circumstances of life, but he did have control over his character and personal choices. And that was the determiner of who he really was, not his financial accumulations or the amount of his possessions. A man's word and his character determined who he really was in a community. I grew up in a small farming town in the 1950s. I remember that even very common people could become respectable members of the community. In a city that is based upon accumulation, those same people would be considered society's failures and rejects.

The modern Nation/State is at war with the family and attacks it in many ways. I previously mentioned modern feminism and its hatred of the family, the wife, and the mother—all symbols of personal enslavement. Another war is the inheritance which the State uses to destroy the family farm and business. Many times a family has to sell their inheritance in order to pay the inheritance taxes. This results with the rich and their corporations and their 'foundations' buying up land and family businesses. I recall that a family that owned a business felt a loyalty to two things: the reputation of their product, and their employees and their families. When corporations take over such businesses their loyalty is to their shareholders. The quality of the product is of secondary concern—public relations can deal with any problems in that area. And during slow periods, a corporation has no problem laying off employees to keep their profit margin and satisfy its 'investors', i.e. speculators.

*

Progress in Biblical terms is moral progress. Biblically, new Technologies must be connected to a moral order. Modern technologies create their own moral order and have no concern with the consequences that new inventions will have upon traditions, relationships, and moral behaviors. In the Book of Enoch, Satan is said to be the god of technologies. While history focuses upon historical revolutions, the most powerful revolutions are technological. The TV changed the world a lot more than WWII. The damage done by a war can be repaired, but the damage done by great technological changes are permanent—at least until the next technological revolution. While the Bible teaches to preserve the personal heritage of every Christian nation and its culture, progress requires that the old ways be destroyed. Any new technologies are said to enhance traditions and personal relationships. Every civilization is based a continuity of the personal and material culture. When continuity dies, civilizations die. Welcome to the New World Order, i.e. New World Civilization.

Once a nation worships material and technological progress, the gates of hell are actually opened. God did not design human beings to be primarily connected to material objects—even objects that appear to be 'alive'. Relationships with other people within marriage, businesses, churches, and schools are the foundation of human contentment. And all of the above exist to promote a personal relationship with God. That is how God created His world. Satan's technology is basically to allow people to escape from the world of creation. When I was young in the early 50s, the number of TV antennas on housetops was limited. Pre TV culture still existed. People would routinely drop in to see their friends and neighbors, to share coffee, cake, and conversation without any appointment. My clan would get together every Sunday evening for times of food and laughter. I was too young to remember what they were saying, but I do remember the constant laughter. Now, people gather together to watch sporting events and there is little laughter.

Man's quest for new and better technological marvels is a war upon God and HIs plans for mankind. Men think that they can remake the fallen world without any help from God or the atoning work of Jesus Christ. Technology saves, not Jesus saves. I hear people say, in the past adultery and fornication were wrong because of the consequences of uncontrolled sexual encounters. However, there is no longer a concern with unwanted babies or sexual diseases that resulted death or madness. [It is worth noting that everyone knows that White Men gave small pox to the Indians, but what did the Indians give to the White Men? Syphilis.] Technology has saved man from the consequences of his sinful lifestyle. From the line of Seth [Abel's brother] we inherit country living; from the line of Cain [The murderer of Abel] we inherit the impersonal city.

*

Biblically, the family clan was a governing agency. Not only does the family educate their own and often discipline their own, but the family and relations operate as a commune by blood. It is an economic unit. "...throughout history the basic welfare agency has been the family. The family, in providing for its sick and needy members, in educating children, caring for parents, and in coping with emergencies and disaster, has done and is doing more than the state has ever done or can do. The state's intrusion into the realm of welfare and education leads to the bankrupting of people and state and to the progressive deterioration of character. The family is strengthened by its discharge of these duties which always lead to the decline of welfare states. The family is the basic economic unit of society, and the strongest one. No society can prosper which weakens the family, either by removing the family's responsibilities for education and welfare, or by limiting the family's responsibilities for education and welfare, or by limiting the family's control of its property and inheritance by usurpation."[27] The potential tyrant's biggest is a strong family system. Total dictatorial power and control can only happen without first destroying the Biblical family and clan unity. That is why just electing a Christian President cannot by itself restore an ordered social order. First, the Christian view of family must be restored. Otherwise, the masses will still be slaves to the State and in need of physical and mental care.

---

[27] P. 181.

You see, the modern state controls its people by becoming a welfare state. Survival means accepting dependence upon the state. Strong families negate the need for a strong centralized government. That is why the government and its agencies promote racial strife, feminism, sexual liberation, centralized schooling, welfare, and inflation. A strong 'dollar' that does not inflate contributes to a stable future and a culture of delayed gratification: a dollar saved today will still be worth a dollar in ten years, plus interest. The local church is to be an enlarged version of the family and collectively performing many of the same functions that a single family cannot provide. It also provides a dating pool where the young are not related to each other.

*

One of the least understood aspects of Biblical Law is its intolerance toward the criminal and those who would destroy the family unit. The family is protected from both the criminal within and without the family. The salvation of the social order is greater than the pampering of evil people. Everyone is expected to be responsible and ethical. If a criminal commits a crime, he is expected to repay the victim several times over: even if it means the selling of the criminal into slavery to pay his debts. Also, repeat offenders are considered a traitor to society and dealt with as you would any traitor: stoning, i.e. the death penalty. Even the young are not allowed to become a spiritual cancer to the social order. Consider the following passage:

Deuteronomy 21:18. If a man have a stubborn and rebellious son, which will not obey the voice of his father, or the voice of his mother, and *that*, when they have chastened him, will not hearken unto them: **19** Then shall his father and his mother lay hold on him, and bring him out unto the elders of his city, and unto the gate of his place; **20** And **they shall say unto the elders of his city, This our son *is* stubborn and rebellious, he will not obey our voice; *he is* a glutton, and a drunkard. 21** And all the **men of his city shall stone him with stones, that he die**: so shalt thou put evil away from among you; and all Israel shall hear, and fear.

A healthy society has zero tolerance for those who would destroy the peace and security of the culture. Also, it is not the role of any agency in society to attempt the reformation of any individual who has declared war upon those around him. Biblically, the motto of life is this: You break it, you pay for it. There are no excuses or the passing of blame. When I used to counsel teens, I always confronted them with reality and their own responsibility for their condition. Everybody wants to blame something in the past, but the past cannot be changed. That is part of one's heritage for good or bad. And no one can change the future. All any one has is today and being responsible for the options you have for today. Ignore the past; make right choices today; and tomorrow will take care of itself. Biblically, if you make a lot of bad choices, you will not have to worry about tomorrow—you won't have any. Modern man thinks that cruel, but archeologists have discovered that when the nations of ancient Israel and Judah followed the above precepts, no one had any locks on their doors. A safe place for families and businesses is considered greater than one person's rights.

There is another purpose in the above strict laws: the laws are designed to teach the eternal nature of both life and death. When the criminal is put to death, it is teaching everyone that not only are there consequences here on earth, there are eternal consequences of greater importance than life on earth: there really is a heaven and a hell. Those who must die for their sins will quickly understand that there is an eternal death for their sins also. Better to be stoned here on earth than to spend eternity in hell. Repentance is open to anyone, even those who are about to die for their criminal mentality. In a sense, the death penalty confronts the criminal with the seriousness of his crime. Crime does not pay and neither does rebellion against God. Public executions are educational to the seriousness of every aspect of life.

*

Anyone who studies the Bible knows one thing: modern society is at war with Biblical principles and the people that teach the Commandments of God. Everyone is free to be spiritual in America, but those who proclaim the laws of God will come under attack. The 'woke culture' and the drive for inclusiveness are not what they say they are; they are Satan's wars against Biblical reality. Satan's servants disguise themselves as those who just want to be free and enjoy the same rights as other Americans. Remember, Satan is the author of confusion and deception. His people are not honest and the will lie if it serves their purpose. Those 'men' in power will not stand up to reality out of fear of being attacked, losing their job, or made to look foolish by the Satanic media. The women's liberation movements are all at war with Biblical reality. Many desire freedom from God, the family, and the responsibility of raising a family. Basically, escaping from the laws of God which require submission to God's social and ethical order.

God designed the males in society to be the warriors, the leaders, and the public defenders of Jesus's Kingdom of God. Throughout history, feminist cultures have failed. One person stated that when women rule in government, they change the purpose of Government into one of being a nurturing order. The natural tendency of women to care and take of people, whether in the family or in nursing, is transferred to the government. The result is a socialistic welfare society where no is allowed to suffer and no one is expected to be punished for any wrongdoing. Every criminal is just a poor little boy who just needs a little understanding and loving care. That is why feminist cultures will side with the criminal as being the victim of an authoritarian, male culture. Back in the 1960s, many college girls would hold up signs, "If women ran the world, there would be no wars."

And ao, the war upon Biblical manhood has become part of American culture, particularly White males. Male leadership is tagged as authoritarian and abusive. There is even something called toxic masculinity. But it goes even deeper than that. God is presented in the Bible as 'male', the Father God. The Old Testament is pictured as being exhibit one of God being ruthless and cruel. In that era, God was masculine and exhibited toxic masculinity. Now, contrary to this, Jesus was transformed into exhibiting man's feminine side along with His mother, Mary. Jesus was sent to represent God the Father to mankind. However, His masculine actions are ignored and his emphasis upon mercy are exalted. The mercy and forgiveness that God exhibited for His people in the Old Testament is also ignored. The Father versus Son dichotomy was created to elevate the feminine Jesus and the matriarchal nature of this world.

Now feminine societies are usually formed in a vacuum of power when men abdicate their proper role in society. After the early arrival of Christians in America, others followed to seek wealth in the land of opportunity. America became a business venture. Men formed a culture where they just wanted to be left alone so that they could purse a life of personal liberty. More and more masculine duties were passed off to other elements of society. This masculine vacuum created problems which resulted in, initially, the government taking over many of the functions of a patriarchal culture. The powers of the government operated as the masculine authority in America. This freed men up to conquer the land and start their own business ventures. I regard this as the birth of corruption in America: for those who did not wish to pursue the more masculine traits of the free market and the dangers of being an entrepreneur, government jobs offered the chance to make money without working up a sweat or having to exhibit masculine attributes. So what happened? The government created a masculine form of rule, enforced by its staff of feminine bureaucrats. The government became the father and everyone else became its family and would be treated as children.

I regard that weak men are attracted to a system where their 'masculinity' is granted to them by the government, not as a result of their personal character. You will never find those with an entrepreneurial personality looking for a job as a government desk jockey. Weak people are attracted to jobs that allow them to pretend to be strong and whose failures are 'subsidized'. The principle—'You break it, you pay for it' does not apply to the public 'servant' I know this sounds strange, but true masculinity is found in the strong family system and the men who take responsibility for the chores of being a Biblical leader. Governments offer weak men vicarious masculinity. That is why very few bureaucrats will ever stand up against an evil bureaucratic system. Their feelings of manhood comes about through their association with a masculine government. Without the government, they are weak and naked.

In the 19th century, the taking of bribes was considered part of a politician's source of income. It was not considered illegal as that is the way governments had operated ever since the formation of the Nation States after the Reformation.

In early America, there were two ways to obtain action by the government: the poor people brought above changes through their voting power; and the rich people obtained changes through the power of their money. Both the *voting government* and the *money government* created new problems. The more power that gravitated toward a central government, the greater the need to control that government. As a result, both poor and the rich operated through a money system. The poor man's vote could be purchased with the promise of forms of government subsidies or favors and the rich could still purchase laws of their own choosing. In a sense, American government officials created of new laws, all operated on the money principle of rule. Governments become the entity that divides up the wealth of a nation: everything belongs to the government and the bureaucrats are the ones who decide who gets their 'fair' share.

As a result, money government became corrupt government. The American Civil War made everyone realize how much money could be made by wars and the bribes that go with emergency wartime contracts. After the Civil War, American government was transformed into a business venture for those who controlled or were able to influence the laws and taxes of the land. And the bigger the government, the more money and power was available for those who were connected in one way or another to the finances of the government. In reality, even though the name 'government' was still used, in reality the United States became a land of political organized crime. The 'Mafia' and the government both operated on the same principles except the politicians passed laws to make their crimes 'legal'. Both exhort money from the masses through the threats of some kind of violence. Both operate protection rackets and instigate 'hits' against those who oppose their criminal activities.

*

Now, during the Victorian era, as men were off pursuing financial gain, the Church's role as the conscience of a nation declined. Men no longer wanted a religion that exemplified the teachings of the Bible about good works and service to others: that became the women's job in the churches. And they did a fine job as multitudes of women started church-based charities. America was transformed into a nation of charities. They were everywhere, serving needs wherever a need could be found. America became divided between the ruthless and corrupt world of business and politics and the feminine world of caring and charitable work. The public realm was considered the masculine realm, and the home was to be a haven from a heartless, male-dominated culture.

It was during this age of feminism that a matriarchal culture was born. As the 'home' became separated from the real world, women felt they were being deprived of becoming part of that world. The Biblical world and the Laws of the Bible no longer applied to the public realm in the United States after 1776, and especially after 1865. When men were off pursuing their own desires, women felt isolated in the 'Christian' home and wanted to become part of the real action outside of the feminine sanctuary where the trophy wife was expected to keep pure. And as government took over education and welfare, more and more the women had less to do in their homes. The house became a prison of sorts, denied its true function as God intended. It was during this time after the Civil War that the churches also became feminized. When the home lost some of its functions, women gravitated to the church as a source of feminine power and action. The female, Christian feminist took over the churches; and more and more men felt uncomfortable in the feminized church. They left in droves. And with it the militant church died and it became like the home, a safe haven in a heartless world. The matriarchal culture was born.

"The matriarchal society is thus the decadent or broken society. The strongly matriarchal character of the Negro life is due to the moral failure of Negro men, their failure to be responsible, to support the family or to provide authority. The same is true of American Indian tribes, which are also matriarchal today. In such societies, women provide considerable portion of the family income because the moral dereliction of the men makes it necessary. A strongly permissive element predominates in child training and the moral failure of the male is transmitted to the next generation. … It should be stressed that, contrary to popular opinion, a matriarchal society is not a society in which women rule, but, rather, a society in which men fail to exercise their dominion, so that women are faced with double responsibility. They must do their own work, and then work to stave off the anarchy created by man's moral failure."[28]

Once the people of a nation abandon the Biblical model of society, there is nothing to hold back the powers of evil. Once the masses no longer believe in the power of the family to mould the future, and once the church no longer storms the gates of hell, there is nothing left but to face the judgment of God upon a nation and its people.

Chapter Eight: Biblical Law and Man's Purpose upon the Earth.

Genesis 1:26. And God said, Let us make man in our image, after our likeness: and **let them have dominion** over the fish of the sea, and over the fowl of the air, and over the cattle, and over all the earth, and over every creeping thing that

---

[28] Rushdoony. P. 203.

creepeth upon the earth. **27** So God created man in his *own* image, in the image of God created he him; male and female created he them. **28** And God blessed them, and God said unto them, **Be fruitful, and multiply,** and **replenish the earth, and subdue it:** and **have dominion** over the fish of the sea, and over the fowl of the air, and over every living thing that moveth upon the earth.

The above verses from the very first chapter in Genesis explain one of the purposes of Man upon this earth. Mankind was not to remain in the Garden of Eden, but to take the blueprint of the Garden and copy that blueprint throughout the earth. Beauty was created by God and when man sees something beautiful, there is an aspect within man that resonates with the beautiful. No one walks through a concrete jungle and feels at peace with the steel and concrete. Those buildings represent functionality not beauty. Men use those buildings to accomplish some other purpose but not to inspire awe and wonder. People can be inspired by a sunset, but not by the sun being reflected off the glass of a skyscraper. One of the purposes of man is to go out into the earth's wilderness and build a civilization and homes for themselves that reflect the glory of God. Men's dwellings are to inspire people to contemplate the God who inspired men to build such structures.

Near my home area, there is a town in the mountains that was built to reflect a Bavarian village. People go there to walk around and eat the fine food served in the various establishments. The same food could probably be served in a strip mall, but it would be lacking an environment in which men feel at peace with their surroundings. Even music is to reflect the joyous and melodic sounds of being at peace with God, one's environment, and one's place in life. God's music is to be a **joyful sound**: music that puts a smile on your face and in your heart. Modern architecture is not designed with beauty in mind, but with aiding in the making of money. Godly man has dominion over the land; Satanic man exploits the land for his own pleasures. Man is not to worship God's natural order, i.e. nature worship, but to find pleasure in the God who created beauty. And to copy that beauty in all that he builds: a place to call home.

Fallen man reflects the personality of his Satanic creator. The natural earth is to be exploited for purposes of gaining personal power and wealth. Other people are treated in the same way. The American Robber Barons had no problem using people and exploiting them in order to enhance their industrial empires. There was a fear that if the employees ever had a surplus of money they would never show up to work under the unsafe working conditions to which they were exposed: poor and hungry people can be depended to show up for work every day and be willing to tolerate the chance of workplace death. Many a worker fell into those giant pots of melted steel. That is why I believe the Corporations reflect what life was like under the Pharaohs and Caesars. Individuals only mattered if they contributed to the glory of the government and its leader. The Pyramids reflected the glory of the Pharaoh, not the slaves who built them. The temples and pyramids that the masses built were not built with beauty in mind, but to reflect the power and glory of the Pharaoh and his gods.

*

No one hears much about man's dominion mandate much anymore. It has been pretty much discredited. It is associated with clear cut forest cutting or strip mining. Christian leaders have neglected to defend these charges or to teach to the Christian nation about the Kingdom of God. I believe the major reason is that the dominon mandate is opposite of the American dream. The dominion mandate is not about making money and material wealth. It is not Capitalism as claimed by Protestant and Reformation leaders. Capitalism was founded on the concept that if everyone pursues their own selfish desires, everyone benefits. In other words, Fallen Man by acting out his corrupt ways will serve the greater good of the world: the baker does not make his bread so he can serve others, but so he can take your money. And yet, that selfish desire ends of serving mankind even though that was not his goal. That sounds legitimate for the family baker, but it does not apply to corporations and those who have the power to exploit people for their own good, i.e. Big Pharma.

In order to escape this mandate of service and building beauty, America developed its own version of Christianity. The leaders of the church were dependent upon the masses for their financial support. A theology of religious capitalism was developed: people by serving their own religious interests were also serving God at the same time. Religious and spiritual 'entertainment' brought people inside the Churches: that is what 'God' wants and that is the goal of the church. America's God loves big churches so Americans built big churches. Americans found that they really could serve God and mammon as long as God received His 'fair' share in the tithes and offerings. Ten percent ain't bad if it puts you in good standing with God. America's new idea of dominion was strictly confined to the church and the maintenance of the building and staff.

"The salvation of man includes his restoration into the image of God and the calling implicit in that image, to subdue the earth and to exercise dominion. Hence, the proclamation of the gospel was also the proclamation of the Kingdom of God, according to all [of] the New Testament. A radical deformation of the gospel and of the redeemed man's calling crept into the church as a result of Neoplatonism. Dominion was renounced, the earth regarded as the devils' realm, the body despised, and a false humility and meekness cultivated. Dominion was regarded as a burden of the flesh rather than a godly responsivity. Especially with Pietism, Jesus was pictured as meek and helpless, pacifist and mild of manner."[29] As a result the church became feminized and men attended church to please their wives or to be an example for the children. Men were created to be workers and builders, not passive pew sitters.

There is a flip side to the dominion mandate: if the church does not accept the challenge, some other entity will fill that void. When God's people create a vacuum, Satan's people rush in to fill the space. Under Christendom, despite the corruption in Rome, Christians transformed the decadent days of the Roman Empire to a Christian civilization based upon Biblical Laws. The local parishes practiced many forms of Christian ministry. The people really did believe in good works as a sign of one's devotion to God. The problem, as always, history books love stories of secret affairs and religious corruption. The common people and their good works gets ignored as that makes for boring narratives: men working, supporting their families, building cathedrals, and basically, staying out of the stuff that historians love to write about. After the Reformation, the newly formed

---

[29] Rushdoony. P. 449.

Nation/States started to exercise the dominion over the earth that the church had abandoned.

The American Revolutionary era marked the transforming of the United States into a nation that rivaled the Kingdom of God upon the earth and the dominion of God's Church. "God grants *dominion* to man under His law, but He does not grant His *sovereignty.* God alone is absolute Lord and Sovereign. To deny God's sovereignty is to transfer sovereignty from God to man, or to man's state. Thus, Tomas Paine, in the *Rights of Man,* affirmed as a fundamental principle the sovereignty of the nation-state, declaring '*The nation is essentially the source of all sovereignty; nor can any* INDIVIDUAL, *or,* ANY BODY OF MEN, *be entitled to any authority which is not expressly derived from it.'* Paine and the French Revolution clearly affirmed their totalitarianism by this statement. The state as god became the source of authority, morality, and dominion."[30] Americans bought the books of Paine by great numbers. His belief in Man and Man's ability to rule themselves and the whole earth inspired men to go to war with England rather than explore peaceful options or to fight using non-military means. After the Revolution, the American Northern Church never sought to establish a church that recognized the dominion of the Kingdom of God. Men won the freedom to pursue 'life, liberty, and happiness.' That is totally opposite to the Sermon on the Mount.

*

Deuteronomy 5:21. Neither shalt thou desire thy neighbour's wife, neither shalt thou covet thy neighbour's house, his field, or his manservant, or his maidservant, his ox, or his ass, or any *thing* that *is* thy neighbour's.

The tenth Commandment is the least mentioned of all the Commandments probably because it is not even considered an important Law. It could be compared to a commandment that might read thus: 'Thou shalt not be overweight.' A law of that sort would open up all kinds of questions: What is overweight? Does body build make a difference? Does age make a difference? Is

---

[30] Rushdoony. P. 451.

weight gain normal in winter? The Biblical Commandment not to covet is almost open to a lot of questions as the American Economic order is based upon the spirit of covetousness. Some 'Christians' feel that any intense desire is coveting some object, title, or gain. In other words, intensely going after some goal has been defined as coveting some goal in life and that has been condemned. The result is that many Christians have been taught a passive acceptance of life. Living intensely has been viewed as coveting life itself and making an idol out of some desire. A basic definition of covetousness is this:

"Thus, what is clearly condemned by the tenth commandment is every attempt to gain by fraud, coercion, or deceit that which belongs to our neighbor."[31] Most have applied this principle to the individual person. Thou shalt not make an idol out of thy neighbor's wife. Which is correct, but it goes a lot deeper than that. The Bible commands Christians to covet the best gifts from God. However, this Commandment has been weaponized and politicized to attack Christian culture and beliefs. This law is being used to destroy Christian Civilization and Western Civilization. That is what I want to focus upon. It starts with this idea: anybody that has something that I do not have or desire to have is illegitimate. A person does not covet what his neighbor has, but he no longer wants his neighbor to have that which he does not have. Those who covet have transformed their sin into being a victim of some form of oppression by those who have something. Those who focus upon a beautiful woman are guilty of 'lookism'. Because I am not good looking, I do not want others to be good looking. So, what does this Commandment really mean for modern America and the current class warfare?

The new American government is based upon disguised covetousness. The income tax was designed to take money from the haves and distribute that money to those who are envious of the haves. Socialism, Communism, and Democracy all are sold to the masses as forms of legalized robbery. If a particular minority desires something, they can instruct the government to supply it to them by taking it from those who have and what they want. The State acts as a collection agency for those who control the vote or those the dictator can use as a weapon to control his enemies. The government can carry out outlandish acts of

---

[31] Rushdoony. P. 634.

confiscation as long as the right group gets their share. The mob is bribed with money the government does not have so it appeals to the covetousness of the masses to support the government's illegal forms of robbery: fiat money, graduated income taxes, and colonialism. .

A modern term used to disguise the covetousness of the masses is the demand for equality. Those who want something are envious of those who have it. The rationale is that the reason that they do not have it is that others have acted to deprive them of it. One form of deprivation is blamed upon discrimination. Some other group is blamed for not allowing the victimized group to enjoy the same pleasures in life as they do. Failures never look within themselves when there is a government that will use their deprivation to enslave the rest of the population. Remember, governments do not care about people, they only use them for those who hold the reins of power. Covetousness is encouraged amongst the losers of society because they are useful, that is all.

Another form of covetousness is assigning some form of special privilege to a class of individuals envied by the social outcasts. The most popular one right now is White Privilege. Success for some is based entirely upon the fact that they received special treatment which others did not receive. It is one group's connections that made them successful. In fact, success is based only upon that one factor. Such things as talent, hard work, family traditions, moral character, special schooling, cultural expectations and personality are not considered a factor for success or failure. The ability of a person to turn their life around is considered impossible as long as a privileged class is allowed to exist. As some state, as long as White people exist, minorities will suffer. The fact that special privileges can be earned is not considered possible. All privileges are a result of some form of social oppression.

Covetousness demands a social order of total equality. The envious refuse to take any blame for their current condition. Success is something that is handed out and if it is not handed out equally, then the government must develop plans to redistribute wealth to restore the natural equal condition of man. **Everyone is born equal, and that equality is supposed to remain equal throughout one's life.** There are no such things as consequences for a person's actions or 'immoral' lifestyle. The lazy and the ignorant are supposed to share in the wealth of the nation. **Wealth is no one's private possession, but belongs to everyone within a nation**—and now the mob demands that the whole world be made equal. That is impossible, so the ruling elites have injected the masses with the ultimate equalizer, i.e. death. Only the privileged will be allowed to live as the earth's population is being reduced to well under one billion, down from over 7 billion.

There are several problems with the goal of a nation of equals: it takes lots of power to force everyone into the same mold, and no nation has ever survived without some obtaining various forms of special privileges. It takes talented people to produce the necessary food and services that everyone demands as their right. Victims do not produce anything and usually do not desire to join the laboring class that does the labor involved in food and material production. **Everyone wants equality of wealth, but few want the equality of work.** Ultimately, the effort it takes to raise some and lower others destroys the producers of society. Few want to work so that other do not have to work.

*

Another social institution that is under attack is the family. The good family produces special privileges for its children. In fact, a lot of success is based upon the values learned in childhood. I grew up in a small farming town, and work was part of the culture. Even in high school, a person was often associated with what part-time job they did for spending money, cloths, and car insurance. I benefited from that climate by adopting a work ethic: I enjoy working and I enjoy even more what I can accomplish by that work. I even volunteer my labor for the satisfaction of helping others. I learned the pride in what one can accomplish brings a lot of personal satisfaction. Those who demand forced equality are never able to take pride in their accomplishments which, in my opinion, produces a real mental handicap. I know how to bring peace and satisfaction to myself without asking others to do it for me. That is the opposite of covetousness. I now take pride when I can help others through the use of my talents.

*

Jesus taught a Biblical principle which, for many, does not sound fair:

79

Mathew 25:14.   For *the **kingdom of heaven*** *is* as a man travelling into a far country, *who* called his own servants, and delivered unto them his goods. **15** And unto one he gave five talents, to another two, and to another one; to every man according to his several ability; and straightway took his journey. **16** Then he that had received the five talents went and traded with the same, and made *them* other five talents. **17** And likewise he that *had received* two, he also gained other two. **18** But he that had received one went and digged in the earth, and hid his lord's money. **19** After a long time the lord of those servants cometh, and reckoneth with them. **20** And so he that had received five talents came and brought other five talents, saying, Lord, thou deliveredst unto me five talents: behold, I have gained beside them five talents more. **21** His lord said unto him, **Well done, *thou* good and faithful servant: thou hast been faithful over a few things, I will make thee ruler over many things:** enter thou into the joy of thy lord. **22** He also that had received two talents came and said, Lord, thou deliveredst unto me two talents: behold, I have gained two other talents beside them. **23** His lord said unto him, **Well done, good and faithful servant; thou hast been faithful over a few things, I will make thee ruler over many things:** enter thou into the joy of thy lord. **24** Then he which had received the **one talent** came and said, Lord, I knew thee that thou art an hard man, reaping where thou hast not sown, and gathering where thou hast not strawed: **25 And I was afraid, and went and hid thy talent in the earth**: lo, *there* thou hast *that is* thine. **26** His lord answered and said unto him, ***Thou* wicked and slothful servant**, thou knewest that I reap where I sowed not, and gather where I have not strawed: **27** Thou oughtest therefore to have put my money to the exchangers, and *then* at my coming I should have received mine own with usury. **28 Take therefore the talent from him, and give *it* unto him which hath ten talents. 29** For unto every one that hath shall be given, and he shall have abundance: but from him that hath not shall be taken away even that which he hath. **30** And **cast ye the unprofitable servant into outer darkness: there shall be weeping and gnashing of teeth.**

Not only does God pass out 'talents' to people on an unequal basis, he appears to reward people unequally. The above is totally offensive to the Socialist, Communist, and Democratic forms of government. Biblically, inequality is the nature of reality. It is this God's reality that people are at war with: God is not being fair. Everyone should not only be created equal, but they should be born with equal opportunities. Even in the above parable, one person was given ten times what another was given. Everyone is judged by God on using what they have, not what they do not have. And, God expects everyone to use their gifts through hard work and perseverance. Individual responsibility is an important lesson to learn about God's Reality. Heaven and Hell are the ultimate dividing categories and life is designed to teach this important lesson: You reap what you sow. **Different levels of sowing produce different levels of reaping.**

*

One of the methods governments use to justify apparent inequities under their rule is to apply a system of meritocracy to justify the inequity of life. It is an attempt to return some of the blame back upon the victim. At least, to restore some social peace amongst the mob. Despite the claims of a tyrant, he cannot be god and he cannot deliver like a god. Even the ruler that promises everyone their heart's desire has to recognize his own limitations. The mob's covetousness needs to be assured that the system is fair, even though the results are not fair. One of the best methods is to install some form of meritocracy. Design tests for each job and those that score well, get the job. However, men are not gods and every test must be designed by a human being who could never know all the factors that go into qualifying a person for a job. I remember one medical school matched the test scores of the medical students with their success as a doctor later in life. The results were embarrassing. The 'C' students turned out to be better at doctoring then those with the higher IQ's and those who performed better in testing. There were factors in that job that could not be evaluated by testing.

Jesus also deals with the issue of special privileges.

Matthew 20:1. For the kingdom of heaven is like unto a man *that is* an householder, which went out early in the morning to hire labourers into his vineyard. **2** And when he had agreed with the labourers for a penny a day, he sent them into his vineyard. **3** And he went out about the third hour, and saw others standing idle in the marketplace, **4** And said unto them; Go ye also into the vineyard, and whatsoever is right I will give you. And they went their way. **5** Again he went out about the sixth and ninth hour, and did likewise. **6** And about the eleventh hour he went out, and found others standing idle, and saith unto them, Why stand ye here all the day idle? **7** They say unto him, Because no man hath hired us. He saith unto them, Go ye also into the vineyard; and whatsoever is right, *that* shall ye receive. **8** So when even was come, the lord of the vineyard saith unto his steward, Call the labourers, and give them *their* hire, beginning from the last unto the first. **9** And when they came that *were hired* about the eleventh hour, they received every man a penny. **10** But when the first came, they supposed that they should have received more; and they likewise received every man a penny. **11** And when they had received *it*, they murmured against the goodman of the house, **12 Saying, These last have wrought *but* one hour, and thou hast made them equal unto us, which have borne the burden and heat of the day. 13 But he answered one of them, and said, Friend, I do thee no wrong: didst not thou agree with me for a penny? 14 Take *that* thine *is*, and go thy way: I will give unto this last, even as unto thee. 15 Is it not lawful for me to do what I will with mine own? Is thine eye evil, because I am good? 16 So the last shall be first, and the first last: for many be called, but few chosen.**

The owner of the land and the possessor of wealth distributed his money to some that seemed unfair. He gave some special privileges. His workers demanded some form of equality and equity of return. Everyone has the right to help those he will and not help others. This forms one of the attacks upon the family system: the heads of families can grant privileges to their own children or to those within the family clan. That is the nature of freedom and it cannot be rectified without a tyrant taking away the right to spend one's money as one chooses. God created a world that has laws and those laws produce consequences. When people are free, they are sovereign over their own acts and there are built-in penalties for every law that God created. When the mob demands that a government suspend God's laws in order to attain equality or equity, the government must then attempt to steel from one class and give that wealth to another class. That brings the government under the condemnation of God. That is one reason that nations rise and nations fall—even governments cannot escape the consequences of God's universe. When a nation attempts to change the laws of God so that everyone can be equal, regardless of differences, it will experience the same consequences of every person who thinks his ways are better than God's ways.

*

I grew up in a Fundamentalist church which stressed the revival experience: a person needed to testify to the church his 'saved' experience in order to be considered a member. I never remember being taught anything about Biblical Laws. Jesus, I was told, replaced Biblical Law with New Testament grace. The church did print a one page list of moral expectations: Most of the items listed were public expressions of sins: smoking, drinking, chewing tobacco, card playing, movie attendance, rock music, and dancing. If a person could avoid the above he was considered a good Christian. Basically, a Christian was known for what he did not do. Biblical Laws were never stressed but laws about the level of social involvement in American culture. Biblical Laws had been replaced by church laws. After all, the Reformation freed men from the legalism of the Roman Church era of Christendom.

Ever since Jonathan Edward's sermon, *Sinners in the hands of an angry God,* Americans have been obsessed with spiritual experiences. The experiences could be very dramatic. When the idea that good works were no longer a sign of one's salvation, the masses wanted some way to assure themselves that they have escaped the fires of hell.

James 2:14. What *doth it* profit, my brethren, though a man say he hath faith, and have not works? can faith save him? **15** If a brother or sister be naked, and destitute of daily food, **16** And one of you say unto them, Depart in peace, be *ye* warmed and filled; notwithstanding ye give them not those things which are needful to the body; what *doth it* profit? **17** Even so faith, if it hath not works, is dead, being alone. **18** Yea, a man may say, Thou hast faith, and I have works: shew me thy faith without thy works, and I will shew thee my faith by my works. **19** Thou believest that there is one God; thou doest well: the devils also believe, and tremble. **20** But wilt thou know, O vain man, that faith without works is dead? **21** Was not Abraham our father justified by works, when he had offered Isaac his son upon the altar? **22** Seest thou how faith wrought with his works, and by works was faith made perfect? **23** And the scripture was fulfilled which saith,

Abraham believed God, and it was imputed unto him for righteousness: and he was called the Friend of God. **24** Ye see then how that by works a man is justified, and not by faith only. **25** Likewise also was not Rahab the harlot justified by works, when she had received the messengers, and had sent *them* out another way? **26** For as the body without the spirit is dead, so faith without works is dead also.

When a person accepts the substitutionary death of Jesus Christ, that person becomes a new person—in a sense, he has a new DNA. That person become the Temple of God and God's Holy Spirit comes to live in that Temple. The result is that person now takes delight in the Laws of God and seeks to exhibit those laws in his life. The Laws no longer bring condemnation but serve as a target or goal for one's life. The Law which formerly had condemned that person now serves as vehicle to express one's new nature. The Age of Christendom from about 450 to 1450 marked a time when many sought ways to express their faith in God by living a life of service to others. Around 1500, trade was increasing the wealth of many. Nations formed which facilitated the exchanged of goods through various forms of currency. It became more and more apparent that the doctrine of good works was interfering with economic progress. A faith was needed that liberated man from good works. Martin Luther 'was chosen' to lead man into a new interpretation of the Gospel message and a new way to find assurance of salvation without the keeping of the Laws of God. Traditionally it was believed that good works do not save a man, but saved men do good works.

This is why R. H. Tawney could write the classic work: *Religion and the Rise of Capitalism.* The new faith of the Reformation made finance capitalism possible. People could take their eyes off of heavenly service and focus upon serving God by producing goods and services—at a profit of course. Charity took on a new meaning—acts of good will practiced by professionals. When the legalism of the Puritans died in the United States, the emotional faith of Jonathan Edwards became an obsession. People finally had a way to know they were going to heaven without having to perform good works. By the time of The American Revolution, Christian and non-Christian could unite in serving the nation and its laws of prosperity and private property.

The Constitution makes no mention of God or any system of Laws. The American people were totally freed from Biblical Laws. With salvation in their back pocket, men were free to create laws the produced prosperity. Americans operated under two law systems: the law of salvation through emotions, and the laws of business designed by men. In fact, many churches combined the two law systems into a Prosperity Gospel. The teaching was that God blesses those who are saved with financial success. Those who succeed in the business world are displaying their salvation for all to see. This became the American Way of Life that became America's message to the nations. These are the laws that Christian and non-Christian alike could export to other less privileged nations. Business laws were considered natural to the created order and thus moral and good.

Chapter Nine: From Biblical Law to the Founding of the United States.

The American Revolution was more than what the nation celebrates on the Fourth of July. The Revolution occurred under the umbrella of Western Civilization as it had developed since the Reformation. From the time of

Descartes (1586-1650) to the philosopher Bertram Russell (1872-1970) I regard this as the age of the great philosophers. This age created great thinkers who attempted to work out the laws of life without using the Bible as the Revelation of God's reality. For the most part, they operated within Western Civilization that everyone could accept as real. Western and Biblical Civilizations tended to limit these men from deviating too far from the generally accepted beliefs that most considered reality. Those that sought to deviate further turned to the Occult and Eastern Mystical avenues of thought. Both of those became very popular in the 19th century. Eastern mysticism became very popular in the 1960s and rock stars and New Age gurus offered ways of escape from any society that still recognized Western Civilization as being real and acceptable. The Occult remained underground as the ritual murders and child sacrifices connected with the occult remained a crime.

It was the mainline philosophers who were popular with the American Founders. I regard the changes produced by the Revolution as representing the changes in American philosophical thought. Some Founders even referred to passages in the Bible, but that may have merely been to make their ideas more acceptable to the common man who still held onto Biblical notions of salvation and the Bible as the domain of truth. Historians make the big mistake in thinking that, because a person quotes the Bible in his writings or speeches, he believes that to be true. Any good politician knows that success, at times, means appealing to the prejudices and thinking of your audience. Telling the mob what they do not want to hear will get you nowhere, especially in a democracy. I have read studies where some have counted the number of the Founders who cited the Bible as a source—means nothing.

When you analyze the Old Testament, it is not a book about establishing a religious government. In fact, the Bible warns about the dangers of establishing a centralized form of government that replaces the family, clans, and tribal orders.

I Samuel 8:4. Then all the elders of Israel gathered themselves together, and came to Samuel unto Ramah, **5** And said unto him, Behold, thou art old, and thy sons walk not in thy ways: **now make us a king to judge us like all the nations.**

6 But the thing displeased Samuel, when they said, Give us a king to judge us. And Samuel prayed unto the LORD. **7** And the LORD said unto Samuel, Hearken unto the voice of the people in all that they say unto thee: **for they have not rejected thee, but they have rejected me,** that **I should not reign over them. 8** According to all the works which they have done **since the day that I brought them up out of Egypt even unto this day,** wherewith **they have forsaken me, and served other gods,** so do they also unto thee. **9** Now therefore **hearken unto their voice:** howbeit yet protest solemnly unto them, and shew them the manner of the king that shall reign over them.

God showed to Samuel that an evil people desire a powerful government as a form of security and this security will come at a price. Every powerful government will become a tyranny and confiscate the people's wealth and children.

I Samuel 8:10. And Samuel told all the words of the LORD unto the people that asked of him a king. **11** And he said, This will be the manner of the king that shall reign over you: He will take your sons, and appoint *them* for himself, for his chariots, and *to be* his horsemen; and *some* shall run before his chariots. **12** And he will appoint him captains over thousands, and captains over fifties; and *will set them* to ear his ground, and to reap his harvest, and to make his instruments of war, and instruments of his chariots.

Samuel lists all of the evils that will occur once the people turn their lives over to a 'king'. (I Samuel 8: 12-18.)

I Samuel 8:19. Nevertheless the people refused to obey the voice of Samuel; and they said, Nay; but we will have a king over us; **20 That we also may be like all the nations; and that our king may judge us, and go out before us, and fight our battles.**

The above is very much like that occurred during the Revolutionary War era. Americans wanted a nation that could support the new business climate and produce prosperity for everyone. Just as the Puritans wanted a nation to be a light unto the world, the United States was to be an example of how a

'Democratic' government could produce the first modern nation that was independent of any god or legal order, but a government designed to support the material desires of the people. Throughout history, nations have invoked some god to provide a common culture and to bring unity to the state. America would establish a new form of government in which the desires of the people expressed through Democracy would be the god of the nation. In the Old Testament, the nation of Israel had rejected God as their King, and the result was an ancient 'democratic' order.

Judges 21:24. And the children of Israel departed thence at that time, every man to his tribe and to his family, and they went out from thence every man to his inheritance. **25** In those days *there was* **no king in Israel: every man did** *that which was* **right in his own eyes.**

America was to become a nation in which everyone was free to pursue happiness in their own way. The government's purpose was to support an order in which everyone really could do what was right in their own eyes. Everyone had the **right** to be **free** to enjoy life and liberty according to his own desires. The common culture and unity of the United States would be based upon the *Wealth of Nations* which was published in 1776. The theme was every man doing that which was right in his own eyes would produce a stable and prosperous nation. No person should ever be expected to serve the State or his neighbor, but in a Capitalistic order, every man serves others by serving himself. The United States was to adopt this concept and produce a nation of people who would naturally get along with others because it was in their selfish interests to do so. No one would be expected any longer to serve a god, his laws, or a state church. This was a truly revolutionary concept: not one god but every man his own god.

*

The Old Testament is about God establishing His Kingdom upon the earth. The nation of Israel was to be God's vehicle for establishing in the minds of the people the type of Civilization that God was seeking to teach to Israel and eventually to all the nations of the world. The secret of God's Kingdom was that it would be a 'Civilization' not a government. The people of Israel kept thinking that a Civilization could only exist by the force of a powerful 'church' or a tyrannical king. The people of Israel were constantly rejecting God and His Laws. Anarchy and chaos were the rule of the day. The problem is that evil and rebellious people can never agree to live by any standards other than their own. A nation where every man thinks he is a god does not lead to any kind of social harmony. Every other person is expected to behave as each individual 'I' thought they should behave. The people wanted no king because everyone wanted to be their own king. So, one of the battles in the Old Testament was between God seeking to teach the people the importance of obedience to His Laws over obedience to some human ruler.

When the people naturally follow the Laws of God instead of their own desires, a common culture is born. The need for a powerful, centralized government is not necessary. The people live within an established and accepted culture without being forced to live as a community. That is why, when the early Puritans expected to set up a Christian government in America, it failed miserably. Biblically, there was no Old Testament example to which they could pattern an American Theocracy. The attempt to establish a nation where church leaders could rule themselves or through government officials subservient to the church only resulted in failure. The rebellious human nature of the people in the Old Testament still existed in early America. A strong 'Christian' government could never make people want to serve God or His Laws.

There was precedent for Biblical Law and a Biblical Social Order during the Age of Christendom in Old England. However, before England developed its own form of Law, it is important understand that it was preceded by the Fall of the Roman Empire and the collapse of Roman Law. When universal laws collapse, order collapses along with it. The opposite of a Lawful order is, yes, a lawless order. Anarchy and chaos marked the end of Rome. A lawful order is essential for every society and civilization. A government that rules without laws is a tyranny. The people live in fear because tomorrow is not predictable. In fact, tyrants rule by creating an unpredictable environment. People must live by abiding by the laws of the day. Laws are designed to make life predictable: that is why God's laws are absolute and totally predictable. Human laws are to pattern themselves after God's Laws—not only in content but in the predictability.

The Greeks formed multiple city states that were constantly waring with each other. In my school days, the Greeks were considered the founders of modern civilization. I enjoyed reading the Greek Tragedies but they were not in any way inspirational. Life was merely man's attempt to impose his personal order upon the chaos of destiny. Destiny always came out victorious. We studied

Roman history over any Roman literature. The Caesars and their grasping for power made for good reading. But again, the political, moral, and financial collapse left one wondering: how could the great Roman engineers who built those magnificent temples, viaducts, forts, wall, and roads not figure out how to run a nation? The problem, fallen man can built bridges but he cannot create or repair his own soul. This is a fundamental problem throughout history. The physician cannot heal himself. One of the purposes of LAW is to restrain evil, but it can never cure evil. This is the reason that every nation that rejects God ends up swimming in evil.

Romans were great administrators and as a result, the rulers attempted to control the whole empire form Rome. "The diverse populations of the Empire, or the upper classes within those populations, might be thoroughly Romanized; yet with the decay of the non-Roman cultures and political systems, public concerns tended to descend into apathy and indifference. The whole imperial structure was grossly overcentralized, and when the center could hold no longer, the bough began to break."[32] The mere establishment of Roman Law and Roman Justice could not make people Romans; it could only restrict people from living under their own laws. This can be seen in the United States. More and more laws are passed to make everyone obey the same laws across many local cultures. The Civil War was about establishing a universal law upon everyone under the control of Washington. Once a nation starts down that road, there is no end in sight. As I write, a universal definition of sexuality is being imposed upon the whole nation. Laws can never create unity and the more that laws are passed to create unity, the further the nation falls into apathy and indifference.

One of the reasons Roman disintegrated sounds very familiar. The urban centers developed a class of unemployed dependents. They formed a separate class that could not or would not integrate into the ideals of Rome. The class came into conflict with multiple other classes. "Between the senatorial and equestrian families on the one side, and the mases of free citizens in the cities on the other; between the freedmen and the native-born Roman citizens; between citizens, urban or rural, and the millions of slaves; between the urban population and the peasants—among all these social elements, little sympathy endured."[33] The thing that make Western Civilization great is that everyone believed that it was the true order of reality. Some may not have liked it, but it still was the only

---

[32] Kirk. P. 129.
[33] Kirk. P. 129.

real order there was. As I write, America has become a nation of multiple civilizations fighting for recognition and lawful support. In Rome, in order to maintain his power, the Emperor would side with the impoverished classes. They could easily be bought with welfare and free entertainment. (Bread and circuses)

Kirk offers some key lessons to be learned from the Fall of Rome. "Through insufferable taxation, levied to pay the soldiers and please the proletariat, the most industrious classes fell." Kirk cites the famous historian Rostovtzeff, "'The men who inhabited it had utterly lost their balance. Hatred and envy reigned everywhere: the peasants hated the landowners and the officials, the city proletariat hated the city bourgeoisie, the army was hated by everybody, even by the peasants. The Christians were abhorred and persecuted by the heathens, who regarded them as a gang of criminals bent on undermining the state.' ... When the barbarian people overthrew the Roman state, many folk in city and countryside doubtless accepted the fall of central power as a relief."[34] Of course, as with all governments, laws were passed and large bureaucracies were formed to enforce new taxes and regulations. The result was that it became too difficult or too expensive to manufacture goods or to sell farm products.

Empires are expensive. For a time, Rome could support itself by conquering and plundering other nations. As a result, the empire grew to the point of being unmanageable and there were no more nations close enough that conquering them would prove profitable. It was at this point that the Empire resorted to new types of laws: the laws designed to save a sinking ship. As I write in 2023, laws and regulations are being added to the American failing empire almost daily. And if not new laws, executive orders are multiplying beyond belief. There are many forms of laws in history, but when a nation is failing, the laws become laws of desperation. Laws designed to raise money; laws designed to appease special interests; laws to control the flow of 'misinformation'; laws to protect those minorities being used to threaten the middle class into submission; and laws designed to penalized those who criticize the ruling powers. These new laws are laws signal approaching disaster. One thing has not changed since the days of Rome: recruiting angry mobs or minorities to keep the productive middle class from using what power they had left to challenge those in charge. The mob is powerless to make fruitful changes: they can only destroy. And that is what

---

[34] Kirk. P. 130.

they are used for—to destroy productive opposition to the failing government elites.

The reason for the centralization of laws of desperation is that the true laws of self-government and local government are no longer affective. When a nation is operating normally, most people naturally take care of themselves, their families and neighbors. There is no need for government intervention on that level of law making and lawful obedience. When the police chief of my small farming town retired after 30 years on the force, he stated he had never fired his gun in the line of duty and only had to draw it twice. That is self-government in action. The need for laws are minimal. Plus, everyone in town believed in Western Civilization and no one felt that the laws of the land were discriminating against him. The laws of an accepted Civilization are much better than laws imposed by governments. Civilized laws people impose upon themselves; laws of government are imposed by force upon the people. The first police force in the United States was not established in New York City until 1844. People believed in the laws of Civilization and abided with them because it was in their own self-interest to do so.

When Civilizations are no longer accepted, then laws are needed to prop up the existing social order. For three hundred years (1611-1914) Western and Christian Civilizations became the commonly accepted laws of life and social order. Governments could be weak by current standards because they were not needed. The most important laws are the invisible laws of an accepted civilization: laws are considered normal and accepted as similar to the laws of science. Everyone knows that anyone who denies gravity is entering into a life-changing experience. (As the saying goes: It is not the fall the kills you but the sudden stop.) Thus when Jesus inaugurated the Kingdom of God into the World, he was setting forth a new law system, i.e. a new civilization. Those who accept a new life from God, have the obedience to the Commandments planted within their inner being. This was truly revolutionary. During the 1000 years of Christendom, the laws of the Kingdom of God were accepted as real, even by those who did not want to be Christians.

*

Luke 17:20. And when he was demanded of the Pharisees, when the kingdom of God should come, he answered them and said, **The kingdom of God cometh not**

with observation: 21 Neither shall they say, Lo here! or, lo there! for, behold, **the kingdom of God is within you.**

Jesus is attempting to teach those people who think of kingdoms in terms of armies, bureaucracies, and armies. In other words—Kingdoms based upon power to control and enforce people toward a particular end. Jesus was teaching the revolutionary nature of His Kingdom. A totally new concept of controlling people through an invisible civilization. Governments and armies have always been synonymous: no army, no order; no laws, and no obedience. Pagan religions and priesthoods were used by ancient empires to provide a religious justification for submission of the people to the laws of the King. This is where the Puritans and the early American Christian really go off the path. These men who had escaped from the religious persecutions in England, still thought in terms of forming governments that would not persecute Christians—at least Christians who believed as they did. The Puritans still thought in terms of establishing a physical kingdom supported by rulers endorsed by the church.

The failure of the early religious founders to understand the nature of the Kingdom of God upon this earth started America off in the wrong direction. Americans devoted themselves to creating a very visible Kingdom that would be a light unto the entire world: the right laws and the right rulers could create a perfect order. Obviously, the Puritans failed and even as I write, the word theocracy as entered into the American language as a belief in a state church or the rule by a Protestant Vatican. With the American Revolution a new form of government was established where the people themselves would replace the God of Theocracy with the people as god. The masses were tricked into believing that now they could write the laws of the land; not so. The Whiskey Tax Rebellion was fought between 1791-1794. The people quickly discovered that the new government was not of the people, by the people, or for the people. The wealthy class quickly took control through laws that oppressed the farming class.

No one understood that the purpose of a government is to support a Civilization of Laws, not a bureaucracy of laws. The tyrannical government of 2023 started in 1776, not in 2020, with a failure to understand that the true nature of government was established by the Kingdom of God. From the very beginning, after Israel had escaped from the tyranny of Egypt, the people were taught the ways of God and His rule over His people. The people were not to replace the pharaoh with their own pharaoh, but with a Civilization based around the laws of God. Early on, "The idea of the rule of God over his people was already there. … There, in the heritage of Moses himself, we shall find the beginnings of their hope of the Kingdom of God. For this was no idea picked up along the way by cultural borrowing, nor was it the creation of the monarchy and its institutions, nor yet the outgrowth of the frustration of national ambition, however much all these factors may have colored it. On the contrary, it is like with Israel's whole notion of herself as the chosen people of God, and this in turn was woven into the texture of her faith from the beginning."[35]

Early on, God was revealing the nature of His kingdom as revealed in how Israel fought its battles against those enemies that would seek the wealth of the newly formed nation. It is important to understand that these Old Testament times are for our instruction.

I Corinthians 10:11. Now all these things happened unto them for ensamples: and **they are written for our admonition,** upon whom the ends of the world are come.

Bright wrote the following:

"It must be understood that the Israel of the early days in Palestine was not at all a nation as we would understand the term. On the contrary, she was a tribal league, a loose confederation of clans united one to another about the worship of the common God. The clans were independent units unto themselves. Within the clans there was recognition of the moral authority of the … elders, but organized authority was lacking. Furthermore, society exhibited no class distinctions, no wide rift between rich and poor, ruler and subject, but rather complete democracy characteristic of nomad life."[36] Remember, God is revealing the nature of His future Kingdom which will be revealed through Jesus Christ. When reading above, the whole situation sounds unworkable. And yet, the same thinking has been applied to the Kingdom of God. Nations need power, and there is no power in a loose confederation of people. Even the disciples of Jesus could not understand how an invisible Kingdom could succeed.

Again, the following passage reveals how people might feel when their security is in principles revealed in the Kingdom of God. "Here we see the clans

---

[35] John Bright. The Kingdom of God: The Biblical Concept and Its Meaning for the Church. Abingdon-Cokesbury Press. 1953. P. 19.
[36] Bright. P. 31.

maintaining a precarious existence, surrounded by foes but without government, central authority, or state organization of any sort. In times of danger there would arise a hero, one upon whom the spirit of [God] rushed (Judg. 3:10; 14:6), called a judge…. He would rally the surrounding clans and deal with the foe. While his victories no doubt gained him prestige, he was in no sense a king. His authority was neither absolute over all Israel nor permanent; in no case was it hereditary. The battle strength of the judge was the voluntary levy of the clans; he had no standing army, no court, no administrative machinery whatsoever."[37]

The nation of Israel was unlike any other nation upon the earth. Of course, this does not mean the people were excited about such an arrangement. The lack of a King and the lack of a standing army certainly invited insecurity. In Israel and in the Kingdom of God, men are to live dependent upon God and his provisions. This is totally contrary to the nations that trust in the material wealth and in their army. The new nation of Israel, in fact, became a nation of famers: unlike the Canaanite cities that surrounded Israel. These cities also produced greater wealth than those poor Israeli farmers. Being surrounded by wealth constantly tempted the people of Israel to adopt the religion of the Canaanites, i.e. Baalism. Despite what you might think, the people of the Old Testament usually preferred the lifestyle of the wealthy Canaanites to their own meager farms. The surrounding religions of Palestine also practiced a religion that featured temple prostitutes—with a variety to choose from depending upon your sexual inclinations. For most, and I mean most, they preferred the riches of the city and the unique pleasures in worshipping Baal. The people who actually followed God during the Old Testament era were just a minority, or a remnant in Biblical terms. During the time of Elijah when the nation numbered about ten million, only seven thousand had not bowed their knee to Baal. [God's plan does not appear to be working very well.]

I Kings 19:9. And he came thither unto a cave, and lodged there; and, behold, the word of the LORD *came* to him, and he said unto him, What doest thou here, Elijah? **10** And he said, I have been very jealous for the LORD God of hosts: for the children of Israel have forsaken thy covenant, thrown down thine altars, and **slain thy prophets with the sword; and I,** *even* **I only, am left**; and **they seek my life**, to take it away. **11** And he said, Go forth, and stand upon the mount before the

---

[37] Bright. P. 31.

LORD. And, behold, the LORD passed by, and a great and strong wind rent the mountains, and brake in pieces the rocks before the LORD; *but* the LORD *was* not in the wind: and after the wind an earthquake; *but* the LORD *was* not in the earthquake: **12** And after the earthquake a fire; *but* the LORD *was* not in the fire: and after the fire **a still small voice**. **13** And it was *so*, when Elijah heard *it*, that he wrapped his face in his mantle, and went out, and stood in the entering in of the cave. And, behold, *there came* a voice unto him, and said, What doest thou here, Elijah? **14** And he said, I have been very jealous for the LORD God of hosts: because the children of Israel have forsaken thy covenant, thrown down thine altars, and slain thy prophets with the sword; and I, *even* I only, am left; and they seek my life, to take it away. **18** Yet I have left *me* **seven thousand** in Israel, all the knees which have not bowed unto Baal, and every mouth which hath not kissed him.

This passage is very important in understanding the Kingdom of God. It is not a populist movement. That is where America began its decline. Christians and their Church are to be a witness to the Kingdom of God. Ultimately, the Church is to be a light in the midst of darkness. The people of the Kingdom are to express the love of God for Man by exhibiting the call to be a slave to the God of their life who saved them from eternal estrangement from the God of creation, i.e. a living sacrifice. That is why the Kingdom of God is not and can never be a populist movement. But the people who came to America did not come here to become poor dirt farmers. Just as the people of the Old Testament changed gods to avoid the difficulties of serving the God of the Bible, so the American church adopted the values of American Civilization. The American Way of Life provided material wealth and the opportunity to live life according to one's heart's desire.

*

It is worth noting how God judges the people who call themselves followers of God when they turn away from Him. God had Assyria invade the nation of Israel and transport many of the people to faraway lands and moved Assyrians into the vacated farms of the people of Israel. As I write, that is happening in reverse. Now, millions of pagans are being brought into the United State and many followers of God are being forced to live with those who have no desire for the Kingdom of God. The problem for the Christians is how are they to live in and express God's Kingdom when the churches, the Government, and the masses have no desire to expect the Laws of God to be valid in the 21st century? Just as in the Old Testament, the American people of God are about to be taken into captivity.

For the Christian, sometimes it is like living in multiple worlds. There was the dominate Western Civilization which ruled for centuries. (1611-1914) However, in 1776, the American Civilization was inaugurated by the Declaration of Independence. That lasted until 9/11, 2001. At the point the various laws (The Patriot Act, and the National Defense Authorization Act) announced the coming of the New Global Civilization. Normal Americans now found themselves considered 'enemies of the state.' Life can get very confusing and that is why Americans feel disoriented right now. The official church still lives in the world of Western Civilization. However, the people of the church live in the modern American 21st century Civilization. However, the laws of the land are there to support the New World Civilization. And yet, for the true followers of Jesus Christ and His Kingdom, they live outside of all three. I will deal with this later, but for now, it is important to understand why life is so confusing and people have trouble communicating reality with others who may not share the same worldview and actually live in another civilization. True followers of the Bible and its Laws feel, at times, like the hillbillies living up in the Appalachian Mountains: cut off from modern civilization.

*

Real life is always messy. The purpose of any civilization or law order is to transform confusion into an order. People need an order. There are those who desire to form an order in which they will be the 'king' of that order. Orders provide power to those in charge and that is one of the goals of establishing a global order. Also, many orders begin with the desire to replace God's order with one of Satanic origin. History is the story of multiple kingdoms and multiple world views in a war for supremacy. The Kingdom of God appears to be invisible if not non-existent. The American Church in order to make itself visible as a spiritual power joined one of the major civilizations. After the Reformation, first the Churches joined the new Nation/States in order to become recognized. The church felt that the power it desired could only be achieved through becoming associated with some earthly power in Western Civilization. Later, the American Church allied itself with the new American Civilization of material wealth and psychic prosperity, i.e. money and happiness.

One great reason for the Fall of Rome was the Empire could no longer provide an order for the people. "Rome had fallen, Augustine says, for want of order in the soul. By their nature, men seek for order: not the unconscious order of swallows or bees, but an order which human intelligence understands. For men, their acts must have significance. Men are miserable unless they find 'a disposition or arrangement of equal and unequal things in such a way as to allocate each to its own place.' They must have purpose in their existence. And what is that purpose?"[38] The Old Testament marks God's intrusion into the earth with His created order. It started with the order of Moses versus Pharaoh. The story of Exodus goes a lot deeper than the movie version. God was replacing the order of Pharaoh with His new order through the nation of Israel.

The early Christians struggled with the Roman order in which they lived and the Kingdom of God which was their life. This positions a Christian in conflict with the principalities and powers of every age. Not only is the Christian to live within the Kingdom so is God's Church. The problem is there are two churches, the visible one and the invisible one. The two are often at odds. A false church and a true church often exist within the same building. As I write, America is internally at war with several civilizations or orders all competing to be the dominant one. Was there ever a time when the Kingdom of God was more invisible? Reality itself seems to be in hiding from mankind. The only order in the United States is enforced by force. The local communities with their church and social expectations served to exhibit an order by voluntary compliance. People complained about the social prison of small town America, but that is nothing like the modern prisons built for those who oppose the New World Order of control. That is why Kirk could state this about a world without a local social order: "Were there no state, with force at its command, there would be no civilized existence—indeed, no human existence at all, except on the most primitive and bestial level."[39] There can be no social order if every man can make up his own order, but some form of universal social order is needed for life to exist without anarchy.

This is why it is important to understand the government of ancient Israel. A centralized government was not needed until the people forsook their mission from God. That is why America had no police departments until the mid-19th century. The Kingdom of God does not operate in any government or in any impersonal urban arena. The Kingdom of God begins with self-government

---

[38] Kirk. P. 161.
[39] Kirk. P. 164.

98

through an understanding of an eternal order that was not created by man. This is why every tyrant and every totalitarian order is at war with the Kingdom of God. Evil men understand better the true nature of God's Kingdom than those who attend American Churches. And Biblical Americans know that to submit to the Laws of the Kingdom makes that person an enemy of Satan's order, i.e. the New Global World Order. The order of God's Kingdom cannot avoid being at war with the New World Satanic Order.

*

Modern Statist Law cannot be understood unless it is contrasted how men viewed law in the Age of Christendom: God's Laws were real, not human constructs. Men could only apply God's Laws; they could not create new laws. "The King himself is under the law; should he break it, his subjects would be absolved from their allegiance. And the law is not merely the creation of kings and parliaments, but rather the source of their authority. At heart, the law is the expression of natural justice and the ancient ways of a people."[40] England under Christendom had a duel law system: Laws of the King and his men [Parliamentary Laws], and Laws of the people [Common Laws]. Common Laws could be described as the legal expression of a society's Civilization or Human Order. Common Laws reflected the values of the masses and not laws imposed upon them by the King. Judges were expected to uphold the ancient traditions and the beliefs of the masses. The above is an example of the Kingdom of God in operation as the yeast the leavens the whole loaf.

Matthew 13:31. Another parable put he forth unto them, saying, The kingdom of heaven is like to a grain of mustard seed, which a man took, and sowed in his field: **32** Which indeed is **the least of all seeds**: but when it is grown, it is the greatest among herbs, and becometh a tree, so that the birds of the air come and lodge in the branches thereof.

33 Another parable spake he unto them; The kingdom of heaven is like unto **leaven**, which a woman took, and hid in three measures of meal, **till the whole was leavened.**

---

[40] Kirk. P. 184.

Jesus explain two important principles of His Kingdom as it operates within a nation or culture: It starts tiny as just an idea, and it is like yeast where just a pinch can make the whole loaf grow. This is how Civilizations or Christian orders start out until a whole nation can reflect the values of Biblical Laws. It all starts with a small group of Christians becoming living sacrifices and exhibiting God's laws of justice and service. That sounds ridiculous, but God promises that there is a power released when Christians become living servants to God and others.

Acts 14:22. Confirming the souls of the disciples, *and* exhorting them to continue in the faith, and that **we must through much tribulation enter into the kingdom of God.**

There is a problem, in order for a Civilization of God to be created within a nation, trailblazers are needed. They are the ones that will live differently from the rest of the nation and for that there will be consequence, i.e. much tribulation. The Kingdom seed is planted by Christians living the Kingdom values no matter the cost. However, God promises that those who live the true Christian Life will be blessed, not with riches, but with propagating reality to the masses. Amazing as it sounds because we all feel we live in an age of chaos and disintegration, that the Kingdom of God has the power of God operating within it. Kingdom Living is a miracle in operation. Because most 'Christians' look for results, the Gospel is popularized to gain immediate results without 'much tribulation.' Kingdom living was never designed to be a mass movement, even though a whole nation will be blessed by God's remnant becoming living sacrifices. That is the miracle of the yeast affecting the whole loaf.

The Common Law under Christendom exhibited some of the principles of Kingdom Living. Kirk describes the nature of Common Law: "The common law is founded upon custom and precedent, although upon *national* customs and usages, rather than local. This common law is an 'organic' development, arising out of centuries of judges' decisions upon the basis of what the people believed to be just. It is 'prescriptive' law, derived from the man-to-man experience of people in community over a very long period of time; it is 'customary' or 'traditional' law. ... The common law has been called 'unwritten law'...."[41] In America, laws today are seen as agents of social change. The laws are not

---

[41] Kirk. P. 184.

designed to restrain evil, but to punish those who refuse to submit to some political or social agenda. These laws are written to overturn traditions and centuries of commonly accepted practices. The LGBTQ agenda is an example of modern laws destroying traditional laws or Common Laws.

The common law system sets limits upon what judges can rule. They are not to rule using their own personal beliefs as a guide, but upon the traditions of the people and their long history. The people naturally resist change or being manipulated by laws that are seen as attacks upon their personal and religious beliefs. The judges had no power to create laws as is the case today. "They must abide by the accumulated experience of legal custom, so that the law will be no respecter of persons, and so that people may be able to act in the certitude that the law does not alter capriciously."[42] The Common Law system also employed a jury of twelve good men who are noted for being trustworthy. In other words, juries were not composed of misfits chosen off the streets to serve the Crown. To sit on one of these juries was considered much like becoming a judge.

There is another feature of common law juries. They did not have to abide by laws that differed from the traditions and practices of the people. If a law went beyond the desires and traditions of the people, the jury could find a person innocent of a law he had broken. Not only that, but the judge or king could not overturn that decision. In a sense, the true Supreme Court under Christendom was the jury. It had the power to declare laws null and void. I have served on several grand juries and we were instructed that we must abide by the laws of government even if we find them unfair. This nullifies one of the major purposes of a jury of common men—not professional juries as in American federal courts today. It is important to understand that Biblical and Christian morals were considered part of the Common Law. This made English Common Law different from other nations. Basically, the American legal system is based upon procedural law and not any common law that was considered higher than written legislative laws.

Kirk states the true nature of legitimate law: "For a body of law to be really enforceable, it must receive the willing assent of the mass of people, living under such a law. Stable government grows out of law, not law out of government. If the political power decrees positive laws, without reference to general consent, those laws will be evaded or defied, and respect for law with diminish, so that

---
[42] Kirk. P. 185.

force must be substituted for justice; precisely that resistance to statutory law occurred in some European countries, over the centuries."[43] This refers to America of another age when a legal system respected the traditional law and the thinking behind that law. Laws are by nature conservative, and that is the beauty of laws--not a flaw. Strong, multi-generational laws are a roadblock to those who would seize power and use new laws to change and control the masses.

The magnificence of the Common Law was this: "Now, the English people looked upon the common law as *their* law, the product of their historical experience; it was not something imposed upon them from above. ... And if the common law was the foundation of order, also it was the foundation of freedom. The high claim of the old commentators on the common law was this: no man, not even the king, was above or beyond the law. ... The Law is a bridle upon the king. ... By the reign of Edward I, in the last quarter of the thirteenth century, the common law was so well entrenched that no king could defy it, whatever else, he might aspire to."[44] This is why very few Americans know about the common law and how the people's laws even kept their king on a short leash. As I write in 2023, there is no political leash to be found and no law greater is considered greater than the American 'King'—and his especially his executive orders.

Chapter Ten: The American Revolution was a Legal Revolution.

---

[43] Kirk. P. 189.
[44] Kirk. P. 190.

The American Revolution was a legal revolution more than a political one. Why? Because in the Constitution there is no reference to any legal system or to any absolute laws. Why? Because Americans were declared free to start their own laws, their own order, and their own absolutes. There was no mention of God or any Biblical principles. Obviously, there was no mention of having a form of Common Law. The people were declared to be the true lawmakers through their representatives—as if the masses knew whom to vote for or the masses could not be manipulated. The Constitution actually opened the door for the nation to be ruled by an elite. The only question was whether it would be a good elite or a corrupt elite.

Before the Revolution, the religious immigrants had already established an order based upon their interpretation of Biblical laws. Also, Blackstone's Commentaries on the Laws of England was accepted as America Law before the Constitution. The big fear among the masses was that England might seek to establish a 'state church' in the colonies. In the minds of the people, that was the really big issue. A tax on tea? Who cares? Many feared that the U.S. Constitution was opening the door to tyranny. The only check on power according to many was the government's own court. I mean, how impartial would they be? Laws and Constitutions should not to be about the powers of the government, but about what the government cannot do, or should never do. Not temporary "no's" but absolute no's. Some of the objectors to the secular Constitution managed to insert a 'Bill of Rights' into the Constitution. However, the rulers totally subverted those rights by stating they only applied to the States, not to the central government. It took four score and seven years, but America's legal revolution became firmly established. Even the American churches were also forced into submission after the Civil War.

The American Revolution ignored the whole purpose of a law order. "Churches and states are immortal corporations: if we break down established laws, thriving customs, and beloved ceremonies, we rashly ignore the lessons of the past and endanger society's future. Our religion, our culture, and our political rights all are maintained by continuity: by our respect for the accomplishments of our forefathers, and by our concern for posterity's well-being."[45] A true nation must be a protector of a people's traditions or it is not legitimate. The American Revolution overturned America's history of Western Civilization. Only one third of the Americans wanted a war against England. That is why the skilled propagandist Sam Adams had to create fake atrocities to push people into supporting the war. Two-thirds were content with the status quo. The American elites were not.

There is a reason a war for independence was needed. Other British colonies achieved independence without a major war of revolution. Why? Wars are the best way to bring about social and cultural changes. Negotiated settlements bring about peace but not change. The American Founders have been idolized because they made sure that was part of the political narrative. These men became the heroes of social and cultural change. Throughout history, revolutions followed a certain pattern: "A revolution begins with relatively moderate objectives, led by men not altogether radical; but as blood is shed and hatred increase, the early leaders of the struggle give way to men more extreme and violent. The old order dissolves into anarchy, but no tolerable new order emerges. Presently confusion becomes so terrible that the recovery of peace matters more to the people than does anything else. And then there appears a 'man on horseback,' a talented military commander often, who restores order at the price of freedom."[46] The American Revolutionary War opened the door to a powerful national government with a centralized bureaucracy.

America has used violent wars, time and again, to bring about today's culture from Hell. America fought its first major war as the First Barbary War (Tripolitan War). It was fought from 1801-1805. Where was this war fought? In the Mediterranean Sea. That is a long ways away Boston. Even today it takes a powered war ship a long time to get there from America. America right away announced its intentions to become a world power. Other wars were fought to bring about total change to America, its people, and its culture. The Civil War was a war of total change in the way multiple governments were expected to rule in this nation: from local to national controls. The Spanish American War changed

---

[45] Kirk. P. 245.
[46] Kirk. P. 264.

the public perception of America as world power. WWI changed the nature of propaganda and its use on the American public. World War II created the idea of globalism. The Cold War created the 'last man standing' world view. If the United States failed to be the world's policeman, the whole global order would fail. There are more, but those who rule the earth can never allow peace to exist. Tyrannies need wars that never end. Peace makes people turn inward and creates a desire to return to the small town environment. They even start thinking that maybe we do not need a powerful, centralized government taking all of our money. People must always be convinced, by whatever methods possible, that they need a tyrannical government, or else that government will make sure that the people will cry out for a powerful government: look at how organized crime operates and you will understand modern politics. You need protection or your business will burn down. Sure enough, those who reject protection have their businesses burnt down. The nation needs billions and billions spent on a military or there will be a war. That is why America has a war for every generation—just a reminder.

Two major factors determined the new American order after the Revolution: The age of Enlightenment and America's blank slate social order. While America did not experience the violence of the French Enlightenment, America did have its share of social and political upheaval. Besides the numerous Indian Wars, there was Shays' Rebellion in Western Massachusetts from 1786-1787, and the Whiskey Rebellion in Western Pennsylvania from 1791-1794. The new rapid urban invasion of immigrants was not an easy adjustment. The newcomers were not always welcomed, if for no other reason than their willingness to work for less money than the citizens. At this time of transition from Colonial American to Industrial America, there was no common culture in which everyone was expected to submit. Americans were free to establish their own cultural expectations. As in all such situations, selfish concerns were more powerful than community concerns. A uniform people and a centralized government go together.

Kirk cites Rowland Berthoff in *An Unsettled People.* In early America there was no established social order. "At the base of the hierarchy lie the economic values, necessary but subservient, of adequate production and equitable distribution of material goods. Upon that system rests the specifically social values of satisfactory relationships among men in a reasonably stable, secure institutional structure, the system with which social history is primarily concerned. But a stable social structure is less important in itself than as the foundation, in turn, for other, loftier values of mind and spirit—esthetic and intellectual achievement of some excellence and perhaps even what is variously called self-fulfillment, redemption from sin, and salvation of the soul."[47] Despite what the Declaration of Independence declares, the private pursuit of one's private goals does not make for a powerful government. The masses must be constantly reminded that, however great their life, they need a strong government. In America, not only do businesses compete, so too do the assorted governments compete for market share.

The new America was based upon a free market system: not only in economics, in churches, but in the social order also. Of course, the free market is sold as the greatest way to establish freedom in the land. It is an evolution imposed upon every area of life and culture—and may the most fit survive. All of life becomes of competition without any religious or ethical restraints. The rules of Old England did not always apply in America. Nothing in the new nation was based upon tradition. The laws of the school playground became the laws of the city. One thing the old movie and TV westerns accurately reflected was what life was like when there were no codified laws and social traditions. In such an environment, the most powerful and the most immoral were also the most successful. During the 1000 year reign of Christendom, the Catholic Church imposed an order upon everyone, including the kings. Americans were searching for an order that would be fair, but in reality, the rulers were searching for an order that would bring some sort of social peace ordained by those who controlled the levers of power. Americans have lived in a divided world ever since the Revolutionary War: the ideals of the Revolution on the one hand, and the reality of America being ruled by an elite of the rich and the powerful on the other hand. .

---

[47] Kirk. P. 442.

"Nineteenth-century America, eager for material gain, often neglected the roots of order in class, family, church, and community; and despite the zeal of evangelical preachers, the common man of the nineteenth-century America sought less earnestly after salvation of his soul than had Bunyan's Christian. Here we can merely suggest the difficulties which the 'permanent things,' the ideas and institutions of an abiding order, encountered in the United States during the era when the American people swept on to the Pacific, and grew more prosperous and powerful than any other great people ever had been."[48] This aspect of America has really never changed. The American people have been at war with other nations and peoples for its entire history. There never has been a time when Americans could establish their own Common Law and a traditional order in which everyone subscribed. Americans do not really share a common legal heritage, but only common fantasies of how the world should operate. For example, many people claim America was founded as a Christian nation, but the government has never operated as if this were true. Believing America was a Christian nation gave the church people a free pass for their failures to confront the evils of their time and their government.

*

Because America lived under a free market system, there were always winners and losers. No one likes to be one of the losers. Whether the losers were result of their own undoing, or because of being oppressed by the more powerful, America had traditions which promised equality and equity. People rarely blame themselves for being one of the losers. Some other entity has to be blamed. During the age of Christendom, the social order provided a vast network of charities to aid the losers which prevented a large disgruntled class of people. The local parish church was the great equalizer: not only in its teachings about heaven and hell, but that everyone in the church was an equal to every other person. People were not measured by status or wealth but as members of a holy community. It is similar to the times during WWII, everyone was considered equally an American contributing to the cause.

---

[48] Kirk. P. 443.

Other than times of war, America really never had a feeling of community where everyone had an important place in life. As stated, America was a land of winners and losers. The winners had to justify their wealth, and the losers looked for someone to blame. Because status and wealth is the ultimate goal in the American social order, there has never been an order in which everyone could feel equal. A successful social order provides a feeling of oneness despite many differences. The Bible teaches that in the Kingdom of God, everyone was created with different talents, but all share an eternal soul and all will be rewarded by God in a fair and equitable manner. A successful nation and culture needs an afterlife in which wrongs will be rectified, and everyone will be rewarded for how well they did in their particular place in the social order. God is the great equalizer. When a nation reject God and the Bible, the 'losers' start demanding the government make things equal on earth, now. With spiritual equality ruled nonexistent, material equality is all that is left.

Oh, by the way, Laws can never create a social order or rectify any wrongs the losers may feel they have endured. That is why Americans have become addicted to laws and more laws. The general feeling that any short-coming or any wrong can be corrected by the right law. Every failed law requires another law. That is the role God has in history: He reveals His Laws.   When a government attempts to play god, i.e. better Commandments, it only makes thinks worse. When a people share a common faith, there is no need for laws to correct hurt feelings. I cannot emphasize enough the necessity of a nation sharing a common belief. And if the common belief is the Bible and its Commandments, they also share a common morality and a sense of community. Governments were created to provide for a common defense of the borders, and to ensure that there is a fair judicial system. When any government attempts to force a common morality upon the people, it will fail. Because all non-Biblical moralities are from Satan. He is the author of confusion and disorder.

As America became more and more prosperous in a material sense, Americans became aware that the nation was developing a class system. The feeling at the time was this: The powerful people take what they can, and the powerful people keep what they can. When people are judged solely by their material wealth, moral and ethical values are of no value. As the saying goes: Money talks. Not everyone can be rich, but that is the class of people everyone wanted to excel in—that is how society judged people. And the church recognizing the nature of America, developed a theology to justify the American Way of Life: God blesses His servants with material wealth. Because America became a wealthy nation in the last half of the 19th century, most people could believe that they were wealthy because they were good. Their selfish lifestyle had God's seal of approval—'just look at my bank account.'

The Constitution developed the idea that America was a nation of laws and the people had the power to change the times and the seasons. Men felt the power of being able to plan and control their own destiny, separate from all others in the nation: each man a king. However, life requires an order in which everyone can feel that they belong and that everyone in that order shares the same values. In a sense, the general order of a nation must take on the feeling of a community of equals. Americans were given personal rights to protect themselves from the intrusion of others into the lives, but individual, solitary rights do not create a community and a common bond. When life is lived in terms of rights, then the laws of the evolutionary jungle takeover.   It is every man and his rights against the rest of the world. Every person then becomes dependent upon the government and their leader to protect those individual rights. That is how nations die. That is the story of America in the 21st century.

Chapter Eleven: Imperfect people demand perfect laws.

One of the primary teachings of the Bible is that all have sinned and fallen short of the Kingdom of God. Not only that, men are genetically flawed and incapable of even making themselves into perfect beings. However, most men do not want to accept that teaching of the Bible. When men fail to accept their own terminal imperfection, they cannot accept it in others, in governments, or in their culture. In fact, one's own imperfection is viewed as a result of imperfections in the others listed above. So, what do men demand a cure for their own feelings of being imperfect? They demand that governments create a perfect order to match their own view of their perfection. It is like a sign on the wall in one place I worked: It is hard to soar with the eagles when you are surrounded by turkeys. That is the predicament of modern, self-righteous man: he cannot cure his own 'turkeyness.'

What people are witnessing in the United States in the 21st century is an effort to create a legal system that will make everyone feel a part of some cosmic order. Everyone feels that their fallen human nature was caused from outside themselves. Biblically, the problem is within man. Man has rebelled against God and man no longer has the human nature that he was created to have. Men still retain within themselves the ideal of perfection but are frustrated when they cannot achieve that ideal. Part of that fallen human nature is man's refusal to recognize the reason man feels estranged from himself and from others. Even if a man were to recognize the precariousness of his situation, the last solution would be one that requires some dramatic action on his own part. God offers no passive cures. God declares in His Word: Take up your cross [death to self-interest] and start following me.

God requires only perfect men can approach the throne of God. As you can see, there is a problem. Now, Biblically, a man can be declared perfect through the atoning and substitutionary death and resurrection of Jesus Christ. However, men want to prove that they can, in some way, make themselves perfect. And if they can do that for themselves, it proves that God is not the god he claims to be. Man can become his own god and cure himself. Fallen Man is at war with God and will never approach God except on his own terms. That problem started with Cain who offered his own form of sacrifice to God, rather than a sacrificial lamb.

That is why the nature of LAW is so important: the right laws can bring perfection down to earth from the heavens. Man could steal perfection from God without having to become submissive and becoming a slave to God. Cain was the first person who sought to revise the laws of God and attain perfection by being a really good guy and by showing God what good works he could perform.

In man's search for perfection, he also expects total equality. No man should in any way be superior to any other man. The problem starts at birth. Everyone is born in different times, in different nations, in different families, under different governments, with different talents, and taught different religions. Evolution creates men equal and yet the total culture makes men unequal. False religions seek to solve this problem. Rituals are a form of spiritual laws that operate invisibly much like governmental laws. Obeying the right cosmic laws and keeping the right spiritual rituals both are designed to dispel man's guilt for being imperfect. Man cannot escape the need for some form of perfection within his body and soul. Many want the government to make others perfect in place of making themselves perfect. Or by displaying one's own perfection by revealing the lack of perfection in others. Men cannot escape the need for some form of perfection—it is hard-wired into our makeup by God.

*

Thomas Sowell describes something like this in his book, *The Quest for Cosmic Justice.* All men stand guilty before God and most men fear that this might be true. It is common for criminals, celebrities, and the very wealthy to donate money to charities and churches hoping God, if there is one, will give them credit for their good works. Throughout history, men have lived in fear of what the gods might do. Men knew they were guilty and they knew they stood naked before the unknowns of life. Rene Fulop-Miller wrote this in 1935:

"The great and primal dream, common to all the peoples of the earth, one which has troubled the mind of man since the dawn of his first beginnings, is an anxiety-dream; for apprehension dominates the earliest and deepest strata of human thought and feeling; dread inspired by the vastness of the universe, and by man's loneliness therein; dread of the mysterious, incalculable, capricious powers with which his imagination peoples the realms of space. … The thousand

111

cares and alarms which life with its concrete perils continually evokes—fear of illness, pain, poverty, loss of love—one and all of them are but circumstantial condensations of an inextinguishable and original terror, which is projected upon the obscure background of the ancient cosmic anxiety-dream of helpless loneliness felt by a creature grown self-conscious amid the eternal silences of boundless space, where deities dimly felt to be inimical hold sway. The omnipresent gods: these spooks, these 'numina,' which are the products of man's animistic thinking!

"The conceptual outlook of our race has from the first been tainted by this horror and disquietude; the first creations of human fancy were the awful forms of hostile demons, inhabiting earth, air, and water; peeping from behind every tree-trunk, awakening with every sunrise, lurking in all that was edible; ever ready to attack, to inflict discomfort and torment and death. The clouds, the fountains, the forest, the steppe—all nature is full of elemental spirits, spooks, kobolds, dragons, devils, which are stronger than man and to whose whims he is subject. Men cannot escape the delusion that his life is passed in a charmed circle that is essentially demon shapes, man endows them with powers and dimensions no less boundless, transcending experience; and he ascribes to them as personalities the terrible characteristics and qualities which he projects into the outer world from his inward experience of primordial dread."[49]

This is the world in which men feel they must confront. The very idea of justice appears impossible. Not only justice between people, but cosmic justice from the gods. Therefore, there are two levels of justice: in time and in eternity. History is the story of man's attempt to construct institutions which would provide man with protection from the unknowns and terrors of life. Generically, the solution was found in Kings and Priests. Some person or organization to save me from the terrors of the day and of the night. "Unceasingly man tried to force the incalculable into a system, to bit and bridle the uncanny powers, to mitigate their cruelty and arbitrariness, and thus to free himself from the nightmare of the world's anxiety-dream."[50]

---

[49] Rene Fulop-Miller. Leaders, Dreamers, and Rebels: An Account of the Great Mass-Movements of History and of the Wish=Dreams that Inspired Them. The Viking Press. 1935. P. 8-9.
[50] Fulop-Miller. P. 11.

When true Biblical Christianity was banished from America, the populace returned to the same problems faced by ancient pagans, except in modernized forms. Consider the terrors faced by ancient man: "Zeus is a capricious, revengeful, malignant demon; and, like their chief, the other gods of the Greek Olympus are pitiless tormentors and destroyers. … Whatever happens here below happens because the gods delight in hurting mortals, to whom, therefore, life often seems not worth living. … How many horrible figures did the Hellenic imagination create in additions to the gods of Olympus: Pan, the god who dwelt on earth, and whose sudden appearances cause unreasoning terror ('panic'). … The notion of such omnipresent malicious powers pervades the religions of antiquity."[51] This fear of gods, who acted like delinquent gods whose behavior could not be predicted, opened the door to the God of the Ten Commandments whose ways were revealed to be open and consistent. Of course, it went much further than that: The God of the Bible reveals the very nature of the universe and the laws that He built into His creation. Not only that, He wanted a personal relationship with His people. Amazing.

At first, the people welcomed a God who was so much different than the pagan gods of other nations. However, there was an element of fear in the God of the Bible. Men knew they were guilty and wondered, would killing a lamb open the door to the judge of the universe? "With distressing clearness, they become emotionally aware of the infinitely manifold possibilities of wrongdoing, recognizing their capacity to resist temptation: and out of this annihilating conviction of guilt developed the thought that man himself must be to blame for imperfections of the world, that he had to atone for the Fall which had brought a cure upon the whole human race."[52] However, very few really accepted the message of the God of the Bible. Men were looking for a god who could be propitiated through some form of sacrifice or ritual, but obedience to the Laws of God went beyond what most people were asking. Also, most wanted a god they could control and would serve their selfish needs: a living sacrifice, not a chance.

*

---

[51] Fulop-Miller. P. 12.
[52] Fulop-Miller. P. 13-14.

The nation of Israel was not a very religious nation by Biblical standards. The nation was surrounded by nations that were quite wealthy and offered religions that did not require moral obedience, only the sacrifice of babies. Evil people will trade a baby for a life of moral freedom. [Why do you think abortion is such a big issue? The killing of babies to gain some type of cosmic freedom has always been popular.] It took time, but the masses finally found a religion to their own liking: a government of the people, by the people, and for the people. Rather than serve an over-demanding God, men could form a government in man's own image. This new 'god' would protect man from the terrors of the day and the night [National defense, daily bread, and moral freedom]. There is a lot more to modern governments than most people realize. The masses will put up with even evil governments if it will but protect their right to be morally free from the God of the Bible and His form of justice.

While few want to admit it, but the modern Nation-State is a religion: a religion the people would much prefer to the Biblical idea of salvation and service. Unless you can see modern Nation/States in this light, you will never understand why the people continually submit to the tyrannical controls upon every aspect of their lives. All men ask is the protection of their moral freedoms under the guise of rights granted by the government. The American Churches submitted to this religious sham because that is the kind of religion people wanted in America's religion of the free market. In an unregulated way, America has always had a 'State Church'—in the same way that a dog always follows his master. Any church that challenged the Master State would always find itself in trouble. This was exemplified when the Southern Church challenged the government of the North. After the South's defeat, the winning side sent infiltrators into the Southern Churches so that they too could support their new master.

*

The road to the master state paralleled the decline of the Biblical teachings about reality. From the Reformation until the 18th century, Church and State were considered co-equals by many: mostly because those in power did not yet feel powerful enough to separate the Government totally from the God concept. The early post-Reformation philosophers felt the need to at least have some form

114

of original cause apart from man. Descartes' 'I think therefore I am' concept still needed a 'god' to support his thesis. John Locke's *Essay on Human Understanding,* a work based upon human reasoning, still felt the necessity of giving a tip-of-the-hat to God. No one dared defy God openly, even though people were beginning to feel He had worn out His welcome. However, that was all about to change.

Mankind discovered a new god that humanity could trust and this god did not care at all about any nebulous and ancient Commandments. This god was Nature that was the 'god' who made man through evolutionary processes. Even before Darwin, men felt that Nature was the one in charge of this earth. Whether true or not, the powers of the State used this new 'knowledge' to separate God from the newly acquired powers of the Nation/State. Modern science is really a counter religion to the faith in the Bible. The findings of science are more nebulous than the founders of that faith want to admit. You see, godless men created a godless method of creating a system that does not need God. Not only that, it must give the appearance of being greater than God. Science developed a method where its reality can be proved in a laboratory, unlike the works of God. Because God reveals absolute laws, secular man must have his own absolute laws. That is why the Nation/State has become so essential in the modern world: only a power greater than 'god' can impose its will upon mankind. Man cannot escape the need for absolutes—that is the way God created this world.

*

I consider the French and American Revolutions as twins as both occurred at the same time and both invoked the same philosophies of social and political life. **The only difference is that the French Revolution was based upon the teachings of Satan and the American Revolution was based upon the deceptions of Satan.** The French hated God openly; the Americans merely dismissed God as a minor factor in political life, i.e. secularism. The philosophical foundation for the 21st demonic global order was laid at this time. The old laws were being removed and new ones based upon reason were being presented to the public. The Ten Commandments were gone and the Commandments of Reason now ruled. That is why the American Constitution lists no laws by which to judge the reality as revealed in the New Order of the Ages. What is amazing is how the American churches became partners in a totally secular form of social order: Satan and God were given equal billing.

Before the laws of the Nation/State could be dramatically changed, the laws of the universe had to be changed. "It was only the remarkable results achieved by experimental science at the end of the seventeenth century and during the eighteenth which gave people courage, regardless of the dogmas of theologians, to penetrate farther and farther into the world of natural causation, and to recognize that, behind what hath hitherto been regarded as the arbitrary will of God, there prevailed a rationally comprehensible and calculable necessity. One domain after another was opened to physical and methods of examination, became susceptible of scientific explanation, was shown to be subject to the working of a few clearly formulated natural laws."[53] The above does not sound like the voice of Satan, but that is how he pleads his case before men. If men want raw power, then Satan will lead them into the very demonic powers they are seeking.

One of the first saints of Science was Galileo. He felt that the language of God could be replaced by the language of mathematics. Science could reduce reality to things that could be observed, weighed, or measured. Then formulas could be derived which spoke the language of reality—a reality that could be tested in a laboratory. God seemed so remote and the Bible so confusing, but mathematics seemed to be derived from inside of man's brain—a brain given to man by nature. Mathematics was the voice of Nature's Bible revealing absolute truths. Truths that were greater than the alleged truths of the Bible and the ancient philosophers. The Bible described man's reality as having some divine purpose. Francis Bacon maintained that Nature revealed no grand purpose upon which man could find any cosmic meaning. With God eliminated, man was now free to impose his own laws upon the people of the Nation/States.

It is these new laws that empowered the Nation/State to establish forms of government previously seen as evil or pagan. "People had now learned to laugh at faith in providence, heaven, hell, and damnation as 'cobwebs of superstition,'

[53] Fulop-Miller. P. 144.

and were setting to work, unhindered by thoughts of God or another world, to mould this world to their liking. 'Nature and reason, those are my gods' exclaimed Citizen Duport in the [French] Convention."[54] At that point a child was rolled out and men proclaimed that from now on, all children should learn not about God, but about reason. In keeping with the theme, the new god was the 'Goddess of Reason.' After this convention, the mobs entered of Saint-Eustache and turned it into a tavern and a public celebration of sexuality. The demonic aspect of the new faith was openly revealed to everyone.

*

The new laws of science were now to be applied to the control of the masses. Not only was Nature the subject of laws, so too could man be subjected to the laws of science. The science of man was a deceitful way of saying that just as man could control nature through mathematics, so man could be controlled through new laws of science. Obviously, this was an attack upon the personality of man given to man in creation. The image of God was just another one of those fictions imported from the past. [As I write, the new AI computers are being developed to totally know everything about every person and use the laws of science to control every man for the betterment of mankind and the salvation of the environment and the earth.] It takes a soul to resist evil and that is why the new social laws are promoting scientific laws that result in the decay of the defiant human soul. That is the real target of the Nation/State. There can be no tyranny as long as human souls are allowed to be publically displayed. Men are Nature's machines and are expected to act as such. Individual personalities are merely animals attempting to differentiate themselves from the herd.

The Laws the Newton taught to the world revealed a mathematical order of reality. It is now the role of the State to develop laws of humanity. Newton led to the control of matter, now laws could be developed to mold humans just like matter had been molded into giant locomotives. It was labelled 'social physics.' "The mechanism of society must be analyzed, the relationship and functions of its several parts must be ascertained. So soon as, in this way, the forces of repulsion and attraction among the 'social atoms' and the laws guiding these had been elucidated, it would be possible, by modifying our knowledge, to modify our lives, and to bring into being 'the only natural and reasonable social order,' in which

---

[54] Fulop-Miller. P. 145.

suffering, injustice, and dread would no longer exist. The useful science of statistics now came to be regarded as capable of demonstrating the possibility of such a 'social physics.'"[55] Remember, this is mankind speaking during the latter half of the 18th century. Their dream has certainly come to fruition in the 21st century.

Fulop-Miller gave this conclusion to the Age of Enlightened Man:

"Now, however, numerical observations were completely divorced from religious faith, being no longer used to demonstrate the divine ordering of the world. Usurping dictatorial powers, number declared itself **the supreme law**, the **fundamental order, the only significance** of the world."[56] (Emphasis Added.) Man had finally understood the true nature of reality and through the powers of reason, he would be able to use the powers of nature to create a world according to man's own liking.

Chapter Twelve: When Laws are transformed into religious rituals, a new god is revealed.

After Biblical Laws were ruled out of order, new laws were created that actually resemble ancient pagan rituals. Just as rituals were created to please the

---

55 Fulop-Miller. P. 147.
56 Fulop-Miller. P. 148.

gods, so the new laws were created to please the new gods of government. The Nation/State has become a modern god because it demands the obedience formerly demanded by the idols of Baal and others like that. Tyrannies must be founded upon a religious order of reality. Those who do not worship this god will be declared law breakers and dangerous to the public order. From a Biblical point of view, only God can create laws. Men can discover God's laws in the physical world, and apply God's laws to human situations. When the tyrant and his colleagues create laws, they are declaring themselves to be gods. Obedience to these gods is an act of submission to the god of those laws.

Because of this new nature of laws, the 'masses' expect the justice system to be perfect as any system of the gods. Every time someone feels they have not received 'justice', they take it as a failure of the gods. As I write, the demand for justice and rights has probably never been greater. One reason is the fact that people look upon the government as a god, and gods are supposed to bless their people. That is why the ancients used to offer sacrifices—both animal and human—they expected benefits form serving their gods. When a government takes over every aspect of life, it takes on the role that God used to occupy within people's lives. The governmental culture replaces the culture of the community, the church, and private associations. These may still exist but they all operate under the auspices of the culture created by the laws of the Nation/State. .

One of the great tragedies of the nationalization of laws and communities is that local relationships have been replaced by legal relationships. Even those who have attempted to help their neighbors have been accused of feeding people without a license. The government with its assorted agencies of help are there to offer tax-supported welfare. Impersonal bureaucrats replace the personal caring of the community. There is another aspect that a Christian society. It is based upon not only the receiving of charity but the blessings those receive who give of their time and money to help those in their community. Modern charity has been transformed into a legal relationship with the impersonal god of government. The same thing happens in the church when people turn service to God into 'legalized' rituals. The Sunday morning service has become a legal obligation to God. One reason for the decline of communities is that the government bureaucrats have replaced those areas where Christians used to serve others. Because we all live in a culture of legalized reality, whether in church or in culture, it never dawns upon any of us that things used to be different before the government tyrant declared himself the god of the people and his bureaucrats are his disciples.

One of the most important aspects of human beings, as created in the image of God, is to serve others as God serves His people. When the State becomes a god, it wants to become the origin of service to man. As with the true God, the state declares that there can be no other gods before it. Not only that, when the State creates people through its educational bureaucracies, it expects people to act in the image of the statist being created by the school system. For graduates to behave as a creature created by God is an act of rebellion against their creator. People must first of all serve the State, no others. If others need help, then it is the State's function to serve that particular need. Statist charity is never about helping people; it is does not want anyone else providing services that have been legally given to the Supreme Power of the land. Just as Christians first look to God for help—'Give us this day our daily bread'—subjects of the State are to look at that entity for their daily bread.

Most people think that Nation/States and welfare are just natural and they cannot imagine any other way. The very idea of people devoting their spare time to help others just goes against the modern American lifestyle: Best leave charity to the professionals. However, government charity is never about helping people. This has been shown again and again. Those groups without political clout have been readily neglected. The welfare checks are not there to help but to buy allegiance to the ruling powers. It is also about something else that is extremely vital in a healthy society: person-to-person contact. [Once I had to deal with a government agency. When I went in, I was assigned a phone booth and I was to sit there and wait for a call.] The strongest bonds, we are told, are to be formed with one's government, i.e. patriotism. All other loyalties are seen as a challenge to the dominance of the tyrant's power. That is one reason Christian schools have often come under attack: they are private forms of personal allegiance. Government schools operate as education factories. The impersonal has a difficult time competing with the personal and that is why the State must seek to suppress personal organizations and their sources of power.

American businesses have partnered with the State in the control of the culture. The corporations want a society where people look to big business for jobs. Those who in the past who had jobs outside of the corporate culture are under attack: the small business, the farmer, the logger, the fisherman, and the repairman. Not only are these workers outside of corporate control, they offer personal relationships with their customers. All human personality is a threat to every bureaucracy or corporate order. The Nation/State operates through legalities to create an impersonal society connected to an impersonal government/business reality. A good example is how teachers and public personalities have come under attack for using politically incorrect language. Everyone is expected to conform to an impersonal culture of conformity.

*

I want to go back to the age of Christendom. It was a time when people were legally allowed to express their Godly image without regulations. England alone was covered with Christian Charites. You have probably never hear about them. After the Reformation, these charities had to be destroyed in order to open the door for total control over the masses. England had monasteries and religious houses built to help people, lots of people. There were over 759 hospitals scattered across England. "There were, in addition, many rest-houses for wayfarers and pilgrims, homes for the aged, feeble and destitute. All these conducted under the direction of the monasteries or religious. Attached to the monasteries were also the schools."[57] As Henry VIII created his own Protestant domination to free England from the Vatican, he also wanted to eliminate all competing powers. So this is what he did:

"In the general scramble of the '*Terror*' under Henry the Eighth, and of the *anarchy* in the days of Edward the Sixth … the monasteries were plundered even to their very pots and pans. The almshouse in which old men and women were fed and clothed, were robbed to their very pots and pans. The almshouses in

---

[57] R. S. Devane. The Failure of Individualism: A Documented Essay. Greenwood Press. 1948. P. 268.

which old men and women were fed and clothed, were robbed to the last pound, the poor alms folk being turned out in the cold at an hour's warning to beg their bread. The splendid hospitals for the sick and needy, sometimes magnificently provided with nurses and chaplains, whose very *raison d'etre* was that they were to look after and care for those who were past caring for themselves, these were stripped of all their belongings, the inmates sent out to hobble into some convenient dry ditch to lie down and die in, or crawl into some barn or hovel, there to be tended, not without fear of consequences, by some kindly man or woman, who could not bear to see a suffering fellow –creature drop down and die at their own door-posts."[58]

The above actions taken by the British Government were 'legal' in the governmental sense of the word. This was more than just greed or the need for extra money, it was a government's attempt to end all competition from other gods, or in this case, God. The stealing from the poor was accomplished under the guise of religion. Whenever a government appears to support a religion, hold onto your wallet. That is not what governments do or were created to do: they are to provide a system of courts and to protect the borders. When any national government exceeds those specifications, it is declaring a war against local governments, communities, and churches. A centralized government can also create a centralized a legal system imposed upon everyone—a system no local agency has the power to resist. Laws represent power and that is why when any nation deviates from the laws of God it does so in order to gain power.

Devane cites Abbot Gasquet: "It [The Reformation] was a revolution indeed, but a revolution not in the ordinary sense. It was a rising, not of people against their rulers, not of those in hunger and distress against the well-to-do, but it was in truth *the rising of the rich against the poor,* the violent seizure by the new men in power of the funds and property which generations of benefactors had intended for the relief of the needy, or by educational and other endowments to assist the poor man to rise in the social scale."[59] Just like most of history, sometimes the real events hide between the publicized events. The

---

[58] Devane. P. 269.
[59] Devane. P. 273.

Reformation may have appeared to be a religious Reformation, but it was, in reality, a legal revolution: What is the source of law in a nation? God or the king?

*

Great historical narratives, like that of the Reformation, are often cover stories for what was truly going on. Evil men operate in the darkness and by the use of illusion. The narrative is to provide a righteous cause that the masses could believe to be true. The Reformation was used as an excuse to destroy the Age of Christendom. It was an age when the masses still believed that God's Laws were real and their application to the social order was to be the true goal of the social and political order. Every age has its criminal element, and historians often record their actions as exemplifying the temper of the times. However, ages are to be judged by the target for which they were aiming. That target during Christendom was the implementation of God's laws upon the order of the age. Even if the criminal element rebelled against those laws, the target still remained as the goal for the majority. With the Reformation, that target changed. However, Satan and his supporters always operate under the cover of deceptive narratives. The Reformation narrative completely covered up the true revolution that occurred: the birth of the powerful Nation/State, and its co ruler, the system of Finance Capitalism. That is the true narrative of this age.

The following describes the true nature of the Reformation:

"The Lutheran Reformation, and the revolution of the German principalities which embodied it, broke the Roman Catholic dualism of ecclesiastical and secular law by **delegalizing the church**. Where Lutheranism succeeded, the church came to be conceived as invisible, apolitical, alegal; and the only sovereignty, **the only law** (in the political sense), was that of the secular kingdom or principality. It was just before this time, in fact, that Machiavelli had used the word 'state' in a new way, to signify **the purely secular order.** The Lutheran reformers were in one sense Machiavellians: **they were skeptical of man's power to create a human law** which would reflect eternal law, and **they explicitly denied that it was the task of the church to develop human law**. This **Lutheran skepticism made possible the emergence of a theory of law—legal positivism**—which treats the law of the state as morally neutral, a means and not an end, a device for manifesting the policy of the sovereign and for **securing obedience to it**. But the secularization of law and the emergence of a positivist theory of law are only one side of the story of the contribution of the Lutheran Reformation to the Western legal tradition. The other side is equally important: **by freeing law from theological doctrine and from direct ecclesiastical influence**, the Reformation enable it to undergo a new and brilliant development."[60] (Emphasis added.)

The Bible and its teachings became imprisoned within the church and the individual soul. The political and financial elites were able to establish a new set of laws which allowed for the development of the world we see today. The very idea that anything in the Bible should have any influence on legislative laws would be labelled ridiculous and the sign of a theocracy. You would hear the cry of the mob at the time of the crucifixion, 'We will not have this man rule over us.' Secularism is the age of Man and God has no place interfering with the laws that men make. The Christian leaders of this age had no fear in turning over the making of the laws to the rulers of the State. They assumed, just as in the days of Christendom, that those in power would be good men who would not make laws contrary to the Biblical description of reality. Another one of Satan's grand deceptions.

Berman writes: "The development of positive law was conceived to rest ultimately upon the prince alone, but it was presupposed that in exercising his will he would respect the individual consciences of his subjects, and that meant respecting also their property and contract rights. This presupposition resided— precariously, to be sure—upon four centuries of history in which the church had succeed in Christianizing law to a remarkable extent, given the level of the cultural life of the Germanic peoples in the beginning. Thus a Lutheran positivism which **separates laws from morals, denies the lawmaking role of the church,** and finds the ultimate sanction of law in political coercion nevertheless **assumes the existence of a Christian conscience among** the people and a state governed by Christian rulers."[61] (Emphasis Added.) Wherever there is power, Satan will

---

[60] Harold J. Berman. Law and Revolution: The Formation of the Western Legal Tradition. Harvard University Press. 1983. P. 29. .
[61] Berman. P. 30.

attempt to infiltrate his people into those positions—always pretending to be good and honorable men.

When the immigrants from England arrived to America, they set about establishing a new law system. Puritans accepted the concept of new individualism as the foundation of any social order. The Reformation was based upon the salivation of the solitary individual. Everyone stood alone before God and each person must seek out his own salvation. The Church became a meeting for individuals who claimed to be saved or were seeking salvation. The Church as a corporate power that parallels the power to the State was seen as too political. Individuals could get involved with politics on a personal level. The corporate church body felt that all laws should represent the desires of the masses and introducing religion would only complicate matters. Whether for good or for bad, the church was to remain separate from the dirty and secular world of political influence peddling. That political world was best left to non-Christians who could remain neutral in regards to religion and politics.

Because salvation was a matter for the solitary individual, the role of governments and their laws were to focus upon empowering the individual through guaranteed civil rights and civil liberties. These newly established rights were applicable to everyone in society equally. This marked the philosophy behind the rising tide of Democratic Individualism. The role of the government was to protect individual from being influenced or pressured from other individuals. In previous ages, the Church as a corporate body of believers could have immense influence upon governments and their leaders. Those days were gone as only the private individual could attempt to influence the elections and the laws that governments make. Religious institutions, it was believed, are by nature biased and could not be objective in the secular affairs of the State.

This reduced the voter to the level of just one of millions. The college professor and a homeless drug user each had one vote. The problem is that the lower classes could be more easily influenced as their common needs for welfare bonded them together into a common voting force. Controlling some block of individuals who could be purchased became the goal of those in power. Obviously the lower classes were more subject to having their vote purchased

125

because of their greater needs. The character and the commitment of a person to the nation had nothing to do with having the right to vote. When individualism controls both the nation and the church, the higher goals of Biblical teachings have no relevance. The nation and the church must do what it takes to make the individuals happy. The church must please those who choose voluntarily to choose one church over another, and those in power must maintain their power by appealing to the baser concerns of the masses, i.e. bread and circuses.

*

Biblically, reality is patterned after the family and the church. Both are patterned after the Trinity: God the Father; God the Son; and God the Holy Spirit. Each are individuals and each are bonded together as one. This principle applies to the family: each person remains an individual within the family, but each is also bonded to the family as a unit. The Church is also to reflect the nature of the Trinity: individuals attending the Church retain their own identity, but they are joining a spiritual and heavenly family that bonds together to create ways serving God as a community. Of course, modern individualism has destroyed all concepts of bonding to any organization or family that becomes bonded together for some greater purpose other than agencies that enhance the needs of an individual.

I regard the individualism of the Reformation as setting the pattern for the modern lonely individual that if anything has bonded to the social welfare State. In a sense, the Nation/State is now performing the role once supplied by the Vatican. Lost in all of this is the Biblical teachings about the Kingdom of God. Church and State both may exit, but they are to exist and operate under the umbrella of reality as defined by God's Kingdom. And how is this reality defined? By God's people living a life of serving and sacrifice, there are displaying the power of God in their lives. For example, the very idea of a government school is totally appalling. The school is to be the ministry of the Church both for instruction but for the building of a godly character. Getting high tests scores mean nothing if that student has sold his soul to evil. The school has become a ministry of the State and is used to promote its agenda.

*

The Reformation, by destroying Christendom, laid the ground for two new civilizations upon the earth. "It was the American and French revolutions that set the stage for the new secular religions—that is, for pouring into secular political and social movements the religious psychology as well as many of the religious ideas that had previously been expressed in various forms of Catholicism and Protestantism. At first a kind of religious orthodoxy was preserved by means of a deistic philosophy—which, however, had little of that psychology which is the heart of religious faith. What was religious, in fact, about the great revolutionary minds of the late eighteenth and nineteenth centuries—men like Rousseau or Jefferson—was not their belief in God but their belief in Man, individual Man, his Nature, his Reason, his Rights."[62] **The Kingdom of Man replaced the Kingdom of God, and everyone said Amen.**

After the Enlightenment, **a new Trinity was formed: Individualism, rationalism, and nationalism.** These became the foundation stones upon which modern Democracy was based. A modern Reformation was celebrated: "Liberal democracy was the first great secular religion in Western history—the first ideology which became divorced from traditional Christianity and at the same time took over from traditional Christianity both its sense of the sacred and sense of its major values."[63] Just as the early church produced its early martyrs when taking on the Roman Empire, so the new global democracy produced its list of martyrs of those of fought to impose to Kingdom of Man upon every area of the earth. Wars were no longer that of merely defending a nation's border, but they became religious crusades. The book *American Crusade* by Benjamin Wetzel "… argues that the Civil War, the Spanish-American War, and World War I shared a cultural meaning for white Protestant ministers in the United States, who considered each conflict to be a modern-day crusade." In fact, the Allied Powers considered the WWI a crusade against the German Huns. These concepts reinforce the idea that the Nation/State has indeed become the new global Vatican power. And 'Christians' treat it as if it were the new universal Catholic church: The new World Order instead of the Kingdom of God. Nations have no business fighting Holy Crusades.

---

[62] Berman. P. 31-32.
[63] Berman. P. 32.

*

When the laws of Christendom were abolished in the name of religious reform, Satan's men were free to set up a new Civilization based upon individual interest and selfish accumulation. The Church and Christians set up charities and gilds to lessen the impact of those who would transform society into a regulated jungle with the winner taking whatever the market will bear. Pope Leo XIII wrote the following in 1891: "Political institutions and the very laws have set aside the ancient religion. Hence, by degrees it has come to pass that working men have been surrendered isolated and helpless to the hard-heartedness of employers and the greed of unchecked competition. The mischief has been increased by rapacious usury, which, although more than once condemned by the Church, is nevertheless, under a different guise, but with like injustice, still practiced by covetous and grasping men. To this must be added that the hiring of labour and all manner of trade are concentrated in the hands of the comparatively few; so that a small number of very rich men has been able to lay upon the teaming masses of the laboring poor a yoke little better than slavery itself."[64]

Because Biblical Laws have been relegated to the Old Testament and Christendom has been renamed The Dark Ages, few today even realize the demonic character of the current situation. R. H. Tawney, the famous economic historian, wrote the following: "Capitalism in the sense of great individual undertakings, involving the control of large financial resources, and yielding riches to their masters as a result of speculation, money-lending, commercial enterprise, buccaneering and war, is as old as history. Capitalism, as an economic system, resting on the organization of legally free wage-earners, for the purpose of pecuniary profit, by the owner of capital or his agents, and setting its stamp on every aspect of society, is a modern phenomenon."[65] Modern governments and those who control them have created a legal order of exploitation and the creation of a new form of slavery—debt slavery. **Workers no longer have souls who have been created in the image of God, but are useful tools for the production of more and more trinkets—in order to establish a global empire.**

---

[64] Devane. P. 276.
[65] Devane. P. 276.

Harold Laski wrote this about an age that no longer was restricted by any theological teachings: "Broadly, we may say that the contribution of the sixteenth century is the destruction of ecclesiastical authority in the economic sphere. This enables property-relations to develop unhampered by theological considerations. There emerged from this a secular State which sought, and found, its mission upon the basis that it replaced the Church as the guardians of social and well-being. It builds its own morality, based upon utility, to suit its new prestige."[66] The oldest trick is to create a controlled opposition. If the people complain about the inequities of Finance Capitalism, the usual defense is this: You don't to live under Communism or Socialism do you? The real alternative exhibited during the age of Christendom is not considered an alternative. Biblical Laws? After all, no one wants to live under a Puritan theocracy. Another false choice.

Chapter Thirteen: Developing an order designed by the new Saviors of Mankind.

While no one thinks about the divine right of kings anymore, however, there is a new form of divine right in modern America: the intellectual elites. Those who are groomed to be leaders are the new chosen ones. Often promising students are chosen in college and then trained because of their 'superior' qualities. Those who enter into the elitist protocols are given special treatment.

---

[66] Devane. P. 277.

They are trained to think that they have been chosen because they are better than the rest of the students. They are led to believe that they are special and that they have been selected because of their special talents. In time, after the number of recruits has been narrowed, other fringe benefits might be added such as sexual and monetary favors. The ego of the chosen is catered to and by the time the training has been finished, the person really believes that he is special. He is also led to believe that his benefits now depend upon his continuous loyalty to his support of his superiors. The pattern may vary, but once a person has become an insider, it is very difficult to turn away, no matter what one is asked to do.

Every tyranny needs not only an evil cadre of supporters, but those who become willing executioners. As I write, American leaders at all levels of society-- from universities, media talking heads, medical doctors and hospitals, military officers and many more still promote the vaxxx despite the death and suffering of millions of people. Those 'anointed' ones know the consequences of not following orders from 'above.' Usually, the highest elites, those who rule the anointed ones, all have an insurance policy in which they can expose their servants. Getting to the top requires a person participate in some evil deed. If the lower elites oppose the will of their superiors, they will be publically exposed and ruined—and their family humiliated. Actually, I am quite sure that some of the anointed ones catch on to what was happening to them, but they continued on as the good life requires that they turn a 'blind eye' to reality. There is a sense that being part of the special elites makes a person feel like he is part of a very special club. Also, the evil consequences of their actions is spread around a large number of others—shared guilt is easily dissipated. Not everyone chooses to be evil, but it was merely what the elites had to do to stay in power. It is little different than a person in the military who kills other human beings. The guilt, if any, belongs to his superiors who gave the orders to kill. And furthermore, the evil that elites do is for the good of humanity: too many people on the earth; so, some must die for a higher good.

There are two levels of divinity involved here: the divinity of one's actions and the divinity one's beliefs. This can be compared to a religious sect organized by Satan. This is an aspect that most do not understand or choose not to understand. Evil exists and it can be communicated on a personal level. There is a sacred relationship between evil people that has real power. There are special ceremonies and rituals that the elites perform together which gives them a demonic psychic camaraderie of shared evil. Another factor is men are by nature in rebellion against God. When fallen men are given power, they have no qualms about waring against the God of the Ten Commandments.

It is this fallen human nature that Satan appeals to when recruiting his special followers. There is a hidden factor when recognizing these elites: they lose their initial image of God within them. In time, they enter upon a road where they become walking dead men on the inside. The corollary of this is that Satan is the great deceiver and his people are trained in this art, i.e. great actors. After all, part of their job, wherever they are installed, is to sell the lie, the Big LIE. It is beyond the comprehension of 'normal' people how evil is a lot more than just doing something wrong; it is an actual 'living' entity that works to destroy God's Laws, and everything in a nation and culture that points toward anything good.

When Satan has established his people on multiple levels within a nation, the culture takes on the personality of Satan. Everyone becomes more and more impersonal. People become fearful of expressing the Image of God within themselves. Society takes on the image of a giant factory and everyone becomes more and more mechanical: a nation of worker bees. Diversions from reality are sought through entertainment or assorted forms of pleasure. Relationships become transitory, including marriage. True friendships become based upon shared pleasures and not the bonding of souls as men have written about in the past. Once a culture becomes impersonal and mechanical, and the intellect has been sufficiently dumbed down through government education, the people are ready for one of Satan's tyrannical rulers who will lead people into the valley of the shadow of death with no escape.

*

It is important to understand the nature of Biblical religion: it is more than just a spiritual club or a system of theological beliefs. Religion tells people what is reality. That is why, when men give their soul over to Satan, he provides them a picture of reality from his viewpoint. In addition, that is why those people who serve Satan really believe they are involved in true reality. God is pictured as the evil one who only subjects man to mindless slavery to some nebulous and cruel deity. Satan is the one that teaches men how to live life to the fullest. That is why the people that keep serve evil cannot be convinced to change their allegiance—it just does not make sense. The real problem on the earth, for these people, is that the masses refuse to give themselves over to the true truth. They hold onto ancient foolishness from the Old Testament. Evil cultures control the thinking of everyone. People become slaves to a false narrative without even knowing it. When doctors keep injecting people, even though they know they are killing many, they keep injecting people. They really believe that they serving humanity for some greater good. Besides, they are living in the only reality that makes sense; so they have no other options than to obey the leaders of the Anointed One's cult. I grew up attending government schools. It never dawned on me that there were other narratives than the official government-endorsed ones.

*

Thomas Sowell writes that cultures have visions of what reality is or what reality should be like. These visions control the thinking of mankind. Every nation has a worldview which controls the thinking of the masses in their day-to-day life. Visions provide a target for tomorrow. The World Economic Forum talks about how the world should prepare for a better tomorrow. Western Civilization was an operating model for life as it is lived in everyone's daily life. The Forum is not a Civilization, but is actually a war upon civilization. The worldviews of the masses are considered to be at war upon the earth's environment. The environment of the earth is being destroyed by Western Civilization. The future for the forum requires the death of modern civilizations. The promoters of the vision consider themselves the anointed ones, i.e. they are beyond human. I believe this anointing is a sign of Satan's connection to the self-proclaimed masters of the universe.

"The rise of the mass media, mass politics, and massive government means that the beliefs which drive a relatively small group of articulate people have

132

great leverage in determining the course taken by the whole society."[67] This intellectual, business, and government class hold different views of reality than those of the common laborer. Intellectuals usually gain their income either from the government directly or from government subsidies. For this reason, they develop the governmental view of reality, i.e. the power to control reality. They are in a position where they can rule over people through teaching students, businesses, or government agencies. Those who are taught or controlled automatically take on an inferior status—much like the doctor and his patient. This intellectual class inherits the tendency to have a superior view over and feels entitled to make decisions for the good of humanity: the masses are the patient and they are the doctor. The masses have been found to have stage four enivromental impact disorder: death awaits all such people.

One of the marks of the ruling elites is that they manage to separate themselves from critical or negative feedback. The working class understands his performance because he will often get on-the-job feedback: often essential to his continuation on the job or performance bonuses. That is not a factor in those connected with governmental programs. Those who work for any government educational institution are often immune from the consequences of their work performance. As I write, it has been revealed that the government worked with the social media outlets for prevent any negative feedback against the government or its prominent figures: censorship was openly used to protect those who were the anointed ones. That is one reason why the great visionaries in the government are rarely confronted with the real world.

Sowell list the four points on how the elite's visions are imposed upon the masses:

1. Assertions of a great danger to the whole society, a danger to which the masses of people are oblivious.
2. An urgent need for action to avert impeding catastrophe.
3. A need for government to drastically curtail the dangerous behavior of the many, in response to the prescient conclusions of the few.

---

[67] Thomas Sowell. Vision of the Anointed: Self-Congratulation as a Basis for Social Policy. Basic Books. 1995. P. ix-x.

4. A disdain dismissal of arguments to the contrary as either misinformed, irresponsible, or motivated by unworthy purposes.[68]

Those who consider themselves superior can follow the above formula and impose their special anointed insights upon the nation. Because the anointed ones back each other up, it appears as if there is a giant consensus of truth. A truth so powerful the masses must obey and submit to the enlightened ones. These same procedures are used by Satan to impose his agenda upon the people called Christians. The Biblical teachings are seen as a great danger to all of society from which the people must be saved. To not resist these teachings will lead to a dangerous theocracy being imposed upon everyone. These Biblical teachings must be curtailed. The Christians are pictured as ignorant followers of ancient beliefs that are totally destructive to the free personality. To tolerate Christians would be totally irresponsible. The Bible is sexist, homophobic, racist, anti-progress, deniers of historic truths, and fearful of science—who needs them?

Sowell also lists the typical formula for the defense of one of the anointed one's failures. As before, it all starts with a crisis, real or not, does not matter: a crisis is needed to impose some agenda. I have observed that the crisis was usually manufactured to impose a predetermined agenda. Often the agenda comes first and then the crisis invented afterwards. If the results promised by the elites does not produce any solution, no problem. Excuses for the failed agenda are manufactured in advance just in case. Those who criticize the results of some elitist program "...are dismissed as 'simplistic' for ignoring the 'complexities' involved, as 'many factors' went into determining the outcome. The burden of proof is put on the critics to demonstrate to a certainty that these policies alone were the only possible cause of the worsening that occurred. No burden of proof whatever is put on those who had so confidently predicted improvement. Indeed, it is often asserted that things would have been even worse, were it not for the wonderful programs that mitigated the inevitable damage from other factors."[69]

---

68 Sowell. P. 5.
69 Sowell. P. 8.

When the anointed ones pass a law, it cannot fail. It was designed to achieve a certain purpose which is not always stated. **I believe that many laws and programs are designed to fail**. Unsolved problems only call for more power given to those in charge and more money to pour into the coffers of the anointed programs that they oversee. It is a grand fallacy to assume that those in charge of any institution are designed to succeed. Sometimes failures serve the elites better than a grand success. Again, you can always recognize the fingerprints of Satan in most events. He is the author of deception and confusion in order to achieve his destruction of the Kingdom of God. When any government exceeds the limits imposed by the Bible upon its power, you know that Satan has had his hand in that process. When governments commit the same evil action over and over, it is not an accident: you are seeing how Satan operates. Satanic failures are one of his most powerful weapons. These failures can be used to blame some enemy of the New World Order: Western Civilization has destroyed the environment.

*

As I write the nature of 'sex' and 'sexual identity' reveals the nature of how the anointed operate and how their agenda also coincides that of Satan's agenda. Probably, the clearest example of an agenda being imposed upon the America people and which reflects the direct connection between the anointed ones and Satan is the nature of sexual identity. In the very first chapter of Genesis, God tells everyone that men are either males or females. Those are the only choices.

Genesis 1:27. So **God created man** in his *own* image, in the image of God created he him; **male and female created he them**.

Therefore, for anointed ones, this is one of the first areas of attack. First they attack creation and the appearance of Man upon the earth. In verse twenty-six in chapter one, God announces that He had create Man on the sixth day—not the six millionth day. From Darwin in 1860 until about 2000, creation was under constant attack, especially in the government schools. Then, the anointed, feeling confident they had won the battle of verse twenty-six, moved onto verse twenty-seven. The very terms 'Male and Female' were now considered social constructs. Children have been forced by the tenants of Western and Christian Civilizations to believe that there are only two categories of sexuality. This is considered nothing but the religious suppression of man's freedom to choose in every area of life. The anointed ones believe in human freedom above all else. Any social, religious, or ethical laws are chains upon man's liberty to choose his own path for life.

Actually, the modern attack upon sexuality started in the 1960s with the college students demanding 'free love.' Such things as abstinence, marriage, monogamy, adultery, and heterosexuality were all considered relics from the past. In the past, there were no reliable methods of birth control. There were no cures for sexually transmitted diseases. And childless families were considered abnormal: children were needed to work the family farm or family business. Children were also considered necessary in order to pass on one's inheritance. Family traditions were considered an essential part of a meaningful life. The greatest joys in the past, when sources of amusement were limited, were to be found in the family. During times of need, the family clan was there to step in and help: before government welfare and government insurance programs such as Social Security, Unemployment Insurance, Food Stamps, and Medicare.

As I proceed, keep in mind that the attack upon reality is foundational is Satan's attack upon the Kingdom of God. Because a person's sexuality is so basic to God's civilization, Satan rallies his troops to focus upon this issue. Those who live outside the Kingdom of God find this topic very pleasing, liberating, and essential to a life of personal freedom. It is not just a normal rebellion against God, but a hormonalrebellion against God. Sexual liberation is one of the most pleasurable ways to express one's rebellious nature. That is why, starting in the late 1960s, sexual 'education' was elevated to a national crisis. The original thesis was the 'teens' do not know how to prevent pregnancies. Abstinence was no longer considered viable, and sexual 'games' without intercourse was also considered not enough. The theory being that teens must be 'taught' how to have sex and not produce children. Somehow, what a small pamphlet could have accomplished was transformed into a major course in education. Obviously, something else was going on besides teaching about condoms and pills.

First, the anointed ones have given themselves the permission to lie. They openly state that lies are permitted if the cause is greater than the lie. Therefore, lies were put forth to justify the initial stage of sexual indoctrination. Think about it: how many hours of training does it take to teach teens something they figured

136

out for themselves in the past? There has to be more to sex education than mere technical knowledge. The youth are being taught an agenda from Satan and his hirelings. They are not being taught the Ten Commandments for sure. Secular governments are at war with God's laws in all areas of life. However, the easiest way to destroy God's laws in the minds of the young is to teach them how to break the one law they want permission to break. After that, the rest of the laws will fall like dominoes. How can you convince teens to accept the sacredness of marriage if you are teaching the young that the act of a true marriage requires pre-marital sexual purity? That is a long time to wait. In fact, marriage and sex are separated from each other. What a very subtle way to declare war upon the God and His Word. The cry goes out: sex now, marriage later.

Whatever the anointed ones set out to do, they will be successful because they are the ones who define success. "There is no possible reply to these heads-I-win-tails-you-lose assertions, except to note that they would justify any policy on any subject anywhere; regardless of its empirically observed consequences. In short, no matter what happens, the vison of the anointed always succeeds, if not by the original criteria, then by criteria extemporized later—and if not by empirical criteria, then by criteria sufficiently subjected to escape even the possibility of refutation. Evidence becomes irrelevant."[70] The reason the anointed can get away with outright deception and outright failures is that they also control those who are the critics of the national agenda—the press, the media, and the politicians. Any other critics are merely conspiracy theories with an ax to grind—an ax of a personal vendetta.

In the 1960s, sex education became a national agenda. All of a sudden, there was a national crisis. Apparently, parents had proven themselves incapable of teaching their own children about sex, or even giving them a book to read if the parents felt uncomfortable confronting the issue. That was the crisis: parents had abandoned their children. The only solution was for the Federal Government to come to the rescue: That is quite a jump. From parents to Washington, D.C. Apparently there were no other options according to the anointed ones. That alone should make a person suspicious of those in charge of the sexual education agenda. Another suspicious action by the government is that their first act occurred in 1964 when the Office of Economic Opportunity made a grant to a Planned Parenthood clinic. So, the first step was to enhance the availability of

---

[70] Sowell. P. 15.

abortions. When I grew up in the 1950s, the first step in an unplanned baby was marriage, or for one of the relatives of the 'guilty' parties to adopt the baby. It was considered a family responsibility and the nature of being accountable for the misdeeds of one's clan. No problem, we take care of our own.

This undermining of the family and the idea of personal responsibility is one of the key issues here. The government does not care about the traditional nature of the greater family or about the life of the baby at all. Those issues are ignored and are not part of the solution by definition. You can tell a lot about an agenda by what is left out of their argument for their plan or agenda. **The anointed only believe in one solution to any problem, their solution.** From 1964 to 1966, Federal grants to sex education grew five times to more than two million. Government funding is much like the mustard seed of the Kingdom of God: a tiny tree soon grows into a tree. In 1970, the first national family planning act was passed. Federal expenditures grew from 16 million to 200 million. In seven years the number of teens using 'family planning' options grew from 250,000 to 1.2 million. [Do not be fooled by the euphemisms: family planning means baby extermination.]

As stated, in order to create a crisis mentality necessary for radical changes, the anointed declare a problem where there is none. So what about the giant sexual crisis that the government and schools were so anxious to promote. Sowell wrote about how the ruling elites, following the pattern, manufactured a sexual crisis. A crisis so bad that only a national commitment on the Federal Government level had to power to handle the situation. Official school boards of education, the *American School Board Journal* and the *PTA Magazine* united in their stand against the new age of sexual and pregnancy problems. Below is the crisis before the government got involved: "But what was in fact the situation when this kind of 'crisis' mentality was being used to push for more sex education in the schools? Fertility rates among teenage girls had been *declining* for more than a decade since 1957. Venereal disease was also *declining.* The rate of infection gonorrhea, for example, declined every year from 1950 to 1959, and the rate of syphilis infection was, by 1960, less than half of what it had been in 1950. This was the 'crisis' which federal aid was to solve."[71] **Remember, government propaganda does not rely upon facts, but upon emotional appeals to a manufactured reality.** The same principle is still being used as I write in 2023.

---

[71] Sowell. P. 17.

The crisis of 1964 resulted in, by 1968, nearly half of all schools in the country—including public and private, religious and secular—installed sex education programs in their schools. Usually the federal government provides financial incentives to start a program, and schools are quick to accept and submit to the terms of the financial aid. As with all government programs, there is the public declaration of their purpose and a hidden agenda. It is the hidden agenda that is rarely mentioned. So, how did these sex education classes do in preventing sexual crises? The results of government sponsored sex education classes reveal the hidden agenda. [Spoiler alert: Government programs are often hidden attacks upon God and His Laws. Everything else is just show and tell.] The results:

"As sex education programs spread widely though the American educational system during the 1970s, the pregnancy rate among 15-to 19- year-old females rose from approximately 68 per thousand in 1970 to approximately 96 per thousand by 1980. Among unmarried girls in the 15- to 17-year old bracket, birth rates rose 29 percent between 1970 and 1984, despite a massive increase in abortions, which more than doubled during the same period. Among girls under 15, the number of abortions surpassed the number of live births by 1974. The reason was not hard to find: According to the Alan Guttmacher Institute, the percentage of unmarried teenage girls who had engaged in sex was higher at every age from 15 through 19 by 1976 than it was just five years earlier. The rate of teenage gonorrhea tripled between 1956 and 1973. [The former head of the Office of Economic Opportunity, Sargent Shriver stated.] 'Just as venereal disease has skyrocketed 350% in the last 15 years when we have had more clinics, more pills, and more sex education than ever in history, teen-age pregnancy has risen.'"[72]

The above documented results are not the result of a failure of government programs, it was part of the plan to 'demoralize' American teens. It was a plan to lead teens away from God and His moral plan for man. Sowell expands upon this. "...the real goal was to change student's *attitudes*—put bluntly, to brainwash them with the vision of the anointed, in order to supplant the values they had been taught at home. In the words of an article in the *Journal of School Health,* sex education presents 'an exciting opportunity to develop new norms. Only in the light of this agenda does it make sense that so-called 'sex education' should

---

[72] Sowell. P. 18.

be advocated to take place throughout the school years—from kindergarten to college—when it could not possibly take that much time to teach basic biological or medical information in new attitudes."[73] Of course, new norms and new attitudes means non-Christian ones. The reason the American Churches did not pull their children out of government schools is that those churches are basically 'State' churches. They expect to align themselves with the winning side, i.e. the government one. America churches know that it is dangerous to publically oppose the Satanic powers of the Anointed Ones.

*

It should become evident that no matter what the government says it is doing, it is controlled by servants of Satan. They lie and the result of their programs and laws are designed to steal power from God and use it to destroy the Laws of God and the people of God. Whether it is welfare laws, crime laws, monetary laws, education laws, environmental laws or any laws that interfere with local responsibilities are not designed to produce an ethical, moral, or self-governing people. Any study of what the Government did to the Blacks after the Civil War or to the American Indians after their defeat on the fields of battle illustrates that the leaders know how to break people's independent will. The goal is to transform minorities into a permanent dependent class. Any group that the government states that they are out to help, will in time, end up in a worse condition. Just as a wild animal raised in captivity can no longer survive in the wild, so people raised by the government no longer know how to care for themselves or their friends and neighbors. The government becomes their god: When false gods replace the real God, the souls of the recipients of government aid are destroyed. Satan's fingerprints can always been seen in government actions that break the God-given spirit in people.

All Satanic intrusions into American life have been through a never-ending system of laws. America has indeed become a nation of laws and of a law-abiding people. However, that is never good if those laws are designed to destroy the Image of God within man. If you understand the true nature of Satan and his form of government, you can then understand the purpose of many American laws. If you understand the purpose of the Church and God's Kingdom upon the earth, then you can understand the evil that must be opposed. However, the

---

[73] Sowell. P. 20.

American Church has surrendered to the American Way of Life and it has no idea that it has traded service to God for service to the State. In 2023, the church is playing church, and the people of the government are free to openly serve the agenda of Satan. This has not happened overnight, but has been in the pipeline since 1776. The problem for Christians is that they think that 200 years of evil can be banished in a day. Let's all protest, or next election, we'll throw the bastards out. Those bastards have to be thrown out election after election after election.

Chapter 14: American has become a nation of laws and that being so, the people expect salvation to come through the perfection of laws, i.e. Evolution through laws.

America is on a pilgrimage, much like the pilgrimage of Christians. However, Christians are on a life-long journey with Christ toward his perfection of the understanding of God and his perfection of the personal and social character. Perfection for the secular American is the search for a series of laws that will transform every American into a secular church: the brotherhood of mankind. It parallels Ponce Deleon's search for the Fountain of Youth. Men cannot create workable laws that supersede God's Laws. Not only that, fallen man cannot create the perfect 'anything'. It is also similar to the Old Testament and false religions; they all believe that laws can save a man from an environment of evil. This is not new, Cain believed he could save himself by offering the works of his own hands, as opposed to the offering of a sacrificial lamb. The Pharisees in the New Testament believed that religious laws and ritual could make a person acceptable to God, i.e. that laws could perfect man.

When men refuse to do anything until they can accomplish the proposed act to perfection, they will end up doing nothing. Sporting games or musical concerts fall short of perfection: that is just the nature of reality. However, when the rulers of a nation demand perfect laws and perfect justice, then the judicial system will fail to produce any justice. Does every trial demand the top lawyer, the best prosecutor, and the perfect judge? Of course not, but that is what American Law expects. In a sense, the American judicial system has become a way of allowing the guilty/rich to postpone justice, sometimes indefinitely, and the innocent punished by expensive court costs to protect themselves from an injustice. The system itself has become a way to punish political opponents who cannot afford a costly defense. The cost of perfect justice has created weaponized injustice. Perfect comes at a price if you have the money.

This quest for perfect justice raises a real red flag. We live in a culture and nation that protects imperfection. Whether drug users, criminals, the homeless, the immigrants, the corporations, Big Pharma, doctors, college athletes, and drunk drivers, are all granted various forms of tolerance. The judicial court system is the one area in American culture in which perfection is demanded. If a speed limiter were placed on every vehicle at 35 miles an hour, around 30,000 lives could be saved every year. And yet, when I mention this to people, most feel the price is worth in order to travel long distances. We need imperfect cars. Think of all the lives that have been lost in America's wars upon an imperfect world. And yet I still hear people say stupid things like: Better to let 99 go free, than one innocent serve time. In other words, if justice is not perfect, then to achieve perfect justice, most must be set from—just in case there was a mistake.

*

At the time of the writing of the American Constitution, some claim that the people wanted a government that forbade lawyers from serving in the government. The fear was that they would create a legal system in which only they could profit. The common man would have to hire a lawyer even over simple matters. As I write, it takes years of litigation to carry out the death sentence in many states. The legal fees run into the millions. The price of perfect justice is based upon economics: many people profit from a complicated and bureaucratic justice system. Wisdom and common sense do not prevail, but only with a technical order and lengthy procedures. The common man is basically excluded from the court system except as a defendant. In the Old Testament, there were no prisons and criminals had to make restitution three or four times the amount they stole. Crime did not pay and the victim was reimbursed. Today, the victim receives nothing and the lawyer everything.

I regard the establishment of a legal monopoly by a group certified as official members of the BAR as a system where insiders were able to construct a government inside the government. Lawyers have not only dominated the elected offices and the appointments by the President, but they also were the ones who became the judges in the nation. These judges set it up so that they could rule any agency and government in America. In the state where I grew up, the constitution was copied from the U.S. Constitution: the counties elected men to the senate and the people elected men to the house. The SCOTUS ruled it unconstitutional. The reason: it violated the principle of one man, one vote. As a result, the three urban counties took over the state and the other 36 became colonies of the major cities. Why? Because that is the kind of government the 'lawyers' wanted—an urban society over a rural, decentralized society.

In the same way, when the voters of that state passed a referendum to forbid the busing of children across town, the SCOTUS ruled that unconstitutional. America from the very beginning set up two governments: one to fool the people and one which had the power to do as it wished. In the early 19th century, a Constitutional Amendment was passed which prohibited lawyers from holding public office. During the War of 1812, the 'British' burned the library of Congress and after the War, the Amendment became lost. That amendment would have prevented an insider class with special titles from controlling the laws of the land. As a result, lawyers write and pass the laws, and judges decide how to interpret the laws. It has become so accepted that when the SCOTUS makes a ruling, everyone obeys. Five judges rule the nation. The article below documents the story of the 'Lost' Thirteenth Amendment.

"In the winter of 1983, archival research expert David Dodge, and former Baltimore police investigator Tom Dunn, were searching for evidence of government corruption in public records stored in the Belfast Library on the coast of Maine.

"By chance, they discovered the library's oldest authentic copy of the Constitution of the United States (printed in 1825). Both men were stunned to see this document included a 13th Amendment that no longer appears on current copies of the Constitution. Moreover, after studying the Amendment's language and historical context, they realized the principle intent of this "missing" 13th Amendment was to prohibit lawyers from serving in government. So began a seven year, nationwide search for the truth surrounding the most bizarre Constitutional puzzle in American history — the unlawful removal of a ratified Amendment from the Constitution of the United States.

"Since 1983, Dodge and Dunn have uncovered additional copies of the Constitution with the "missing" 13th Amendment printed in at least eighteen separate publications by ten different states and territories over four decades from 1822 to 1860. In June of this year (1991), Dodge uncovered the evidence that this missing 13th Amendment had indeed been lawfully ratified by the state of Virginia and was therefore an authentic Amendment to the American Constitution. If the evidence is correct and no logical errors have been made, a 13th Amendment restricting lawyers from serving in government was ratified in 1819 and removed from the U.S. Constitution during the tumult of the Civil War. Since the Amendment was never lawfully repealed, it is still the Law today. The implications are enormous."[74]

It is worth reading the whole article in the link below. That explains why the American legal system has become the ruling body in America and why the

---

[74] https://www.thelibertybeacon.com/missing-13th-amendment-found-no-lawyers-in-public-office/

laws are so written that only a trained insider can understand them. Actually, some laws are unintelligible until a lawyer and a judge tell everyone what they mean. America has no book of Common Law that everyone can understand. As mentioned, Blackstone's Commentaries on the Laws of England was a book owned by early Americans before the lawyers' class developed a Book of Lawyer Law. This is why the people do not make the laws of the land. This is why no matter who gets elected, nothing changes. Congress is a show and the class of rulers that operates through a hidden system where the judge and lawyers classes are just the visible part of a ruling network of secret elites.

*

It is important to understand that the very corrupt system of American Democracy has been installed upon the American people that few people question. Democracy has been replaced government-imposed perfect equality. The quest for cosmic justice goes beyond the right to choose one's own lifestyle. In early democracy, as the saying goes: everyone had the right to go to hell in their own way. That is traditional freedom. It is the right to fail and the right to experience the consequences of one's decisions. That is no longer tolerable. One reason is this: Christians who make the right choices are blessed by God and they experience good results. Those who reject God will experience the true consequences of rebelling from God. In a nation ruled by servants of Satan, this is not tolerable. Those who follow the Commandments of God must not experience anything better than those who reject the Laws of God. This is how God built the world in which we live; and for a reason—after death we will all experience the true consequences of living for God or against God. That, of course, is Heaven or Hell. Satan does not want people to experience reality before its time. You see, consequences are there in life to alert everyone to the much bigger, cosmic dangers of bad decisions. Satan does not want people discovering the true nature of God's reality. He does not want to lose his faithful servants. In Satan's world, there are no bad consequences. That is the worldview that Satan's governments seek to install up the land.

*

As I write, Cosmic Justice has been elevated to perfect Social Justice. In order to achieve the overthrow of God's reality, it requires a government of immense power. When people choose evil, God judges them in this life, even before their ultimate final judgment. When people are under such judgments, the government must intervene to destroy God's judgment. In a sense, the social justice government is at war with God. That is never a good thing to do. Eventually, that leads to the nation coming under the judgment of God. Many books have been written on why nations rise and fall, most do not want to investigate the powers of God in any national failure. Because God uses natural forces or He raises up enemies to weaken or destroy that rebellious nation, the secondary causes are considered the real cause of the decline. The primary cause is God and that really is the rest of the story.

Sowell cites Milton Friedman: **"A society that puts equality—in the sense of equality of outcome—ahead of freedom will end up with neither equality nor freedom. The use of force to achieve equality will destroy freedom, and the force, introduced for good purposes, will end up in the hands of people who use it to promote their own interests."[75]** (Emphasis added.) The new equality is being imposed by law upon Americans as I write. It is even illegal to use the wrong pronoun when addressing transgenders. All those who refuse to work also must be made equal to those who work through a guaranteed annual wage. President Lyndon Johnson said the following about the quest for cosmic justice:

"You do not take a man who, for years, has been hobbled by chains, liberate him, and bring him to the starting line of a race, saying, 'You are free to complete with all others,' and still justly believe you have been completely fair."[76] Cosmic Justice claims that allowing everyone to start at the same starting line is not equality. The goal is to provide everyone with the tools so that he could finish at the same time as others. Equal opportunity is not equality became everyone does not have the same chances of success. The role of the government is to pass laws that promote the equality of outcome for those who have failed to achieve the same tools of success as others. Whether it is derived from a disruptive

---

[75] Thomas Sowell. The Quest for Cosmic Justice. The Free Press. 1999. P. 6-7.
[76] Sowell. P. 11-12.

family, a poor neighborhood, bad schooling, or any number of other reasons, some people have been subjected them to inadequate qualifications. In a system of Cosmic Justice, the person who experienced many of the above scenarios is still allowed to compete on an equal level. The goal is to make the race to success handicapped as you would a golf tournament where the average player can compete on equal terms with the pro golfer. The government is in the role of handicapping life.

There are two main points here: the government's justice is designed to destroy God's idea of justice as found in Christian and Western Civilizations. Second, modern justice can only be achieved through a powerful Nation/State system. These two goals are basic to the American judicial system. The enemy is not corruption in government or business, but the American people who insist on holding onto their ancient dogmatic beliefs. Sowell illustrated the danger of attempting to 'save' people through laws and welfare. This can be illustrated in the history of Blacks in America. Their current problems ae based upon the fact that slavery permanently damaged their ability to function outside of the plantation mentality.

Sowell writes: "The prevalence of fatherless families in the black ghetto, for example, has been widely explained by the lack of legally constituted families under slavery. But if one proceeds … to actually seek out the facts, an entirely different picture emerges. A hundred years ago, when blacks were just one generation out of slavery, the rate of marriage in the black population of the United States was slightly *higher* than that of the white population. **Most black children were raised in two-parent families, even during the era of slavery, and for generations thereafter.** The catastrophic decline of the black nuclear family began, like so many other social catastrophes in the United States, during the decade of the 1960s."[77] (Emphasis added.] The breakup of the Black community was a direct act of sabotage. The Blacks were needed as the 'Brown Shirts' to discredit Western Civilization and open the door to the New World Order. **The laws of the 1960s were never designed to help the Blacks, but to weaponized**

---

[77] Sowell. P. 15-16.

them and promote their manufactured anger against the White people of America.

*

The foundation of an order based upon secular laws is that men are not fallen creatures who are alienated from God but that they are sick and need a cure. A famous lawyer in the early to mid-20th century was Thurman Arnold. He served under FDR and later defended those people accused of being Communists. He wrote this in his book, *Symbols of Government.*

"From a humanitarian point of view the best government is that which we find in an insane asylum. In such a government the physicians in charge do not separate the ideas of the insane into any separate sciences such as law, economics, and sociology; nor then instruct the insane in the intricacies of those three of these three sciences. Nor do they argue with the insane as to the soundness or unsoundness of their ideas. Their aim is to make the inmates of the asylum as comfortable as possible, regardless of their respective moral deserts. In this they are limited only by the facilities of the institution."[78] The Bible teaches that men have rebelled against God's Laws and has been infected with a disease called sin. The cure can only be found in the substitutionary death and resurrection of Jesus Christ. The first purpose of God's Laws is to force men to recognize their rebellious nature and that they cannot cure themselves. Men are incapable of obeying the laws under their own power.

As Arnold points out, modern governments have replaced Jesus Christ as the cure for what ails men. The power of government laws can direct men into the proper channels of behavior and thus cure them from their addiction to traditions and religious ideologies. The cure is replacing the laws of men with the laws of a governing elite who understand the nature of the masses, i.e. an unruly mob. Arnold continues:

"The advantages of such a theory for purposes of thinking about government are that we escape the troublesome assumption that the human race is rational. We need not condemn polices which contradict each other solely on

---

[78] John H. Hallowell. The Moral Foundation of Democracy. University of Chicago Press. 1954. P. 10.

the ground that the action of government must be logically consistent…. **The theory eliminates from our thinking the moral ideals which hamper us whatever a government institution takes practical action**…. It frees us from the necessity of worrying about names, and arguing about the respective merits of communism, fascism, or capitalism—arguments which have the unfortunate effect of creating phobias against practical and humanitarian measures."[79] (Emphasis added.) Humans by placing labels upon the various solutions to be used in the government's insane asylum restrict the cures that might help mankind. Communism should not be rejected just because it goes against American patriotic and American prejudices.

Arnold recognizes the power of laws and that the dictatorships of the 1930s were able to accomplish great things because there were no traditional or ideological limits upon their ability to take the necessary actions to heal society. "Arnold sees no essential difference between communism, fascism, and so-called 'capitalistic democracy.' They are all engaged in the same activities, albeit rationalized differently, and with the exception that some are more cruel than others. 'In Russia, Germany, and Italy, where old ideals were suddenly wept away,' he wrote in 1937, 'a certain necessary realism has compelled these governments to recognize that the political party is always the real government. They therefore dragged political machinery out into the open and made the political leader the nominal as well as the actual governor. This enables them to use political techniques more frankly and openly.' If I understand him correctly, Arnold is saying that the dictatorships have the virtue of doing frankly and openly what our parties must do deceitfully and less openly. Our political system will reach maturity, he suggests, when we can build a political organization in America that can operate with equal frankness. In Germany, Russia, and Italy, he says, 'trials became an admired method of political propaganda,' while 'in this country the trial of political issues by the Supreme Court of the United States, while it was actually political propaganda, was supposed to be something else.'"[80]

---

[79] Hallowell. P. 10.
[80] Hallowell. Page. P. 12.

Arnold was an active part of FDR's regime during the 1930s. That period marked the end of traditional Capitalism and the introduction of Socialism into the American mentality. However, it was not labelled that, but only a New Deal. Arnold felt that the names people apply to politics really have no connection to reality. "Democracy, he tells us, has changed in recent decades from a creed to a political fact. The 'principles' of democracy ... were once worshiped as fundamental truths, and democracy was once regarded as a set of guiding principles. Now we know that democracy is simply 'a name for a type of organization controlled by voters.' And we have discovered that 'it is immaterial whether democracy is morally beautiful or not'. We are no longer troubled by the fact that political platforms are 'inconsistent with political action.' **Politicians have learned to use the techniques of advertising, where slogans take the place of truth**. The have learned how to take polls on public question and thus ascertain the best way in which to frame their appeals. **Principles and political platforms have become 'more and more of a ceremony and less a matter of belief.'** To those who write them."[81] (Emphasis added.)

The reign of FDR marked a launching of a whole new set of agencies backed by laws and more laws. Political programs operate with laws which means on the force of laws. Many attempt to disconnect the police powers of the state when new programs and agencies are created: there are very few voluntary laws. Behind it all is the belief that the people of the nation can be 'helped' by changing the old laws. The fantasy of Cosmic Justice is the goal to justify of every change being brought about today. There is a dream that salvation can come about with the power of government and the laws necessary to bring about a New World Order where everyone can be controlled for their own good and the good of mankind. The problems of the world were caused by every man doing that which was right in his own eyes and totaling upsetting the balance of nature and of a communal existence. The new laws of the Social Credit System will finally bring mankind into harmony with nature, with each other, and with the powers that rule the earth.

*

---

[81] Hallowell. P. 16-17.

It is important to understand the significance of Cosmic Justice. Those ruling elites have set as their goal something that God cannot do. Only a secular government, separated from God, can deliver on the promises of true Cosmic Justice. There is no Cosmic Justice under God's reign, but only under the controls of all-powerful government, i.e. a government with the powers of a god. God's justice could be summed up in this: You break it, you pay for it. God's world is a world of consequences.

Psalm 7:9. Oh **let the wickedness of the wicked come to an end**; but establish the just: for the righteous God trieth the hearts and reins.

Job 4:17. Shall mortal man be more just than God? shall a man be more pure than his maker?

Cosmic Justice is an attempt to be more just than God. When men fail, the government is there to pick them up. When men experience the consequences of their 'sins', the government is there to 'save' men from those consequences. The first reason men seek cosmic justice is that the world as it exists fails to conform to the desires of men. Men in their dreams, desires, and choices keep running into a wall called God's created reality. The very idea of equal outcomes was tested in some of the American communes in the 19th century. Believing in equality, everyone in the commune received the same material benefits regardless of their personal contribution. There was equity for all. Those communes failed. It turns out that equality and equity come at price: no wants to work so that those that do not work can attain an equal share.

One college professor thought he would teach equality of outcome upon his class. Everyone received the same grade regardless of their test scores results. The overall affect was that everyone's test scores declined. The incentive to excel vanished. The Bible recognizes this flaw in sinful man. That is why the Bible teaches this: **If a man shall not work, neither shall he eat. When men want to eat, they will drop their opposition to work.** Sowell cites the dilemma of a ship sinking with three hundred on board and only two hundred life jackets. Equality and fairness demands that no one be given a lifejacket because one hundred will drown through no fault of their own. In economics and on that ship, not everyone can be saved. The laws of life are not fair, but that is a reality that many do not want to face.

Another feature of Cosmic Justice is to demand reparations for past injustices. For example, money will be taken from those who never owned slaves and given to those who were never a slave themselves. "A historian writing about Czechoslovakia, for example, said that the policies of this newly created state after the First World War were 'to correct social injustices' and to 'put right the historic wrongs of the seventeenth century.' Presumably, no one from the seventeenth century was still alive at the end of the First World War. One of the many contrasts between traditional justice and cosmic justice is that traditional justice involves the ruler under which flesh-and-blood human beings interact, while cosmic justice encompasses not only contemporary individuals and groups, but also group abstractions extending over generations, or even centuries."[82] The problem is that the modern selective process is racist. Whites, who were drafted to fight a war for American business interest, their ancestors are not even considered for reparations for the terrible deaths many of those draftees [Statist slaves] suffered.

Once a nation starts to impose Cosmic Justice, it declares itself to know better than God, the nature of reality. The First Commandment declares the men can have no other God before the real God. The problem with God's Commandments is that there are consequences that no nation can avoid. There is no defense against God's judgments. When the Nation/State sets itself up as a god, it is declaring war upon God. As I write, the United States is under the judgment of God.

Hebrews 10:31. *It is* a fearful thing to fall into the hands of the living God.

---

[82] Sowell. P. 31.

Chapter Fifteen: The Dual Laws of American Democracy.

The problem with systems of laws is that there are various levels of laws within every nation. There are laws that support the idol of the government, a government that is a tool of a mafia elite. The actions of modern governments parallel those of organized crime, except on a greater scale. The ability to tax a captive people is just another form of extortion: it operates on the principles of a protection racket. Just pay your taxes and the audit enforcers will not 'break your legs.' That is why every government gravitates toward a monopoly over the land over which it rules. Just as criminal mobs had a territory over which they controlled, there were mob wars over who had the rights to a particular territory. The mobs expect to have a monopoly of force under its control, including having the police leaders on the payroll. Those that submit to the rule of the mob are allowed to live in peace. That is the type of government that exists in the modern world: a protection racket controlled by mafia dons, i.e. Congress.

The above represents one set of laws inside a 'democratic' Nation/State. There are another set of laws which represent 'social control' laws: Laws of expropriation and laws of control. The modern Nation/States have expropriated the Biblical ideal of absolute laws for their own purpose. Biblical Laws are based upon the reality created by God. They are not laws of expediency, but laws that are based upon God's own nature and His creative powers that copy that nature. God is the source of all laws. When states seek to become gods, they borrow the idea of laws from God. The State's laws are designed to reflect, not the reality of creation, but the reality of the State's power. Technically, Statist laws are legislated commands with penalties for non-compliance. Some are mere laws of convenience, as in traffic laws. Traffic laws are not designed to reflect God's created reality, but are really just rules of a game like chess. However, laws permitting usury should not be considered laws in the Biblical sense. Like many laws, this law is designed for the benefit of those who make the laws. Biblically, usury is anti-law, as in anti-Christ.

Despite all of the names given to modern governments, it is vital to understand this: "Whatever the form of government, by whatever name it is called, it is always … rule by some elite, a minority that rules either by deception or violence."[83] I always look for the fingerprints of Satan when I look at events. When you see government by deception you know that evil people are in charge. It is vital to differentiate modern governments from the type envisioned by many in the founding of the United States. The goal by many was to form a confederation of individual states that could unite in order to provide for an external defense, i.e. the border, and to maintain peace between the assorted local governments. It would be a very limited government. In the first seventy-five years, the big issue was, who would control the money, and who would be able to separate legitimate laws from laws of power. Would the states control the circulation of money? Would the central government supply the money for

---

[83] Hallowell. P. 1.

everyone? Or, would the banks create the currency of the land. How can the assorted state governments and the national government know what is a bad law and what is a good law? Do the people of the nation have more power than the people of a state?

It may not come as a surprise, but many think the modern Nation/State is a sham. It makes up its own definitions of 'natural rights', 'justice', and 'laws' to suit the needs for more power. It works this way: the state claims to be totally secular with no connection to God or God's Laws. However, that makes the state look for what it really is—a tyranny being imposed upon the masses. Calling itself a government of the people does not make it so. The tyrant, i.e. the government, has no clothes and his nakedness is revealed for what it is, i.e. a slave owner controlling the masses. The State needs to put on some fake clothes and that is where the rights, laws, and justice come in. It uses those categories to fool the people into thinking that their slavery is the price everyone has to pay for a government that 'cares' for them and their 'rights'. Remember, freedom is the enemy of rights. Modern rights can only exist by limiting the people's freedom.

Hallowell describes what many say about the modern state when they are being honest" "For it is not by reason that the destiny of men is determined but by deception, fraud, and force. Government, whatever the name applied to it for propaganda purpose, is always rule by the few in their own interest. Indeed, Pareto [*The Mind and Society*] tells us, 'the art of government lies in finding ways to take advantage of ... sentiments, not in wasting one's energies in futile efforts to destroy them.... The person who is able to free himself from the blind dominion of his own sentiments is capable of utilizing the sentiments of other people for his own ends.'"[84] Those men who are capable of rising above their own humanity know how to become the ruthless type of individual it takes to rule over the masses. Think about it: What kind of person drafts young men to die in battle to protect the special interests of the ruling elites? A person who has risen above moral and human sentiments.

What few want to admit is that, when men liberate themselves from God, they open the door to Satanic deception. To become fully human requires a

---

[84] Hallowell. P. 3.

person stay in contact to the God who made him human. Without that humanity, men become irrational and can be manipulated by irrational ideas and techniques. "...Pareto, Marx, Sorel, and Freud are all agreed that men are motivated more by irrational considerations than by rational ones."[85] The elites are there to assure their subjects that everything man does is perfectly rational; all the while they submit to the government of the invisible ruling powers. When all of the visible and hidden taxes are added together, men work from six to seven months out of the year for their 'governments'. "IF justice, natural law, and natural rights refer to no objective reality, if democracy is but a word, then these words can be used in any fashion anyone wants to use them, and there is no way in which we can challenge his right to do so."[86]

Once people reject God's revealed nature of Man, then anyone who has control of man's language can manipulate them into whatever direction they wish to lead man. The famous quote from Lewis Carroll's *Through the Looking Glass* explains the power of a nation's leaders to control the words of a nation:

"When I use a word,' Humpty Dumpty said in rather a scornful tone, 'it means just what I choose it to mean — neither more nor less.'

'The question is,' said Alice, 'whether you can **make words mean so many different things**.'

'The question is,' said Humpty Dumpty, 'which is to be master — that's all."

(Emphasis added.)

Those who run a government for their own purposes, will also define words to justify their actions. Politically correct language is used to divert the masses away from the true meaning of words. Americans have all been trained to speak Orwell's *New Speak*. That is also the reason Satan has been at war with the King James Bible: it is a dictionary of the true meaning of important words. Governments first rule by changing the language of the people into one that

---

85 Hallowell. P. 4.
86 Hallowell. P. 7.

keeps them from understanding the real world and the true nature of reality. Slavery to the State means liberation from God, but the leaders tell everyone that means Freedom, Justice, and Personal expression. Satan plays word games to keep the masses from even knowing their true condition.

Thurman Arnold who served under FDR, was not afraid to speak the truth: surprising coming from a lawyer. "The basic cause of our political confusion in America, he says, arises from a naïve faith in the existence of the 'thinking man.' The 'thinking man' of the popular mythology is the man who is able to discern right principles and to prefer them to false ones. The 'thinking man' is the man who is able both to discriminate and to act upon the basis of sound reason. No competent psychologist, Arnold says, believes in the thinking man. He knows that such a man does not exist. ... Arnold points out that 'in advertising the thinking man' has gone so completely that a modern advertising agency would be amazed at the suggestion that the best way to sell goods is by making a rational appeal. ... Only when government becomes as enlightened as the modern advertising agency and frees itself from all rational scruples, can government really do the work for which it is designed."[87]

The modern Nation/State rules by advertising its mission. It sells it as a product such concepts as justice, rights, and protection. None of those are part of a government as outlined in the Bible. Just as the government illegally, I should add, immorally prints fiat money which it sells to the masses at face value; it also creates fiat rights, fiat justice, and fiat protection—just take the jab. Arnold wrote: **"To believe in the objective reality of law, justice, and rights … is infantile.** He quotes with apparent approval, however, another writer who describes the adult personality in this way: 'And now, when you have ceased to care for adventure, when you have forgotten romance, when the only things worthwhile to you are prestige and income, then you have grown up, then you have become an adult.'"[88] (Emphasis added.) While that was written before WWII, it sounds very much like the World Economic Forum that everyone will own nothing and be happy. Even the old fake lies of law, justice, and rights can be

---

[87] Hallowell. P. 7-9.
[88] Hallowell. P. 9.

eliminated under the Great Reset: Governments will finally be able to reveal their Satanic lies and there will be noting anyone can do about it. Go spend your guaranteed annual income—if you have been a good boy.

Arnold understood the nature of Satan's Great Reset in the 1930s: "Arnold apparently believes that only when we learn to regard the mass of citizens as patients in need of psychiatric therapy can we make real progress toward the solution of our social and economic problems. ... [Hallowell concludes.] "Unless we recover our capacity to distinguish truth from falsehood, goodness from evil, beauty from ugliness—unless we recover, above all, our sense of humor that is founded upon the rationality of man—there is grave danger that we, too, shall succumb to the horror that is held out to us as **the promise of being made as comfortable as possible.**"[89] (Emphasis added.) The time is coming when no one will dare proclaim: I demand my rights. Patients in a government ward have no rights.

*

One way to keep people from coming to understand that they live under a fiat government is to create as many diversions and misdirections as possible. Never allow the masses to see behind the curtain that masks the real world. Every false and fiat government thrives on racism, homophobia, religious fundamentalists, White Supremists, culture wars, crime, inflation, depressions, foreign wars, and high crime rates. And they all need resolution from a strong government. However, the real need for a strong government arose from another place. The above issues are the governmental magicians' right hand to divert people away from his left hand. And they all need resolution from a strong government, but the real cause of the above issues has been totally neglected.

However, there was a greater issue happening in history which really laid the groundwork for strong Nation/States. What was the magician's left hand? The left hand was the Reformation and the consequences of that religious revolution. Previously, for a person to be complete and accepted he needed to belong to a community: the family, the clan, and the church. Those outside of

---

[89] Hallowell. P. 11.

such groups was considered an outcast. People became themselves by their submission to some group and became complete within that group. Only outcasts were solitary individualists. The Reformation gave birth to modern individualism: men were to look for a world where they were not dependent upon anyone or any organization in their pursuit of happiness. The new solitary individual needed something to protect his individualism—rights granted to him by the Nation/State.

Hallowell cites a couple of authors who explain the new concept of the 'master-less' man. In a sense, a new kind of law was born: man is a law unto himself. Submission to the law of another person is perceived as a limitation upon one's divine individuality—man as a god. Reinhold Niebuhr wrote in *The Nature and Destiny of Man* the following: "If Protestantism represents the final heightening of the idea of individuality within terms of the Christian religion, the Renaissance is the real cradle of that very unchristian concept of reality: the autonomous individual."[90] The great political philosopher, G. H. Sabine wrote this:

"The individual human being, with his interests, his enterprise, his desire for happiness and advancement, above all with his reason, which seemed the condition for a successful use of all his other faculties, appeared to be the foundation on which a stable society must be built. Traditional differences of status already began to seem precarious. Not man as a priest or a soldier, as the member of a gild or an estate, but man as a bare human being, a **'masterless man,'** appeared to be the solid fact."[91] (Emphasis Added.) The real modern horror of slavery is that they had a master in a culture that glorified the masterless man. This is one of the major problems the modern factory and corporation had to overcome: somehow turning a free individual into a worker bee. The first method was turning workers into wage and debt slaves: a form of White Man's slavery.

In the Declaration of Independence, Men were placed upon this earth to be guaranteed 'life, liberty, and the pursuit of happiness.' Believe it or not, this is

---

[90] Hallowell. P. 70.
[91] Hallowell. P. 70.

what men who follow the teachings of Satan were placed upon this earth to strive for and achieve. The principalities and powers who desired to rule over men recognized an opportunity when they saw it. The State would appeal to men by promising that their allegiance to the Nation/State would guarantee the lifelong pursuit of the above dreams. The American Revolution was based upon the Reformation/Renaissance view of man. Certainly not the Biblical view of man. That is why the Constitution does not mention God or His Laws within that document. A new set of laws were created which liberated mankind from the Laws of God. That is the American definition of freedom—a freedom which the powers of government wished to bestow upon all those who would recognize the American Democratic Government as representing the final stages in man's hope for a life of sensuous delights. The new government can lead mankind to a new kind of heaven—one here on earth.

*

The American Church and the American Business Leaders worked together to create a new nation dedicated to social peace, financial prosperity, and the freedom from unnecessary ethical restraints. American Church Capitalism, became the foundation for the resulting economic order. The Church developed a theology which supported the new outlook for the people who supported the church. No one wants a church that preaches sacrifice and service. In order to pursue the American Way of Life, salvation had to be made easy. Just as everyone wanted easy credit with time payments, so people wanted a theology where people could serve God with a little effort every Sunday. Over a lifetime, that adds up to a lot of time 'serving' God in the Church "Service." Plus, a person also would put a few dollars in the offering every Sunday just like he paid off his credit card a few dollars at a time. Jesus said His Church could storm the Gates of Hell. The Kingdom of God could defeat the enemies of a Christian Civilization. As an alternative to this, the American Church was transformed into a fortress: a place where people could celebrate Christian values safely behind the walls of the Sanctuary. [Kind of like a wildlife sanctuary where animals can live free from their predators.] Instead of storming the gates of Hell, the church put up gates to keep Satan's Stormtroopers out.

While many refer to America as a 'Christian' nation, its laws were not based upon Biblical Laws. America is a Christian in the same sense that the corrupt Abe Lincoln was called 'Honest' Abe. The Christian nameplate on America was a way disguise its true war upon Biblical Christianity. Americans did build a lot of Church buildings which became a symbol of America's faith: especially the picturesque white church in a small town with that steeple on top. In the South where I live, many churches have their own cemeteries; a church family's history can be traced in those country churches. It is very meaningful to a family but not much beyond that. It can be a kind of poetic associating tombstones with the church's mission. [In some churches, the long covered pot luck dinner table is right next to the tombstones—I mean you can rest your dinner plate on a tombstone if you so desire.]

For most Americans, material wealth symbolized God's favor upon their lives. Christian living areas became protected by laws. [Called Blue Laws today.] Before welfare, those who lived wicked lives were not subsidized by the government. Everyone could see the walking dead who had lived lives engaged in the pursuit of physical pleasures. Every town had a 'skid road' or a 'ghetto district' where those who led immoral lives would congregate. The middle class American was proud of his standing before God and his bank account. There were laws to protect the successful people by keeping the immoral and the failures confined to certain districts in town. The 21st century marked the end of safe districts made by stricter laws in family areas which were strictly enforced—such as anti-loitering laws. Living in such a protected and moral community gave people the sense of living in a 'Christian' nation. Now those safe havens have been ruled discriminatory.

Chapter Sixteen: The Christian worldview and the foundation of Law.

Laws are to reflect reality and God is the author of reality. God and reality cannot be separated. The early Church sought to write a series of creeds that attempted to secure a systematic doctrine of Biblical reality. Modern man has completely lost touch with reality and thinks that men can pass laws which create their own reality: there is no reality in an evolutionary world unless the king of evolution, Man, declares something so. Biblically, true Laws define the real world; today, man's laws define man's real world. There is no reality until man announces it to be true. One school of American Law were called positivists: a law is what man says it is. "In fact, jurisprudence is declared by these legal positivists, relativists, and analysts, and analysts to be completely autonomous of any moral or religious considerations. ... Whether a law be good or bad, just or unjust is no concern of the pure science of jurisprudence, for pure jurisprudence is concerned exclusively with the norms or standards set up in the various legal systems.... [The law] is concerned with law as a logical system derived from a basic norm, whatever that might be."[92] Could be called procedural law: justice is achieved when men follow the correct procedures as set out by law.

There is another school of legal thought espoused by Roscoe Pound. [Not to be confused with Ezra Pound.] This school believes that laws should satisfy the interests of society. "Laws should be passed that satisfy the 'human wants and desires.'"[93] The problem is that the wants and desires keep changing and these laws must balance between stability and change. Laws must be, in a sense, living and growing with man's evolution. It is the courts role to decide what the interests of a changing culture are. Pound views laws as a means for social control and to accomplish human engineering. Laws are the means a government can tell the masses which behaviors will result in their punishment. All laws resemble speed limit laws in which the State can dictate any speed it desires for any particular road. [Years ago when I travelled through Montana, the speed limit on some roads was 'reasonable and prudent.']

Because there are no absolutes but merely interests, society becomes a clash of various interests, lobbyists, all seeking justice for themselves. What is not recognized is this: the institutions/groups which have the most powerful lobbyists are protected and advanced by the Central Government in Washington, D.C. Justice means furthering their agenda. In fact, in the 21st century, the Federal Government is attempting to eliminate all competing 'interests' other than its own and those groups that support the Grand Global Reset. The illusion is to create a Nation/State based upon the universal brotherhood of man and his unity with the earth. The theory is that everyone shares a common interest and a powerful government can impose that commonality upon everyone. Just like the Theory of Evolution, so is the theory of mankind's common humanity. However, having bodies that more or less resemble others does not make everyone the same, in any sense of the dream. Only those that submit are considered the correct products of evolution. More than being politically correct, men must become evolutionary correct.

*

Biblically, there are also those who are Biblically correct or not. The most important division is the separation of the believers from the non-believers.

---

[92] Taylor. P. 280-281.
[93] Taylor. P. 280.

There could not be any wider gap: some destined for Heaven, and some destined for eternity in Hell. That eternal separation starts now, in time, and creates two classes that cannot be united. That is just the beginning. There are racial, cultural, and national differences. Even within the same group there are differences of parentage, of talents, and locality of birth. A child born in Cactus Flats, population 275, will be totally different than those born in a major city. I grew up in a small farming town and even in that town there were major differences between farm boys and 'city' boys. They even dressed differently: farm boys and town boys could be identified by their clothing style—or lack thereof. If the boys in my home town of rural White guys were noticeable different in their ways of thinking, how can a nation be brought together as one? One reason Hitler is still hated so much is that he believed no nation can unite divergent people into one unified nation. The mantra was this: One Race, One Nation, and One Law—and a leader the people can unite around. That belief totally destroys the hope for a New World Order.

Taylor states the real problem in the United States:

"The great illusion of modern 'post-Christian' democrats and humanists is that true community can be created between men without the grace and power of the risen Christ. In the very same year in which James Meredith was forcibly admitted to the University of Mississippi, the Supreme Court prohibited the saying of the Lord's Prayer in the public school system of America. Such apostate humanists apparently expect men to live as brothers without believing in God as their creator, to found a community of men without any common life of sacraments and creed to bind them together, and to think as one while remaining utterly individualistic and self-serving."[94] What the Bible teaches is totally rejected as even possibly true: Sinners and followers of Jesus Christ can only be united by some form of compulsion or force. The global rulers recognize this: that is why a system based upon a social credit score tied into a centralized system of digital banking/money is set to be introduced. Everyone will have their behavior linked to their ability to bank and to spend money.

*

---

[94] Taylor. P. 308.

There is an additional problem with the new government control through the social credit system. It will result in people becoming more and more cautious about who they associate with. What happens if your friend becomes tagged by the government as an enemy of the State for non-compliance to governmental regulations? In the world of Evolution, friendship is merely a human construct and needs to be abandoned if it disrupts one's credit score.. Evolution does not create human beings, it evolves 'intelligent' animals. Modern man passes laws with 'animal man' in mind. The Social Credit system is built upon the thesis that an animal humans can be conditioned as you would caged animals. God-created beings have God's image within them. People are not animals and any attempts to treat them as animals will fail. Laws that refuse to take into account God's image within man will produce several results: false laws create rebellion; false laws create mental disorders; false laws create human conflicts; and, most importantly, false laws invite judgment from God. God and His Laws are not socially constructed and cannot be changed without suicidal results.

It starts with another idea as mentioned above: Individualism. Laws that treat humans as individuals and individuals alone will result in the atrophy of the human personality. Eventually, you have a nation of Zombies who function as 'human' robots: an animal with carrot and stick conditioned responses. Or, a man that can only think in terms of sensual reality: All that is real comes to that person through his fives sense. That is not how God made man: God has revealed to Man through the Bible a reality that is beyond the senses of man. If God had not revealed reality to man, he would never discover it through 'Science.' There is another thing in 'government world' that is lost when the laws of the State treat men as beings that are governed by laws and laws alone: humans lose their soul, i.e. his God-given unique, eternal personality.

Jesus inaugurated the Kingdom of God upon His resurrection. It is a civilization that binds people together under a common legal system: the Laws of God. That Kingdom is the bond that was created to bring people together into a community. The community exists separate from any Government and its laws. That works out fine as long as the government is content to operate as God planned for human governments to operate: create a safe environment where people are free to live their lives within God's Kingdom. These is the primary roles of a Godly government: A nation that is threatened by an external enemy must be resisted if the people want to be free from foreign oppression. And, the government must protect the people from the criminal and immoral elements that would make a stable social and economic order impossible.

There are places in the world, I am told, where every store's inventory is behind the counter: if you want to buy something, you ask for it. Up until quite recently, stores in America could have their inventory on display where people could take it and place it in their cart. Now, some stores are starting to lock up certain consumer goods. That is a sign the 'law and order' has broken down. That means that other areas of social and economic life are also failing. Most people do not realize that the Kingdom of God is not a government and it can only successfully exist within a lawful order. The Kingdom is not an underground black market moral crusade or something that exists only inside a church building. When the Godly role of government fails, all other aspects of society fail with it. Yes, governments are from God, but they are assigned a primary task of protecting a culture from enemies both foreign and domestic: nothing more; nothing less.

*

There is another aspect of God's Kingdom that few recognize. The human personality develops in time. God places His image in the unborn child at conception. That image is like a seed. It not only takes time to develop, but it needs an atmosphere where people can freely interact in a safe and trusting environment. If you watch TV crime shows, you know that a husband or wife cannot be made to testify against each other in a court of law. It is founded upon the thesis that trusting human relationships require an atmosphere of reliance and confidentiality. Ideally, the family should fall under the same limitations: a man's home is his castle with a drawbridge. However, other close associations are now coming under the control and intrusion of the government. Even the doctor/patient confidentiality is no longer protected by law. Because all medical information has been digitized, and transmitted to a person's insurance provider, there are no secrets—especially if you are covered by some government medical plan. In the name of 'protecting' the 'individual' the government must oversee all interactions between two or more people. Yes, wherever two or more are gathered together, there is government involvement. The government has replaced God in those circumstances.

The primary reason for the Income Tax is so that the government has access to how you make every dollar. Getting tax dollars is secondary to obtaining the information all about every person. There is no getting around such an invasion of privacy: it's the law. The human personality needs privacy in order to develop properly. No one wants to work out the life on a stage or before a camera. The person would become very self-conscious and fearful of expressing his human and imperfect human nature. Even mature Christians do thinks that they do not want recorded or revealed. Not only that, everyone needs persons they can trust without the fear of the government forcing information to come out into the open: no person should be required to testify against his closest friends. The law treats everyone as either a criminal or a future criminal. The laws state that the government has a 'right to know' things that might violate the safety of the public order. That is, crimes must be prosecuted before they are committed. Because one home has witnessed a crime, every home must be supervised to prevent repeat occurrences of such wrongdoing. Of course, such invasions of privacy do not apply to the government's own operations.

The Bible reveals which behaviors are to be called crimes. Thought crimes are only between a person and God. When the government starts thinking in terms of 'thought crimes', it is elevating itself to the level of a god. In a sense, the tax forms are almost like a personal confession to one's priest, except your priest is not your government. By the way, the Bible restricts taxes to those areas of life that are impersonal: tariffs, tolls, licenses, and head taxes. Income taxes, inheritance taxes, property taxes, and any tax the quires the violation of your own privacy from the government. Of course, America has passed multiple laws which violate the Biblical restrictions placed upon potential tyrants. **Only people who are allowed to have secrets from the government are a free people.** That is why every tyrant passes laws which require that a person testify against himself, i.e. tax forms and other required documents, and those other people that trust him.

One of the purposes of God's Kingdom is to create a community of those who are obedient to God's Laws: not the laws of the King. Modern thinking portrays the dualistic world of individualism versus collectivism. Each person is to be secure within **his own mind** and his own ideas, and **his body** is to be part of a culture formed by the laws of man, i.e. ruling elites. That is not how God created His people. Man's personality can develop only in relationship with God and with his community. "Man is called by his Creator to love the Lord his God with all his 'heart' and his neighbor as himself. ... The common error of both individualism and collectivism, in typically humanistic fashion, is that they take their starting point in man, whether that be the individual or the group. The biblical view of man in society transcends this dilemma. In the light of the Word of God, we know that God created man for community with his fellow men and as a social being. This means that man does not find his purpose in himself as Locke supposed nor in the group as Karl Marx supposed but in the God who made him."[95]

The modern State finds any close and private community a threat to its monopoly over the lives of its subjects. That is one reason that politically correct relationships are promoted by the government and the media. For example, the traditional English Men's Clubs where men could meet and discuss ideas have come under attack. Also, the memberships are limited to a certain type of individual. A tyrant thinks that whenever men meet in private they are plotting some intrigue like in the days of Rome when very few Caesars died of old age. Those in government know that they are at war with God and people who serve God, and that is why they fear any organization with closed and exclusive memberships. Biblically, people need such 'behind closed doors' places to develop their Biblical personality. For the tyrant, that is not a valid reason. There is only one community and it is a public one, open to the eyes of the Overlords. Of course, those in power are entitled to have their own, members-only meetings, such as the Bilderberger meetings.

In the Middle Ages, the church buildings were considered places of sanctuary. A person could actually flee to the church for protection. This was especially true if the person was wrongfully convicted or was guilty of some

---

[95] Taylor. P. 423.

political crime. Even ordinary poor criminals could seek refuge within a church. In England, such a person was then allowed to leave the country, never to return. The King's Law could not touch a man who sought refuge in the church. Interestingly, the main meeting place within a church building is still called a sanctuary. The basic belief is that the church had its own law system which was separate from the King's Laws. This dual nature of laws served to protect men from the unruly whims of a tyrant.

Gradually, the governing powers sought to end the idea of the church being a separate nation within the Government's domain. "For Marsilius [of Padua] peace and order cannot be secure if there is at any moment a possible conflict of jurisdictions. Thus he sought to establish the internal sovereignty of the new rising state of Europe by ending the several jurisdictions existing within it; hence existing ecclesiastical immunities must be abolished, and churchmen made altogether subject to the civil government."[96] In early America, before the Civil War, the national government had to share its authority and jurisdiction with multiple 'lesser' jurisdictions. In a sense, a person might find sanctuary in another city or another state where the total rule of the national government was not recognized. I you want to know one of the real reasons for the Civil War, you will find it in the war upon competing jurisdictions. The Lincoln regime could send a telegram to any place in the Northern States and have some newspaper editor, some elected official, or some minister arrested for publically opposing the war. The Civil War ended political sanctuary in the United States. There were times when churches sought to reestablish a limited form a sanctuary when a few attempted to hide or help 'draft dodgers' to escape from the Draft Board. Of course, today that has all changed. Americans cannot leave their nation without the proper paperwork: people can attempt to run but they cannot hide.

*

Early in Christian history, the Apostle's Creed was published.

I believe in God,
the Father almighty,

---

[96] Taylor. P. 469.

Creator of heaven and earth,
and in Jesus Christ, his only Son, our Lord,
who was conceived by the Holy Spirit,
born of the Virgin Mary,
suffered under Pontius Pilate,
was crucified, died and was buried;
he descended into hell;
on the third day he rose again from the dead;
he ascended into heaven,
and is seated at the right hand of God the Father almighty;
from there he will come to judge the living and the dead.

I believe in the Holy Spirit,
the holy catholic Church,
the communion of saints,
the forgiveness of sins,
the resurrection of the body,
and life everlasting.

Amen.

This creed states that God is both the creator of the earth and of man, and sovereign over the whole earth. He is in control of history and all reality operates according to His laws. "God is the makers of heaven and earth, not Satan. History culminates in God's plan and triumph, not in Satan's victory."[97] As evil as times appear at times, God will be victorious over Satan and his evil rebellion against God and His people. Christianity is built upon the belief and the hope of God's victory over evil—an evil that shall never appear again, forever. "This declaration immediately **makes God the source of all ethics, of all morality, and of all law**. In all non-Christian systems, the source of ethics and of law is the state..... Either God is the true source of morality and law, or the state is."[98] (Emphasis added.) The purpose of creed is to quickly and dramatically reveal the teachings of the Bible. Creeds define orthodoxy and will reveal anti-Christs by those whose views are different from those defined by the Bible as expressed in the creeds.

---

[97] Rushdoony. The Foundations of Social Order: Studies in the Creeds and Councils of the Early Church. Presbyterian and Reform Publishing Company. 1972. P. 5.
[98] Rushdoony. The Foundations. P. 5.

The next creed was the Nicaean Creed. This further established that the events of Jesus' life are real history. One of the earlier challenges to Christianity was Gnosticism. Without getting sidetracked, the Gnostics believed that Jesus was the absolute, and the Demiurge created the material world. These two were polar opposites and they cancelled each other out. This allowed Man to become the supreme force upon the earth. In a sense, most religions copy the Gnostic lead in making Mankind the last remaining power upon this earth. "In all non-Biblical faiths, the essence of religion is the attempt of man's imagination to impose a pattern or ideal upon history."[99] The Biblical view of history with God using the events of time to mold His people into His Image is negated. Secular history is heading for some kind of man-made utopian order. The very idea that God is using history for his own purposes is denied. Only Man can rule over time and history.

It is important to understand that many of the issues facing Christians today also confronted the Christians in the early days of Christianity. Arius of Alexandria [256-336] created the doctrine of Arianism. Basically, the god of Arius was unknowable. He exists but cannot communicate to man. He may be a presence or a force, but he cannot be categorized or subjected to a theological definition. Men need to explain the existence of this earth, but they do not want that creator to have any power over this creation. Kind of like today's belief in ancient aliens that planted the first human seeds upon earth. Just like the god of Arius, ancient aliens imposed no laws and have no ethical standards. Both are invisible forces that operate behind a curtain and only vaguely reveal themselves.

Arianism became the doctrine adopted by rulers. It could be used to support their empire and by adopting Arianism; they could declare Christianity illegal. The Christian God and His Revelation did not support an all-powerful Emperor or Caesar. The Christian God revealed the Laws of God that were superior to the Laws of the Empire. But the Caesar knew better than to attack the God of the Bible directly, but used the words of the Bible to introduce higher laws than the Laws of the Bible. Under Arianism, Jesus was just one of many divine manifestations in history, "...all serving to unify the Roman Empire as the divine

---

[99] Rushdoony. The Foundations. P. 9.

human order. Their Arian bishops were thus inescapably statist in their orientation and faith. For them, the empire was God's true order, and the emperor God's present manifestation and power on earth."[100] The American Church in many ways has adopted an Arian view of government while superficially hiding behind Biblical labels. The State is the Supreme Law giver and Christians are to obey their leaders as their Christian duty.

The corollary of Arianism is the idea that men can also become a god as Jesus became one also. Jesus taught mankind that everyone had the potential to become part of the universal divinity. This opened the door to the rulers of a nation to claim that their powers were divine and that the laws of the land were given to the nation by a form of divinity. **Of course, once the state becomes divine, resistance is both wrong and futile.** The Laws of the State become the laws derived from the powers of the universe. The American Church has gladly submitted to the laws of America because America is a 'Christian' nation and must be obeyed, even if those laws are declared to be more powerful than the laws of the Bible. The Laws of the Old Testament were merely for that nation and that time, but modern man can rise above such laws and create laws that will lead the Nation/State to form a new utopian order.

*

In 381 A.D., Christians met at Constantinople to defend the certainties proclaimed by the Christian faith. People hate certainties because they are viewed as limiting man's freedom to develop his own lifestyle. Today, mankind worships something called 'Choice'. The God of the Bible limits man's choices. "Everything associated with roots and uncertainly is today despised by the self-styled new elite. Marriage, morality, family, law, order, certainty, and above all, Christianity, are hated with a passion. Man's freedom is to avoid all certainty except himself; the quest for certainty is seen as the quest for death. Life for these men means uncertainty and rootlessness."[101]

---

[100] Rushdoony. The Foundations. P. 14.
[101] Rushdoony. The Foundations. P. 18.

In the 1960s, the 'hippies' believing in something called 'A Happening'. Some spontaneous event just starts to happen and everyone parties or acts crazy in some way. It is irrational, unplanned, and emotional: it is the feeling of the divine moment that releases the true character of life: a moment of ecstasy that just happens. An orgy of feelings that overwhelm everyone at the same time. It could be compared to meeting someone in the park, having wild sex, and then moving on, without ever knowing the other person's name. Ecstasy came out of the moment to be enjoyed without any rules or restrictions. That represents the philosophy of modern man, i.e. the total freedom of the moment. Living during those times, I remember people do something totally unexpected and irrational in the name of being free from social restrictions and ethical controls. A person who submitted to expected social roles was not considered free.

Both the modern and ancient revolutionaries had one undeclared purpose. We live in a time where mobs randomly riot and burn cities. The mobs are actually making a theological statement: "This hatred of roots and of certainty is basic to revolutionary activist. The revolutionist destroys things of value precisely because they have a value apart from him. Only what he decrees can stand. [Not White Men's Values.] The revolutionist destroys roots, values, and laws because they speak of certainty, and he is at war with certainty. This is the basis of revolutionary destruction. It seems senseless to those who fail to realize **that destruction basic to revolutionary faith**."[102] (Emphasis Added.) The burning of cities is an attack upon a Christian White culture that has resulted in a spiritual and material prosperity the rootless revolutionary despises.

There is another aspect of Christianity that is hated: the unity that is a result of believers forming a close-knit community. Christianity creates a social and cultural unity that non-Christians despise. The mob wants the unity of an orgy, not the unity of a common faith and a common commitment. Satan's war against Christian unity has also infiltrated the American church. The new unity is one of a common desire to have a faith that does not require any commitment to any truth that requires public actions, i.e. works, or a life of personal sacrifice. The idea that Biblical Laws apply to every culture regardless of time is one

---

[102] Rushdoony. The Foundations. P. 19.

thought that had to be asserted by the early Church. The New Testament Church was not only an extension of Old Testament Israel, but a continued Revelation of God's *eternal* propose for His people. The unity of the early Church was based upon the truth of God's Laws for all time, not merely a religious club or a religious political party.

*

Growing up under government schooling, I learned a lot about ancient Greece and the glory of Athens and its literature. This time was pictured as the Golden Age of Man—before Christianity arose and declared war against what it called the pagan gods of the Greek pantheon of gods. The constant warfare between the multiple Greek city states has been largely ignored. The glory of Roman culture and empire were founded upon the teachings handed down from the Greeks. I remember reading the Greek plays and the pictures of those outdoor amphitheaters as being special. There is a magnificence to Greek architecture that amplifies the teachings of the Greeks. American cities cannot compare to the beauty of the Greek cities. And yet, the life of the common Greek 'citizen' is largely ignored. Rushdoony describes the Greek mentality as following:

"The lot of man was a sorry one, and the processes of the universe confounded, confused, and shamed man with frustration, defeat, decay, and death. It is customary for humanists to portray pagan antiquity as a golden age, a time of joy and a human self-realization and dignity; the portrait represents mythology. Pagan man held to a basically pessimistic outlook. *Fate* destined man to an ultimately dark and shadowed end, and man's todays were clouded by life's basic hostility to man. It was no less rue of the barbarians that for them life was basically frustrating.""[103] The Romans said this about the early Christians: "Those people sure know how to laugh." It was this joyfulness that separated the Christians from the terror of the night found under pagan beliefs who constantly felt oppressed by the profusion of the pagan gods. Jesus Christ was the God of certainty and the Laws of God could be trusted to be true regardless of the times. God and His Laws were unchanging. God ruled and controlled history, not chance.

---

[103] Rushdoony. The Foundations. P. 31,

*

Another Church Counsel occurred in 431 A.D. The temptation of those days was how to define the nature of Jesus. Those who opposed the Biblical definition of Jesus as God's only begotten Son, sought to define Jesus as a man who through his holy life was elevated to a God by the Father in Heaven. Jesus was not our savior, but a saving example in which we all could aspire. Satan's promise in the Garden of Eden that men could become gods was looked upon as a truth that transcended whoever said it. When Jesus asked His disciples to follow Him, they were to follow Him into divinity. Many believe that Truth is where you find it, regardless of the source. The deity of Jesus Christ might not be true, but people can still worship the process that can make any person into a god. Jesus became a god when he chose to unite his will with the God in Heaven. Someone, anyone can do it.

As a result of this belief, the Emperor or the State could become gods walking upon the earth. This belief liberates the ruling elites from normal restrictions placed upon human beings. Remember, it is not the common man that the ruling powers are seeking to elevate to godhead, but themselves. This is one of the major reasons the Overlords are at war with Biblical Christianity: Men want to become gods and they do not want any other gods upon the earth than themselves. You cannot understand modern governments unless you understand that the elites consider themselves divine and are a class separate from all other human beings. This is why these leaders have no qualms about sending people off to war or injecting the whole earth's population with deadly and experimental vaxxxines. Of course, their divinity does not come from God, but from Satan who endows certain creatures with Satanic powers and a Satanic lack of conscience.

With the resurrection of Jesus Christ, the war began between those who believed in the divinity of Man and those who followed the teachings of Jesus, the Son of God. Because more Whites in the United States believe in Jesus as the one and only Son of God, there is a war against the White Race: Satan's followers are not taking any chances. The Overlords of man claim divinity for themselves so they live in fear that those who know God personally will expose their Satanic connection. Again, power either comes from God or it comes from Satan; there are no other sources of power. The election process of modern democracy has been severely compromised. No one will ever get elected who believes in the divinity of Jesus Christ and the legitimacy of God's Laws. Satan will call out his best propagandists to make sure that does not happen. Satan is the author of deception and confusion and his powers to influence elections are beyond belief.

Every civilization or Nation/State needs something that could be called divine, such as the English divine right of Kings, or in American Democracy, the voice of the people is the voice of god. If the God of the Bible is denied, then some other source of divinity must be imported to legitimize the right of a few to rule over the many. Any laws must carry with them some sense of authority. Why should the masses give up half of their income to the various assorted forms of government? Some form of order must be imposed which makes the necessary sacrifices just part of the way the world is—there is nothing anyone can do about it. Of course, emperors have claimed to be divine throughout history. The current American Overlords and the ruling elites of the New World Order have also connected themselves to the divine powers of Satan.

The early Christians in Rome were faced with the choice between two divinities:

"The political order embodied and manifested the divinity inherent in being and salvation was therefore in and through this high point of power, Caesar. 'Salvation is to be found in none other save Augustus, and there is no other name given to men in which they can be saved.' [**Acts 4:12.** Neither is there salvation in any other: for there is none other name under heaven given among men, whereby we must be saved.] Conflict between Christ and Caesar was thus inescapable. Rome was quite willing to recognize the church and give it an approved states as a legitimate religion provided that the church recognized the superior jurisdiction of the state and the political order as the true and primary manifestation of the divine. As Francis Legge noted, 'The officials of the Roman Empire in time of persecutions sought to force the Christians to sacrifice, not to an of the heathen gods, but to the Genius of the Emperor and the Fortune of the City of Rome; and at all times the Christians' refusal was looked upon not as a religious but as a political offense.'"[104]

One reason the American Church has been captured by the American government and culture is that it failed to understand the divine nature of the American system of government and the American Way of Life. The government expects 'Christians' to send their children to public indoctrination centers called schools. Even private and home schools are subject to inspection and governmental accreditation. The government expects Christians to sacrifice their children to the goddess of American wars—both foreign and domestic. The government expects its subjects to fill out extensive information about themselves for purposes of taxation and control: citizens are entitled to privacy, but not subjects or civilians. Pagan gods could hardly demand more of their worshippers.

One of the purposes of the Church meeting at Chalcedon was to establish the foundations upon which the Church and the State could occupy the same territory. "...Chalcedon prevented human institutions from professing to be incarnations of the deity and able to unite two worlds in their existence. The state was reduced to a human order, under God, and it was denied its age-old claim to divinity for the body politic, the ruler, or the offices."[105] Today, no one questions that the Nation/State is the greatest power upon the earth. The laws of the State become laws greater than any Biblical Commandments or Christian doctrine. There are no appeals beyond the declarations of the State. Freedoms only exist as granted by the State. There is no freedom that is above the power of the State to deny. Freedom is permission. *"Permission form the state to exercise certain areas of activities could exist, but not a liberty apart from and beyond the state grounded in man's creation by God."*[106] There is no ground upon which any man can appeal beyond the power of the State.

As I write, more and more, Christians are losing control over their own bodies and their own minds. In times past, that was not even considered a freedom, but just the way the world works. A King might pass laws, but he was not allowed to take away a person's humanity. Through forced injections, a Christian loses control over his own body. And further, through massive

---

[104] Rushdoony. Foundations. P. 64-65.
[105] Rushdoony. Foundations. P. 67.
[106] Rushdoony. Foundations. P. 68.

programs of propaganda and drug-induced compliance, Christians are losing control over their own minds. After WWII, the Americans wanted to know how the Soviet Union was able to control its population despite killing over 60 million of them. American leaders were told the secret was Sodium Fluoride. It pacifies that part of the brain that controls a man's ability to resist orders from a superior force. Sodium Fluoride is a poison—just read the warning label on your toothpaste—but delivered in small amounts can be the perfect weapon of mass control. It was sold to the public as a preventative for tooth decay—yes, chemotherapy for cavities. Very few questioned the real reason for adding it to everyone's drinking water. Obedience to the master State is considered expected. Today the command to drink the water has morphed into 'Take the Jab.' That is a Command-ment from your god.

*

The Bible declares that we all live in a fallen world. Not only has man fallen from the original perfection of Adam and Eve, but nature and the animal kingdom haves also fallen from their perfect role in maintaining a healthy earth. Today, the cure for mankind's problems and shortcomings are to found in statist actions. There is nothing that cannot be cured if the power of the State is directed toward a cure. What used to be called sin is now merely a social disorder. In times past, God would send droughts and storms as judgments upon a sinful nation. Now that is called climate change. Through the proper application of geoengineering, the climate can be controlled and God's judgments can be prevented. Modern governments act as God blockers.

Christians in the New Testament era, recognized the significance of the Kingdom of God as God's invading force. "In antiquity man had been bound to the state but 'freed from God. Orthodox Christianity freed man from the state by binding him to God, who is man's true ground of freedom and fulfillment."[107] However, with the American Revolution, the American Church reverted back to the days of antiquity where the city States had total control over the lives of its subjects. The Church bought into the heresy that the State was required to be neutral in all doctrinal matters. The State became the ruler over the visible world

---

[107] Rushdoony. Foundations. P. 80.

and the Church became the ruler over the invisible world. Because Finance Capitalism needed a secular order in order to operate efficiently, the Church went along and gladly became a building where the invisible world could be experienced. The opportunities for immense wealth in the new land made everyone a believer in the power of government to unleash the 'horn of plenty.' In the 1950s, it was popular to decorate the Thanksgiving table with a woven basket with fruit emerging from the wicker horn. That symbolized the abundance that a secular government could produce. People might give God a tip of the hat, but everyone knew the true source of life's abundance.

*

Another important creed was the Athanasian Creed, named after, of course, Athanasius (299-373). Secular political thought does not understand the nature of the Trinity. This is important to understand even though it can be a little technical. I mean, what does the Trinity have to do with political power? Good Question? Answer: Everything. Non-Christian political history swings back and forth between total control [Tyranny] and total freedom [Anarchy]. Or as the TV show, *Get Smart,* stated, a war between Control and Chaos. Philosophically, it is the war between the ONE and the MANY. The Trinity is best understood in the nature of the family. The family is a creation of God and it is based upon the Trinity. In the Trinity, the Father, Son, and Holy Spirit are all real 'individuals' and yet they are all God. The family is real and yet it is made up of real individuals. It only makes sense if you understand the nature of the Trinity and the family is built upon that model of created reality.

In the same way, the government is real, but so are the lessor governments under its order. The family-controlled school is real. It operates separate from the government and yet it is part of the national identity as much as the government. The elite's argument is that if other governing entities were allowed to exist, there would be chaos. Everyone would be doing their own 'thing' and society would collapse. The central government provides a safe environment for all other governing entities to operate safely. A non-Christian order cannot imagine a social order without someone in control to tell everyone what to do. The Overlords fear that if a nation relinquishes any of its obsession with control, the people will end up destroying the peace obtained through multiple laws governing every aspect of their behavior.

*

The Christian church is based upon a hierarchy of talents and positions of authority. It is not a democracy. The fallacy of democracy is that the man in the street knows how to run a nation. Does the man receiving a welfare check understand the danger of a fiat money system? How about gold and silver as money? That is why politicians will often appeal to the emotions of the mob in order to gain support. While the Bible has some simple doctrines, there are others that are not so easy, such as the nature of the Trinity. That is not easy to understand. Democracy breeds the idea that the simplest ideas reflect the true nature of the world. If the mob cannot understand something, it must not be true. In fact, the myth of the common man and his ideas about realty have come to govern the church also. The American Church has been reduced to preaching John 3:16 and little else. Governments have been reduced to just getting votes. And businesses have been reduced to satisfying the shareholders. Populism will always lead to destruction.

The Overlords use this idea to maintain that without their manipulation of elections, the mob would run the country into the ground. The Christian idea of order is one of multiple orders. Each order operating separately, but each one thinking in terms of the greater good for everyone. And yet how is that to be obtained? This is where the Bible gets unpopular. In a nation, there will be multiple forms of government, each having domain over a small part of realty: the local school, the church, the local government, the various private associations, the local businesses, and the local labor unions, all have power within their domain. The labor union protects its members, but its expertise does not allow it to run a school. Each special area of controlled freedom will contribute to a great order. Of course, all domains are expected to rule their domain under the ethical demands of God and His Word. The question modern man always asks: how can a people run a nation of multiple orders and levels of power without having to submit to the controls of the Bible? No one can. It is impossible. Hence the need for a tyrannical government in order to prevent anarchy—every man doing that which is right in his own eyes. Without God's Word, every man ends up doing that which is right in the 'eyes' of the elite.

There is a problem: God so designed reality that evil people cannot be trusted in any level of power and control. A nation needs good people who understand the nature of God's laws in order to survive. When a nation does not produce good people, then an all-powerful government must step in and seek to impose order upon chaos. **God has so designed his world that it takes a nation of good people in order for freedom to exist**. The first level of government is self-government. Everything begins on that level. When that level of government fails, then only an all-controlling government can bring order to society. That is why when a society rebels against the Commandments of God, tyranny will always results. Rebellious people invite tyrants into their midst. When there are no divine laws, there will be Satanic laws. There is no middle, neutral ground between good and evil.

Chapter Seventeen: The modern goal is to use laws to make people equal, create liberty, and ensure the equity of outcomes in a statist order.

The Overlords of Nation/States believe that the power of modern omnipotent governments, i.e. tyrannies, can create a new utopian order. Having defeated God, men can now build a heaven upon the earth: a 21st century tower of Babel, so to speak. Biblically, the foundation for a good nation is a secure border. The Bible relates how to dwell safely in one's own land.

Leviticus 25:18. Wherefore **ye shall do my statutes**, and **keep my judgments,** and do them; and ye shall dwell in the land in safety. **19** And the land shall yield her fruit, and **ye shall eat your fill**, and dwell therein in safety.

There can be no freedom, no liberty, and no equity if people cannot dwell safely in their own land. A nation cannot be a nation without a secure border, and a people cannot prosper if foreigners, i.e. immigrants, can take the fruit of their labor.

Another thing to understand is how words are defined in the Bible. The Bible is, among other things, the definer of words. Because tyrants will change words to suit their own propaganda, the Bible keeps the words stable over time. The Bible has no Orwellian 'New Speak'. Word manipulation is one of Satan's tools to confuse and deceive the masses. So let's start with the word 'liberty' in the Bible.

Luke 4:18. The Spirit of the Lord *is* upon me, because he hath anointed me to preach the gospel to the poor; he hath sent me to heal the brokenhearted, to preach deliverance to the captives, and recovering of sight to the blind, **to set at liberty** them that are bruised....

After the fall of Man in the Garden of Eden, men became enslaved to a material existence. The world became a place where men could satisfy their sensual and selfish fallen, and 'human' nature. While God gave man senses, they were not to become ends in themselves. It is like those who live to satisfy their taste buds and become fat and eventually in poor health.

I John 2:15. Love not the world, neither the things *that are* in the world. If any man love the world, the love of the Father is not in him. **16** For **all that *is* in the world, the lust of the flesh, and the lust of the eyes, and the pride of life,** is not of the Father, but is of the world. **17** And **the world passeth away, and the lust thereof:** but **he that doeth the will of God abideth for ever.**

Biblically, those who live for the sensual things in life, become emotionally bruised. The liberty to indulge in sensual pleasures brings only temporary delights. In time, the senses became satiated, and more intense or more corrupt sensual outlets are sought. Men become chained to a sensual treadmill from which there is no escape. For most people, the goal of sensual novelty takes both time and money. Not only that, but in time, other areas of life suffer: wife, kids, neighbors, and job. Men were not created to live by 'bread' alone. When men do that, they neglect the reason God created men and the ways that God grants true fulfillment—enjoyments that will last forever. The following is the life of those who use their senses but do not live to satisfy them:

Galatians 5:22. But the fruit of the Spirit is love, joy, peace, longsuffering, gentleness, goodness, faith, **23** Meekness, temperance: against such there is no law.

The liberty the Christian enjoys is the above and those, when embraced, provide a life of spiritual delight—without any of the negative consequences of the selfish and sensually absorbed lifestyle.

The liberty of God sets people free from their self-destructive and sinful lifestyle. The Bible calls this sensual life a form of bondage, i.e. slavery. This why the Bible does not condemn slavery, but only those who become slaves to sin—a slavery that leads to eternal death. God's liberty sets the captives free.

Galatians 5:1. Stand fast therefore in **the liberty wherewith Christ hath made us free,** and be not entangled again with the yoke of bondage.

And now the most important point which the American Church has failed to teach. The true liberty results in a lifestyle of fulfillment through the form of service for which God created us, called us, and wishes to see lived out in our lives.

Galatians 5:13. For, brethren, **ye have been called unto liberty**; only *use* not liberty for an occasion to the flesh, but **by love serve one another.**

*

As revealed above, there are two forms of liberty in this world: the liberty to serve others without the burden of guilt or personal baggage, and the right to serve oneself through the pursuit of sensual inputs to one's mind and lifestyle. A Biblical government is there to protect the right of people to live a life of service without undue restrictions. However, that form of liberty will never win an election. When a government politicians uses liberty to win elections and gain the loyalty of the masses, it is appealing to the animal nature of mankind. You can judge the moral temperature of a nation by looking to see what kind of liberty is being promoted by the politicians. There is another form of liberty that started in the American Civil War: politicized liberty. Liberty was transformed into a sensual feeling or a right protected by the government. About this time, the word was re-designed to create an emotional response needed to fight a war or win an election. That is another reason I regard the words of the Bible as being so important: the Book prevents important words from becoming a tool of Satan to subvert the thinking of men.

I came across a book written in 1930 on liberty by Everett Dean Martin which understood how 'liberty' was losing its true meaning. "Liberty and popular government are much the same, and the idea of liberty has become so associated with patriotic emotion that it has become more a matter of pride in history—or in popular fictions about history—than a clear, rational concept. We are inclined as a people to substitute emotion for thinking in dealing with most of the important concerns of our common life, and our attitude toward liberty is no exception."[108]

In fact, America debate no longer exists. The public, through the media, has been conditioned to respond to 'hot' works like a bunch of Pavlov's dogs. You know the words: Racist, White Supremist, Sexist, anti-Semite, right wing extremist, and fascism. There are more, but when these words are introduced into an intelligent argument, intelligence ends. These words are like waving a red flag before a bull—the charge is on.

During the Civil War, the slaves needed to be liberated. You know when a word has become a hot word when there is only one response to the use of a word. In the Civil War that response was to kill Southerners. Other solutions to freeing the slaves were not considered because liberty became absolutized and that demanded an absolute solution: WAR. The word surfaced again in a dramatic fashion in the wartime propaganda of WWI. The Allies were fighting for LIBERTY against the evil Huns. WWI used propaganda techniques to create a nationwide 'mob' hysteria. After the War, the people thought 'liberty' had been secured and there was no need to protect it. "Since the war, we have had to witness a widespread cynical tendency to subordinate many of our traditional American ideals to the end of material prosperity."[109]

Martin felt that because Americans no longer knew the true meaning of liberty that the nation was in danger of losing true liberty. That certainly came true after the crash of 1929. With the election of FDR, a bunch of new laws were passed which were designed to destroy traditional liberty and rebrand it into the narrow band of economic liberty. New laws were said to provide for the salvation of the nation as people learned to submit to a multitude of new regulations. FDR's New Deal promised to liberate the masses from poverty in exchange for their former ideas about freedom from government intrusion into their lives. Now the masses exchanged **freedom from Governments** and accepted economic freedom by becoming dependent upon a new form of **dependent freedom**. Everyone became dependent upon some government program in order to survive. Those government handouts now became an essential part of American government. Gone were the days when localities could work together in freedom

---

[108] Everett Dean Martin. Liberty. W.W. Norton & Company. 1930. P. viii.
[109] Martin. P. viii.

to solve their own problems. It has been maintained that the Depression of 1929 was designed from the beginning to destroy traditional liberty. It was to be replaced by the freedoms enjoyed under socialist governments found in Europe.

*

It is interesting that Martin sees one of the greatest dangers to American liberty is religious Fundamentalism, or as he calls it, religious fanaticism. Even as Americans were losing their liberties through the continued propagation of WWI style propaganda, Martin believes that Americans were in danger of losing their liberty because of religious Fundamentalists. It is interesting that a man who recognized the danger of politicizing 'liberty' writes about the dangers of religious liberties. This has been a problem throughout American history. Liberty has come to mean liberty from something else, rather than the liberty to do good things without government interference through restrictive laws. Actually, Martin wanted to be liberated from the masses who believed the Bible was true.

Martin does recognize the battle for liberty throughout history based upon two primary definitions of liberty. "The first is realistic and is based upon experience; the second is idealistic and is based upon emotion. The first stands for self-discipline, the second for spontaneity. The first holds that liberties are a human achievement; the second holds that liberty is a natural right, a gift of nature. The first conceives of liberty as an outcome of culture and a means to culture; the second maintains that liberty is an escape from the burdens and artificialities of civilization. The first stands for individual responsibility; the second says, Let the people rule. ... The second philosophy enfranchises the man and makes crowd domination possible."[110] As you can see, these two views of liberty as expressed in 1930 still exist in 2023. The problem begins when the government feels the two groups must be integrated or when laws are passed to favor one over the other. The first one is close to the Biblical view; the second is closer to pagan views. In a word, most people accept the libertine view of liberty which the Bible condemns as rebellion against God and His Laws. Whatever, the two forms of liberty cannot be reconciled. In fact, historically, the White race has traditionally followed the first view, and the Black race the second view. Thus the

---

[110] Martin. P. 6-7.

disciplined, self-reliant form of liberty is called racist. One author found this out when he wrote a book about the importance self-discipline and delayed gratification. He was labelled a racist and almost lost his teaching position.

There are also consequences of the two ideas of liberty. One produces a culture of progress; the other produces a culture of experiences rather than a vision of a better future. The first one operates on its own without the necessity of protecting it from the intrusion of outside cultural forces. People left alone, without government subsides, will develop a culture of liberty to make a better world for their children. The second lifestyle needs some sort of protection or subsides to protect it from the consequences of living by the standard: eat, drink, and be merry, for tomorrow we die. The first tends to support a monogamous marriage, while the second tends to produce a serial form of sexual encounters. In the libertine sense, the first culture restricts many of the liberties enjoyed by the second one. Obviously, a lifetime commitment to a marriage partner really does limit a person's opportunities for new and unusual experiences. Raising a child really limits one liberties. As you can see, the two cultures will naturally segregate themselves from each other. It has nothing to do with race, but with the fact that contrary cultures cannot mix: unless the government moves in and forces integration of opposites.

The United States is in decline because, since the 1960s, it has attempted to stay neutral in the liberty wars. That is until 9/11. After 9/11, traditional liberties were deemed dangerous: they allowed terrorists to have liberties, and therefore should be denied to everyone. America could no longer allow the first type of personal and private liberty. As a result, the government felt it could no longer even trust Americans. Many felt that the end of the first type of liberty was a war upon conservative and Christian beliefs as their form of liberty was too dangerous, i.e. extremist: people not dependent upon the government are dangerous. As a result, the Overlords of America decided that they could no longer trust those Americans who refused to join the party of subsidized pleasure seekers. You see, sensual seekers have one major flaw: they will not risk their lives to preserve a culture or a nation. Death ends all pleasures; so why would anyone die for some cause that may become obsolete in a few years?

Another great principle learned after 9/11 is that laws cannot save a nation. Every form of social-control laws have been enacted and still the cultural 'extremists' keep carrying on defending liberty number one. As a result, new laws are pending to deny culture style one people the right to engage in any banking activity. In other words, even though laws cannot save a nation—they never have—laws are being passed to accomplish something they are very good at: destruction. Governments have a religious faith in laws and they will not renounce their faith in their power to bless and condemn according to need. They have no choice. No matter what a government does, true liberty based upon Biblical reality, keeps rising up. Mankind has never quite understood that God create REALITY. Declaring war upon the real world with new laws just *ain't gonna* work. No matter how many laws a government passes, the power of God cannot be negated. His Kingdom of responsibility and accountability will prevail.

*

Another thing to consider, is the promotion of 'liberty' merely a con game imposed upon the American opinion? When Americans are granted sexual liberties, are they being conned out of the liberties that really matter? The American Overlords could not care less what the masses do in their spare time. That is the area where phony liberties are granted. "Hey people, you have the liberty to sleep with whomever you want. But don't quit your day job." So who really benefited from mankind's liberation from the Laws of God? Those in government, those in education, those in medicine, those in business, and those in the military. The very idea that the above groups should operate within the Laws of God is not even considered today. They all have been liberated so that they can set up their own institutionalized empires of exploitation. Martin believes that modern society has moved from the first form of liberty to the second form to accommodate those who could be utilized for some secular agenda.

A good example can be found in the American Civil War. While the goal was said to be the liberation of the slaves, that was not how it worked out. True liberty under God was transformed into universal equality. After the Civil War, giant corporations grew up from the huge profits made during the war: second rate food and supplies were supplied to the troops at top of the line prices. These corporations transformed the working class into wage slaves. The conditions in the new factories were dangerous and degrading. Workers were forced to work for subsistence wages under brutal and deadly conditions. Ten per cent of the steel workers died on job every year. In one ten year period, two thousand railroad brakemen died on the job—not counting all the other rail-related deaths. Corporate White slavery replaced Black plantation slavery. And forget the ex-slaves, they were no longer needed to create a centralized government. They were basically abandoned—until they were needed to further change society through other agendas. Ex-slaves became the elite's social wrecking ball against those who might resist the New Global Order.

Martin explains the evolution toward new forms of slavery. "It began in the Eighteenth Century and was greatly accelerated in the Nineteenth, when the Industrial Revolution brought opportunity to individuals to exploit their fellowmen. Individualism became the slogan of industrial magnates. They resented and resisted all legal control over their behavior. But industrialism had created great changes in social conditions—overwork, long hours, city slums—abuses which made the workers as a class demand that something be done to bring under the law the men whose economic power was by putting them into the position of tyrants above the law."[111] It is a long story, but the care of workers was passed onto the government. The beginning of a welfare state was begun to help the businesses avoid the true cost of the abuse of people—both of workers and consumers.

Martin next lists the American version of Christianity for the breakdown of classic liberty. While Martin's Biblical understanding is suspect, his analysis of social and religious trends is quite accurate. When Christians came to America, their theology was changed to meet the needs of the hour. He noted that there were three great changes to the Christians understanding of the Bible: the nature of salvation; the methods of evangelism; and the purpose of the Church upon the earth. The early Puritans believed that salvation was limited to those God had chosen. Salvation was not for everyone. Being part of a Church was an exclusive

---

[111] Martin. P. 7.

club in which only a few could join. As a result, Deism was introduced to the land where those who followed Western Civilization were doing God's work. God has created the earth and man, planted within him assorted talents, and then left man alone to work out the salvation of the whole earth. America's educated elites adopted this form of religion. Most of America's Founders were Deists. It was up to the elites to transform the wilderness into an empire. The third area of religion was the introduction of Great Awakenings and a religion of the masses was created. Christianity became an experience, not the adoption of any particular theology. After all, since the Reformation there were thousands of different interpretations of the Bible. Men can debate doctrines, but one's personal experience can become quite real. There can be no debate about one feels to be true. No one doubts their own revival experience.

Christian liberty became fundamental to the American Church. Everyone who subscribed to American and Western Civilization thought of themselves as part of God's plan upon the earth. People could disagree about what constituted salvation, or what a church should be like, but everyone agreed that Western Civilization was the greatest example of Biblical principles in the history of the earth. The nation exemplified a secular, inclusive church. While the nature of religion might bring local and private differences, everyone agreed that America was a Christian Nation that was placed upon this earth to spread the **American cultural religion** throughout the whole world. America was a light set upon a hill to bring civilization, American Civilization, to all of the non-Americas, i.e. pagans, everywhere in the world.

*

The Biblical doctrine of the Millennium was secularized and transferred to the American Nation. The huge numbers of dead Yankee soldiers were considered a human sacrifice that purified the American mission in this world. These soldiers had not died in vain; their deaths liberated America from the sin of slavery and opened the door to America becoming the Kingdom of God upon the earth. Christianity "...was transformed into salvation of the citizens of the American Republic in this world. This led to the prophecy frequently expressed by reformers in the Nineteenth Century, that the millennium was at hand and that the Kingdom of God was to be set up in the Republic of the United States. **Thus the State, with its program of legislation, was burdened with the task of the perfection of the individual."[112]** (Emphasis added.)

This new form of Christianity transformed everyone into a nation of amateur theologians who believed in Democratic Biblical interpretations of the Bible. Similarly, American Democracy meant that the common man could determine the true laws of God's New Israel. Every new convert could found a church and teach his unique doctrines as the real truth that God has given to him as free individual. Every person that had a dramatic conversion experience felt he was gifted with a prophetic ministry. America became a nation of people who felt that the government should aid them in the conversion of their neighbors though laws demanding everyone exhibit Christian virtues. This could be labelled Christian Socialism as the government was expected to promote Christian values and punish those who refused to acknowledge Christian Civilization. In the 19th century, in the United States, there existed a condition that could be called religious anarchy. This was a result of the downfall of Biblical Christianity and not teaching about the Kingdom of God. As Corporations and the Federal Government were uniting to form a new reality, people were seeking some form of alternative reality to steady the feeling of being lost in a work/consume world. [During this time, Spiritism also became immensely popular. Ouija Boards and séances became common party entertainment.]

*

With multiple sects promoting new Biblical revelations, Christian ideas permeated speculative culture. In this sense, America became a Christian Nation. As a result, the Nation/State was to take on the appearance of a Christian State: the message of the millennium must be taught both to Americans and those in other nations. The American Way is the only Way. Martin feels that the Christian Church's obsession with evangelism creates a 'crusading' spirit that is dangerous doctrine. "Christianity is a crusading religion. And so the idea of the church at war with the world came to America, and to the evangelistic reform psychology were added an impulse to crusading and an attitude of intolerance. Liberty

---

[112] Martin. P. 8.

cannot prevail against such an attitude, for we get from it a sanction for manipulating and regulating our fellowmen. We Americans, of all nations on earth, are the most obsessed with regulatory ideas."[113]

Martin assumes one major belief: One God is out to evangelize the whole earth. He has no idea that there is an enemy of God, Satan, who is the master manipulator and controller of mankind. Wherever Satan is allowed to have his people empowered, persecution of believers will be in operation. We live on a piece of land where Satan and God are at war with each other. This war cannot be avoided. However, the true Church is to expand its 'power' through service. People reaching out to others in need is the primary form of evangelism. Also, when Christians preach the Laws of God over every fallen institution in society, they are acting as ministers of God protecting the poor and lower classes from being exploited. I regard it regrettable that the American Church did not join with the working class in the demand for civil working conditions in the newly formed Corporations. The secular labor unions were taken over by Communists and Zionists. Because of that, the Church missed a great opportunity to teach the masses the true meaning of Christian liberty.

*

Recall that there are two kinds of liberty: one is the liberty to do that which is right, and the other is the liberty to do that which is wrong. The Masses desire the latter and every politician knows that those are the ones he has to appeal to in order to get their vote. No one gets elected promising hard work and discipline as the only way to live. In fact, only a few churches will even promote those virtues in the abstract: telling stories of Daniel and Jonah. Mass appeal became the foundation of both religious and secular thinking. Mass appeal devolved into mob appeal. There is one major problem with mobs: mobs are very good at rioting and destroying property, but mobs do not pick up garbage or remove graffiti. Throughout the Old Testament, God almost always worked through a remnant. This can be seen in the mob that came out of Egypt with Moses. As soon as Moses was gone for a few day, what did they do? They went back to worshipping the Golden Calf of Egypt. They had seen the Red Sea part, and they

---

[113] Martin. P. 9.

had seen Pharaoh's army drown in mass, and yet they did not really believe in God enough to trust him with their lives. When times got tough, they returned to the idols of Egypt, i.e. their traditional ways of thinking.

That is why that those who wish to change any order, have to understand the nature of true liberty and not the liberty of the masses. The Christian message offers true liberty, but you will never fill the churches teaching about that. When the American Church took of the spirit of democracy, the message of the Gospel was democratized for the masses. Martin wrote: "There is a myth that the rank and file of humanity, acting as a mass, want liberty. There is a legend that it is they who have achieved what liberties we have, that all that has made for human progress, has been won by the great, nation-wide, spontaneous uprisings of the people. Is this legend based on fact? Historically, it is not. It is doubtful whether liberty has ever been won permanently by a mass movement. Furthermore, the masses on the whole have persistently been indifferent to their own liberty. ...more Americans fought on the English side during the Revolution than on the Colonial side."[114]

The American Church had a problem from the beginning. The mythology that America was a nation that were united in certain foundational beliefs is really not true. Americans were united behind liberty only in so far as it enabled them to make money and keep their money. And yet Americans have never been united by common beliefs, but by a common mythology. Americans believed in high ideals, and those ideals were worshipped, but they were not expected to become a part of one's personal life. Except for times of wartime propaganda, Americans believed in themselves. Liberty, in the common man's eyes, came to mean the 'right' to do as one damn well pleases. And what pleased most Americans was to make money. This did produce a nation of great material abundance, but America also became a nation without a soul. Even the churches lost their soul as riches were interpreted to mean the blessings from God which the regular church goer saw as his right. When protestors today claim America should put into practice the ideals of the Declaration of Independence, they do not understand the real American history. America's grand myths were there to

---

[114] Martin. P. 10.

cover up America's overwhelming desire for wealth: "Make everyone equal, you got to be kidding: you want money, work for it."

In the 19th century and the early 20th century America, every American appears to have owned a Bible. That became a symbol of one's belief in the American Way of Life. Martin discusses the contradictions of American Christianity. Americans believed in the teachings of the Bible, but they lived by an Americanized version of those teachings. If the American Capitalist order disagreed with a church's interpretation of the Bible, then obviously people must be reading the Bible in the wrong way. The American Church fell in love with the ability of the masses to produce wealth beyond belief. Just as Esau in the Bible who sold his birthright, Americans sold their birthright for the right to sit at the table with everyone else united in pursuing the same dream. The great prosperity that Americas enjoyed through the unrestrained search for wealth, resulted in a nation where the pursuit of material wealth became the new god of America. No institution, especially the church, could hope to oppose this materialistic way of life and hope to become accepted in American culture. A Church standing in judgment over the American Way of Life could not survive. The masses wanted a church that supported the American Dream, not one that taught the Kingdom of God. Americans wanted to serve themselves first, not live to be an example of Christian service.

Chapter Eighteen: The establishment of Christian Liberty under the Roman Empire.

As American Christians no longer have the liberty they enjoyed in the past, it is essential to understand how Christians won liberty for themselves in the past. However, this is where Christianity has been perceived as a contradiction of its own beliefs. It has fought to establish liberty for themselves, but often oppressed others who were not Christian. It has fought against rulers who oppressed the Church, but use rulers to oppress those of other faiths. Christians have been a big supporter of individuality, but expected people to conform to the cultural norms of a nation. The Church is supposed to be a peacemaker, and yet it almost always supports the wars of the nation in which it resides. The people who become Christians claim to have renounced riches, and yet wealth has been declared to be a gift from God, i.e. blessings. Churches are supposed to bring people together, and yet church feuds and actual battles seem to be the trademark in Christian Churches: where two or three Christians are gathered together you will have four different opinions on every issue.

Whenever Churches have gained power in a nation, they have established State Churches in alliance with the ruling powers. State and Church have always formed a symbiotic relationship. In order to control the masses, both need each other to control both the spirit and body of men. The State can pass laws, and the Church can impose sanctions, i.e. excommunication, or banishment. In fact, where the two are not united, a Nation-State cannot be successful and it can never become an Empire. Again, where the two powers are not in accord, one or the other will establish a dictatorship to maintain order. Part of the reason for the social unrest in 2023 America is that there is no common faith that bonds the people and nation together. Individualism, rights, and personal entitlements have destroyed any chance of the American people uniting behind any common culture. The myth of the Christian nation did serve to unite the people together even though it was just an accepted mythos: Everyone wore the same meaningless badge. People would say: When push comes to shove, we are all Americans. Such American slogans were important but they were meaningless.

*

For about three hundred years, Western Civilizations united most 'civilized' nations into an internal peaceful order. There could be protests, riots, and severe issues with small groups of activists, but they remained just that, a minority. America had its labor 'riots' in the late 19th century, and America had its Vietnam War protests of the 1960s, but neither sought to overthrow the American government. Yes, there were the Indian wars, and violent racial battles, but these were localized and not attacks upon the government in Washington, D. C. Despite all of the above, the severest attacks upon the Church and the Government have come about from the Intellectual class and those involved in Government supported education. Ironically, the most powerful opposition to the American Government and the American Church have received money from the government that writes their checks. Even Christian colleges have produced some of its most profound critics.

The Age of the Church has been depicted by the elites in America as one of oppression. They have compared that oppression with the ruling class of Ancient Athens. That age was pictured as the age where intellectuals were honored and their beliefs controlled the leaders of the government. Plato and Aristotle controlled the thinking of men for a thousand years without any army or government to force their views upon mankind. They ruled by the power of their mind and their ideas. That is what every college professor dreams about—being able to put his views into action without opposition from the masses and the stranglehold that religious beliefs have over their lives. These intellectual elites rally around politicians who treat them as the experts; they love being honored for their opinions and their sought after advice from the rulers.

The hero for the ruling elites was Galileo. He was able to attack the Church and its doctrines through the power of science. He did not defeat the Church's views through quoting some intellectual source, but through the power of science. Science had the power to make the Church look silly and to introduce a higher power than 'God' into the cultural and governing debates. While even Church people could debate the nature of God and His powers, few could raise up some argument to defy the proven doctrines of science. Modern Man cannot be true to himself without the right to pursue intellectual truths over doctrinal truths. Doctrinal truths require that men bow down to some college-appointed or church-appointed authority. Science only requires that men observe the Laws of Nature and acknowledge their legitimate authority over Man. However, those same laws give man the power to use nature to conquer the world through the technologies gained from a scientific understanding of Nature's God.

Modern anti-Christian thinking pictures modern man in pursuit of truth. Religion is pictured as blocking both Truth and Progress. This has been repeated so many times in government education and in the media that the masses have come to believe the Truth exists apart from the Bible. Not only that, but secular truth is the real truth because there are no preconceived idea in secular truth: outside of the facts that there is no God; no revelation from God; and that Man is in anyway hindered from his sinful nature from discovering the truth. Modern Men do not believe any the above three ideas can be not true. Therefore, when Christianity confronts any of mankind's basic assumptions, there can only be one solution—the elimination of Christianity from the social media and other public outlets. Eternal progress cannot proceed without the silencing of churchly authorities and their opposition to change and progress.

When Christianity is allowed to influence the masses, the call goes out for restrictions placed upon free thinking, free sex, and free choice. Modern Man perceives that those who believe in the Bible would make liberty and freedom impossible to adopt. Modern Man admits that in the past there was a need for some form of religious beliefs. The fear of Hell and the rewards of Heaven helped maintain an orderly society before modern methods of social control were understood and implemented. The fear of Hell has served that function but modern man has replaced hell with the new methods of social control. Proper behavior is rewarded here and now and improper behavior is also implemented in the here and now. The rewards of Heaven, and the punishments of Hell were just too far off to really be affective. Now, negative consequences can be applied virtually immediately—such as when a person attempts to make his next purchase, only to discover that his funds have been blocked.

Yes, the Bible has been used to produce men of Christian character, but those character traits are strictly self-imposed. In other words, good character is optional. However, during bad times, most do not adopt optional beliefs. Honesty may be great, but if you are hungry, honesty may lead to one's own starvation. In a Democracy, the people are free to adjust the laws of justice depending upon the needs of the time. Absolute powers chain people down to a predetermined response regardless of the circumstances. Democracy gives the people the right to change 'absolutes' into laws of necessity for the times. "The principle of making the individual conscience the judge of law, and in last resorts the final justification of disobedience, is psychologically necessary for any free people. No people can remain free unless they can make their authorities clearly understand that there ae some things they may not attempt, that is, they may not offend the moral sense of responsible citizens."[115] The problem is that each individual will have a different idea what constitutes a 'responsible citizen.' Even if put to a vote, does 51% of the people constitute a moral majority? Can a 5-4 SCOTUS decisions really declare new moral absolutes?

*

When people talk about liberty, people ask: how did the Church come to have the moral authority over the masses? Actually, the early Church adopted this concept of reality from the Roman political structures. The name Roman Catholic Church reveals a lot in that name. "Christianity had its origin among the oppressed masses of the Roman Empire. After three centuries of conflict with imperial authority, the Church conquered Rome. For the seceding two hundred years it was the official religion of the Empire. And after political Rome perished its imperial spirit survived as the Church. In the social chaos which followed the invasion of the Barbarians ancient civilization declined, and the Church represented about all the order and culture there was. It is inevitable that its attitude toward spiritual independence should have been modified by the changing conditions through which it passed."[116] The Church along with its multitude of monasteries preserved Roman civilization and prevented the total loss of historical progress.

---

[115] Martin. P. 47.
[116] Martin. P. 48.

Just as the Roman Empire had a Caesar, a Pontifex Maximus, it was just natural for the Church to appoint its own Pontifex Maximus, the Pope. This Roman aspect of the Christian Church is a most neglected part of Church History. The Church patterned itself after the Roman Temples. In fact, many of the early churches took over the old pagan temples and converted them into church meeting places. The church, instead of pattering itself after the family, adopted the temple form of worship. In many ways, the structure predates the message. Worship became formal and ritualized. And in time, the Church started building some of the most magnificent temples called cathedrals. Worship evolved into being inside a building rather than an act of serving others.

It is vital to understand that the early church grew up without a 'Bible' as we know it. People may have heard about Paul's letters and the Gospels, but obviously, this was a long time before Gutenberg and the availability of printed books. As a result, the early church grew up under cultural influences of that age. This is very similar to the American Church which grew up in the Age of Enlightenment, Revolution, and the Industrial and Financial Revolutions. Most institutions survive by being populist, in the same way American Churches in the 21st century adapted the message of the Bible to satisfy the needs of the modern Americans. And it goes a step further, people read the Bible through the eyes of their culture. And even more, people look upon the Bible stories as picture in movie versions of Biblical events. For example, in the movies, David is pictured as people think a 'Jewish' boy would look like. However, David probably looked more like a red-haired, freckle-faced Irish lad. That is the true history apart from the movie version.

If we can understand how the image of Christianity was changed by the Roman culture, we can understand how the American Church was changed by American Culture. Martin explains the Roman times in the following:

"During the last century before Christianity, the Roman people lost whatever love of civil and even political liberty they had ever had. Their armies had conquered both the barbarians of Western Europe and the peoples given to luxury, corruption, venality and ambition. The city was crowded with a vast proletariat composed of landless peasants, indigent plebeians, freemen and slave gathered from the ends of the earth. This proletariat led by desperately partisan politicians, who to gain its favor fed it at public expense out of the spoils of war and the proceeds of the public sale of captives into slavery, furnished the human material for a long series of revolutions, which ended in the dictatorship of Augustus and his successors."[117] The land of Palestine during the time of Jesus was part of the Roman Empire and the province of Israel reflected a similar culture. Jesus was one of many revolutionaries of the time. Some wanted an open revolt against Rome, and others sought escape through assorted spiritual solutions. In a sense, there were many who had a message for their times and Jesus's message was just one amongst the cultural and spiritual anarchy.

The days of Rome were filled with intrigue, political upheaval, and despair for the masses. "Many were filled with fear and disgust and world-weariness. There was widespread feeling that life was not worth living; there was talk of suicide, a growing conviction of the vanity of the things of this world and of the sinfulness of humanity. People sought consolation in thoughts of death and an afterlife. ...there existed among the suppressed classed all sorts of fantastic cults, each with its special divination, its oaths of secrecy, its rites of initiation, its tutelary deities, its miracles, its hopes of the millennium, its promise of salvation. It would seem that in the beginning, Christianity was but one among many similar cults."[118] This is important to understand. Today, Christians feel that there has never been an age like modern, pagan America. Life is tough for the true believer, and everyone is talking about the end of time. People are looking for a religion of escape from the challenges faced by those who attempt to live by the Bible.

In the second century A.D., Christians lived in perilous and uncertain times. Many Christians adopted beliefs similar to cults of the time. As the new faith grew stronger and stronger, the government felt the need to suppress a faith that was leading many away from emperor worship and the gods of ancient Rome. Christians were seen as guilty of treason. As people lost confidence in the future, they developed ways to escape into cults of poverty, chastity, prayer, fasting, or public confessing sins in order develop Christian humility. As Rome was well on

---

[117] Martin. P. 60.
[118] Martin. P. 63.

200

its way to decline, more and more looked forward to an afterlife. There seemed little hope for a tomorrow being better than today. With social chaos on one side, and Roman government persecution on the other side, Christians came to believe that some kind of major cataclysm would transform the world in some miraculous way.

This was a time when Christians started developing a new idea about liberty. With a life in Christ, Christians believed Jesus had liberated them from those aspects of life that held them in bondage to the times. This liberty also freed the Christian from the laws of the Empire which restricted their ability to practice their faith. Christians developed laws separate from the Laws of Rome. Roman Laws were perceived to be man-made laws as opposed to the Laws of God. "If he [the Christian] did not openly defy the power of civil authority, he certainly offered it effective passive resistance. He denied its every claim unless supported by his conscience. In fact he denounced and condemned the whole existing order of society. Christians stubbornly challenged and disobeyed Roman authority in refusing to bow before images of the emperor. Christianity did more: it proclaimed a set of values so radical as to be positively revolutionary and subversive of the established institutions and ways of life of the ancient world…."[119] This belief in an internal liberty freed Christians to live a public life contrary to the values of the times in which most felt to be basic to life.

In time, a common Christian belief system was established. The random activities that resulted from the fall of Empire began to be organized under the umbrella of Biblical ideas. It is amazing what people can accomplish when they all share the same moral values and are attempting to accomplish the same goals. The decline of Rome and the decline of the United States share a common disintegration of social unity. Both Rome and the United States shared an ideal of some form of liberty. In Rome, a person was free as long as he acknowledge Caesar to be the god of the Empire. Just pay allegiance to that concept, and you now have liberty to even worship a lesser god of your choice. And in the United States, the Pledge of Allegiance symbolized a person's devotion of the primacy of the State in the affairs of men. The chaos of Rome resulted in the eventual

---

[119] Martin. P. 65.

formation of a new civilization: Christendom. Even the kings had to acknowledge the supremacy of Biblical Law or face excommunication. [If a leader was excommunicated by the Vatican, the people did not have to pay their taxes.]

[The Age of Christendom has been called the Dark Ages. It has also been called the Age of Faith. No age is heaven yet, but when people put their faith in practice and there are no great empires, no great wars, and people just go about living their lives according to the Bible, the Age of Faith becomes the Dark Ages. Nothing happened here, just keep moving on.] As the American Church submitted to the new American Civilization, a new civilization was born, a secular one. It is known as the Enlightenment. America developed a civilization based upon the hopes of the Scientific Enlightenment and the practically of technological progress. The Age of the Machine and the Age of Enlightenment-- anti-Christian thinking--produced the secular American Empire. The new hope of the world: abundance and personal freedom. Somehow, the American Church was able to adapt its theology to find success in America's new civilization.

Chapter Nineteen: The Goal of Liberty is supposed to result in Equality—and yet it does not.

In the minds of Men, liberty and equality are often associated. When a government declares political and financial liberty for everyone, the result is never as expected. Most often liberty produces inequality. The result becomes a mad scramble to find the fault, i.e. the 'guilty party', and change the nature of the governing system to produce equality. It is worth noting that the Bible is all about inequality: predestined or not; chosen or not; heaven or hell; saved or not; talented or not; and the 'accidents' of birth. Modern man believes that Man can overcome these problems through installing Democracy at every level of government and culture. In Democracy, men can make their own rules and not be subject to the rules of some religious or political elite. There is one big problem: even though Men deny it, all men are born with a fatal flaw. Men are fatally imperfect. Men are so flawed that nothing men have done has worked to cure the flaw of being in rebellion against God's reality. Not only that, men are willfully committed to not accepting God's Revelation of reality.

Modern man attempts to cure Man's inequality through the changing of three primary categories: Race, Religion, and Culture. Long before 'the woke' culture of the 21st century, men recognized that the promises of American Democracy and freedom were not what they were sold to be. The American Revolution was fought with either high ideals or false ideals depending upon your point of view. After the War of Independence, many minorities began to feel that freedom and equality were only for White men with an English heritage and who were Protestant. American history can be seen as a 200 year war against the above three categories of entitlement. It is my contention that once people exclude the teachings of the Bible about reality, there will develop frustrations with a world that they cannot control. The Bible does not contradict itself, but men's attempts to replace its teachings with their own ideas will contradict themselves. [I know some say that the Bible contradicts itself, but the reality is, men read the Bible with their own assumptions which they read into the Word. The result is apparent only contradictions.]

However, despite that, people go about creating a world they can control. This is key to understanding American history. If White, English, Protestant,

Males created the founding ideals of America, that is where the problem lies. The solution from the beginning has been a war against White people, their English Western Civilization, their King James Bible, and male superiority. While the above grouping believed equality could be attained for themselves, there was not a belief that equality could be attained for those outside of The Club. Those who were not in the club constantly sought ways to destroy that club and to elevate everyone else on the graves of those in that Club. Joining the 'Club' by adopting the values of that group was not considered an option for the vast majority. [A minority of multiple races, nations, and culture have joined the 'club' and have been readily accepted. **Only those who share worldviews can attain equality within any grouping.** The problem can be seen in the Middle East: Jews and Muslims belong to separate clubs.]

This question of superiority, equality, freedom, liberty, and equity are all religious questions that really cannot be solved by secular man. It is quite embarrassing to take on God's reality and lose the argument to Him. Some feel that just ignoring the arguments about God's realty is best. Rather, men should go about pretending that they had won their battle against God. So Americans based their ideas about men as if men really were created equal in all things. Then after that, pass laws to make things equal through the power of force. One of the biggest problems is not admitted openly: every group thinks they are superior to other groups, especially those groups who oppose their particular view of superiority. "Men have associated attitudes of superiority with their own situation whenever they have had the power to enforce their views. Puritans were reluctant to give equality to Quakers, Protestants were reluctant to grant equality to Catholics, Christians were reluctant to grant equality to Jews, whites have been reluctant to grant equality to Negroes."[120] When any nation sets about to create national equality for everyone regardless of any differences, it is laying the groundwork for civil war.

Grimes offers a solution to America's equality problem. One of the best ways to break up the 'superiority' problem in America was through immigration

---

[120] Alan P. Grimes. Equality in America: Religion, Race, and the Urban Majority. Oxford University Press. 1964. P. viii.

and migration. "In general, the path to equality has led through the large urban centers, where diversity of religion and race has been historically brought about by immigration and migration. For generations of immigrants the urban centers have provided not only a gateway into American life but have in turn shaped the conditions and values of that life. When immigration was restricted, following the First World War, American Negroes commenced that extraordinary migration into the cities which has in turn so vitally affect the politics and values of America at large. ... The close proximity of diverse people in cities has necessitated the norm of religious and racial equality in these areas in the interest of domestic peace...."[121] The city has been a symbol of the power of man to overcome the problems associated with the Biblical message. As mentioned earlier, when Cain was denied the 'salvation' of the Garden of Eden, he founded the first city to provide for his allay his fears:

Genesis 4:14. Behold, thou hast driven me out this day from the face of the earth; and from thy face shall I be hid; and **I shall be a fugitive and a vagabond** in the earth; and it shall come to pass, *that* every one that findeth me shall slay me.

Genesis 4:16. And Cain went out from the presence of the LORD, and dwelt in the land of Nod, on the east of Eden. **17** And Cain knew his wife; and she conceived, and bare Enoch: and **he builded a city**, and called the name of the city, after the name of his son, Enoch.

In my government schooling, the City of Athens was held up as the ideal form of government. In modern history, Paris and London were pictured as the best of mankind's cultural achievements. Up until 9/11 and Covid-19, New York was held in equally high regard. The city has the power to make its own laws and produce prosperity without factories and farms. The best minds can meet at the cafes, clubs, and restaurants. Because of the diversity, every person can locate a group of people who believe and act as he does. Because of the size of the city, every person is able to isolate himself from those who would criticize his ethical and personal values. In fact, in order to survive, people must learn to get along with those who are totally different. Everyone in the city is dependent upon all the others and at the same time not needing to personally interact with those he

---

[121] Grimes. P. ix.

chooses not to associate with. A Catholic does not have to like the Jewish market owner, but they tolerate each other out of a mutual self-interest. Cities are built upon the idea that people who do not like other groups will tolerate them only because they need them to survive. In one city where I lived, someone started a 'Yellow Pages' for businesses that would subscribe to certain Western Values. The courts ruled that kind of 'Yellow Pages' was illegal and unconstitutional. Businesses are to be judged only on the product or service they provide: that is the law of the city. In the same way, no one could publish an 'Italian Yellow Pages.'

In the Bible, the ability of the City to supply 'all' of man's needs without God leads to mankind's worship of the city—symbolized as the Great City of Babylon. Babylon, possibly, is more than just one city here, but of mankind's worship of the city as the source of liberty, equality, fraternity, and prosperity. There is also the fraternal of like-mined sinners who unite in their evil doings, i.e. Gay Bars. In the town and village there are social controls which bind everyone to a common ethical behavior. In the small town, there is a similar force much like the Church's power to excommunicate. Being ostracized in a community separates a person from the binding power that resides within the town and community.

When God judges the city and all that it provides, the following is everyone's reaction.

Revelation 18:15. The merchants of these things, which were made rich by her, shall stand afar off for the fear of her torment, weeping and wailing, **16** And saying, Alas, alas, that great city, that was clothed in fine linen, and purple, and scarlet, and decked with gold, and precious stones, and pearls! **17** For in one hour so great riches is come to nought. And every shipmaster, and all the company in ships, and sailors, and as many as trade by sea, stood afar off, **18** And cried when they saw the smoke of her burning, saying, **What _city is_ like unto this great city! 19** And they cast dust on their heads, and cried, weeping and wailing, saying, Alas, alas, **that great city, wherein were made rich** all that had ships in the sea by reason of her costliness! for in one hour is she made desolate.

Grimes points out the two social powers in the United States:

"It may be said that there exist two constituencies behind American politics—one, essentially cosmopolitan and urban-oriented, which seeks to push forward the policy of equality the other, essentially provincial and rural-oriented seeks to maintain in religion, race, and politics in superiorities of the past. White, Protestant, rural America pulls in one direction; urban America, with its diversity of religions and races, pulls in the other. The differing compositions of the constituencies give rise of different values."[122] The above was written in 1964, but it sounds so much like 2023: the ruling elites hate the White, rural, and Protestant Americans who claim superiority and sow discord amongst the masses. That is why, as I write, many are calling for the end of White Supremacists, and Fundamentalist, i.e. extremist, and Christians.

Grimes concludes his introduction and belief in the power of modern urbanity: "The **urban majority is proving to be a liberating force in American politics**, redistributing freedom by equalizing the claims of the contestants. Equality is proving practically, to be a standard which satisfies at once the requirements of power and legitimacy. It is a second-best solution in which none has perfect freedom; the fist-choice claims of some for superiority are put aside in order to avoid the subjugation which would be the worst solution for others. American politics has always made a pragmatic adjustment to its immediate needs, tempering its idealism with expediency. Today, ironically, **the imperatives of urban life are making expedient the fulfillment of the future ideal of equality.**"[123] (Emphasis added.)

*

Religions are by nature exclusive. Equality in religious beliefs is a contradiction. A religion by definition is exclusive or it would not be a religion but only a philosophy or worse, a cosmic opinion. And yet, the American philosophy of society attempts to make every religion somehow equal. Exclusive religions are divisive and for that reason, cannot be allowed to enter into politics. No candidate should be allowed to run on a ticket that endorses one religion over all the others. The problem is that almost everyone belongs to some religion or feels

[122] Grimes. P. ix.
[123] Martin. P. x.

spiritually connected to some primary beliefs. This can be seen in the battle over the killing of babies—not just unborn children, but children being murdered after birth. In the thesis of killing a baby and the antithesis of not killing a baby, how do you obtain a synthesis? A nation can have two political parties, but can it have two infallible religions? Actually, the American Civil War was caused by two religions—Deism versus Christianity—in total conflict over slavery, and the ways it should be abolished. It was labelled an irrepressible conflict between two irreconcilable differences. In paint, how do you make the colors black and white equal? You can mix them together and form a gray tone. But that destroys both the White Paint and the Black Paint. The same problem can be viewed in the racial conflicts of the Civil War: how can anyone reconcile two different views of god or two different racial cultures?

Most nations are organized around some primary belief system. You can tell what beliefs dominate a nation by what beliefs are beyond free choice. Are there certain beliefs that if expressed publically would cause an outrage from the dominate media? Here are a few of America's beliefs that are beyond free choice and beyond discussion: Doubting the Jewish Holocaust; believing in White racial superiority; challenging global warming; stating men are superior in some things over that of women; attacking the efficacy of modern 'miracle' drugs and injections; challenging America's fiat money system; not believing in sexual diversity; and publicizing the corruption of American Democracy. Yes, America has its own religion which stands above every other religious beliefs. The above statements represent America's State Church. That is why all other religions are equal except the Woke religion of 2023—that is America's new superior faith. All other faiths are judged by their acquiescence to that faith.

When England taught the divine right of kings, the king was free to set up a State Church. "The issue of religious freedom could not arise as long as there was believed to be only one church, one doctrine, one pathway to salvation, and that the one legally sanctioned by secular authority."[124] Many Protestant Reformers thought it impossible for any nation to subscribe to multiple religious creeds. Religious beliefs support the culture of a nation and no nation can thrive if the

---

[124] Grimes. P. 4.

people be divided over the primary beliefs of law and order. Contradictions cannot be equal. It was the role of the divine king to enforce intolerance in order to create a national unity. The Reformation started the age of individualism. The principle of free choice was applied to every area of life. Every person not only became his own king, he expected to live in a culture and nation where he could also be sovereign over his own life's choices. The very idea of obeying anyone else was considered a sign of slavery. That is why, ever since the Reformation, governments, religions, and social philosophies have been at constant warfare: **every individual is his own king, his own priest, and his own judge.**

The result was the Age of Democracy where the people ruled over themselves: every man a king. Somehow everyone's free choice was to be equal with everyone else's free choice. Tolerance reigned as the sign of modernity. As I write, even criminals are being set free in the name of tolerance. About the only way a person can become a criminal is to be intolerant and demand some kind of order imposed upon everyone. Ironically, as the people of America are demanding more and more tolerance for others, tolerance for other nations is evaporating as with the morning fog. Other nations must be forced into a universal New World Order of total intolerance. I always say, when you see mass insanity, look for the acceptance of Satan and his ruling principles.

In England, the Church and the State became one under the King. The United States had no such king to unite the two which presented new problems. Obviously, the new United States government was not about to submit to the ethical standards of any church or any other institutions. I regard the Declaration of Independence as setting a new pattern for the ages. In a sense, the State itself was to be the new king. The State was to become a secular god and people were to look to the powers of the state to form a new unity. Every other social, political, and business institution was now under the new divinity of the State. And under Chief Justice Marshall, the Court declared itself to be the supreme law of the land—above any other state or local government in the United States. [Marbury v. Madison 1803] The location of total sovereignty was not totally settled until after the Civil War and the passage of the 13th, 14th, and 15th Amendments to the Constitution. As I write in 2023, the Central Government has declared itself sovereign over every person's 'private' life and his personal opinions. A person's social credit score rates everyone's degree of submission to the new divinity.

Everyone's primary loyalty is to the Nation/State. All religions must submit to that entity as the Supreme Law of the Land. An oft-cited example of the new American culture that was being formed was the banishment of Roger Williams from the state of Massachusetts. The Puritans had established a unity of legal and theological orthodoxy. Roger Williams challenged that principle and was banished from the land. He challenged the orthodoxy of his age. What is not admitted is that every age has an orthodoxy that the masses are supposed to accept: what was WWII but the attempt to impose a one world view upon another nation. After the war, a global, political orthodoxy was imposed upon Germany. As always, the winners are allowed to promote their orthodoxy upon everyone else. In school I learned about the times when religious orthodoxy killed tens of thousands of people, i.e. those so-called religious wars. In the 20th century, political orthodoxy killed over a hundred million people. [As I write, medical orthodoxy is being imposed upon the whole world. Already, a billion people have been either killed or disabled from the injection.]

*

Toleration is one of the key concepts in a 'Totalitarian Order'. All of the groups subject to the control of the tyrant are to tolerate each other. This is the key to maintaining centralized power. All social and religious dissidents are to tolerate each other. These multiple groups prevent any one group being able to unify any opposition to the ruling elites. Forced toleration or integration keeps the groups from recognizing their true enemy, their controlling leaders. Tyrants use the 'divide and conquer' technique to keep themselves in power: let the people fight amongst themselves. Toleration is one of the words or concepts that has been sprinkled with holy water to make it sound so good. However, toleration never applies to the enemies of the tyrant. There is no toleration for those in opposition to the ruler: these people are White Supremist, political extremists, propagators of misinformation, religious fundamentalists, sexists, homophobes, right wing fanatics, and anti-Semites. For the above, there can be

210

no toleration for they are enemies of the 'people' and a peaceful social order. You can always tell who is in power for they have the power to declare which groups cannot be tolerated in a tolerant order. The cry for toleration really means being tolerant toward those groups that support the rule of the tyrant.

Generally, modern concepts of tolerance, freedom, and equality are limiting concepts that define whose behaviors are guaranteed as long as they keep them private. For example, everyone is equally free to worship any god they want or to believe whatever they want as long as they do not tell anyone. Solitary privacy is the true, modern freedom. However, as I write, privacy is being eliminated through the introduction of Total Information Awareness traced by AI computers. It is not by accident that sexual liberation is being pushed at the same time that personal beliefs are coming under attack. Intellectual and religious freedom has been replaced by sensual freedom. The masses are free to have as many orgasms as they want as long as they are tolerant toward the multiple ways people choose to produce an orgasm. Equality really means equality in being tolerated or tolerating others in ways determined by the elites to be the proper and approved behaviors. Everyone is equal in the need for obedience to the tyrant. Everyone is equal outside those areas not controlled by the tyrant. There can be no tolerance for those who oppose the leaders and the laws of a tyranny.

Religious toleration falls under the same category as sexual toleration. As long as a person's religious beliefs are confined to the realms of the spiritual, the person is free and is also expected to be tolerant to all other forms of spirituality. However, spirituality is something that occurs only within one's mind or 'soul'. In a sense, everything inside a person's skin belongs to himself, but every thing outside of his skins falls under the supervision of those in power. Only those Commandments which apply to a person's thinking process, such as envy, are allowed. However, 'Thou shalt not commit adultery' is strictly personal and cannot be applied to those who choose to live without regard for religious moral and ethical norms. Equality really means just this: everyone is equally expected to submit to the norms of society and government.

*

Because equality, freedom, and toleration are often connected, it is important to understand that the government and its tyrannical leaders do not have to tolerate any person, business, or institution. Supposedly the Bill of Rights was ratified to set guidelines for toleration by government. The government was supposed to tolerate the people's owning of guns. The government was also supposed to tolerate free speech, even if that speech is considered misinformation. The government was also supposed to tolerate religious doctrines and expressions of that faith—even if the lifestyles of certain religions did not conform to accepted social norms. And finally, the central government was to tolerate the laws of the respective states. Of course, with the defeat of the South in the Civil War, the government in Washington, D.C. no longer had to tolerate anything it did not desire to tolerate. Dictatorships must be tolerated by the people and there is nothing that the government has to tolerate. Those who expose the tyrants for the dictators that they are, they cannot be tolerated. Those who expose evil are mentally unbalanced conspiracy theorists and disseminators of false information.

*

There are also religions that support political beliefs. Some are tolerated and some are not tolerated. Zionism is a religious expression of what is called a Jewish Religion. The two are joined at the hip and you cannot have one without the other. To oppose political Zionism makes a person an anti-Semitic person. To oppose the Vatican does not make a person an anti-Italian. A person can oppose Russian policies without being labelled an anti-Orthodox Church. And yet the American Government and even Protestant Christians are not allowed to criticize Zionist/Israeli practices. This is an example of selective toleration. When you see such things, you need to look for the power behind such contradictions. During WWI and WWII, American Germans were not tolerated to say anything positive about their native lands. In fact, that policy still exists today.

Religions and nationalities have often been connected. Christianity has been predominately had a Caucasian connection. Caucasian missionaries and Caucasian Bible translators spread Christianity throughout the earth. Even in 2023, Caucasians dominate the Christian publishing industry and the major

Christian private schools and colleges. Today's war upon White Supremists is a backdoor attack upon Christianity. Fundamentalist Christians are predominantly White and are considered both extremist and anti-modernity. They are associated with conservative politics, private schools, creationism, conspiracy theories, and even believers in the Biblical doctrine of the flat earth. Most of these views and the people who espouse them are generally not tolerated in American culture. Yes, they are tolerated but only in a negative way: the same way a handicapped person might be tolerated doing something he really should not be doing. These 'Bible thumpers' are not considered equal to others in American culture.

Modern America deals with groups that are not tolerated by denying them the avenues of power that other groups can attain. American culture and educational institutions act as gatekeepers. The American school system is designed to only promote those who have agreed to sacrifice personal beliefs in exchange for a good degree. For example, it is very, very difficult for a fundamentalist Christian to get advanced degrees in the social sciences and in the physical sciences. For the gatekeepers in American, those who have beliefs that are not acceptable to the established order are nether tolerated nor are they equal. This form of inequality is allowed in the name of supporting a unified view of reality.

Chapter Twenty: The Goal is to Equalize Races—By Whatever Means Necessary.

Another great divider of mankind throughout history has been race. Generally, those of the same race tend to share certain personal characteristics or cultural traits that makes them more comfortable around their own kind: Despite the modern denials that races are actually different and that acknowledging racial differences is an act of racism. Contrast this with the Democracy and its absolute value of equality. Actually, Democracy has become an absolute value. In order to impose the New Order upon the masses an impossible goal must be set before the forces of Democracy. **Equality is the perfect impossible goal.** Different races, cultures, and religions must all be made equal. It must be understood that impossible goals are chosen for a purpose. The masses are manipulated to sacrifice for a goal that can never be attained. This means that more and more force must be applied to the masses. **And because the goal cannot be attained, the application of force need never end.** Another impossible goal is the elimination of carbon and nitrogen which serves the same purpose.

I want to devote some space here about the racial issue because that has been an issue in the United States since the first Indian war. Americans have had to fight other races and nations throughout its history. Americans have had to fight American Indians, American Mexicans, and American Blacks multiple times. At the times of these wars, most thought that these wars were cultural, not racial. However, after the first Indian Wars against the Pilgrims in New England, the Pilgrims recognized that the wars were not racial, but religious. The chief of the New England tribes stated that if the Indians started farming, building fences, and living in permanent housing, their gods would die. One of the least documented facts about Black slavery is that the slaves held onto their African pagan religions. Slave owners gave their slaves Sunday off in order for them to practice their religious beliefs. The owners agreed amongst themselves that it was better that they did not know what happened on Sundays.

*

In order to impose equality upon a nation, then the racial, cultural, and religious differences must be ignored. Another aspect of race/culture/religion is that they have a different views about the future. Almost everyone thinks tomorrow should be better than today. One reason people go to school or work hard is to make tomorrow different than today. If everyone is equal, then everyone should have the same vision for tomorrow. If some are followers of Satan and some are followers of Jesus Christ, they will see reality in totally different ways. It cannot be avoided. Followers of Jesus work for a better tomorrow because God controls tomorrow; followers of Satan, eat, drink, and make merry, for tomorrow is uncertain. Two very unequal beliefs. The hidden agenda to so control the world so as to eliminate inequality, even when today and tomorrow lifestyles cannot be reconciled. Only slaves and prisoners are all equal because both totally controlled tomorrows. In fact, the Fall of Man was a result of Satan demanding EQUALITY with God. Sin is foundational in the attempt to make un-equals become equals. Satan's world view is to equalize everyone that God has made unequal—including men and women.

Consider what makes men unequal from other men. The war against inequality is a war against God and His order of inequality. Total tolerance also means man's tolerance for Satan and his corrupt followers. Ironically, at same time that the Overlords are promoting tolerance and equality, they are making some people more and more unequal: you too can have your five-year-old sexually transformed before your eyes. The goal of Satan is to normalize the grossest of sins and require everyone, by law, to tolerate those sickest acts of rebellion against God's laws. In a world at war with God, there can be no limits to tolerance. **For a Christian to be intolerant toward evil is against the law of the New World Order.**

*

Ever since 1865, the powers of Washington, D.C. have been used to elevate the Black Race and to prevent Whites from rejecting Blacks because of their cultural and ethical choices. There have been two forces at work: Black hatred of their history and welfare. The government has prevented the Blacks from elevating themselves through a welfare system known to destroy the 'soul' of a person. The Indian Reservations have been a laboratory to understand how to create demoralization through the granting of unearned money. People need to be motivated in order to develop personal character and self-initiative. The Biblical doctrine is this: if a person will not work, he shall not eat. And that law is written into our very being. Fallen Man needs motivation in order get out of bed in the morning. Fallen man dreams of some utopian order where his every need is met. This allows a person to pursue sensual pleasures to his uttermost wants. Far from being a dream world, Government utopias destroy the soul of a person. The techniques used to destroy the American Indian have been used to destroy the character of the Black race. Government guaranteed income results in people seeking stimulation through sex and/or drugs. [Those who promote welfare are the true racists.] See how it works: the government destroys the Black's motivational IQ through welfare, and then tells them that it was slavery in their past that caused their inability to achieve real equality.

*

One thing that keeps evil men from really becoming totally corrupt is God's gift of consequences. Even people who reject the Laws of God discover that breaking God's Laws has built-in results that are not always good. For a child, falling down hurts and he quickly learns not to fall down. The same rule applied to hot water, fire, and other acts that result in pain. There are also social laws that carry with them consequences. The person who acts like a real jerk on the job may find himself looking for another job. If there were a law that everyone was expected to tolerate jerks, then that person would never be allowed to experience the real world of his environment. We all live in a Fallen World occupied by Fallen Men. Governments create laws to keep the criminal element in check, while the people develop cultural laws to keep people's anti-social behaviors in check. Cultures define anti-social behaviors and the people enforce the consequences of personally constructed obnoxious behaviors.

There is another element of human behavior: blood is thicker than water. People naturally prefer to live around those who share similar racial and cultural histories. In fact, similar groups often form a very strong bond. For the tyrant, this is considered very dangerous. People can only successfully resist the powers of a totalitarian order in groups. Lone gunmen are mere terrorists, i.e. criminals, but they cannot bring about change or overthrow a government. During the Middle Ages, i.e. the 'Dark' Ages, the Catholic Faith united people into a common culture. This culture was so strong that even kings had to submit to the laws of a

Christian culture. There were even laws about how Kings could fight a war, and the kings obeyed those laws for fear of excommunication. Excommunication denied the king the right to tax his people—which the masses were more than glad to obey the Church's command to withhold payments. You see, even Kings were forced to experience the consequences of their wrongful acts.

*

With the Reformation, the power of the Vatican to force compliance to its cultural and political laws was broken. The power of Christendom to enforce universal laws and cultural expectation upon everyone was lost. With the breakup of Christendom, a period of anarchy developed. This was a time of the so-called 'religious wars.' These were not really religious wars, but actually power struggles for those men who wished to start their own kingdom in the midst of global anarchy. Every potential 'king' knew that the people in the Age of Christendom were bonded together by a common faith. Therefore, if he wanted to gather people together in his new nation, he needed to bond them to their king and his kingdom though a common faith. The king did not care what faith that was, as long as the people would be willing to fight and die for that faith. If he discovered people in his area believed in Luther or Calvin, then that became the new national faith. If he discovered the people were still devoted to the Vatican, then that became the new national faith. These wars for power were only secondarily about religion. **These wars were wars of power that needed the power of religion to control the king's new subjects.**

After the world had settled down and new boundaries were established upon the maps of the world, something strange happened. There is one power the kings never counted upon. The new kings may have thought that if the Vatican were eliminated, the king could not only be the supreme ruler over the land, he could also become a new Pope. Like in the days of the Roman Empire or ancient Egypt with its Pharaoh, the goal was to unite 'State and Church' into one unified power. This unified power could not only execute the criminal in its land, but it also had the power to send political rebels to everlasting damnation: the King had power over the bodies of men, and the King/Priest had power over the souls of men. Upon this basis, tyrannies of ultimate power could be created. Not only that, there was no other power that the people could unite around to resist the government. There were no higher powers that could stand above both King and his Priests.

*

Contrary to the kings on this earth, the New Testament announced a new kind of invasion upon the land that was totally revolutionary and cultural changing: The Kingdom of God. God's Kingdom does not have an army or a visible form of government and yet has power to infiltrate every aspect of life. While men and governments may war against the Visible Church, their real enemy is God's Kingdom—His invisible presence upon the earth. One of the weapons governments and tyrants use to maintain power is to divide the people into waring groups. Civil Wars are the ultimate weapon against the Kingdom of God's expression in any nation. That is the reason Lincoln wanted to start a Civil War and refused to negotiate any kind of settlement. He was doing the work of Satan and Satan wanted to divide the people of America into as many pieces as possible. By refusing to work out a peaceful solution for the ending of slavery, he used a violent and terrible massacre to permanently divide the Whites and the Blacks from ever unifying against the formation of a totalitarian order. Of course, Lincoln was not that smart. He received his instructions from his god, Satan.

The Kingdom of Satan, which controls almost all modern Nation/States, is at war with the Kingdom of God. It is the united kingdoms of this earth that are seeking to establish a New World Order that will totally destroy God's presence upon this earth. The problem for the American Church is that it has no idea what the Kingdom of God is. The church believes that the Kingdom will only became apparent after the Christians have been removed to heaven, i.e. the Rapture. As a result, the Kingdom of Satan has been allowed to create its own American Civilization without any opposition from the Kingdom of God. As I mentioned, the King James Bible created a Civilization based upon the Bible. This Civilization rose up spontaneously from the people believing in the Bible and applying it to their everyday lives. As a result, Christian and Western Civilizations were established and permeated the entire world. As Jesus said, His Kingdom is subversive and infiltrates a culture like yeast in a loaf of bread. When His followers no longer act like God's righteous yeast, the Kingdom of God cannot infiltrate the King's false kingdom of Satan. A corrupt nation is the result.

The American Civil War attempted to establish an American Civilization that would supplant all other civilizations. It started with the destruction of the Southern culture and then proceeded to destroy Western Civilization through the intense promotion of Finance Capitalism after the war. In fact, it is not a coincidence that WWI and WWII were fought between White people—the race that had established Christian and Western Civilizations. To keep these civilizations from reappearing, social conflicts were used to infiltrate every aspect of Biblical teachings. Feminism and Racism were introduced into American culture at the same time. New values were promoted that went to the heart of former civilizations: civil rights and freedom without moral restraints.

*

With the freeing of the slaves all at once with no plan to gradually change the old culture into a new culture, racial violence was instigated to keep the races from uniting together to work out some peaceful solution. Prior to the Civil War, most Blacks and Whites moved freely about and recognized each other's differences. Slaves were even allowed to own guns and roam freely. By creating a survival of the most fit after the war, the races had to compete for very limited resources. The Southern economy had been destroyed, along with its farm tools and farm animals. Food was scarce and there was not time to reestablish the farms and the markets necessary for food production. This was deliberate as little aid arrived from the North to help reconstruct the South. Reconstruction did not mean economic reconstruction, but the forced integration of the races into the Northern concept of a social order. This was the true beginning of the modern 'race' issue. Race became a tool to make everyone dependent upon the central government in Washington, D.C. to impose its order upon American culture.

Part of the new reality was to create a Civilization with a zero sum nature. In the White versus Black competition for limited resources, every thing a White person owns was taken from the Blacks. Right after the war, there was a zero sum condition in which each race had to stand together to obtain what they could to survive. However, as times improved, those who were industrious and hardworking could actually produce more than enough for themselves. Good times produced surpluses that reward those who know how to farm or to manufacture products. Because this was not to the advantage of the Overlords, the South was kept in a condition of extreme poverty up until WWII. At that time, the North needed the people of the South to help in the war effort. The South was deliberately kept in a zero sum economy. If a White man hires another White man--that means a Black man did not get the job. A poor economy did not produce an excess of jobs.

An important book explaining the nature of economics was written by R. H. Tawney, *Religion and the Rise of Capitalism.* There were many books like it and even Benjamin Franklin's famous book *Poor Richard's Almanac* taught a secular view about success and obtaining wealth. The production of wealth was viewed as a product of what was called the Puritan Work Ethic. Most people do not discover gold in their backyard; most have to work for it. That is the basis of every solid economy: you reap what you sow. Actually, these concepts go all the way back to ancient Israel.

Job 12:11. He that tilleth his land shall be satisfied with bread: but he that followeth vain *persons is* void of understanding.

Job 12:24. The hand of the diligent shall bear rule: but the slothful shall be under tribute.

The Southern White person built up their culture based upon Biblical principles. [Despite the movie image, only 5 percent of the male population owned slaves. Most had to work to become wealthy] In fact, the early Puritans became wealthy because of their belief that a Christian served God by working hard. Also, his life was to display publically his Christian character of thrift and self-sacrifice. Those raised in Christian homes were taught the value of self-discipline and delayed gratification as essential to the Christian life. Christians opposed personal debt believing, as the Bible teaches, that the borrower is servant to the lender.

Proverbs 22:7. The rich ruleth over the poor, and the borrower *is* servant to the lender.

The above and many verses created Western Civilization and men lived by these principles because they believed they were from God. People who believe with all their heart the teachings of the Bible will incorporate them into his lifestyle and the culture around him. The very idea of a welfare culture or a government that is the source of money and wealth is contrary to Biblical teachings. Biblical Civilization has been the source of Christian wealth for centuries. The growth of the welfare Nation/State was not about aiding the poor, but about destroying the true source of success and wealth. Connection to the Government is more important than a connection with God. The role of the government since the Civil War has been to place an alternative view [Non-Puritanical] about success and wealth into the minds of the Black race: every Black man is entitled to wealth and only racists prevent the Blacks from being financially equal with others.

*

Okay, the scenario has been set after the Civil War by creating economic chaos with a zero sum economic order which has created nearly a two-hundred year racial conflict. The White Race, that still retained their Puritan work ethic skills, are now guilty of stealing form the Blacks who do not share that culture. The King James Bible was not part of their African heritage. Their tribal warfare and slave selling culture did not provide them the necessary tools to compete in a highly competitive work environment. Every tyranny survives by showing there is a great need for a totalitarian order. Racial conflicts were the perfect excuse to enhance the American government's quest for increased power. The groundwork had been perfectly planned before the Civil War and after the War, racial conflicts were pictured as a normal part of history. The ignorant White public [Government schooling] were the perfect fall guys as they have been conditioned to accept their racial guilt for the crimes of slavery and the ensuing racial battles. False flag racial killings and lynchings were added to the whole mixture to make everyone believe that America had an irrepressible racial problem.

When the Church no longer proclaims the Kingdom of God and its presence in America, then Satan is free to install his kingdom upon the earth. Satan's minions are free to use the full Satanic powers of deception and delusion. And because so many of the unsuspecting fell for this manufactured reality, no one would ever stop to think that there real dark powers involved in the whole historical political drama. One of the facts that support my idea is that the American government and its agencies have played a key role in instigating racial conflicts and hatred. In the early 20th century, a revived Klu Klux Klan was created and that group was programmed to commit multiple false flags with staged lynchings—all with photographers standing by to record the events for history—and to be published over and over. Many at the time believed that the revived KKK was financed by the Federal Government. The joke among its members who were quite poor was this: the only people who could afford the membership dues were government agents. False flags have been part of the repertoire of all governments since the beginning of time. False flags have all the mark of a typical Satanic deception. He refuses to play by God's rules.

The agencies that worked up hatred amongst the Blacks, also worked up White guilt to prevent the White people from defending their own Western Civilization and the nature of their Christian beliefs. The Christian and Biblical doctrines have been under attack since the first Christian settlers landed on North America. If there is one constant of history is this: wars of migration are as much a part of history as the wars between governments. When Noah and his sons exited the ark, their descendants spread out across the earth. In time, as the land became crowded, tribes kept expanding—often encountering smaller tribes as they went in search of greener pastures. There were no property deeds and the ownership was determined by a people's ability to defend their land from other tribes. You only owned what you could defend. One of the major functions of any government is to protect the borders—from tribes migrating across the earth. **People have always had to defend their land, their dwellings, their culture, their religion, and their families from those who would destroy it.** Somehow, today that is considered evil and unacceptable.

History is not orderly and rarely peaceful. However, when the early Christian immigrants arrived in North America, something changed. Maybe for the first time in history, immigration became an evil. Land ownership became sacred, even if only a few thousand Indians occupied huge amounts of land. Why the sudden change in thinking? I believe it started with the Reformation and the resulting formation of the new and powerful Nation/States. There was a secondary cause that is rarely noted: North and South America were occupied by tribes that were totally subservience to Satan. Their practices of human sacrifice, ritual torture, cannibalism, homosexuality, and constant warfare were trademarks of Satanic powers, and of those who served those powers. Christians were invaders of, not just a land, but of peoples who Satan wanted to maintain ownership over. The invaders were not just people looking for a new land, but people who carried with them a different spiritual authority than the current occupiers of the Americas. Religious wars could not be avoided. There was plenty of land, but the question was this: Which God should rule over that land. Yes, land is vital to every religion: religion and the land must be united to avoid civil wars. [The American Civil War was to decide which 'God' should rule the land called the United States.]

As settlers moved into America, it was more than a battle between immigrants and the current occupiers of the land. It was a war between the Kingdom of God and the Kingdom of Satan. The Kingdom of God is a civilization and the settlers not only wanted to build farms, but to establish a Christian Civilization where none existed before. God commanded His people to go throughout the world and to spread the Kingdom of God amongst those who were held captive by the spirits of evil. Even good people are not perfect and Christian made mistakes. [One missionary was offended by all of the women walking about topless. So, he ordered a whole bunch of t-shirts to pass out. A few days later, all of the t-shirts had two holes cut out in them.]

The success of missionaries spreading the Bible and Western Civilization is a neglected part of world history. Missionaries changed the world. The average life expectancy of the first missionaries to Africa was three months. And yet, they kept pouring in to spread the messages of the Bible. However, a Christian prosperous and safe order attracts evil people who wish to benefit from the law and order that the Christians have established. It has been said by some: First came the missionaries and then came the British troops. And yes, once missionaries had established some kind of moral order and the beginnings of a civilization it made it easier for nations to develop in other ways. The problem missionaries encountered is common to all of history: Evil and good people will share this earth until Satan is finally defeated. Historians love to lump races together; they do not separate the white hats from the black hats. However, it was White Men who carried Biblical Civilization throughout the earth. Many primitive nations gladly welcomes the blessing of a moral culture. Today, missionaries are considered racist for 'imposing' Christian culture upon pagan cultures.

*

Therefore, as I traverse through American history, it is essential to keep in mind the reality of the true events: God and Satan were at war for the abundance this land would produce. Both were aware that with abundance comes global power and influence. The United States not only became the center of Christianity and the producer of tens of thousands of Christian missionaries, it also produced those intellectual who wanted to spread a secular agenda throughout the land. Yes, America aslo produced Satanic missionaries which few know about. Christian missionaries operate openly, while Satan's missionaries operate through deception and illusion. Satan's servants will spread their gospel through corporations, war, trade, finance, and American entertainment. Western Civilization was at war with American Civilization from the very beginning. Most history books were written by those promoting and defending American Civilization: What Kingdom of God?

A good example of how American history can interpreted is illustrated in the infamous Salem Witch Trials of 1692. That event, where about 20 people died, has become part of just about every American history textbook. Actually, the trials took place in Salem Village which was a small suburb of Salem, Massachusetts. Whatever else about the event, there were real Satanic manifestations occurring in that little village. The people lived in a time when Satan operated quite openly in Europe and the United States. These blatant acts of some spiritual force could be quite frightening. Remember, at this time, Americans were still under attack from the Satanic powers of the native tribes. It could easily be perceived that Satan had opened a second front right in their own village. And, it was Christians from the surrounding area that put an end to the whole affair. It was not a military operation but concerned Christians that took it upon themselves to end the spiritual panic attack. Rather than make Salem Village a poster child for all Christians, remember these people lived on the edge of civilization and there were any number of things to fear: Indian attacks, droughts, plagues, and bad harvests. One bad event could spell disaster for the whole community. [After 9/11, people saw terrorists everywhere. People were urged to report any suspicious looking person to the police.: That guy in the grocery line sure looks like a terrorist.]

*

It is important to understand the context of American slave history and the problems that were created by that institution. Many more White slaves were transported to North America than Black slaves. In fact, only about 5 per cent of the total number of slaves transported out of Africa arrived in what would become the United States. At the time, slavery was a global institution, and those that transported Blacks to America were generally part of Global business cartels. British cotton factories need a steady supply of cotton and it was the need for this constant supply that created the huge plantations of the American South. While the movies picture these plantations as only cotton fields, they were in reality small cities or even big cities. Everything a plantation needed had to be manufactured in house. Many of the slaves were skilled tradesmen. Also, picking cotton only occurred six weeks out of the year. [For dangerous jobs on the plantation, White laborers were brought in to clear swamps of snakes, etc. No owner wanted to put an expensive slave at risk.]

When slavery ended, the freed Blacks were weaponized to destroy White Christian civilization. What the Indians could not accomplish through the front door, Blacks would be used by attacking through the back door. Those in control of American Civilization did not want the freed slaves to succeed. They were to be used as cannon fodder in the continuing war against the Kingdom of God. Again, I am re-writing American history from the perspective of the spiritual battles that have been going on since the Garden of Eden. Textbooks will cover the wars between the farmers and the big cities; between local and centralized governments; between family businesses and giant corporations; between assorted concepts of progress; between Protestants, Catholics and Jews; between local businesses and foreign ones; between paper money and metallic money; between land owners and renters, etc. In other words, American history is told as the story between all kinds of different conflicts. However, the story of the biggest conflict of all is never mentioned: the battle between the two spiritual kingdoms and the laws that are part of these opposite civilizations. There can be no compromise between the God of the Bible and Satan's war against God's special creation: man and God's rule upon the earth. .

Now, Satan operates in the United States behind words and concepts, not openly with public human sacrifices. He does not promote his kingdom by openly flaunting evil, but he offers a better way than the ways of God. Satan's kingdom offers freedom, equality, the pursuit of sensual delights, material wealth, a life a continuous amusements, and a life where man is in total control of his own destiny. Basically, Satan offers a way of escape from God's Kingdom and a life of service to God and others. The first step in his war against God in American was to create an ideal that everyone could accept as being a neutral ground between God and Satan's concept of reality. The answer was secular Democracy: let the people create their own reality where neither God nor Satan was in control. The masses could actually be their own gods and not have to make a choice between two waring spiritual entities.

There are several assumptions that every American is supposed to agree upon as true: Democracy, equality, equity, tolerance, diversity, freedom, choice, personal rights, civil rights, and cultural protection. I suppose the list could be longer, but most of the above categories only apply to those chosen by the Overlords to be used for their purposes. White's culture does not quite qualify for the universal protections offered to others as it would serve no good toward the goals of a New World Order. The first immigrants to North America were at Jamestown in 1607 and Plymouth in 1620. [Recall, the Witch Trials were in 1692—very, very early in period of the Indian Wars and their demonic religious beliefs.] Both Jamestown and Plymouth were founded by religious refugees. They were seeking to found a colony free from non-Christian controls over Christianity.

*

America started out as a Christian nation, but that quickly ended. In time, many followed the path to America because of the riches that were being generated. Early on, it has been stated that in three years a person to earn enough money to buy his own farm or start his own business. American was considered by secularists as a New Atlantis; by others a 'horn of plenty'; and by others a life of adventure. Whatever the reason, cooperation among divergent groups would become the grease that would oil the wheel of prosperity. Religious differences needed to be put aside for some greater goal. And it was so. Money does talk and the American Church part of the grease that would oil the wheel of riches for everything. It was in 1741 that Jonathan Edwards preached his famous sermon, *Sinners in the Hands of an Angry God.* I regard this sermon as a religious revolution: experience replace doctrine. The Kingdom of God was replaced by the Church experience. Theology was replaced by emotion. An emotional experience liberated everyone from the necessity of serving God through establishing God's Kingdom on earth as it is in heaven.

Religious differences that formerly divided people could now be united without having to argue about doctrinal differences. America now had a religion of its own, i.e. a democratic experience which was not based upon any ideas that might separate the people. If you had an experience, you were part of the club. Of course, the real necessity for unity was so that everyone could work together to create an American Empire of Business. Religious differences in the past divided the people and prevented them from uniting together for a common purpose. This new American faith that united everyone created a mentality in which the same good business principles could be applied elsewhere to produce a nation of people who share the same prosperous experiences. The American Way of wealth creation became the only way for a universal salvation through prosperity. Amen.

As mentioned earlier, the American South attempted to hold onto the old style Christian beliefs of community and service before wealth. The idea of a Kingdom of God upon the earth was still alive in their minds. [Forget the propaganda and the movies, only 5 per cent of the Southerners owned slaves— and women and Blacks owned a lot of those slaves.] Those who believed in the rule of God attempted to put into practice Christian values in every area of life. Communities really were small towns where the people actually did take care of each other. They took to heart the idea of serving God through serving others. That is why the business community needed to put an end to the Southern Way. The impersonal Corporate model of living needed to be installed in order for everyone to adopt the work/consume culture of the Corporate materialistic living. That is why just about every movie about the South pictures an underlying and hidden evil behind the façade of neighborliness. Bad people just cannot bring themselves to believe that good people really do exist: they must be hiding the evil that resides inside their own heart, i.e. there are no really good people. Life is jungle warfare, and to the victor go the spoils. That is the reality as practice by the American Robber Barons.

Chapter Twenty One: The techniques to keep race the central issue in American History.

After the Civil War, racial conflicts were created through the government's creation of a Black army of about a quarter million Blacks. They were not a paid army, but were expected to live off the land. Remember, the White Southern men has been killed by the hundreds of thousands. They had been disarmed, and their farms largely destroyed where the Union Army had traversed through the land. Not only were the Whites left with very little, so were the Blacks. There was no Marshall Plan for the South. Not only that, the Whites that survived the War were still considered the enemies of the United States. Just as Whites settled in Jamestown and Plymouth, the Black race could be used to found a new nation based upon new principles of unity totally apart from any ancient religious beliefs. Christian unity would be replaced by racial, sexual, religious, and financial unity. However, this will not come about except through the destruction of Western and Christian Civilization.

In America, Race and Religion have been the two great obstacles to becoming a nation of one people and one God. Grimes wrote: "The amicable accommodation of religious differences in America has been a significant achievement of our political experience; our ability to achieve a similar accommodation of racial differences has been our most conspicuous political failure. ... That is to say, religious convictions, or the lack of it, is contained within the individual; it may indeed never become known but remain a well-kept secret of the soul. Religious conviction does not necessarily appear on sight, as it were, as something to be remarked upon."[125] Grimes starts out with associating 'race' with skin color. That alone creates a problem where there is none. It assumes that people are so superficial all they can see is the color of one's skin. In other words, White people are unable to see the soul of a person.

In the pre-Civil War South, the races were probably as close as any other racial mixture in history. It took a giant war to teach the races to hate each other because of the terrible carnage imposed upon the Whites of the South for something that was none of their doing. The Southern people and their wealth were destroyed because a small minority owned plantations. Not only that, but the image of the plantation was placed within the minds of the North by the fictional and false book, *Uncle Tom's Cabin.* Wartime propaganda was used to create weaponized racism. One common practice before the war reveals the lack of racism. If the master had a son about the same time as a Black boy was born on the farm, the White child was declared to be the master of the Black boy. They were then to look after each other for the rest of their lives. Yes, there was a master/slave relationship, but it was based upon mutual friendship and caring.

---

[125] Grimes. P. 41.

Skin color had little to do with the lifelong relationship formed. In fact, Christians with the financial means, would often purchase slaves so that they could teach them about Jesus Christ and eventually free them.

Those that wanted to weaponize race, emphasized the skin color in order to ignore the real reasons the races were divided. Skin color was chosen because it was the one thing that could not be changed, at least, easily. **To talk about cultural or religious differences was to talk about things that could be changed. And the Overlords do not want change, they want eternal conflict. They want skin color to be the reason, the only reason, there are racial divisions and conflicts.** The Bible teaches the real reason for conflicts:

Amos 3:3. Can two walk together, except they be agreed?

The story of American racism is this: how can America get two races to walk together who do not agree? All other differences, such a religion, cultural, and ethical are said to be no big deal—it is the skin color. That is why many believe that if Americans can inter-marry and produce a new common race of tanned people, the racial problem will have been solved.

Grimes writes: "Early in the nineteenth century, modern white racial theory developed as a legitimizing myth to support the social condition of white superiority achieved through colonialism and slavery."[126] This was the beginning of the mythology that America could not have become successful without racism and colonialism. In reality, race became politicized by the War of 1812. England feared that the United States was becoming too strong. One thing that made England great was its great intelligence service and its ability to create propaganda. England ruled through its ability to get its enemies to fight each other. Through misinformation and false flag operations, England could keep its enemies from becoming too strong. After the War of 1812, England pulled its magic upon the United States.

British Intelligence funded the Abolitionist movement in the United States. This group called for the immediate freedom of all slaves and even sent newspapers into the South calling upon slaves to revolt and kill their masters. Also, spies were sent into the South who were noted as Fire Eaters. They were apparently well funded and had the talent to rise in power throughout the South.

---

[126] Grimes. P. 49.

Their job was to stir up hatred in the South for the North. England's goal was to start a civil war and divide the United States into two nations—neither of which would have had enough power to threaten English rule. This was the first instance in the United States to weaponize slavery. The Abolitionists preached an intense hatred and some of them called for the killing of every White person in the South—as slaves had done in Haiti earlier.

This is why those who do not understand the nature of evil and those who are servants of evil, cannot understand history. There are men placed in high places who are not 'real' men as we would think of them. They have been assigned a role to play and evil men are more than willing to carry out some important role in the drama of time. Image the ego trip of those who are trained to become world leaders and agent provocateurs. In fact, when I read books about the South today, these men who stated some really evil provocative statements are still quoted as representing the average Southerner of the time. The problem with Satan and his servants is they do not play by the rules; actually they play by Satan's deceptive rules of lying and the spreading of disinformation. What makes it worse, their disinformation comes from what historians refer to as a credible source—after all, and he was elected to be a governor in a Southern state. Again, an historian that does not understand spiritual warfare cannot write about true history. He will accept Satan's lies as being the real deal.

While slavery was defended by those who had a great financial interest in the continuation of cotton production, it was also defended by Southern Christians who sought to end slavery but in a peaceful way. The North's call for an immediate end to slavery did not make any provisions to mitigate the anarchy that would follow. It would be like the green party taking over the United States and stating: Starting Monday morning, everyone must take public transit. That is what the South faced. They had no choice but to defend slavery until something could be figured out what to do with three million unemployed slaves. By demanding freedom for slaves and unwilling to negotiate any kind of settlement, the war became an inevitable conflict. Just as planned. Christians also had a problem with those who called slavery an absolute evil, despite what the Bible stated about its legitimacy. Christians felt that they had to rise up to defend the Bible. Satan is very wise in creating evil situations and then placing Christians in the line of fire for defending God's Word.

Wartime propaganda has a lasting impact upon historical truths. No one tells the truth during times of war. Preaching the truth during war can be called an act of treason. For a Northerner to say anything good about the South or the innocent Southerners who were not slave owners, was considered pure evil. Many Northerners [About 40,000] found themselves in a Federal prison for telling the truth about the war. Grimes argues that the political conflicts after the war were a result of those who attempted to defend slavery or to defuse the tensions of racial conflict. After the war, there was only one acceptable viewpoint about race and the compatibility of turning America into a racist-free nation. In the post-war era, the elevation of race became a litmus test for all governmental policies. Grimes writes about this issue: "The larger applicability of these arguments survived the Civil War to leave a lasting assumption in the minds of some that the races of man were by some law beyond human control inherently and eternally unequal. Although constitutions and statutes might protect or even prohibit slavery, in the long run what was really at issue were those 'truths' which might be judged as unalterable by constitutions and statues, those truths which lay at the core of one's belief in the equality, or inequality, of races. Theology and ethnology thus remained authoritative sources for discussion."[127]

The above statement signifies that any intelligent discussion of racial issues is beyond question. Those who have alternative views are considered outside the proper limits of social debate. Also, what is completely ignored are the cultural, religious, and ethical backgrounds of the different races. Even if people have the exact same IQs, people just do not become 'equal' in one generation. The Bible refers to the multigenerational effects sin upon a family tree:

Exodus 34:7. Keeping mercy for thousands, forgiving iniquity and transgression and sin, and that will by no means clear *the guilty*; visiting the iniquity of the fathers upon the children, and upon the children's children, **unto the third and to the fourth *generation*.**

Deuteronomy 34:7. Thou shalt not abhor an Edomite; for he *is* thy brother: thou shalt not abhor an Egyptian; because thou wast a stranger in his land. **8** The children that are begotten of them shall enter into the congregation of the LORD in **their third generation.**

---

[127] Grimes. P. 50.

Deuteronomy 34:3. An Ammonite or Moabite shall not enter into the congregation of the LORD; **even to their tenth generation** shall they not enter into the congregation of the LORD for ever:

People become damaged as a result of their past choices and the environment in which they have lived in the past. It takes several generations for assimilation to do its work. If people have been involved in pagan worship, their traditions influence them to the tenth generation. The **Amorites** were people known to indulge in adultery, child sacrifice, homosexuality, prostitution, idolatry, and witchcraft. The Moabites were also a pagan nation. The Blacks that came out of Africa worshipped false gods, i.e. Satan, and did not have any moral traditions as found in many Europeans nations. Passing an Amendment making them equal to Europeans and having full access to the public process would not work. Intelligent people know this. People carry their past heritage within their mind and are not easily expunged from their consciousness, or even their unconscious. The immediate and complete emancipation of a people fresh out of Africa was a tragedy ready to happen. That was the plan.

The Fundamentalist concept of being 'born again' immediately has heavily influenced American politics. The preacher persuades someone to raise their hand, or say a short prayer, and suddenly, he is a new person. However, the person who has had his sins forgiven, if it was a real encounter with Jesus Christ, but his whole personality, family history, and cultural history remain the same. The Bible talks about working out one's salvation with fear and trembling. It takes time to be liberated from one's past, especially when you are an American living in a propaganda State.

Philippians 4:12. Wherefore, my beloved, as ye have always obeyed, not as in my presence only, but now much more in my absence, **work out your own salvation** with fear and trembling. **13** For it is God which worketh in you both to will and to do of *his* good pleasure. **14** Do all things without murmurings and disputings: **15** That ye may be blameless and harmless, the sons of God, without rebuke, **in the midst of a crooked and perverse nation**, among whom ye shine as lights in the world....

A man's salvation occurs on two levels: First, he is transformed from a slave to sin into a servant of Jesus Christ. However, his past, his childhood

232

training, his culture in which he grew up and lives, and his previous life's choices all remain intact and part of his being. When a person works out his salvation, he is allowing God's Word and the power of the Holy Spirit to transform his old habits and ideas into new one's patterned after God's Word and becoming part of the Kingdom of god upon the earth. A person is to approach this process with much trepidation because it is so easy to fool oneself that a person is doing God's work when in actuality he is merely carrying out patterns of thinking from his 'past' life. If God cannot create a totally new person instantly, neither can any law or Constitutional Amendment. The great danger is to 'baptize' one aspect of one's personal history and declare it is from God. That is the 'fear and trembling part.'

Satan is highly intelligent and his servants follow his orders. He knows that if you tell the slaves that they are now totally equal with everyone else, he starts to think in those terms. He starts demanding all of the same rights and responsibilities as those who have been raised since childhood in a certain way. I was raised on farm work—lots of it. That became part of my character and even when I worked in other areas, the character traits I learned as a farm boy were included in that endeavor. That is true of every human. Those raised on welfare with have a different outlook and a different work ethic than someone raised on his father's farm. A boy raised on a plantation, working under a field boss, will have different life experiences and attitudes than a boy raised working in his family's business. Therefore, a newly proclaimed 'freed' slave will become angry and frustrated when he fails at endeavors he was never trained to engage in. And to make matters worse, it takes several generations to become a totally new person who can operate 'efficiently' in a totally new culture. There are no miracle cures for a person's past bad experiences.

That is why, after the Civil War, when the freed slaves went forth to conquer the South as empowered by the law, they were met with resistance. In states where the Blacks were able to control the newly formed state legislatures, they ran the states into bankruptcy and used state funds for their own private means of becoming rich. Open corruption was the norm. Black juries would immediately find a Black defendant 'innocent' regardless of the evidence. [This was a major reason that there was post courtroom justice imposed. A Black could kill a White man on main street and be declared innocent.] Laws resisting the imposition of African values or pagan beliefs upon Southerners were called 'Jim

Crow' laws. Whites, defending their heritage and systems of justice and ethical values, passed laws to protect Western Civilization.

*

The Puritan Work ethic had incorporated itself into American culture long after the last Puritan had died. Americans were able to conquer the wilderness in such a short time because they were relentless workers. Take a walk through some heavily wooded area and imagine clearing that land with just an ax and a saw. I cannot imagine such a task without power tools. Imagine building a log cabin by hand and carving the joint to build a cabin that could withstand the wind storms and the snows. That was the Puritan ethic. What does a person do if his only skill is picking cotton? Freedom without skills could only survive through government payments or through theft. In fact, after the Civil War, the north authorized the Blacks to steal what they needed as a form of reparations, i.e. back wages. After the War, when Blacks were hired, they would stop working as soon as their supervisor left the work scene. That was the plantation mentality. Actually, many plantations used task oriented work: when a slave completed task, the rest of the day was his. An ambitious slave could finish his task in about four hours. Often, a slave would put a couple 12 hour days in so he could take four days off and visit friends and relatives in nearby plantations. The new factories were not conducive to workers trained on the plantation.

This difference in life histories led most people in the South, Black and White, to develop their own form of segregation. Neither felt comfortable in the other's culture. This created a legal dilemma. Laws were passed that required the two races to totally integrate their cultures. Obviously those who passed those laws were not expecting freed Blacks to enter into their neighborhood. Because the differences in the races was considered merely a matter of skin color, the whole history of race relations was turned into a war against those who kept maintaining that a person is not formed by his skin color but by his entire history over several generations of experiences. In fact, most Blacks think that Western Civilization is merely 'White Man's' ways and have no relevance to the Black personality as he experiences it. It is like a law would requir White Men to enter into a Black urban culture and learn to adjust to that way of life. Urban street life is nothing like the small farming town: different skills are needed for survival in each one. Each race is 'inferior' in the other's culture and the wisdom needed to survive in either in what both would consider a strange land.

234

The problem was that the freed slaves were supposed to adapt to Western Civilization without much training. Civilizations are based upon traditions learned in childhood from one's parents who were raised by their parents to learn a particular way of life. As stated, I believe that intelligent forces are at work in every nation and culture: forces for both good and evil. Because the American Government was founded upon the principle that good and evil do not exist and there is no competition between the two, laws passed upon this understanding do not reflect the real world. Democratic Laws at best are peace treaties between competitive interests who have somehow worked out some kind of compromise. The whole idea of America's Laws, not based upon the reality of Biblical Law, attempts to remake the world through a secular understanding idea of reality.

A good example of America's understanding of races which has no understanding of Biblical realty can be seen in the following by a former government minister to China written in 1881. He was talking about American rejection of Chinese immigrants, but the attitude reflects the secular American view of races and cultures.

"I know of no people who have seemed to me to have **so many prejudices of race as ourselves**. Whether it is due to our long contests with tribes of savages, the natives of the vast territory which we have occupied; or to the institution of slavery which took upon itself among us, **the very worst features which slavery has ever exhibited**, whether it is a pride of stock stimulated by our successful conquests over the many difficulties attending the settlement of a new, and in some respects, an inhospitable region; or whether all these have combined to produce the result, it would seem that a Negro, in times now passing by as we may hope, or a Chinaman still, **meets with a less ready reception from us than in any of the European nations**.... And all the while we cry out, with what to Heaven must appear **the grossest delusion and hypocrisy**, that **these other races resist** our influence—that they will not assimilate. **We hold them all at arms length** and **then throttle them because** they will not approach nearer to us. This is our boasted liberality and generosity."[128] (Emphasis added.)

---

[128] Grimes. P. 61-62.

The above represents that non-Christian, non-Western Civilization, and the non-American Way of life view of the culture of the United States. The original America was based upon Western and Christian Civilization. The Constitution changed that into an American Secular Civilization based upon English Civilization. The British idea of a global empire became part of America and the idea of a ruling elite class was also adopted. The myth was developed that any old country boy could become President with a little hard work became part of American lore. Later, the rags to riches story was added to the lore. Then the melting pot myth became incorporated, but this myth did little more than create a national mythology to justify the impossible. Most Americans expected immigrants from wherever they came from to do what the European immigrants had done earlier—throw out the old country values and put on American ones. When other races and cultures started arriving in great numbers, Americans expected these groups to do what their ancestors had done. When these intruders held onto their old ways, Americans resented that and considered it a rejection of their most cherished beliefs. Why would not every race want to adopt the American Way of Life over that of their own? If other races did not wish to become true Americans, they were expected to form their own 'ghetto' where their ways could be hidden from public view.

This attitude was labelled by those who believed in traditional American values as White Supremacy, i.e. the worst form of racism. Grimes cites Josiah Strong who said this in the 1880s: "There can be no reasonable doubt that North America is to be the great home of the Anglo-Saxon, the principle seat of his power, the center of his life and influence."[129] For the Yankee Christian, America was the New Israel of God. For the secularists, America represented the finest result of Nature's evolutionary process. After WWI, and the loss of American lives and the influx of foreigners who did not act like true Americans, the White Race, began to isolate themselves from the rest of the world. Americans were proud of their heritage and the feeling that every White person was a true American. A minority of Americans felt that what made America special was the mixing of all races. They wished to form a multi-racial and multi-religious nation. However, the majority passed Laws in the 1920s to limit immigrants who did not share European values. This was probably the last time where those in power felt that

---

[129] Grimes. P. 62.

their nation was chosen to be either a New Atlantis [secular] or a New Israel [religious].

It was this era where many believed that it was the government's role in life to convert the immigrants, Indians, and ex-slaves into 'Anglo-Saxons'. Why would they not want to become identified with the greatest nation in the history of the world? The Indians who had no desire to join the club were placed on reservations. There, their children were removed and placed in government schools and trained how to become Anglo-Saxons. Removing children from their families in order to reprogram the Indian proved to be a dismal failure: government programs cannot replace the family in a child's life. Segregation was another form of reservation in order to preserve the American Heritage. Despite the narrative, it was not racist in the sense that those races and immigrants that adopted the language, culture, and clothing style of the dominant Whites generally found acceptance. I grew up on the West Coast after WWII. There were a large number of Japanese living in our area. In fact, our town had been turned into a Japanese internment camp during the war. Yet, the Japanese were not considered foreign as they talked, dressed, and acted like the dominant culture. A Japanese moving into a neighborhood might even increase the property values as they loved to transform their yards into things of beauty—which might motivate others to spruce up their landscaping.

Americans kept passing law after law in an attempt to save their cultural personality and national identity. Americans sensed that they were being invaded by those who did not even like Anglo-Saxons and their form of Finance Capitalism. One of the most significant foreign invasions started in the late 19th century. Eastern European and Russia Jews arrived in droves. They formed their own ghettos in urban areas, especially New York. They also brought with them something Americans were not ready for: their own history, their own culture, their own religion, their own books, and their own special identity—which they had no intention of changing. It was like another nation had invaded the United States. These people were very good at using America's own ideas to gain power inside the nation. They understood the new media inventions that traditional Americans failed to understand. They knew that the future lied in entertainment and the control of the national information. The older Americans still thought in terms of local government, the small town paper, and the entertainment of friends, neighbors, churches, and communities. The Jewish way of life found a home in the urban culture which was just beginning to become dominant. In a sense, the Jewish Immigrants did not seek to assimilate, they created their own dominant culture. Americans, in time, were expected to assimilate into Jewish Business Culture and entertainment culture.

Because those areas of business and culture were new and urban, they were, in a sense, without legal restrictions. Also, the Jews brought to America a new image of the immigrant: a key ingredient in the making of an American Stew. Actually, the new American Stew became like a virus that infected the American thinking: it was a meme. Growing up in a government school in the 1950s, the melting pot image and the American Stew were repeated off. They became, in the minds of the young like myself, as real as rain and sunshine. We were told America was unlike any other nation upon the earth; our doors were always open to strangers. The reason Americans went to war was to save this image as America being the greatest nation and most helpful upon the earth. This heritage must not be allowed to die and Americans fought to defeat evil wherever it manifested itself: that was the official mantra.

A New York Jew, Emma Lazarus, wrote the poem which was inscribed upon the Statue of Liberty:

"Give me your tired, your poor,

Your huddled **masses** yearning to breathe free,

The wretched refuse of your teeming shore.

Send these, **the homeless**, tempest-tost to me,

I lift my lamp beside the golden door!" (Emphasis Added.)

This poem was written to change the image of the type of immigrant welcomed to America. Bailey Aldrich, editor of the *Atlantic Monthly,* viewed that the immigrants arriving to the United States as the 'menace alien.' But it really was too late, as the Jewish Immigrants were able, in a few decades, own many of the newspapers, movie productions, banking institutions, and radio network. When Henry Ford attempted to expose the danger being inflicted upon America, he discovered it was too late. If you want to stay in business in America, you must repeat the immigration mantra—welcome wretched refuse. Ford discovered this: No melting pot belief, no loan.

In the 1920s an effort was made to stop the influx of the refuse, but WWII was used to change all of that. The same people who had taken over the entertainment, banking, news media, and radio, 'hired' Winston Churchill to whip up sentiment to declare a war upon Germany. [At the time of WWI, there were more German Americans than English Americans in the United States.] During the Depression, Americans were beginning to fear the power of this new class of immigrants. This new class not only understood the nature of propaganda, they had to tools to promote it. Despite this, there was a rising tide of fear that America was being taken over by a people that did not share the traditional American and Anglo-Saxon values. Hence the propagandistic buildup of Hitler and his 'persecution' of the innocent Jews in Germany. What followed was one of the greatest propagandistic ploys in the history of the world. After the war, laws were passed to protect the Jews. All of their tools of control now became firmly established. Eventually, it even became against the law to question the beliefs of those who controlled the information in the United States. To resist their version of history was to become a supporter of Hitler. A new form of excommunication was spread throughout the land. People were allowed to say the most outrageous things about Christians and their churches, but not a word could be said in defense against the authors of those accusations. They had the LAW on their side. Freedom only applied to those attacking Christianity.

In this overview, the defense of America was shifted away from defending the nation's long ethical history and its traditions derived from Christian Civilization. Now, to defend America against the immigrants who held different beliefs was considered racist. This continues to this day: to defend White culture against Black culture is considered racist. The only issue is skin color. Whites are not allowed to defend their long history and its values. Whites are not allowed to reject alien cultures that would destroy their culture.

Insert: One thing must be constantly kept in mind: the whole subject of race, and law have been totally secularized. History is based only upon what men can see and touch. Mankind came out of the Evolutionary chain of being, and there is no physical evidence that man has a soul and that he is nothing more than an example of what Nature can accomplish, given enough time. That is why, when Christians add a spiritual element into any social narrative, they can easily be accused of applying their personal prejudices to the reality of the hour. That is why, when Christians oppose the Jewish 'race/religion' of attacking Christian values, they are accused of being 'anti-Semitic'. Of course, no one is ever accused of being anti-Christian or considered a violator of a Christian's human rights. That is why race is considered skin color and not a racial heritage. From Evolution, there is no such thing as a soul and no race could ever claim to be created in the special image of God as the Caucasians claim. Actually, that rule only applies to Caucasians. There is hardly a race that does not consider itself special with a heritage and religion different from all others. The races' self-identities are considered historical truth; the Caucasian Bible sees history in a different light. That is why the Bible is considered a compilation of 'fables'.

*

And now, back to my story. American history, in the 1930s, begin to focus upon non-Caucasian races and their religions. The dominance of White Man's religion and civilization came under a massive attack. Coincidently, the 1930s was the era of the Great Depression and the coming of age of radio entertainment. Times were tough, but everyone had access to a radio and could join with the rest of America in experiencing some of the best entertainment of all time. Because there was no video, the radio shows had to rely upon great writing. They were also expected to portray American values. When I watch a TV show, I will usually read something at the same time. However, it is impossible to read while listening to a radio show: your mind must create the video part of the show—that requires an active participation of your mental processes. The listeners mind must create its own special affects by the sounds on the show: you hear a gunshot, and your mind pictures that gunshot.

However, while Americans struggled to survive during this era and got totally caught up in the fictional world of radio, there were great cultural changes happening out of sight from the masses. FDR created a political revolution and transformed the United States into a socialist nation. Americans came to look to Washington, D.C. for their salvation. The Depression, everyone was told, was a national problem—far beyond the ability of any community to grapple with. Even the individual states struggled to find financing. Some even issued wooden coins as a substitute for the lack of U.S. coinage. There was another thing, the public's addiction to the new radio medium, nationalized American culture. Who wanted to attend a local playhouse when there was much superior talent on the radio? Americans became united like no other time: for the first time in history, the family gathered around their radio to be entertained by people they did not know: people who were not personal, but entertainers. This changed the way people perceived themselves: personal character was replaced by one's image. In previous times, the family might gather around the piano and sing together or attend some local event with just plain old neighbors. However, the man on the radio can play the banjo a lot better than one's neighbor.

This new mindset enabled the Overlords to now nationalize problems. There may not be any racism in your town, but America as a whole was now a racist nation. Everyone became a convicted social criminal. [Just as we are now being told that every person is destroying the earth's climate and is contributing to the death of the earth. All stand guilty as charged.] During the 1930s, the American and International Jewry were preparing for a war against Germany. The history of Germany and its invasion by Eastern European Jews after WWI was eliminated from the official German story. The Communist revolution in Germany during the 1920s was no longer talked about. The financial war against Germany after the War totally destroyed the German mark. German's saving were destroyed. The Intellectual and professional leaders of Germany became dominated by post WWI invaders. When Hitler came to power, International Jewry declared war upon Germany. Jews rioted in New York City. They went into stores, removed anything produced in Germany, and threw it into the Hudson River. Huge rallies were staged to picture Germany as an enemy of the United States.

The above is important because the events were used to cover over the takeover of American culture and its historical narrative by a non-Caucasian race/religion. To divert attention from the Jews, they set about uniting the Jewish interests with those of the Black race, and to some extend with the Indians. The three races were combined to picture America as a racist nation and the American Western Civilization as being White Supremist. Christianity was attacked because it did not support the religions of the Jews, the Blacks, and the

Indians. Of course, it was skin color and race, not religion, that is the poster child for the attack of White Christianity. By the end of the 1930's, everything was in place to go for the final attack—a giant war was declared against the White, Protestant [Lutheran], and isolationist nation of German. [Remember, it was Nationalist Socialism, not international Communism.]

Here is how Grimes summarizes the rise of the American Propaganda State:

"It was not until the Second World War that Americans awoke from the appalling apathy that that had characterized public opinion racial discrimination in the past. Hitler's anti-Semitism, in part echoed by American fascist groups in the late 1930's, together with the atrocities committed by the Nazis in the name of Nordic superiority, caused a revulsion against race theory in this country that led in turn to a re-examination of public policy as well as private sentiment. No country which had seen the lynching of 119 Negroes (according to the Tuskegee Institute records) during the decade of the thirties could fight a war against blatant racism with entirely clean hands. As the war with the Nazis brought home to many Americans the evils of racism, so the global struggle for power after the war had its effect on our public policy."[130] That represents the official narrative and that story was used to disable White Christians from defending themselves. Somehow, such defense was associated with Nazism.

When a nation is at war, everyone wants to know what they are fighting, sacrificing, and dying for. War opens the door to change and the planting of new ideas into the minds of the public. America was pictured as a nation that had a "Nazi" past and it is time that it cleansed itself of that evil by sacrificing the lives of their boys against the racism of Germany. After the War, the Empires of the world began collapsing and new nations were being formed—non-White nations. This was also the start of the Cold War, the newly formed nations became the target for both Communism and Americanism. The competition to form an alliance with the 'third world nations' became like a giant political game between the Soviet Union and the United States. This game required that America appear to be the global champion of the non-White people. Because the other nations were not Christian, the image of America needed to be changed. The United

---

[130] Grimes. P. 65.

States became the champion of every race, every creed, and of every color. These new nations needed to be won over politically, not religiously.

Racial conflicts were planned long before WWII in order to raise 'Black Consciousness' and to plant new ideas into their minds. In 1909, the National Association for the Advancement of Colored People was founded. In 1910, the Urban League was established. In 1917, the Universal Negro Improvement Association was added to the organization attacking the White Establishment and Western Civilization. These organizations coincided with the rapid growth of the Jewish influence throughout the United States. America was more and more labelled a racist state that, from the very beginning, started with the theft of Indian lands and their subsequent genocide. White, male, Christian America was under attack, and yet it was done indirectly through anti-Christian, i.e. non-Christian, groups. White Christians now became the source of evil and it was time they turned over their leadership to minorities who were not connected to America's evil racist and religious past. Because Western and Christian Civilizations were dominated by White Males, these civilizations were attacked for the very reason they were White and Male, i.e. dead White Males.

I understand that to write like this makes me into a conspiracy theorist, however, I prefer the name, Conspiracy Revealer. Satan, the grand conspirator, has not changed his *modus operandi* since the beginning of time.

Psalm 2:1. Why do the heathen rage, and the **people imagine** [fabricated ideas] a vain thing? **2** The kings of the earth [the ruling elites] set themselves, and **the rulers take counsel together**, [conspire] against the LORD, and against his anointed, *saying*, **3** Let us break their bands asunder, and **cast away their cords** [their laws] **from us.**

Ezekiel 22:25. *There is* a conspiracy of her prophets in the midst thereof, like a roaring lion ravening the prey; **they have devoured souls**; they have taken the treasure and precious things; they have made her many widows in the midst thereof. **26** Her **priests have** violated my law, and have profaned mine holy things: they have **put no difference between the holy and profane**, neither have they shewed *difference* between the unclean and the clean, and have hid their eyes from my sabbaths, and I am profaned among them. **27** Her **princes in the**

midst thereof *are* like wolves ravening the prey, to **shed blood**, *and* to **destroy souls**, to get **dishonest gain. 28** And her prophets have daubed them with untempered *morter*, seeing vanity, and **divining lies** unto them, saying, Thus saith the Lord GOD, when the LORD hath not spoken. **29** The **people of the land have used oppression, and exercised robbery, and have vexed the poor and needy:** yea, they have oppressed the stranger wrongfully. **30** And I sought for a man among them, that should make up the hedge, and stand in the gap before me for the land, that I should not destroy it: but I found none. **31** Therefore have **I poured out mine indignation upon them; I have consumed them with the fire of my wrath: their own way have I recompensed upon their heads**, saith the Lord GOD.

Nations and people conspire against God, but the results are always the same. The means used to conspire against God's people vary, but the goal is always the same. They currently conspire to destroy the White Race and all of the beliefs, laws, and values that go with them. Christians must not focus too hard on the particular weapons being used, but must focus on the goals of those who are manufacturing the issues. As I write, many Christians are doing everything they can to prove that they are not racists, etc. The Church should rather be promoting the Kingdom of God. The Church should focus upon what they are doing to serve others—no matter how it appears to their enemies. The problem with going on the defensive is that once defended, the attack will only change to another topic, ad infinitum. The Church is to be known by what it is doing, not by defending itself from Satan's critics.

*

One of the problems of the civil rights movement is that they too have focused upon the negative. Those minorities in the past who felt they were not getting their own fair share, developed parallel economies and communities to attain their own rights. When the Chinese in California were not getting the bank loans they thought were their right, they formed their own bank. In fact, that bank developed into one of America's major banks. Minorities that form a community are able to attain rights not given to them automatically. In terms of school and neighborhood segregation, the goal should have been to develop better schools and better communities, rather than seek to enter into already established schools and communities. The slave mentality or the African culture, apparently, prevented the freed Blacks from working together as other minorities in the past have done. Of course, when the Blacks went to the central government to attain their rights, they contributed to the enslavement of the whole nation. Everyone's behavior came under the observation and control of the Overlords. Whites were no longer allowed to form their own businesses and schools—they were expected, i.e. compelled to hire minorities or include minorities in their private endeavors.

The whole idea of rights that were designed to protect people from the government, have morphed into the government controlling everyone in the name of equality and equity. This total transformation was to be accomplished through the miracle of laws. Just as people think that they can be 'saved' by imposing behavior laws upon themselves, they also think a nation can be 'saved' imposing lots and lots of laws upon everyone. In 1776, the leaders taught that that the masses could 'save' America from the England's excessive taxation through the making of their own laws. The right to pass separate American laws could save the land from England. Later, when one section of the nation had different laws than that of another section, the North invaded the South to unify the laws of the nation. What are wars, but the imposition of one law system upon that of another nation? Or to separate a people from laws they oppose. Actually, salvation by law started with the early Christian immigrants, i.e. the Puritans. They believed that by the passing of laws requiring church attendance they could 'save' the new land. This thinking has never stopped, as America now has more laws than ever, believes that laws can save a nation from some declared evil such as social segregation: if the government can merely lock everyone in the same room, they will learn to get along.

In the 1940's, the nation became obsessed with laws about the making of social harmony between the nations. In 1939, the year WWII officially began, a Civil Rights section was created in the Department of Justice in order to enforce Civil Rights laws. In 1941, FDR established by executive order, the Fair Employment Practices Commission. President Truman in 1946, created the President's Committee on Civil Rights. The committee stated: "'We need to guarantee the same rights to every person regardless of who he is, where he lives, or what his racial, religious, or national origins are.' In 1948, again by executive order, President Truman prohibited racial segregation in the armed forces."[131]

---

[131] Grimes. P. 69.

More Civil Rights Legislation were passed in the 1960's. There was the Civil Rights Act of 1960 and then again in 1964; The Voting Rights Act of 1965; The Fair Housing Act of 1968 and the famous War on Poverty Act of 1964. This War ended up costing America some 2 trillion dollars. That program and Johnson's War on Vietnam started the deterioration of the America dollar the road that led to today's tens of trillions of debt. America survived by transferring America's debt to foreign nations by forcing them to purchase dollars in order to buy oil, i.e. the Petro Dollar. A law that is now forcing those nations outside of the West to form their own 'petro dollars' which is ending the ability of the United States to colonialize the dollar. Yes, when the West got rid of their colonies and granted them 'freedom', their enslavement was continued through various forms of debt and dollar manipulation. This form of financial colonialism does not require an army to enforce it. It is accomplished by imposing American Laws upon the whole world: those nations that oppose American domination find themselves facing a revolution within their own borders. America after WWII, patterned its laws after observing how the mafia controlled people—a global protection racket. Obey American Laws or face internal revolution.

All of the above Civil Rights Laws promised a cure for America's racist dilemma. When the laws failed to deliver as promised, the Blacks felt there was a grand conspiracy of White Supremists. "Behind the racist tensions of the 1960's lay a Negro generation acutely aware of extreme frustration."[132] America is so convinced that laws can save people that it keeps passing more and more laws. And when those laws do not achieve their intended goal, they pass more laws. It is impossible for any government to admit that laws cannot save anyone: they can only punish. Tyrants rule by laws and without the promise of salvation by laws, the tyrant starts losing his power. In the same way in the New Testament, the Pharisees and Sadducees ruled over the people by promising salvation through their laws: keep their laws and God will find you acceptable in His sight. Their war against Jesus was that he promised a plan of salvation that did not include keeping of the ritual laws created by the religious elites. If the people do not need the Pharisees and the Sadducees, then what will they do to earn a living?

The Overlords of America are in the same position as the religious overlords in the New Testament, i.e. salvation by laws, our laws, and only our laws. God

---

[132] Grimes. P. 70.

created a reality where crime could be diminished by Laws, but laws can never make people into good people. Making a law that forces neighborhoods to integrate their housing polices does not make everyone into good neighbors. Integrating schools does not create Black students who prefer books over basketballs. And then, everyone wonders why the laws are not working. No one ever comes to the conclusion that the legal system is attempting to replace God's roll in the universe. Salvation by law has been in effect ever since Satan caused the fall of Man. Cain attempted to satisfy God through an offering of his best works. And when God rejected his form of salvation, he became enraged and killed his brother who sought salvation by grace. For six thousand years, men who reject God's plan of salvation think that they can create a better plan more in keeping with the need of their Satanic Overlords.

The race issue is not a race issue, it is a bold attempt to condition mankind into the Satanic delusion that men can save themselves through law. If the right law is created and enforced with enough power, utopia can be achieved. The Social Credit system is the tyrant's ultimate dream in that thousands of laws can be enforced through Total Information Awareness and Total Surveillance. No one will be able to access many avenues necessary for life if they violate one of the laws. With that system, there will be no escape unless you do not mind living without water, electricity, cars, banking systems, and food. Otherwise, you are still free to enjoy personal sensual and private experiences. You are free to have sex with whoever you want as long as you do not discriminate against any person because of race, religion, or personal beliefs. Everyone should have an equal opportunity to be your sexual partner.

As you can see, the issue of race has been a tool to condition the masses to accept the Social Credit system. Despite all of the laws, money, and programs, racism still exists. However, the Social Credit System offers a legal system that will overcome all of the shortcomings of past laws and wars against poverty and racism. Of course, it is not going to stop there. Any person who holds on to any Biblical belief or Law can also be separated from the means to continued normal life. Anyone is free to survive in the wilderness as long as it is not on public land. The following is Alan Grimes conclusion about American's racial problem as written in 1964:

"A vicious cycle tends to develop in which poverty makes inadequate schooling inevitable; poor schooling perpetuates prejudice and ignorance, which in turn perpetuate poverty. ... The importance of education, which has so successfully proven to be a solvent for religious antipathies, is becoming more evident in the area of racial conflict. Once again the role of the Supreme Court in recent years as the national moral sensor cannot be underestimated. It is not alone the legal effect of its views in gradually achieving integrated schools and other publically sponsored social institutions which has been significant, but the equalitarian social values which have guided these decisions and brought an awakened public conscious to bear upon the problems. Education, broadly considered, serves not only to transmit traditional values but occasionally to transcend them. **Recent public opinion survey have repeatedly shown that racial prejudice is a function of ignorance.** 'The higher one's education,' one social scientist has written,' the more likely one is to believe in democratic values and support democratic practices. All the relevant studies indicate that education is more significant than either income or occupation. .. The more poorly educated whites are the strictest segregationists, the best educated whites are the least segregationist. **The higher the level of education the lower the level of racial intolerance.**

"The passages from racial exclusiveness to racial diversity, like the passage from religious exclusiveness to religious diversity, has been historically accompanied by a democratic change in social basis of politics. As was the case with religious diversity, **toleration** marks the first step toward equal toward equal acceptance. Yet toleration, whether in religious or racial matters, implies a superiority and can therefor never provide a satisfactory, equitable solution to the problems of a heterogeneous and pluralistic society. It may expect then that **'white supremacy,'** like the semi-official Protestantism of early America, will lose its appeal as a social value as a new equalization of opportunity is more and more realized. Equality thus emerges again as the second-best alternative to that of claimed superiority, with race becoming as irrelevant to public power as religion did. Such a solution to the problem of racial diversity will be a departure from the practices of the past, yet it will be a realization of **the equalitarian principles of the Declaration of Independence**...."[133] (Emphasis added.)

The above statement represents the official American orthodoxy. Those who oppose the approved racial agenda are uneducated, poor, and White. Those who accept to new America are like those Protestants who gave up their

---

[133] Grimes. P. 83-85.

dogmatic Biblical beliefs and melted into the new American racial stew—the melting pot. Any dogmatic beliefs, whether in race or religion, must be excluded from the public mind. Democracy, freedom, toleration, and equality are all the foundations of the new American order. As I write, those wanting to be included in the American culture of total tolerance have been labelled the LGBTQ+ crowd who believe they are the new normal. They are the new American Founders of a new nation dedicated to liberty and the goal of life, liberty, and the pursuit of happiness.

Chapter Twenty-Two: The American Future belongs to the City.

It has been said that the Bible is a book designed for rural folks. Individuality thrives in the city; communities are formed in the village and the farmlands. One of the reasons is that people in the country need each other and are dependent upon working together. In the city, the individual has only himself to trust. The individuals of the city form a crowd; the people in the village form an extended family. The village built the small church; the city built great cathedrals. In the city, the exterior of the person is most important; in the country, one's interior values are vital and people can see through a false identity. The image of God within man matters little in the city: a man creates his own image: man is created in the image of his own desires. The man who attempts display his Godly image in the city will find that he will be labelled as a real bumpkin, a country bumpkin. When the Blacks moved to the North, 90 per cent settled in the cities. This was an important matter in the development of their character. The White Protestant Christian, even if he lived in the city, was raised in the values of the Christian village. That was for most of American history considered the American Way.

There is more to the conflict between races than skin color and because of that, the reconciliation between the races cannot be based just upon tolerance. Plus, tolerance operates on the lowest common denominator—being forced to get along with someone you do not like, i.e. you tolerate them. God planted within mankind the desire to be united with others. That is what the true Church is supposed to offer to people. Paul wrote the following:

Ephesians 4:2. With all lowliness and meekness, with longsuffering, forbearing **one** another in love; **3** Endeavouring to keep the unity of the Spirit in the bond of peace. **4** *There is* **one** body, and **one** Spirit, even as ye are called in **one** hope of your calling; **5 One** Lord, **one** faith, **one** baptism, **6 One** God and Father of all, who *is* above all, and through all, and in you all. **7** But unto every **one** of us is given grace according to the measure of the gift of Christ

Because this desire to be one with others, it frustrates mankind when they cannot achieve unity with their own powers. Satan is the author of rebellion and destruction. His only means of uniting people is in a common hatred of God, His Laws, and His people. When you see a nation spouting forth hatreds on all fronts, you see that Satan is on the loose. People criticize the 1950's for being a bland decade, but it was also the decade when there were no mass domestic hatreds. Generally, everyone accepted Western Civilizations as having been the belief that had conquered the world in the 1940's. The 50's were also the first TV age and the nation of was caught up watching the same shows. The new fall lineup of TV shows was a big event, similar to the new line of 1950's cars that came out in September. People rushed to the showrooms to see what the new cars looked like.

Superficial as the 1950's might have been, there was peace in America and everyone was pursing common dreams. It is said that the 1950's lasted until the death of President Kennedy in the fall of 1963. President Johnson took the nation into war, created racial strife, started student riots over the draft, and placed America on the road to financial ruin. From November 22, 1964 to May 4, 1970, with the Kent State shootings, American was undergoing a revolution like none other since the American Civil War. Hatred was everywhere. As a result, the unity of the 1950s had disappeared, never to return. There was no common civilization or religion that Americans could agree upon. I might add, most of the strife was confined to urban areas. Small towns were still holding parades on the Fourth of July to celebrate the nation they remembered. There could not have been massive social change in the 60's without the giant urban centers, the huge State universities, and the TV to bring the new hatreds into everyone's dinnertime experience.

Maybe one common trait of the 60's that brought white students and black protestors together was a shared hatred of the current system, i.e. civilization. There was even a crossover as White students joined the Black protestors in seeking to establish a new order replacing the old one. Both groups felt that if they were empowered to make the laws, American could become just like a Hippie Commune or a national Woodstock. The Blacks united behind the dream of Martin Luther King and the urban riots; and the students united behind the protests and sex, drugs, and Rock 'n Roll. Living during those times, it was felt by many if the nation could all just sing the same music, the nation could be healed. Of course, riots, sex, and drugs are only the unity of Satanic deception. For the Hippies, all people need in life is some unifying external hatreds [The draft boards and the war.] and some internal sensual experiences [Music and drugs.].

*

Unless a person views history from the perspective of the Kingdom of God being at war with the Kingdom of Satan, everything seems to be in eternal flux. Everyone has a different idea on how to restore order and who to blame for the current disorder. In the 1960's, the Supreme Court did as much as anything to destroy the old order and create a new order founded upon permanent social conflicts: Black versus White; urban versus rural; and government versus Christianity. Of course, the cover story for these conflicts was equality, democracy, and separation of church and state. Laws that did not produce equality were unconstitutional; laws that allowed religious expression in publically supported institutions were unconstitutional; and laws that gave too much power to the old rural order were unconstitutional. The Constitution in the hands of the Court was used as dynamite to blow up everything that hindered the creation of a totally new civilization. This was a *legalized* Revolution, fought under the color of a living Constitution that could grow with the changing mindset of the 'people.' Of course, it was the Court that decided how to interpret this new mindset.

Maybe one of the least mentioned aspects of national reality is the subtle affect Supreme Court rulings have had on the nation and how they affect the national mindset down the road. For example, the rulings on school prayer and the ruling on separate but equal schools totally changed the nature of education. Intellectually, the placement of Black children in White schools had the affect making scholarship only for Whites and that Blacks needed to be athletes in order to succeed in that culture. Black children who made great grades were intimidated by the Blacks who did not do well. It eventually created a system where Blacks were graded differently than Whites. And of course, the school prayer and parallel issues led to an amoral and anti-Christian school system. That

252

was a major factor in the destruction of Western Civilization which had been the common and binding force in American culture.

In 1962, the Supreme Court ruled in the *Baker v. Carr* decision that one man one vote standard must be the standard in ALL elections. That led to the elevation of mob rule in elections. Many states had Constitutions like my home State of Washington. The Senate was made up of representative from the 39 counties. The House was made up of those elected by the most populated areas. Power was thus divided between the urban 'mob' mentality and the rural farming mentality. It was also separated the Conservatives in the Senate from the liberals in the House. It also separated the farming and rural control of the Senate to the urban control of the House. In order to pass legislation, both groups had to agree on basic issues. The United States Constitution operates on a similar pattern where the populists states are not allowed to turn the less populist states into colonies of the mob ruled urban centers. That is what happened in my state as a result of that ruling which stated both the House and the Senate must be based upon population alone. In Democracy, only the popular mob can have a voice in government. As a result, the 36 counties of Washington State became colonies of the 3 counties where most of the people lived. Money flowed out of the small towns into the big cities to build infrastructures, roads, and urban renewal projects. Small towns died in the name of voter equality.

The rural counties were dominated by independent farmers, loggers, and fisherman. These workers held onto the traditions of Western Civilization and of the ideas of the Founders of America. They held onto the religious beliefs of Christianity and the patriotism of the local community. Under that system, rapid change became difficult and traditional values had to be respected by all. The radicals who wanted a new order based upon socialism were frustrated by the conservatives who tended to own their own businesses and valued their neighbors and the traditional community values. This one decision allowed the majority of any state to dictate the policies for the whole state based merely upon their socialistic values. Other values were now undemocratic and needed to be restrained from those who wanted to rebuild the world according to their visions of a New Order, the urban order.

Technically, the United States was transformed from a Republic to a Democracy. Throughout history, democracies fail for two reasons: the mob can be manipulated to vote a certain way; and they understand that they can vote themselves benefits from the Treasury. This results in political corruption as the politicians always expect to be in on the graft. When the voters hire someone to steal for them, it comes at a price. Hey, everyone is getting rich, so why worry. The problem is this: soon the treasury runs out of money and is forced to borrow to keep the gravy train from stalling out. More and more money must be borrowed to keep everyone happy. Another problem with borrowed money is that it requires interest payments. When interest payments are made, it removes money from circulation, which produces either a recession or the need for more borrowing. Democracies always declare war upon the two principles of a working civilization: You break it, you pay for it; if you do not work--you do not eat. The voters/mob would never allow those two principles to ever be enforced. Civilization is the enemy of the hungry and bored urban horde. .

As a result of *Baker v. Carr,* America became nation where whatever the mob wants, the government must create laws to support the mob. If one-third of the people own houses, and two-thirds do not, then the majority are free to confiscate property in the name of some greater good. The traditional argument against such fears is that the Constitution protects the minority against the majority. However, the judges work for and supports those in power. That is why freedom of speech is now subject to not spreading false or misleading information, as defined by the government. And, of course, Congress shall make no law from restricting the ownership of guns. That protection is meaningless. The government runs the mobs which give the government permission to do as it damn well pleases—as long as the government promises that the people's check is in the mail. Originally, freedom was established through localized centers of power. If you do not like the laws in one county or one state, you are free to move elsewhere. No court battles, no protests or riots, just move. That is the best freedom of all—the freedom to move wherever within a nation: a nation where regional differences are legal.

In 1811, the noted jurist James Kent wrote Commentaries on American Law. He wrote:

"There is a constant tendency in human society, and the history of every age proves it; there is a tendency in the poor to covet and to share the plunder of the rich, in the debtor to relax or avoid the obligations of contracts; in the majority to tyrannize over the minority, and trample down their rights; in the indolent and the profligate to cast the whole burdens of society upon the industrious and the virtuous....

"Society is an association for the protection of property as well as of life, and the individual who contributes only one per cent to the common stock, ought not to have the same power and influence in directing the property concerns of the partnership, as he who contributes his thousands."[134]

Basically, when the mob is allowed to rule, they will demand that those who have be compelled to give of the wealth to those who do not want to labor in order to obtain the needs of life. Mankind is at war with the following principles established by God when Men chose the rule of Satan over that of God:

17 And unto Adam he said, Because thou hast hearkened unto the voice of thy wife, and hast eaten of the tree, of which I commanded thee, saying, Thou shalt not eat of it: cursed *is* the ground for thy sake; in sorrow shalt thou eat *of* it all the days of thy life; **18** Thorns also and thistles shall it bring forth to thee; and thou shalt eat the herb of the field; **19** In the sweat of thy face shalt thou eat bread, till thou return unto the ground; for out of it wast thou taken: for dust thou *art*, and unto dust shalt thou return.

Here again, those who contribute to political thought have no understanding of the spiritual realm and the battle against the image of God within His people. Satan is at war with God and His Kingdom. Satan's kingdom seeks to turn the mob loose upon those who are attempting to live by the Laws of God. The Overlords know their best chance at defeating God's rule is to control the rabble who want nothing to do with Biblical Laws, especially the Laws against

---

[134] Grimes. P. 101.

envy and covetousness. When people live in a lawful and orderly society, those who follow Biblical principles will generally find success in their endeavors. The elites cater to the covetousness of the lower classes and it is to those motives that election promises are directed.

Democracy always leads to the poor taking that which is not theirs and are unwilling to do what it takes to attain success and wealth. Several decades ago, a college professor wrote a formula that worked almost every time for a teenager to escape from yhe poverty cycle of his culture: Graduate from high school; do not get married or have children until later; get a job, any job, and keep it for at least two years; and save as much as possible and do not go into debt. The students rioted on his campus and demanded he be dismissal on the grounds of racism. Why follow that formula when the welfare route is much quicker? They had helped pass laws which encourage a different route which did not require work, self-discipline, and delayed gratification. The American nation has passed laws which penalizes those who attempt to follow the traditional ways to success.

*

In 1841, Samuel Jones of Boston wrote *A Treatise on the Right of Suffrage*. The following is an excerpt from his book:

"The owners of property therefore have a deep interest in the affairs of the government; and an interest, too, which others have not. It is reasonable that they should have an influence and an agency in the government, in some degree commensurable with their interests. It may he emphatically asked, why persons having no property should have a right to interfere, by their votes, in the disposition of the property of others, or in the election of legislators and public officers whose most important duties are exercised in matters involving the rights of property?....

"It should be kept in mind, that the owners of real estate have all the personal and other rights possessed by others; and it seems but just that they should have an additional influence, in public affairs, equal to their additional rights as owners and of the whole territory of the country. And the public good most evidently requires that they should have this additional influence. They, as a class, combine, in the greatest degree, all those qualifications which entitle them to the confidence of the whole body of the people, and which furnish the best guaranty that they will always give their suffrages, intelligently and honesty, and under the influence of patriotic motives. And why should they not? The whole country is their own."[135]

There is one problem in the above argument, as the Bible states: For all have sinned and fallen short of the Kingdom of God. In the leaders of a nation become corrupt, then the successful will become corrupt also. Every time a nation falls into evil times, a revolution seeks to create a sin-proof form of government. There have been times when those with property used it to turn the rest of the nation into slaves. As I write, evil men have forced 80 per cent of the American population to take a vaxxx that is not a vaxxx, but a DNA controlling injection. The national mob unknowingly accepted this plan to either sterilize everyone, or to cause a massive die off to 'save' the planet. When Satan takes over a nation, there is no system, law order, or Constitution that can protect the people from their own destruction. That is why limited suffrage must be confined with multiple units of localized power. That prevents the rich and powerful from creating giant monopolies and cartels. Without the diffusion of power, evil men will always aim for the total control of everyone.

The Bible adds a different system of government than the above mix. First of all, governments are localized. There should be no standing army. Men can only be drafted to defend the borders of a nation. There should be no property tax—no one can lose their property for not paying taxes. There can be no personal income tax—a tax which is based upon self-reporting to the government one's private life and activities. There can be no inheritance tax—what you earn and save is for your children, not for the state. Only impersonal taxes are allowed, such as tariffs, licenses, and tolls. Money must be based upon forms of wealth such as gold and silver—no funny paper, i.e. fiat money. Every fifty years all loans are cancelled—this prevents both government deficit spending, and it prevents people from becoming wage slaves. The above practices will usually prevent a corrupt evil elite from taking over a nation. No form of government

---

[135] Grimes. P. 102.

founded apart from the rule of God through His Laws can survive for long. Evil people, whether an evil mob or an evil ruler, cannot succeed if the Bible is their Constitutional limit on governmental power. .

*

One of the goals of 21st century America is to destroy the family farm through an immoral inheritance tax and the lack of a Jubilee Year when property must be returned to its original owner. The intent was to protect the farmer's inheritance for his children. If bad harvests cause him to lose his farm to save his family, his inheritance would not be lost for his children. Biblically, the farmer not only produces food, but he produces hard-working honest children. Local farmers often produce a community as they all need their neighbors at times and they all must be neighborly at other times. If a farmer's barn burns down, his barn insurance is his neighbors. The Christian life was meant to be lived in town and village where people's moral life and commitment to others matters. There is no such need in the urban Darwinian jungle where only the fit survive.

In 1930, Professor William Gee wrote *The Place of Agriculture in American Life.* The following is an excerpt from that book:

"There is nothing so characteristic of the farmer as his *individualism*.... Conservatism at times greatly irritates the progressive elements in society, but it has often kept the world from running amuck. And the farmer is notably a conservative.

"The farmer vote is generally conceded to be a more thoughtful vote than the heterogeneous city vote....

"A recent study by the author tends to confirm the existing opinion that *thrift* and *frugality* are virtues more prevalent in the country than in the city....

"Nowhere else as in the country is there exhibited a like *democracy* of attitude....

"The farmer is the most *religious* element of our population....

"The very foundation of our civilization are laid in the *sacredness of the family ties*.... Statistics show that there is a larger proportion of divorces in the city than in the country....

"The chief danger in the cityward drift is that we may fail to carry over into our new urban majority those country characteristics that have made our national life great. The city environment can never foster independence of action, conservatism, democracy of attitude, thrift, and frugality, religiosity, and the strength and purity of family life as does the country..."[136]

As I write, foreign nations or foreigners and America's superrich are buying up farmland by the tens of thousands of acres. Also, farmers are losing their chickens and cattle also through by some form of planned elimination. At the same time, soon all cattle will be injected with mRNA vaxxxes of some kind. Both farmers and the foods they produce are under attack. What is going on is still being debated, but what is obvious, the American farmer is under attack with the goal of transforming what farms remain into corporate farms, controlled by government environmental regulations. The American farm family is being changed into a rural version of the urban employee: Big box farms become like their counterpart in the city—big box stores. With the urban government soaking up the tax funds, small cities which served as nurseries for Christian character, are also dying.

Up until the last few years, it was not politically correct to attack Christianity directly. Even those who promoted abortion regarded it as a personal choice. But it has become more that: the supporters of abortion now regard it as an act of worship to their Satanic beliefs. Yes, even Satanism can now be promoted openly. However, while Christianity is still under attack, attacking Satanism is considered some kind of cultural crime. What has changed? First, everyone recognizes that the American Church as a Biblical Church has failed. It is a private club open to all, but still just a club. Second, the church has adopted a Gospel of counseling, not the Gospel of Jesus Christ. Adjustment is more important than confrontation of the changing culture. Third, the Laws of God are really only taught by White Christians and thus those who promote those laws are

---

[136] Grimes. P. 113-114.

labelled White Supremists. Fourth, the social media has created a culture of individualism and social isolation. Belonging to a group is less important than finding a niche on the social media. Fifth, the American educational system has emphasized relativity and the progressive nature of truth. Dogmatism is totally out of touch with the American mindset. Sixth, Americans have been taught that anything old is obsolete and out of date: Fashions, styles, musical tastes, and even ideas change with the times. Old people have not a clue about what is happening. The churches are dominated by old people who are similarly out of touch. Seventh, the Bible throughout the last two thousand years has been promoted by White Men. Eighth, Biblical Laws are racist as they condemn other cultures and their ethical standards. Ninth, Christianity is divisive and cannot lead to unity within any nation: it condemns those who disagree to eternity in hell. Tenth, even most people who attend church admit that it is just a ritual that makes a person feel good just in case there really is a God.

As Christianity has died, so has the civilization died that it created. Even American culture and its Constitution were founded upon the leftovers of Western Civilization. The country church and emotional services were popular on the frontier for lonely homesteaders, but the Industrial Revolution and the closed frontier created a different American than the one of the American Revolution. The government founded in 1789 really has no connection to 2023. Just think about how the world has changed since then and then think, why should people be satisfied with the same form of government, and the same laws? The old Republic must die in order for a true Democracy of the people can be established. Republics are divided into separate localities and power centers, but Democracies unite everyone under a form of government that is designed to bring people together into one. Republics teach separate but equal, but Democracies teach forced unity and equal.

Chapter Twenty-Three: The Laws of the Crowd Apply to the Democracy.

The Middle Ages were considered the Age of Faith followed by the Ages of the Reformation and the Renaissance. After that, the 18th century has called the Age of Enlightenment. Then the 19th century which was the Age of Industrial and Scientific Revolutions. The 20th century could be nothing but the Age of World Conflicts. The 21st century is the age of the Mob: better yet, the manipulated mob. Actually, the Age of the deceived mob thinking it had been empowered. One of the great myths is that the social media empowers people to become whatever they want to be. A person is free to write his own fictional autobiography and pretend it is real. And because no one knows you personally, your secret will remain a secret.

There is a flaw in all of this: the government and its agents its agents are also free to write fictionalized accounts of reality. The aliens are coming; Russia is your enemy; the dollar is just as sound as gold and silver; the jab will protect you from dying from whatever virus is being promoted at the time; everyone is equal and only evil people make them unequal; changing laws has the power to change people; the government responds to the wishes of the people; and there are no celestial limits to what man can attain. However, like many modern beliefs, there is a Satanic element to all of the above. The Mob does not see itself as a group of fallen and rebellious creatures in God's created order. Satan places within the mob the idea that their goals can only be achieved by their uniting for some sort of violent act: mobs vote by rioting and destruction. The mob is above other cultural powers in that the mob believes that only by destruction can men be freed from the evil rulers of modernity. In a sense, the mob sees itself as having god-like powers, as the mob cried out in the 1960s, Power to the People. In fact, there is a feeling of unity as everyone bonds himself to the powers of the mob taking action. The mob becomes an anti-family.

The mob is the creation of Satan's plan to destroy God's concept about human beings. The mob seeks power, not from God, but from the god of chaos and anarchy. When people join in a mob, they really do sense some form of spiritual power: that is power from below. People will do things when swallowed up by a mob that they would never ordinarily do. People say, I could never believe that was me doing those crazy things. When people gather together to defy some aspect of reality that they want to change there are only two ways change can be achieved: through passive resistance and through violence. For example, if the government outlaws some activity that the Bible mandates, the Christian and the Church will just keep doing it. During the 1980's, there were attempts to destroy Christian schools, mainly in Ohio and Nebraska. Christians kept on doing what they knew to be right. Some pastors were actually jailed. Some parents sent their children out of state to protect them. When I lived in Seattle at that time, a neighbor took in a high school student who was sought by the police in Nebraska. His crime, attending a school not authorized by the state. Eventually, Christian schools became accepted nationwide. No riots, nothing was burned down, and no shots were fired. Open defiance proved, at that time, that good people working together can change the laws of the land. [Times have changed and today those Christians who commit acts of open defiance are considered 'terrorists' and enemies of the State. There are even re-education camps built to house such open resistance to the new divine order of the laws of the land.

*

Modern American 21st century Democracy could better be described as government by the mob, of the mob, and for the mob. But it is not a mob in rebellion against government, but a new form of tyranny where the elites create a permanent state of mob rule. The Overlords create a mob mentality in the people, and the cry out, we must do what the people demand. The mob is promised that their 'sinful' deeds will be tolerated and they need no longer fear the repercussions of breaking the laws of Western and Christian civilizations. The mob is promised that their equality can be achieved without their having to conform to outdated Standards of behavior. The mob can be assured that their success in life will not be tied to any behavioral choices they choose. The mob will be protected from the religious fanatics who have discriminated against them in the past. The unruly and immoral mob has always been a majority in any nation, despite the form of government or any particular time in history. The mob in the New Testament, when given a choice between freeing the criminal Barabbas and freeing Jesus from jail, chose Barabbas. This is more than just a story about Jesus, it represent how democracies always function.

Matthew 27:15.   Now at *that* feast the governor was wont to release unto the people a prisoner, whom they would. **16** And they had then a notable prisoner, called Barabbas. **17** Therefore when they were gathered together, Pilate said unto them, Whom will ye that I release unto you? Barabbas, or Jesus which is called Christ? **18** For he knew that for envy they had delivered him.

19   When he was set down on the judgment seat, his wife sent unto him, saying, Have thou nothing to do with that just man: for I have suffered many things this day in a dream because of him. **20** But **the chief priests and elders** persuaded the multitude **that they should ask Barabbas, and destroy Jesus**. **21** The governor answered and said unto them, Whether of the twain will ye that I release unto you? They said, Barabbas. **22** Pilate saith unto them, What shall I do then with Jesus which is called Christ? *They* all say unto him, Let him be crucified. **23** And the governor said, Why, what evil hath he done? But they cried out the more, saying, Let him be crucified.

24   When Pilate saw that he could prevail nothing, but *that* rather a tumult was made, he took water, and washed *his* hands before the multitude, saying, I am innocent of the blood of this just person: see ye *to it*. **25** Then answered all the people, and said, His blood *be* on us, and on our children.

26 Then released he Barabbas unto them: and when he had scourged Jesus, he delivered *him* to be crucified.

Those who can persuade the mob can control the actions of the rulers who fear any mob under the control of the hidden leaders of a nation. Some call it Mobocracy.

*

The first task for any tyrant who wants to rule through mobocracy is to know how to form a mob. The first step is to create victims out of people who through every fault of their own have been left behind in multiple areas where others have succeeded. Because America advertising has created a land of envy and covetousness, it is easy to appeal to the failures in life as having been cheated. It is a conspiracy theory that excuses those whose lack of motivation, i.e. laziness, has left them feeling left out of the good life—the one you see on TV. There are almost an unlimited number of people when you live in a nation where riches are on display everywhere—particularly the athletes, the movie starts, the recording artists, and the cable shows which feature the lifestyles of the rich and famous. When studies have been looked into those who took part in many riots, it was surprising to find that many had good jobs. These people have been led to identify with those who are failures. Blacks have been taught to be eternal victims. Rich Blacks still identify themselves as ex-slaves or consider poor Blacks their brothers. In fact, the identification of all multi-racial Blacks as being African of heritage, has been an important part of creating Black racial unity—far exceeding their actual numbers. A 50 percent Philippine and a 25 per cent Black is considered a Black person, not a Philippine. In fact, the very large number of Philippines and Asians in America have not been organized into a mob. Mobs have been organized around those who are at war with Western and Christian Civilizations. Those races who have strong religious beliefs are difficult to form into mobs. [There are religions that are more political than being a religion and those are not really mobs but religions of hate.]

*

The American educational system has long since abandoned education in favor of producing various forms of class and racial hatred. Before a mob can be formed, a class of people must be prepared to have a mob mentality. That is one of the functions of American Education. "Young people are being corrupted, discouraged, deflated, frustrated, over-burdened, and deceived. If you are a parent you need to find out who is trying to alienate your children's affection and persuade them to abandon the principles you have taught them. You need to find out who is teaching the young to hate family loyalty, Christian morality and Christian individuals, hate honest scientific investigation, hate independence, self-responsibility and achievement."[137] The above is a warning to parents that their children are being turned into a controllable mob in the school that is supposed to be educating them.

When you destroy a child's heritage, they become morally and culturally homeless. And when they look around for companionship, they gravitate toward others who are in the same homeless situation. However, because homeless souls cannot bond, they, in reality, become a mob. Mobs are looking for a leader to tell them who they are and what they are to do in life. Of course, the Overlords have designed modern American culture to appeal to these spiritual naked individuals. These students are like those lost in the woods and then someone comes along and tells them—I will lead you out of the woods. Not surprisingly, the mob is instructed that they can establish their identities by partaking of the numerous sensuous pleasures offered to them. You see, you do not need an ideology to bond with lost individuals: you just need to share the same experiences. The party atmosphere of college is designed to form sensual mobs.

During my years in the 1960's, a shared hatred for the Vietnam War and President Johnson created a bond with strangers. I was amazed how quickly people could become 'friends' just by joining into a motivated mob. Also, a good leader can easily impose his will upon any undirected mob. This is possible because Western Civilization and the American culture of trust had broken down. I regard the cover-up of the assassination of JFK as the beginning of the fall of trust. There was no internet back then to hold the mainstream media up to any scrutiny—everybody trusted Walter Cronkite—but something did not seem right. President Johnson was a known 'criminal'. Then there was the Gulf of Tonkin Incident, and we were all off to war. The CIA introduced the drug culture into the college campuses, and the 60's rock groups gave expression to an angry generation. Those of us raised in the Leave it to Beaver culture felt like the 60's had killed that idyllic world. The minor problems that Beaver faced had now become global issues and there were no Ward and June Cleaver to guide us anymore: no one to say, it is okay, you or we can handle it. I still remember the loneliness I felt as I sat before my Draft Board pleading my case.

Mobs did not form in the 1950's. The civilization of that era provided an environment of reality: whatever a person desired could be found within that

---

137 Erica Carle. The Hate Factory: Teaching Children to Hate. Author House. 2008. P. xv.

culture. If a person felt incomplete, the problem was not in society, but in himself. Most people in America still believed that the Image of God resided in man, and that any culture that encouraged that image to express itself was considered adequate. The Overlords needed to break down that image. It first started in the State Universities, and then spread to the lower schools. Darwinian Man replaced Godly Man. In the 1970's, this view of man spread throughout the culture. All kinds of self-help books were published and psychological healing retreats became popular. Usually located in a pristine environment, these retreats promised to restore man to some kind of wholeness where he could feel at home with the world again. The 1970s was considered the decade of 'Me'. The camaraderie of the 60s had passed, and everyone was faced, all alone, with the task of finding a job—often with a meaningless degree. A person might reply when asked his major: I have a degree in the history of student revolutions. Just the degree you need to become an 'associate' at a box store, or if you are lucky, a coffee Barista. [Yes, I know the word meant bartender until 1982 when it became applied to a person who servers coffee behind a counter. Also, the word 'associate' had a more dignified meaning, such as a law firm associate or business partner.]

*

So, how was the image of God within man destroyed so that a mob mentality could be installed in its place? Remember, spiritual forces are at work here. It is a lot more than just animals responding to physical stimuli, i.e. Pavlov's dogs. Also, remember, men have souls designed for communion with God and others. Crowds or the mob have no element of Christian or Godly power. There really are dark forces or powers that can take over a crowd and turn it into a herd of stampeding buffalo. [When herds of buffalo in the old west would stampede, they destroyed everything in their path. Whole farms could be destroyed, including the people living on the farm. One herd actually destroyed a whole town made up of wooden structures.] Mobs not only destroy physical entities, they also destroy ideas and the reputations of people. Every mob demands satisfaction in their thirst for power, i.e. Satanic power.

I call mob logic, the logic of the illogical. It may sound incongruous, but one of the weapons of the mob, that is demanding tolerance for its behavior or beliefs, is intolerance. The mob is based upon the belief that everyone is equal and the enemies of the mob who insist upon tolerance for themselves means those people are not equal, i.e. and thus are asking for tolerance. Intolerance is directed at someone who is stepping away from the crowd. The politicized mob requires tolerance for everyone except those who are not part of the mob. During the World Wars, patriotism, loyalty, and nationalism were created to create a national mob: all equal in supporting the war. Those against the war were not tolerated. Those people who expressed intolerance toward the mob was an act of superiority against those who did not measure up to their own anti-war standards. Mobs cannot accept any behavioral standards except their own. Those that seek to bring in any outside ethical standards into a mob are quickly intimidated into compliance with the inclusiveness of the mob. A moral mob is a contradiction. This is where the problem of creating a nation of crowds becomes a problem. The mob demands a culture of total equality for everyone, but only for those inside the mob. All others must be confined to a FEMA camp for re-education into the brotherhood of the mob. Mobs subsist on emotion, not logic.

The crowd or mob must be intolerant of those who are not tolerant: intolerance cannot be tolerated. The American mob mentality, i.e. the woke agenda, is totally at war with those who do not conform to the standards of American mob culture. "Nothing destroys liberty as surely and quickly as the spread of intolerance. ... Tolerance is mutual respect. ... The ignorant man always believes he is right; the educated man seldom."[138] Martin wrote the above in 1930. Because of American education, this idea has been turned on its head. The college students have been transformed into the new ignorant class. College education has become an indoctrination center for mind control. The radicals of the 1960's, in time, took their views into the universities and put into practice their hatred of Western Civilization on a grand scale. I have purchased a number of college textbooks and I have not found one popular textbook that defends Western or Christian Civilization. Textbooks have become promoters of intolerance to the American Way of Life.

The result of this training, i.e. indoctrination, college graduates have become an elitist mob. The old mobs were controlled by emotional thinking, the new mobs are controlled by elitist anti-Christian, and anti-American thinking. The new mob believes in its ideas and considers other ideas as misinformation,

---

[138] Martin. P. 93-194.

ancient ideologies, and products of a rich man's culture. Textbooks will state that because America has not produced a culture of equality, it is seriously flawed and needs to be replaced with a culture of equal distribution of, not only of opportunity, but of the wealth that used to be derived from hard work or advanced degrees. Now take the following quote from 1930 and the angry depression farmers, etc. and apply it to today's college-educated mob.

"Hence, intolerance is the device by which the ignorant, the unadjusted, the mentally immature, strive to lord it over the community—always of course in the interest, not of their own power, but of 'Eternal Right.' The less a man has in him, the more intemperate he becomes in the vindication of the right. Intolerance leads to the dominance of the less civilized elements of the population. For tolerance is a civilized attitude toward life and only the magnanimous man attains it. **The dominance of the intolerant is always and everywhere a revolt against civilization.** And the converse of this statement is also true: wherever men are in revolt against the advance of civilization, they develop a spirt of intolerance."[139] (Emphasis added.) It started in the Berkeley riots at the University of California in the 1960's. The mob kept shouting, 'Hey Hey, Ho Ho, Western Civilization has to go.' History does repeat itself as the mob in the New Testament who demanded the criminal Barabbas over Jesus. This time it was Communism over Western Civilization.

Martin continues on about the nature of the crowd. "The crowd mind [Think Woke Mind] is essentially a conformist mind; and this is so even when the crowd is openly indulging itself in antisocial behavior. Crowds seldom interpret their motives correctly. Each crowd fabricates a system of obsessive ideas which serves to disguise its real motive, to disarm opposition, to justify its behavior in the minds of its members and hold them together in 'the movement.' The ideas of the crowd become stereotyped, standardized. Having made up its mind, it refuses to listen to the expressions of dissenting opinion. Objectors are thrown out, howled down, thrust aside, trampled. ... Dissent on the part of its members is disloyalty, treachery. ... **Every crowd, if it has the power, will resort to censorship and will ruthlessly destroy those who resist it. It wants freedom of speech only to spread its own propaganda, meanwhile making strenuous efforts**

---

[139] Martin. P. 195.

to prevent contrary propagandas from getting a hearing."[140] (Emphasis added.) Remember, the above was written in 1920, not 2020.

The above scenario is repeated over and over on College campuses. Conservative speakers or those speakers who challenge the woke agenda, are shouted down to silence their message and prevent the meeting from taking place. There are often subtle threats of violence if certain speakers are allowed on campus. Universities often cancel certain speakers in the name of maintaining peace on the campus. The mob mentality has taken over the American Educational System. This not an accident. Religious views or professors who defend traditional religious and political thinking have a difficult getting tenure, or even getting hired in the first place. An American mob has replaced a culturally free environment in which people are allowed to behave in a legal manner. This politically correct mob laid the foundation for the current political tyranny imposed from Washington, D. C. A manufactured mob was used to train the people to submit to a governmental mob used to impose tyranny upon the people.

The mob mentality is one area that Americans traditionally have had a problem with. The first Amendment guarantees freedom of speech, and yet that freedom of speech is being used to silence the speech of those outside the mob. Not only that, the tyrant will often place his people inside the mob to direct their actions against those who oppose the policies of the tyrant. Freedom of speech is being used to destroy freedom of speech. "Freedom of speech is, I believe, the liberty on which all other liberties depend."[141] As I write this, the following was on the internet today:

> Microsoft founder and billionaire Bill Gates called for the use of artificial intelligence to combat not just "digital misinformation" but "political polarization."

> He is only the latest to call for the use of either AI or algorithms to shape what people say or read on the internet. The danger of such a system is evident where free speech, like resistance, could become futile.

---

[140] Martin. P. 196
[141] Martin. P. 197.

In an interview on a German program, "Handel blatt Disrupt," Gates calls for unleashing AI to stop certain views from being "magnified by digital channels." The problem is that we allow "various conspiracy theories like QAnon or whatever to be blasted out by people who wanted to believe those things."

Gates added that AI can combat "political polarization" by checking "confirmation bias."

Confirmation bias is a term long used to describe the tendency of people to search for or interpret information in a way that confirms their own beliefs. It is now being used to dismiss those with opposing views as ignorant slobs dragging their knuckles across the internet — people endangering us all by failing to accept the logic behind policies on COVID, climate change or a host of other political issues.[142]

Of course, it is not the politically correct mob that the ruling elites fear, it is those on the internet who oppose the imposition of government-controlled mob rule upon everyone. The excuse for censorship of free speech is often to protect the nation from idiots, the vocally immoral, and those who promote treason. "Censorships exist ostensibly to stamp out error and vice; their real purpose, however, is to stamp out the truth. ... Men who are officially occupied with the prevention of error have little time for the pursuit of truth."[143] [Again, written in 1920.] There are plenty of fools on the internet, just as there are plenty of fools on TV and inside government. Some say that an AI computer is capable of weeding out truth from error. Does that mean that an AI computer will start teaching creationism or ask for the saving of aborted babies? The only reason a government would ever submit to the rule of an AI computer would be if it supported the current tyranny. A computer that told a President to resign would quickly have its power shut off, at the least.

[142] Jonathan Turley. https://jonathanturley.org/2023/02/15/free-speech-is-futile-gates-goes-full-borg-on-ai-censorship/
[143] Martin. P. 199.

Chapter Twenty-Four: Democratic Rule versus Mob Rule.

America started out as an Republic, but after the Civil War, the nation was transformed into a Democracy. However, the next step was the creation of American Mobocracy. A Republic separates powers and keeps laws on a local level to be the primary focus of the nation's people. After the Civil War, a new kind of individualism was born. American has always been occupied by people who considered themselves individuals, but the individual lived within an environment or culture of responsibilities and obligations. The post-Civil War Amendments created a new relationship between men and their government. Previously, the people had rights to protect them from the government. Now, the people had rights to protect them from other people. The private individual was born and who was empowered by the government to live apart from any civilization of community controls. The government became of the people, for the people, and by the people—the people as individuals. This was the real revolution in America, not the one in 1776,

The local community, which formerly acted as the protector of the individual from outside influences, was transferred to the central government. When the community was murdered by the government of Lincoln, the local individual was exposed as not having a true self. No man becomes an individual all by himself. He grows up with other people and the way a person interacts with these work to develop a person's character. A feral child turns out to be little more than a higher form of an animal. All are born with genetic tendencies, but these tendencies can only develop through the interaction with others. For the tyrant, this is a problem. This maturing process creates individuals who have the power to stand alone within a local culture. The South was noted for its strong local cultures which created some fantastic individuals. It is these individuals that Lincoln sought to extinguish by destroying Southern Culture. Dependent creatures, with no other source of identity, fit in perfectly with any totalitarian order.

One of the first writers to observe the change was Gustav Le Bon. He wrote the book, *The Crowd,* in 1896. He was able to see the future. He was one of the few to recognize that the very foundations of government were changing. Many have written about the changes brought about by the Industrial Revolution, the

Scientific Revolution, and the Financial Revolution of the 19th century. However, Le Bon recognized maybe the biggest unreported revolution—the necessity of governments to appeal to the crowds, the masses, and the mobs of society. In the past, local organizations or churches might have political clout and those in power might have to appease such entities in order to maintain control. Political order started in the local forms of government. There were times the masses might riot or fight each other in the streets, but governments could, for the most past, ignore the masses. The masses were expected to obey regardless of who was in power. If the masses got out of hand, there was always the military to restore order. However, in the 19th center the old centers of the real power were collapsing. Lincoln's War contributed to the collapse of local centers of control. When he freed the slaves, and when he destroyed the traditional Southern culture, the individual became lost in a sea of social and cultural anarchy. The days of local and self-government were destroyed and some new form of order was needed to place the old.

LeBon wrote in the late 19th century: "The present epoch is one of these critical moments in which the thought of mankind is undergoing a process of transformation. … The memorable events of history are the visible effects of the invisible changes of human thought. … Two fundamental factors are at the base of this transformation. The first is the destruction of those religious, political, and social beliefs in which all the elements of our civilization are footed. The second is the creation of entirely new conditions of existence and thought as the results of modern scientific and industrial discoveries."[144] However, what is not always mentioned is the fall of Western and Christian Civilizations. Civilizations are the invisible rulers over the masses. Just as fish live in water, the masses live in a civilization. The people do not always make conscious decisions based upon some aspect of freedom of choice, but just make decisions based upon the accepted worldview in which they live. The masses do what everyone else is doing.

The modern idea of personal freedom is totally different from that which existed during the 1000 year reign of Christendom. Freedom was not political—like choosing your king—and it was not religious—like choosing your religion.

---

[144] Gustave Le Bon. The Crowd. Ernst Benn Limited. 1896, 1952. P. 13-14.

Those accepted parts of a culture in which everyone unquestionably believes define a civilization. Just as fish cannot live outside of water, the masses cannot live outside of a Civilization. In a sense, this actually frees men from having to make too many choices. Freedom becomes something entirely different in a Christian culture. Freedom means not being restrained from serving God and others in ways that God has called a person and the talents given to each person. When people do not have to fight over what Civilization a nation should adopt, they are really liberated to pursue issues that really matter: relationships within a community.

"While all our ancient beliefs are tottering and disappearing, while the old pillars of society are giving way one by one, the power of the crowd is the only force that nothing menaces, and of which the prestige is continually on the increase. The age we are about to enter will in truth be THE ERA OF CROWDS. Scarcely a century ago the traditional policy of European States and the rivalries of sovereigns were the principles factors that shaped events. The opinion of the masses scarcely counted, and most frequently indeed did not count at all. ...the voice of the masses has become preponderant. It is this voice that dictates their conduct to kings, whose endeavor is to take not of its utterances. The destinies of nations are elaborated at present in the heart of the masses, and no longer in the councils of princes."[145]

The decline of the Church and Christendom opened the door to the Kingdom of Satan and its power to replace the controlling powers of Christian culture with the controlling powers of the individual rebel against God and His Laws of Civilization. "The entry of the popular classes into political life—that is to say, in realty, their progressive transformation into governing classes—is one of the most striking characteristic of our epoch of transition."[146] Western and Christian Civilizations acted as a great restrainer upon the evil nature of man. When Civilizations are strong, the general perception becomes that men are really good at heart. If men can but be granted freedom, there will become some sort of millennial paradise upon earth. The thinking is that Civilizations, rather

---

[145] Le Bon. P. 14-15.
[146] Le Bon. P. 15.

274

than restraining evil, act to suppress the good that dwells in every man. If these old orders can be cast aside, then the true man can be released: That is Satan's message to the liberated masses.

Men believe that God's Laws do not limit the evil that men can do, but actually keep men from becoming the gods that Satan promises if men will but cast off their chains, i.e. Biblical Laws. Religion and religious culture are the opiates of the people that keep men from knowing what they can do when their own power is released. Two political systems are offered to the masses as replacements for the old order: Socialism and Communism. Each promises to create a national commune where everyone can do as they please without having to worry about consequences. Governments are there to provide a safety net whenever a person falls. Men dream of some idyllic Atlantis where the people could unleash their inner most desires and not feel locked into a culture or religion that imprisons fallen man in a strait jacket of rules and social controls. Le Bon saw the danger in this new order for the masses: "The dogmas whose birth we are witnessing will soon have the force of the old dogmas; that is to say, the tyrannical and sovereign forces of being above discussion. The divine right of the masses is about to replace the divine right of kings."[147]

When Satan unleashes his kingdom, men operate under the illusions he plants within the minds of man. Men think if they can just rid themselves of the God concept, then they would be liberated from Laws, obligations, responsibilities, and guilt—much like any other god. This age of the liberated individual followed the release of Charles Darwin's *Origen of the Species.* Even though many did not want to admit it publically, Darwin killed God and provided the key to the jail cell in which the Bible had enclosed mankind. The new scriptures for the common man is science. Darwin proved that science can answer the true questions of life. It was during the 19th century that Comte launched the science of man, i.e. sociology. More on that later, but the masses transferred their faith from the old order to the new order of man, science, and the new power of collective man. I might add, there is also fake science: fake

_____

[147] Le Bon. P. 16.

walks on the moon; fake vaxxxines, and fake news. However what the masses do not know, but the new powers that can defy God are also FAKE.

*

In the late 19th century, England recognized they had a problem with the emergence of a mass society. Previously, people would submit, more or less passively, to the demands of the nation. Children in factories, men going to war, and the terrible conditions of the new factory and urban cities. The masses were involved in merely the need to survive. The industrial revolution at first needed an abundance of laborers—that is why the factories turned to small children for cheap labor. However, in time, it seemed that the industrial revolution was keeping too many people alive through cheaper foods and with improvements in the quality of life, i.e. sanitation. Thomas Malthus wrote *An Essay on the Principle of Population,* in 1798. He predicted that the Industrial Revolution was improving conditions so much that in time, the growth of the population would outstrip the ability of the earth to feed the masses. The population then was estimated at one billion, compared to today's seven billion. It seems the fear of too many people goes back a long time. The real fear is that the Overlords understand that there are a lot more people than there are ruling elites. The fear of the masses revolting against their rulers became desperate by 1900. Something had to be done.

What England did in the late 1800's was to adopt a national welfare program to keep the masses in control before a better solution could be implemented. It is similar to the 'Bread and Circuses' of ancient Rome except England offered Bread and National Glory. The greatness of being an Englishman was indoctrinated into everyone. William Shakespeare wrote the following:

"This royal throne of kings, this sceptered isle, This earth of majesty, this seat of Mars, This other Eden, demi-paradise, This fortress built by Nature for herself Against infection and the hand of war, This happy breed of men, this little world, This precious stone set in the silver sea, Which serves it in the office of a wall Or as a moat defensive to a house, **Against the envy of less happier lands,--This blessed plot, this earth, this realm, this England."** (Emphasis added.)

William Ernst Henley (1849-1903) wrote the poem *My England.*

WHAT have I done for you,
  England, my England?
What is there I would not do,
  England, my own?
With your glorious eyes austere,
As the Lord were walking near,
Whispering terrible things and dear
  As the Song on your bugles blown,
    England—
Round the world on your bugles blown!

He also wrote the poem *Invictus,* which glorifies the English national spirit.

Out of the night that covers me
Black as the pit from pole to pole,
I thank whatever gods may be
For my unconquerable soul.

In the fell clutch of circumstance,
I have not winced nor cried aloud.
Under the bludgeonings of chance
My head is bloody, but unbowed.

Beyond this place of wrath and tears
Looms but the Horror of the shade,
And yet the menace of the years
Finds, and shall find, me unafraid.

It matters not how strait the gate,
How charged with punishments the scroll,
I am the master of my fate
I am the captain of my soul. (Emphasis Added.)

In a sense, England became every common man's god upon the earth. England's history does reveal a number of heroes, and a number who became heroes only after their death. The freedom and leisure that the upper classes enjoyed did produce men who devoted themselves to intellectual achievements. Men [Or White men as the critics like to say.] became philosophers, playwrights, scientists, generals, men of letters, financers, Industrialists, theologians, missionaries, explorers, businessmen, evangelists, philanthropists, barristers, and of course, many kings and queens. I know of no history that I enjoy more than the reading of English history. It created the Western Civilization that ordered public life for three hundred years. That Civilization spread throughout the world and became the standard of what was called 'civilized man.' It is this nation that the masses were taught to love and to serve—as long as they both shall live.

This history led the British to conquer much of the world. Young British men fought and died throughout the world. Their graves not only mark the extent of the British Empire, but its success in selling *England* as an idea to the masses of the land. Maybe the most successful example of this is how the British just kept dying and dying in WWI without any rebellion. The French army grew tired of the killing and many, and I mean many, just refused to go on fighting. A normal human reaction if you read any of the accounts of trench warfare. England is typified by the last words of Captain Smith to his crew on the Titanic: 'Be British.' Everyone knew that those words carried a tradition which everyone was supposed to uphold. The masses did not think they were serving ruling elites, or some business class, they served England and their King. This era reveals how brilliantly England was able to create laws that everyone wanted to obey because they were the laws of the people, i.e. Common Law.

*

America is a lot different than England in many ways. If you read behind the American Propaganda history, you will find a history of riots and battles from the very beginning of America's history. There was the Whiskey Rebellion of 1794. Then the Shay's Rebellion of 1785. Then Fries's Rebellion of 1799. In fact, there were around seventy or more riots or acts of 'insurrection' in America in the 19th century, not counting the battles of the Civil War. America was a nation of unruly masses who adopted anti-government stances. America did not become a 'great' nation in itself until the massive propaganda campaign of the First World War. America has always had a problem with the mob. The laws of the land have never been hallowed as in England. Americans have never had a king or a King's Law. Also, I have a lot of history textbooks in my library which picture America as nation of people who have been exploited by a ruling class of 'Robber Barons' or other ruling elites, or elitist organizations such as the American Medical Association.

This history of American violence can be quite revealing. Le Bon reveals that the mob can serve one important function. When the laws of a nation are perceived to be illegitimate laws, the people respond by disobeying those laws. If there is one thing true about the United States it is this: the masses have never treated American law like it came from any divine source or even from respected authorities that place a righteous law above the law of the rulers. Le Bon again:

"Civilizations as yet have only been created and directed by a small intellectual aristocracy, never by crowds. Crowds are only powerful for destruction. Their role is always tantamount to a barbarian phase. A civilization involves fixed rules, discipline, a passing from the instructive to the rational state, forethought for the future, an elevated degree of culture—all of them conditions that crowds, left to themselves, have invariably shown themselves incapable of realizing. In consequence of the purely destructive nature of their power, crowds act like those microbes which hasten the dissolution of enfeebled or dead bodies. When the structure of a civilization is rotten, it is always the masses that bring about its downfall."[148] It is my contention, when the Declaration of Independence and the U.S. Constitution rejected Biblical Laws, the chance of a true universal American Civilization was made impossible. America came under the judgment of God dating from 1776. Ever since that time, America has become a nation of lawbreakers who feel no allegiance to the American legal system: it is merely the powerful imposing their wills upon the less powerful.

If the laws of the land are not considered divine, the people come to believe that all laws are mere matters of expediency: Laws are created to benefit

---

[148] Le Bon. P. 18.

one class over another. That is why the Caesars claimed to be a god: that would validate their rule in the eyes of the masses. Why did Kings claim the divine right to rule? To confirm the laws in the minds of the people. When the American Revolution established a secular nation, there was no divinity in the land. Laws became a means where the rich could exploit the people for their own gain. The feeling is this: if the rich can pass laws to line their pockets, why cannot the poor also pass laws to enhance their bank accounts. There is nothing in any law that mandates obedience except the power of the sword—which governments have in their sheath. Control the government, you control the laws. Control the laws, and everyone not protected by those laws becomes a slave to the lawmakers.

Actually, there was a source of divinity in the post-Revolution government: the voice of the people is the voice of God. The masses were told that they were now in charge of their own lives and could make their own laws. And many actually believed that. That is one of those great American myths that rulers use to seduce the masses into obedience. In the Declaration of Independence, a lie was planted into the minds of men in order to enlist their powers to fight a war against England. The lie: all men are created equal. A more true statement might be: all men are created human. In that they are equal. But equality is not a Biblical doctrine. In fact, equality is the soil from which revolutions and civil wars are born. When a man is told he is equal and discovers he is not equal, then someone must be blamed for his current condition. Paul teaches that God is sovereign over all men and each man according to his place in life.

Romans 9:9. For this *is* the word of promise, At this time will I come, and Sara shall have a son. **10** And not only *this*; but when Rebecca also had conceived by one, *even* by our father Isaac; **11** (For **the children being not yet born,** neither **having done any good or evil**, that the purpose of God according to election might stand, **not of works, but of him that calleth;) 12** It was said unto her, The elder shall serve the younger. **13** As it is written, **Jacob have I loved, but Esau have I hated. 14** What shall we say then? *Is there* unrighteousness with God? God forbid. **15** For he saith to Moses, **I will have mercy on whom I will have mercy, and I will have compassion on whom I will have compassion. 16** So then *it is* not of him that willeth, nor of him that runneth, but of God that sheweth mercy. **17** For the **scripture saith unto Pharaoh**, Even for this same purpose have I raised thee up, that I might shew my power in thee, and that my name might be declared throughout all the earth. **18** Therefore hath he mercy on whom he will *have mercy*, and whom he will he hardeneth. **19** Thou wilt say then unto me, Why doth he yet find fault? For who hath resisted his will? **20** Nay but, O man, who art thou that repliest against God? Shall the thing formed say to him that formed *it*, **Why hast thou made me thus? 21** Hath not the potter power over the clay, of the same lump to make one vessel unto honour, and another unto dishonour? **22** *What* if God, willing to shew *his* wrath, and to make his power known, endured with much longsuffering the vessels of wrath fitted to destruction: **23** And that he might make known the riches of his glory on the vessels of mercy, which he had afore prepared unto glory,

When a nation invokes God's laws over the land, the people will come to understand that God is sovereign over the people and the culture. There is an acceptance that life may not be fair in one's own eyes, but God is fair even though men are not. In the school playground, everyone wants to be the quarterback— no one wants to block for him. When a society's laws become mere human constructions, then the laws of the playground become transferred to the general culture. In God's culture, people are created to play a special role in their place in society. Greatness is not in the accumulation of wealth or social status, but serving others where God has planted you. Because Americans have been obsessed with their own personal equality, everyone pursues a life of being more equal than others. Because of that, America has become a nation in search of everyone wanting to become a king over some personal domain, and not pursue a life of personal service and believing that one's reward is from God, not man. Job writes of the folly of every common man thinking he can run the world better than those appointed to office.

Job 19:10 Delight is not seemly for a fool; much less for a servant to have rule over princes.

The primary form of government in the Bible is self-government. Once that has been achieved, that kind of person is free to enter into service to others.

Proverbs 25:28. He that *hath* no rule over his own spirit *is like* a city *that is* broken down, *and* without walls.

From a people that have no walls, we have become a nation that has no borders and with that, anarchy follows. When people demand equal rights to create their own laws, God judges that nation. One of the ways that happens is that the masses grant equality to the children and the women. And they become rulers equally over the nation. Americans say that such equality is good. God says it will bring a nation under judgment.

Isaiah 3:4. And **I will** give children *to be* their princes, and babes shall rule over them. **5** And **the people shall be oppressed, every one by another, and every one by his neighbour: the child shall behave himself proudly against the ancient, and the base against** the honourable.

Isaiah 3:12. *As for* my people, children *are* their oppressors, and women rule over them. O my people, they which lead thee cause *thee* to err, and destroy the way of thy paths. **13** The LORD standeth up to plead, and standeth **to judge the people.**

Chapter Twenty-Five: In those days there was no king in Israel: every man did that which was right in his own eyes. (Judges 21:25)

When America was founded as a secular nation, there was no longer a 'king' over the land, i.e. King Jesus. [The battle cry of many Americans during the war was: No King but King Jesus. However, that changed quickly.][149] Under a Democracy, every man became his own king. Every man became a law unto himself because everyone was equal: no man could tell another man what he could or could not do. Another name for such a condition is mob rule. There have been multiple urban riots in the history of the United States. Most history books have neglected these riots because they do not fit into the official narrative. The only riots that make it into the textbooks are the urban racial riots—those damned White people causing trouble again. Actually, it is not race but the false belief that everyone is equal or everyone must be made equal. In the city where the government has the power to force some kind of equality, resistance in the form of riots will occur. Anytime a source of power attempts to use that power to force a lie upon the masses, there will be resistance.

One of the problems America had from the beginning is that it had few established classes such as in England and France. America prided itself on being a classless society: everyone begins life at the same starting line. However, Americans came to believe that the differences between people's amount of success represented some unfair hierarchy of favoritism hidden within the culture: there was something called systemic favoritism which favored some class of person over another. This creates a real problem because there is no way a person can succeed if the race is fixed from the beginning. Every person more successful than himself must have conspired against him in some way. The crowd, being a majority, feels it should be able to exert its power to change the social order to allow everyone to succeed and obtain a share of society's wealth. One's man inferiority has been caused by someone else's superiority. The mob cries out for social and equal justice, or the cities will burn. The blessings of society are perceived to be a zero sum endeavour: one man's success has cause another man to fail. This is why America has a history of riots and social conflicts.

---

[149] The battle cry during the Spanish American War was this: Remember the Maine, and to Hell with Spain. Times had changed.

The problem with American mobs is that they operate on the basis of images placed within their minds. Because mobs and crowds operate upon images and emotions, they are easily manipulated. The mob is open to suggestions planted by the ruling elites. One of the purposes of American education is to create a crowd mentality. It starts by so designing a child's education that he will be a real loser: he has been schooled to be incompetent. If this sounds too fantastic, remember the kingdom of Satan is operating within the United States. **Satan may oppose intelligent design being taught in the schools because the child is to learn all about 'intelligent' chaos.** Nature, not God, is the source of all order. However, nature is not perfect and it is up to man to bring order out of chaos. This is the first step in producing an army of young men who believe that when they join with the mob, i.e. chaos, **they can impose their order upon the chaos of American life.**

Remember, the school is not to produce ideas in the mind of the student, but images. One of the first images planed into the student's mind is that of the Boston Tea Party. Through the chaos of the staged event, order was produced through the American Revolution. Growing up in government schools, the images of American wars was a big part of every text book. Wars, riots, chaos, and change are all bundled together. In the textbook, these wars all produced victories for the American Way of Life and the American Empire. In the 1950's, we were repeatedly told, America had never lost a war. Somehow, the ability to kill others was a good thing. The impression was that America only fought a war when provoked by others. American violence ended up producing a better world with the evil scoundrels having been eliminated. It never dawned upon any of us that there were alternative to wars and that a lot of people made a lot of money off of wars. Americans were a good people and they did not do evil things.

In the 1960's, everything changed. The student rioters of that era eventually became the textbooks writers of today. The schools were still producing incompetents, but a new style of mob was being produced. The new mob no longer believed in the goodness of American Laws and Wars. American laws were designed to keep the rich White people in control of the nation. The old order imposed the restrictions of Biblical and Western Civilizations on the nation. The racial and student riots were a product of the previous generations believing that violence produced good results by the tearing down of the old European orders. Of course, that is the goal of the kingdom of Satan in the United States. His takeover of American Education enabled him to use the proclivity of Americans for violence for his own purposes.

American urban areas have always been hotbeds of violence. Remember, America rejected God and Biblical Law from the very beginning. Even the churches rejected the teachings of the Kingdom of God in favor of the ever popular revival meetings or positive thought teachings. Revivals produced 'Christianity' without Biblical Laws. Why? Because Satanic laws had already been installed as the foundation of the American Way of Life. The Churches did not mind opposing the sins of the individuals Americans, but it surely did not want to oppose the Satanic takeover of American Law. Remember, the Reformation split the churches into a thousand different solitary churches. These little private clubs had no power over the populist mob that was quite content with the money that a person earned by supporting the American Way of Life.

The mob was a willing executioner of the old order of what remained of Christendom. Today, the mob is doing the same thing by tearing down the last vestiges of Western Civilization and the American Way of life. The one thing that has remained common is that Satan is still in control of the American Crowd. Whoever is in control of the American Mob controls the nation. "Crowds are only capable of thinking in images are only to be impressed by images. It is only images that terrify or attract them and become motives of action. For this reason theatrical representations, in which the image is shown in its most clearly visible shape, always have an enormous influence on crowds. Bread and spectacular shows constituted for the plebeians of ancient Rome the ideal of happiness and they asked for nothing more. Throughout the successive ages this ideal has scarcely varied. Nothing has a greater effect on the imagination of crowds of every category than theatrical representations."[150] That is why false flag events will often focus on the killing of teenagers and younger ones. The picture of the

---

[150] Le Bon. P. 68.

dead at such an early age creates a dramatic image in the public mind. False flag events are theater: they must be vivid and dramatic.

The Randolph Hearst newspaper chain is given credit for starting the Spanish American War. He told his reporters to send a lot of pictures to his office. He reportedly said: You give me the pictures, and I will give you the war. He knew the value of controlling the masses through visual images. The America TV networks have made Hearst look like a true amateur when it comes to planting images into the minds of the American TV mob. People were persuaded to take an untested vaxxx through the image of people apparently dropping dead on the streets of Wuhan China. The people who control the images the masses see on their TV are the true rulers of America. The schools have created a dumb-downed populace and the Overlords produce the images of reality that the mob readily accept uncritically: in school, learning means you memorize and repeat back, uncritically. The schools claim that they teach their students by applying 'critical' thinking to the alternative media. Students will be asked to look at some alternative media and then be asked to compare what that site is saying when compared to government reports or network news. Students are not asked to think critically about the 'official' version of realty as taught in the schools or on the media. **If** the mainstream media and the government reports are true, then everything else is fake information. What should be questioned is that big **IF.**

*

"To know the art of impressing the imagination of crowds is to know at the same time the art of governing them."[151] However, while those conducting political campaigns use the imagery to control the voting of people, it is important to understand that mobs are not restrained by any laws. [One of the most affective campaign ads showed a nuclear bomb going off as a result of trigger-happy Goldwater becoming President. It was quite an image. So the people voted for a corrupt Johnson over the patriotic Goldwater.] Of course, advertisers also focus upon creating images in the minds of potential customers. But what I want to write about is how American has been a nation of illegal mobs for its entire history. Laws are very affective in Cactus Flats, but in urban centers, laws

---

[151] Le Bon. P. 71.

are far less effective in maintain an orderly civilization. There are no mobs in Cactus Flats, but there are in urban, anonymous centers.

In urban centers, the mobs are more likely to feel that they have become the victims of laws rather than being protected by such laws. The solution has been a war declared upon laws that do not benefit the mob. However, there is a hidden facet of the mob that is rarely mentioned. Most mobs do not just happen. No one has the power by themselves to get up in the morning with the idea of starting a riot. In reality, it takes an inner mob who have the skills to direct a mob into its appointed task. Mobs are the army of the Overlords. They take orders like any other army and are mostly used as diversions from the real problems of society: focus here, not over there. During my era of the 1960's, everyone was focused upon the racial and anti-war riots and demonstration. At the same time, Western and Christian Civilizations were being replaced by the New Order of the Ages. That is one Revolution that never made the news. When those riots had served their purpose, they suddenly ended in unison. The Overlords had won their war and called their troops back to their 'barracks'. The American culture of the 1950s had been killed and buried, never to rise again. Now the Overlords could begin the roll out of their New Order of the Ages.

So what is happening behind the scenes when there is blood in the streets? There is a fallacy behind every age when the people are showing their displeasure with current events. "The idea that institutions can remedy the defects of societies, that national progress is the consequence of the improvement of institutions and governments, and that social changed can be effected by decree—this idea, I say, is still generally accepted. It was the starting-point of the French Revolution, and the social theories of the present day upon it."[152] People thought that by destroying the old order a new order could be imposed upon the land and everyone would live happily ever after. That is the giant lie placed into the social thinking when Satan's kingdom is operating within a nation: the world can be made perfect by a benevolent dictator. Guardians of truth and justice can change the nation for the better with the proper controls. That is the stuff they

---

[152] Le Bon. P. 86.

teach in schools. Only a very powerful ruler can solve the problems of the current chaos and anarchy.

However, the Biblical view of reality is entirely different. A nation is not formed by a leader or by creating a Constitutional Committee. The very idea that the founders of America could create a nation is foolishness. Or that the Supreme Court has the power to change a nation for the better. Leaders, if they are to be successful, must build upon a society and culture that already exists. Almost two hundred years after the ratification of the United States Constitution, the Supreme Court declared that a Separation of Church and State was part of the original document. In the same way, the Court decided that the killing of babies was also part of the original 'intent' of the Founders. People are led to believe that the Court had thus changed the nation: Change the laws and you change the people. More foolishness. Bad laws can only be successful if the people are not already bad themselves.

"…institutions are the outcome of ideas, sentiments, and customs, and that ideas, sentiments, and customs are not to be recast by recasting legislative codes. A nation does not choose its institutions at will any more than it chooses the color of its hair or its eyes. Institutions and governments are the product of their racial and cultural heritage. They are not the creators of some epoch moment, but are created by it. Peoples are not governed in accordance with their caprices of the moment, but as their character determines that they shall be governed. **Centuries are required to form a political system and centuries needed to change it.** Institutions have no intrinsic value: in themselves they are neither good nor bad."[153] (Emphasis added.) The Founders of America did not create a nation. The nation had already been founded by the people that came here and established patterns of life that were based upon a Biblical Civilization. It was the King James Bible that created the values of a people before any nation attempted to impose values upon the people.

In fact, the Founders were at war with the nation that had been established over several hundred years—a nation without a centralized government. The Articles of Confederation attempted to reflect the values and

---

[153] Le Bon. P. 86.

the beliefs of the people. However, the Founders were influenced by the European Enlightenment thought. This system was based upon mankind's liberation from God. The Reformation liberated Man from the Vatican, but it was now time to create a new Reformation that liberated mankind from the God of the Bible. Biblical doctrines were interpreted as limiting man's potential. Men were destined to be the new gods of the earth, and needed to be liberated from the doctrines of the Bible. This is what the Founders believed. Some stated it openly, while others attempted to believe in an undefined god: Transcendentalism and the power of mankind were to become the new gods: gods both Christians and non-Christians were expected to accept as the gospel truth.

Le Bon understood the power of the common man's beliefs and how they shaped the culture in which he lives. These beliefs are an accumulation of centuries of a people living under a foundational assumption about the reality of the world. If you read the history of England, it might surprise you about the continuity of shared ideas that persisted over a thousand years. The assorted peoples that formed England had a 'racial' idea about the world that drove them in a certain direction. There were political conflicts; there were internal wars within the nation; and there were different 'cultures' within the nation, but somehow they were all Englishman. The assorted people formed a common race, a race that was greater than their internal conflicts. That is a mystery that is difficult for the modern American to understand. There were patriotic parades during the times of war, but everyone seemed to have a different idea about being an American. An Englishman had a history that seemed to bring unity to the Nation. American history has been one of one conflict after another. Even the 'motto' life, liberty and the pursuit of happiness means different things to every American.

I believe that is why the United States has been involved in one external war after another, and civil unrest has been constant ever since 1776. It seems, every group wants to impose its idea of America upon everyone else. Every group wants to establish laws that will bring about the America of their dreams. This is where the understanding of the Bible is essential. The Book lays out the foundations of a culture and a working social order that Americas never seemed to grasp. In short, a Biblical nation is founded upon One God; One Law, and One People. Americans could never agree upon any of the above. **If my One God it means a common acceptance of a universal law order that precedes any laws, America never had that.** The Puritan immigrants believed in the freedom of religion, but they could not agree upon a common interpretation of Biblical Laws. Religious freedom for the early immigrants meant a nation of 'thousands' of Biblical religions.   That will not create a unified nation. Only a universal acceptance of a common foundation for all laws can bind a people together.

For a time, early Americans did accept Blackstone's Commentaries on the Laws of England, but after the Revolution, the nature of laws became politicized. Laws did not come from a long common law tradition as in England, but were something the more powerful imposed upon the less powerful. Every out-of-power group sought ways to gain power so that it could pass the laws of their ideal nation. And if certain groups had no chance of obtaining any power at all, they rioted. Because the Constitution did not incorporate any definition of true law, it left it the people to fight over their version of laws. In a sense, the Constitution laid the foundation for civil unrest as each group sought to impose their law system upon everyone else.

And finally, there is no way Americans could come to any idea of who they were racially. Early on, Americans were mostly Englishman. Soon America was flooded with the Irish, Italians, and people from Germany. Today, those might be called one race, but not back then. Each group brought with them centuries of tradition that transcended a common skin color. There is a reason that the French, the Spanish, the Germans, and the English fought one war after another. They really did not consider themselves one nation or even having a common racial heritage. Freedom in America was more about allowing each group, each interpretation of the Bible, and each cultural heritage having a separate space from the others. Some of the urban riots were based upon differences that went back to their mother countries.

Americans have a history much like England, but they are less aware of their history. English people have a holy reverence for their thousand years of traditions. Americans have adopted a different view of reality: they have a reverence for the Constitution but only as a relic from their heroic past. Today, to call oneself a 'Constitutionalist' means, in many eyes, you could be suspected of being a terrorist. The Constitution is a symbol of the past but it has nothing to do with an American heritage that applies to today. For centuries, English traditions meant something to the people of that nation. A tradition that formed their institutions. The only traditions that Americans have really been proud of is America's ability to finance, and produce the weapons of war. Americans from the very first Indian Wars have been a nation of fighters. Manifest destiny was complete with wars against the British, French, Mexicans, and, of course, the Indians. Then once that was complete, America started its destiny to becoming a global empire. First the Spanish American war, then WWI, and then any other nation that stood in America's global destiny as being a light unto the nations. In the 1850s, America established the Yangtze River Patrol in China. **Americans had gunboats on the river from 1854 to 1947.** That is a long ways away from Cactus Flats. This reveals how early in America's history that the leaders of America wanted to establish a global empire with worldwide military outposts. Amazing.

Americans have inherited a history which they did not choose. And as Le Bon notes: "Moreover, it is in no way in the power of a people really to change its institutions. Undoubtedly, at the cost of violent revolutions, it can change their name, but in their essence they remain unmodified. … The destinies of peoples are determined by their character and not by their government."[154] As I write, it is the American government that is at war against its own people and the remnants of their hope in the United States as a good nation. The American government has been at war with various peoples its entire history. God blesses and protects a righteous nation and only in God can a nation's borders and traditions be protected from its enemies. America's war against the world has now turned inward—the last land it has not conquered—or so it thinks.

When the people will no longer publically profess the doctrines of the Bible, [Since the Declaration of Independence], they will look for 'natural' laws. What is not recognized is this: Americans had already abandoned the God of the Bible

---

[154] Le Bon. P. 87.

long before Thomas Jefferson declared it to be so. The problem: Nature's God is also fallen and imperfect. Since 1776, the nation has sought blessings and power from Satan's promise in the Garden of Eden to man: ye shall be as gods. In that absence of Biblical Law, and an understanding of man's fallen character, men will seek out other sources of power and blessings in opposition to God: the kingdom of Satan. Because of this, God has allowed the American government to now declare war against a wicked and perverse generation. It no longer fears the people of God and it knows there is nothing to fear from those who have aligned themselves with Satan's kingdom—after all, that is where the American leaders obtain their power.

*

Biblically, character building starts with the family. Then the church, parental education, the community, and local governments. That is why the Bible has been labelled a book for the small town. The above institutions are not available in the urban centers. Every city is on its way to becoming a Babylon. Americans love their cities because they have become a sources of great wealth. In the Bible, the symbol of the city is Babylon. For me, Babylon is a system of commerce and riches that has invaded every city. Every city represents a rebellion against the order of God. It then installs Satan's order which has produced a lifestyle based upon the acquisition of material wealth at the expense of personal character. The Bible states that such a system will come under his judgment.

Revelation 14:8. And there followed another angel, saying, Babylon is fallen, is fallen, that great city, because she made all nations drink of the wine of the wrath of her fornication.

Revelation 18:9. And the kings of the earth, who have committed fornication and lived deliciously with her, shall bewail her, and lament for her, when they shall see the smoke of her burning, **10** Standing afar off for the fear of her torment, saying, Alas, alas, that great city Babylon, that mighty city! for in one hour is thy judgment come. **11** And the merchants of the earth shall weep and mourn over her; for no man buyeth their merchandise any more: **12** The merchandise of gold, and silver, and precious stones, and of pearls, and fine linen, and purple, and silk, and scarlet, and all thyine wood, and all manner vessels of ivory, and all manner vessels of most precious wood, and of brass, and iron, and marble, **13** And cinnamon, and odours, and ointments, and frankincense, and wine, and oil, and fine flour, and wheat, and beasts, and sheep, and horses, and chariots, and slaves, and souls of men. **14** And the fruits that thy soul lusted after are departed from thee, and all things which were dainty and goodly are departed from thee, and thou shalt find them no more at all. **15** The merchants of these things, which were made rich by her, shall stand afar off for the fear of her torment, weeping and wailing, **16** And saying, Alas, alas, that great city, that was clothed in fine linen, and purple, and scarlet, and decked with gold, and precious stones, and pearls! **17 For in one hour so great riches is come to nought.** And every shipmaster, and all the company in ships, and sailors, and as many as trade by sea, stood afar off, **18** And cried when they saw the smoke of her burning, saying, What *city is* like unto this great city! **19** And they cast dust on their heads, and cried, weeping and wailing, saying, Alas, alas, **that great city, wherein were made rich all that had ships in the sea by reason of her costliness! for in one hour is she made desolate.**

American history is more than we are told in our school textbooks. One of good thing that Thomas Jefferson promoted, to his credit, was the ideal of the American farmer. His opposition was Alexander Hamilton who wanted to model America after the philosophy of the city. The question was always about what type of institutions the American government should promote to become the model upon which to build a nation. The problem was what type of character America should develop in order to achieve a chosen future for the nation. This choice and its consequences is rarely mentioned. Jefferson lost, and the future American was to be modeled after a secular, i.e. Satanic, view of reality. Few think of the choice as being a choice between God's and Satan's idea of personal character. No one talks about the spiritual warfare that determined the future of the nation. After all, a secular nation cannot introduce the spiritual conflicts that produced anti-Christian American history.

The last thing the Overlords want is someone with character. That is why they promoted the urban agenda in America. That agenda is even more visible as I write: homosexuality is good, perversion is good, and transgenderism is good. In fact, drug use is okay if controlled. Guns are bad. Satanism is good. The Bible is bad. Self-control and delayed gratification are bad. Sensual pleasures are the real purpose in life. In a sense, nothing has changed since the days of Alexander Hamilton. America was to be a nation in pursuit of wealth. The citizens of America are to serve their masters—the merchant class. As Calvin Coolidge stated: "After all, the chief business of the American people is business. They are profoundly concerned with producing, buying, selling, investing and prospering in the world." The statement has been mocked at times, but he stated the truth. Alexander Hamilton would have been proud.

Le Bon wrote this: "Peoples are governed by their character, and all institutions which are not intimately modelled on that character merely represent a borrowed garment, a transitory disguise."[155] One things revolutionaries do after having attained power is to take over the education of the young. The beliefs of the revolution must be passed on to the next generation or the revolution will have failed. Educational institutions are formed, and because revolutions are based upon establishing a New Atlantis or similar dreams, the institutions revolutionaries develop will reflect a false reality. By that I mean, a reality that does not reflect the reality of God's creation, but the reality created by man's rebellious mindset: man's laws are better than God's Laws. The revolutionaries adopt a common fallacy. "Foremost among them the dominant ideas of the present epoch is to be found the notion that instruction is capable of considerably changing men, and has for it unfailing consequence to improve them and even to make them equal."[156]

One of the silliest ideas is that by passing laws to force the young to attend a government school, that their minds can be changed for the betterment of mankind. All revolutionaries believe something like this: We have the power to destroy the old laws and introduce in their place, life-changing laws. Just like the Pharisees in the New Testament, men believe if they could produce the right laws and enforce those laws upon everyone, the world could be saved. The school system and the media, in the past, were responsible for creating great national myths which could bond the nation together. The belief in Democratic Laws based upon the desires of the masses has been the one idea that has held Americans together: we are not obeying the rich and the powerful, we are obeying ourselves. And as Americans, we are always free to change any laws we do not like. "General beliefs are the indispensable pillars of civilization; they determined the trend of ideas. They alone are capable of inspiring faith and

---

[155] Le Bon. P. 89.
[156] Le Bon. P. 90.

creating a sense of duty."[157]   The Overlords love to impose their laws and pretend that they reflect the will and wisdom of the people and their heritage. Yes, of the people, by the people, and for the people. And all Satan's people said Amen.

*

During the 1960's in the United States, the nakedness of American Laws were revealed. The Vietnam War was a war about the making of money for the Defense industry. The War was also about the control of the Golden Triangle and its lucrative drug trade. The Draft Law made every young man a potential slave to the powers of the government. At the same time, there were no laws to protect the value of the dollar and destroying the value of the people's money. America no longer inspired faith in the American Way of Life. While the government could appeal to patriotism in past wars and use modern propaganda to manipulate the masses, a fatal flaw was revealed to the Overlords: if they did not control the media, they could not control the people. In fact, the media that opposed the war was quickly changed to an entity that could be used by the Overlords. I believe the whole Watergate affair was like a test case to see if a controlled media could totally turn the masses against one of the popular presidents in history. In 1972 Nixon won the election with almost a unanimous Electoral College victory. Then the media was turned against him, and the masses were convinced Nixon should leave office. Why? Because the TV, night after night, told the masses that Nixon had to go. In fact, despite his obvious lack of charisma, he was probably one of the most honest Presidents in recent memory. Maybe that was his problem, he was a terrible liar. He just could not pull that off. He might start to lie and end up telling the truth.

A true revolution had occurred in the 1960s, and no one seemed to have noticed. Reality was now what the media said it was. Everything on TV was about Watergate for a long time. People were glued to their TV's to watch staged hearings. No one had time to time think about anything else. If someone did start to think outside the box, the media could bring up the gas shortages and those terribly long lines. In the meantime, Democratic Laws had been replaced by the Laws of the media. Reality was just what the media said it was. Corona-19 is going to kill half the population, so get the safe and effective Vaxxx. The people I

---

[157] Le Bon. P. 143.

knew who watched a lot of TV could not wait to schedule their 'lifesaving injection.' We all live in TV world. Or die, as the case may be.

Chapter Twenty-Six: The United States of violence.

I want to start by stating that I understand that every nation has had its times of social unrest. The peasants and the serfs were not always happy being peasants and serfs. And, sometimes, there were two groups who thought their man should be king. But America, which prided itself on being the ideal democracy, a light unto the world, has had a history of riots and internal violent social conflicts. In a sense, sometimes America's serfs actually did go to war with America's 'land owners.' The problem with any Democracy is that it creates a nation of winners and losers. And sometimes it goes deeper than that and it creates winners, losers, and more losers. Because of the way Presidential elections are held in the United States, Lincoln was elected with about 40 per cent of the vote. Thus 60 per cent voted against Lincoln. That is a lot of losers.

The second problem is that those losers can be subjected to laws or even a war they did not support. All people can say is his: Lincoln's war was not a popular war but it was fought within the rules of democracy, more or less. There is another problem in that the votes of the nation can be manipulated and controlled. A majority of the voters could have been bribed in some way. Actually, political campaigns are based upon not so subtle forms of bribery under the color government spending. Senators and Representatives are elected to obtain more money for a state from Washington than it sends to Washington. More winners and losers. There is another level of 'corruption' in a democracy. Once a Representative or Senator is elected and goes to Washington, he can also be bribed. After all, he bribed the voters to get elected, so why should not he be subject to 'legalized' bribery? A Senator can be offered a speaking tour where he is well paid, or he could be offered a giant book deal. Or he could be offered to be the head of an important committee. Offering positions of power can also be a bribe. Or, sometimes Senators are offered lucrative jobs should they lose an election. All of the above are considered legal bribes. Obviously there are many illegal bribes such as advice on which stocks to purchase and when to sell them.

Now everyone knows the above is going on all the time, especially the losers in the election process. So, why should anyone be forced to obey laws that the winners imposed upon the losers? Not only that, the losers look upon the laws as serving special interests, not the interests of the nation as a whole. That is why I believe there is little mention about how laws in America are really not laws at all from the Biblical perspective. Laws are perceived as a zero sum activity: favors granted to one group means taking favors away from some other group. Once a nation abandons God's laws, the laws really are selective enforcement of reality as perceived by the winners in any election. Because there are no divine laws in a nation, no law can be said to be a violation of reality as there is no absolute reality apart from God. Even the Constitution has been shown to as flexible as cooked piece of spaghetti. Each generation is able to say: this is what the Constitution really means.

The above reveals why America has been a nation of civil violence since its founding. Laws equal power and every group is seeking ways to find power. The weapon of choice for those who have been denied power is violence. Of course, this places Christians at a disadvantage in America because their weapons are spiritual, not matches. No ruler ever feared Christians calling down the judgment of God upon an evil tyrant. Every American ruling tyrant knows which group he has to fear and which groups he can easily ignore or suppress. Because of the fallacies of a national Democracy, American history has documented that the United States has had to be one of the most violent nations in history. When people lose local control over their environment and school system, and when national corporations are allowed to treat the population as if they are alive to serve the greater good of the company's stockholders, people will riot.

There is another fallacy of Democracy that has led to constant battles: the idea that in America everyone can do as they want is ridiculous. Everyone is told that society is composed of people who have individual rights. That can never work. Communal life can only survive and prosper if people are willing to accept the restrictions of culture as being necessary for any kind of workable harmony. The Kingdom of God that was inaugurated by Jesus upon His resurrection is mankind's only hope for a riot free culture. Most men are willing to accept restrictions upon their lives if they believe that they are from God and His Revelation. However, in a Democracy, the power of the majority is that they have the right to impose their rules over the minority. That never sets well, especially when everyone knows that in the next election or in the next Supreme Court ruling, today's truth becomes tomorrow's error. Why should anyone be forced to obey laws that are only temporary?

While many worship the U.S. Constitution as being one of the wisest documents in history, it is also one of the biggest pieces of propaganda in history. Not only is it secular, it promises things it cannot deliver. All men are sinners and need to have their sinful nature controlled. However, if the definition of sin is based upon the vote of a legislature or the vote of sinners, then it becomes pretty difficult for any government to perform its designated role as outlined in the Bible. As I write, sinful acts are being promoted as the ultimate in human freedom. Anti-social behavior is being elevated to the level of the purpose of life in a free society. How can anyone feel really alive if they are not allowed to publically enjoy the expression of human depravity?

That is why the U.S. Constitution, when it separated itself from Western and Christian Civilizations, opened the door to eternal conflict. Civilizations serve to place limits upon sinful and rebellious behavior without people having to decide for themselves which moral universe they will choose to live within. Under a civilization, many issues are not to be voted upon. They are considered the real world and no one is allowed to decide what time the sun should arise or any other issue that is considered having been created by God. Civilizations can only grant freedoms that exist within a designated 'playing field'. The Kingdom of God reveals the true rules of life which are unchangeable. Democracies promises that the rules of life can be established by sinful men who wish to give expression to their inner most fantasies. And what do men do when they do not get their way—especially if they have been given the right to get their way—they riot.

*

Not only did the Constitution start America on the wrong foot by allowing all laws to be decided 'by the people' but it purposely left out any divine sanctions to limit what the people could decide: you want the sky, then the sky is yours. Also, the Declaration of Independence, or the Declaration of War against England, set up an ideal of government that was not connected to the real world. Since when can a government promise everyone the right to pursue happiness when all sinners have different ideas of happiness? And the same with liberty. Liberty can only exist within a limited space. One man's liberty comes at the cost of someone else's liberty. Some things in life are not within the power of any government to grant. When a government makes promises that are impossible to fulfill, the people get restless. And the most ridiculous of all is that the Declaration stated that all people are created equal. Equal at what? Equal in in IQ? Equal in musical ability? Equal in athletic talent? As I write, unequal people are running around screaming that they were denied a job because some employer believed that some people are more qualified than others. So what happens, the losers start a riot because someone refused to recognize the truths of the Declaration of Independence. The Declaration of Independence was not only a declaration of war against England, it was also a Declaration of War against God and His Laws.

The problem is this: when people run up against the laws of God in their life, and experience the consequences, whom do they blame? The government says there is no God. They either blame the government or other people for their own rebellious spirit and behavior. That is why the book I am citing here has the following title: *Dissent: The History of an American Idea.*[158] It could also be called, Sinful Temper Tantrums: An American Idea. Instead of a child holding his breath and stopping his feet, adult Americans riot. Young describes what most consider the American view of political reality: "It is the story of religious dissenters seeking refuge in a New World; Native Americans defying the onslaught of European settlement; political revolutionaries launching a government 'of the people, by the people, for the people'; enslaved Africans resisting their oppressors while creating a new culture; immigrants fighting to assimilate into American society; women persevering to gain equality; and minorities demanding their share of the American Dream. It is also the story of a countless number of Americans who prodded, provoked, and pushed the United States to actually be the nation it imagined itself to be."[159] When reality is denied, every ugly guy wants to date the prom queen.

The above list of activities calling for new rights, no matter the cost, keeps growing. Reality is the enemy of all the new dissenters. Somehow being a male is

---

[158] Ralph Young. Dissent: The History of an American Idea. New York University Press. 2015.
[159] Young. P. 1.

no longer a question of anatomy, but what one believes. So many of the dissenters have their own version of truth; however, they present it in terms others will accept. A good example are the first Indian wars in New England. The early settlers were intent upon teaching the ways of God to the Indians. They also wanted to teach them the ways of Western Civilization so that they could easily integrate into the culture of the immigrants. Enough Indians converted that ten small Indian villages were established. The heads of the tribes in that area launched a war against the converted Indians and the Whites who converted them. He stated: If we build fences and take up farming, if we have permanent wives who are helpmates, if we adopt White Man's culture—Our Gods will die. The chief was correct: the first wars were not about race or land, but about the fact that no land can have two gods: one god or the other must die. Bu because, modern Americans do not believe in God, He must be eliminated from any discussion and narrative of the past events: secular explanations must explain every event.

Many of the 'dissenters'—euphemism for violence—latch onto the idea of natural rights. However, the only thing 'natural' in Darwin's world is the survival of the most fit, i.e. most violent, the stronger over the weaker. Jefferson invoked 'Nature's God' instead of the Biblical God, but the god of the fire and the god of the storm is not a very dependable god. The god of Nature does not care about mankind. Somehow, the virtues of the real personal God were transferred to the impersonal god of the earthquake and the volcano. Young gives one idea of dissent as this: "On the broadest level, dissent is going against the grain. It is speaking out and protesting against what is (whatever that *is* is), most often by a minority group unhappy with majority opinion and rule."[160] As I write, the White Race, and Western Civilization are under attack by assorted racial and sexual 'minorities.' It is often pictured as if these are extraordinary times and nothing like this has occurred in the past. However, the war on White Culture has been continuous throughout American history. The White Race has been found guilty and must submit to the attacks that are deemed justified. History, as pictured above, is the story of one righteous cause after another helping to build America

---

[160] Young. P. 3.

into a better nation. To oppose these rebellious minorities is to be on the wrong side of history. That is the story that the Overlords of narratives want everyone to believe. Minorities are the new prophets and operate as the vanguard of the next new civilization. Minorities operate as an Evolutionary force which causes weakening civilizations to die in the favor of a much stronger historical force.

Bacon's Rebellion is probably the first war in the New World where Whites were killing Whites. The war ran from 1676-1677. Actually, it was a war over Indian lands. The best farming lands in Virginia were owned by the wealthy landlords. The poorer Whites were restricted to less than ideal land. Now good lands were still held by the Indians but the poor Whites were not allowed to farm on fertile Indian Lands. Nathaniel Bacon wanted to drive the Indians out so that the poor Whites could obtain good farming land. After all, the Indians just hunted the deer, etc., on the land and the White settlers could put the land to a lot better use through growing profitable crops. The Governor of Virginia, William Berkeley, refused to allow the expansion of White Men further west. Reportedly, around 400 Virginians formed Bacon's army which chased the governor back to Jamestown and then they torched the city. England sent troops and they spent several years quelling the rebellion. This event really set the stage for similar events in the area.

In 1676, Bacon issued his *Declaration of the People.* It presented the issues concerning the reason for the rebellion. It contended that taxes raised for public works were diverted for other uses. The lower classes felt that only the upper classes were given government jobs. The upper classes were able to monopolize the trade with the Indians, and, yes, even then race was an economic issue. The White folks felt that the governor favored the Indians. That probably had a lot to do with the lucrative fur trade with the Indians. The point here is that America has a tradition of violent conflict going back to the very beginning. The Mayflower landed in Massachusetts in 1620 and this battle occurred just fifty-six years later in Virginia. Several similar battles were fought elsewhere patterned after Bacon's rebellion. It is this mentality that the ruling elites have attempted to suppress. Even as I write, the Overlords have attempted to divert dissent into a racial thing to prevent the races from uniting against their true enemy, their Overlords. [Worthy of note, Bacon did have a number of Blacks in his army.]

This attitude was actually expressed in the American Revolution. While only a small minority wanted war with England, war propaganda was used to start an armed rebellion. Two-thirds of the population, at least, did not want a war. About one third were content with the way things were and about one-third were still loyal to their mother country. Like many wars, it was a question about power and who gets the money from the taxation of the masses. In fact, England was entitled to tax the colonies, if for no other reason, it was the British army that provided protection on the colonies' frontier. The British had fought the French and Indian war with their 'nickel' and were seeking some reimbursement for their war expenses. I do not buy the argument that a war was needed to establish a separation from England. Other colonies became free from England without a war. Here again, America had a tradition of solving problems through bullets.

*

There is a corollary to America's use of violence to solve political differences. Early on in America the Puritans could not figure out what to do with those who disagreed with the Bible. This was really a big issue at the time and the way it was eventually solved has plagued the United States. The Puritans had to decide what to do with those who declared war upon traditional Christianity. In the early communities where people depended upon each other for survival, maintaining unity was vitally important. The two posterchild's for this problem were Roger Williams and Anne Hutchison. Both with exiled from Massachusetts. Roger founded Rhode Island, and Anne returned and was hung. She became a great martyr for 'freedom.'

However, because of this, America went to the other extreme until the modern age of political correctness. For most of American history the First Amendment operated to protect the sinner and the idiot. [Except during times of war when the laws of treason were enforced.] However, for much of early America, force was used to create a uniform culture. During the Revolutionary War, those who favored England were tarred and feathered to enforce public loyalty in the land. Ironically, after the war was won, those who remembered the punishment of those during the war, insisted upon a First Amendment to protect them from the same people who had silenced public opinion. Of course, since 9/11, there is no longer a First Amendment, and with the new Woke culture, even being out of touch with current ideologies can land one in trouble. America is back to force to ensure uniform public opinion. The modern form of 'tar and feathering' is to bring charges against an offender of 'free speech'. Tthe defendant will spend years and dollars defending himself. Even if found innocent, the person's life has been destroyed.

You see, when you throw out the Bible, life becomes a little more complicated. There is no longer any standard by which a uniform culture can be obtained. The result is that the Kingdom of God and the kingdom of Satan have been at war in the United States continually since 1776. Throughout history, force has been used to maintain a legal order. Without the Bible, it becomes impossible to know when to use force and when to allow a limited form a freedom. The mistake the Puritans made was to base the public order upon the church service and the maintaining of proper doctrines, but it is the Biblical public Laws which must be forcibly enforced. The personal Commandments, such as not coveting, is not in the role of the State to enforce such a law. However, fornication is its various forms can destroy a social order. Biblical culture is based upon the family and laws must be enforced against such acts that would destroy the family. People have no problem with the State violently enforcing laws that only act to preserve the power of the State, so why shouldn't the Kingdom of God that operates to preserve a culture of sanity for the masses be allowed to protect itself? When the family breaks down, so does the mental, spiritual, and moral health of a community decline. The ultimate result is criminal anarchy. The problem is that the laws that protect the Kingdom of God have been transferred to the American State, which is now controlled by the kingdom of Satan.

There is no such thing as a law-free State or even culture. Evil men, if given free reign, will destroy a culture, and eventually, the government. There has to be limits. The problem becomes dangerous when evil free speech is subsidies. The assorted forms of media in the United States are often given subsidies. Christian and conservative Medias in the United States will never obtain major advertising, such as for new cars or soft drink ads. However, secular publications are subsidized with no apparent limit. Maintaining a Christian culture and nation boils down to this: people must be good themselves in order for a culture or nation to be good. When I was young, getting a divorce was very difficult. The laws encouraged people to work things out. Also, the sacred vows 'till death do us part' were written into the law codes. Now, that would be considered discriminatory and oppressive. Evil people demand evil laws.

The best laws affirm what the people are already doing and act to preserve that order. The worst laws are the ones that demand that people do what they are not doing. This thinking attempts to change people through laws. **From the very beginning America was at war between the two types of laws: preserve a culture or change a culture**. This aspect of America's history is neglected. The Revolution is said to have settled the conflicts of early America once and for all. That is a lie. I want to cover just a couple of the events that preceded the Revolution and which directed America into a particular direction in the nature of its laws and legal culture. I consider these early conflicts the major reason the United States became a secular—anti-God—nation from the start. The American Empire could never be built if Americans considered Biblical Laws the true nature of a government and a nation. Yes, there were battles between Christians and governments before the Revolution, and this is what the Overlords feared most. The Christians who believed the Bible as a source book for laws had to be defeated. This was accomplished by exploiting the narrow minded view of Law as taught by the Puritans.

*

In the 1600's, America was still very closely tied to England. What happened in England affected the people here in America. After all, the early settlers were from England and they belonged to English colonies under English rule. The politics of England made their way to America. There was a revolution in England in 1689 called the Glorious Revolution. Two events followed: Parliament passed the Declaration of Rights which limited the power of the King, and the Toleration Act was passed which ended the intense persecution of Protestant Dissidents. It was this persecution which had led the dissidents to come to America. Persecution makes people desperate and desperate people do desperate things: risk the voyage to a new land; fight the natives there; and then experience famine and plagues. Everyone knows all about the slave ships and their crowded conditions, but that was really normal conditions for most people. The Mayflower was no different. Basically you were locked below deck with 102 people (And a crew of thirty), many of the passengers were experiencing sea sickness and diarrhea—For Ten Weeks. Also, there was not a lot of fresh air below deck.

Thus, when these people endured this for their faith, they were not about to set up a secular government in which all non-Christians were welcome or secularists who despised Biblical Laws. These early Christians were labelled as being intolerant, but they had every reason to be: They had paid a great price to come to America. In time, the Mayflower adventure resulted in many others coming to America who just wanted to get rich quickly. The Glorious Revolution marked the negation of the policies of Charles II who hated Christian dissenters and had persecuted them: His men attacked Christians in their churches; he threw many in dungeons; and his men often destroyed the farms of Christians. John Bunyan, the author of *Pilgrim's Progress,* spent a total of 17 years in a dungeon for unauthorized preaching. One of the last acts of Charles II was to remove Massachusetts colonial charter. James II took the next step and dissolved their colonial government and combined New England under the rule of New York and New Jersey. The king appointed Sir Edmund Andros as regional governor.

"The Puritans were infuriated when Andros levied taxes by executive order, issued a decree requiring religious toleration, commandeered a Puritan church in Boston for Anglican worship services, abolished the General Court, and set up restrictions on town meetings. Many colonists protested, but they were quickly thrown in jail. When the news of the Glorious Revolution arrived in Aril 1689, hundreds of jubilant Puritan insurgents took to the streets in an uprising against the reviled Andros. They imprisoned the governor general and seized the fort in Boston Harbor. Andros escaped, but Massachusetts was back under Puritan control and remained so for the next three years while they waited patiently for the Crown to reissue their charter."[161] However, although Rhode Island and

Connecticut had their powers restored, not so with Puritan Massachusetts. Their State now became a royal colony and their governor was appointed by the Crown.

It gets a little messy, but it is important to understand the nature of the general population: insurrections were common. The second in charge under Andros was Nicholson. He refused to acknowledge the Glorious Revolution and the new regime of William and Mary. He remained loyal to the Catholic King, James II. New Yorkers now regarded him as a papist. Jacob Leisler who had emigrated from Germany, led a revolt against Nicholson. Leisler's group ousted Nicholson. Leister appointed himself and his son-in-law as the new heads of government. Leister "encouraged the lower classes to attack the property of the wealthy English elite, and freed debtors from prison."[162] They held power for thirteen months until British troops arrived to set things right. He and his son-in-law refused to hand over power. They were tried for treason and hung.

"When Protestants in Maryland got word of the Glorious Revolution, they too took to the streets. Vowing to annihilate the papists in the colony, John Coode and a group of militants calling themselves the Protestant Association deposed Lord Baltimore's Catholic regime and seized control of the government. They petitioned William and Mary to establish a Protestant government and the Anglian Church in the colony. The request was granted...." Just another violent transfer of power in the New England Puritan area. However, the Puritan theology and their philosophical thinking became part of American literature which still resides in many people's thinking today, especially the idea that America is/was a Christian nation.

That thought was used in multiple world wars to motivate the masses to help defend Christian America. The people would not have volunteered to defend a Catholic America, or even a secular America. People love to state that America was never a Christian Nation—and they are right. The reason people think this way was that every war was fought for God and Country: the people thought the government was talking about the New England Puritan idea of God and nation being one. The government rejected the idea of Biblical Laws as

---

161 Young. P. 31.
162 Young. P. 32.

interpreted by the Puritans, but the leaders had no problem invoking the idea of God watching over a 'Christian', i.e. Puritan State. Propaganda does not need to be logical or true.

After all of this religious fighting, America was welcoming many immigrants into the nation who were not Puritans. People were arriving who did not have a history of religious persecution. They came here for the money. The above conflicts were largely over how religion would be integrated into America. A new America was being evolving: religion was dying and businesses were writing the future. There were two goals by the Overlords: disestablish Christians; and develop a universal, inclusive American philosophy. [I must keep inserting the idea that Satan and his minions were involved in the process.] The nation of America must rise above its founding. White Christian Puritans must no longer be allowed to assert their narrative of history or be allowed to teach a narrow definition of religion. As I write, these goals have been achieved, totally. .

*

Ever since the death of Christendom with the Reformation, there has been a war on how to organize the whole world into some unified civilization that would be like Christendom, but not Christendom. Two of the most often criticisms of Christendom is that it was White and it was Biblical. I could add that it believed in Biblical Laws and it believed reality could be known and understood through God's Revelation. Modern Americans, who are seeking to create a New World Civilization, i.e. Order, are at war with Christendom and are creating a historical narrative that attacks Christendom at what they feel are its weakest points: racism, and Biblical morality. Young writes:

"By 1700 misunderstanding, condescension, competition, and conflict had become the accepted manner of dealing with the Indians. By 1700 Puritan theology and attitudes in New England had taken such deep root that they still permeated American philosophical, religious, social, cultural, and political thought. [White Supremacism] By 1700 slavery and the plantation system had become so entrenched in the South that a century and half later it was to lead to the most devastating and bloody war in the nation's history, and a century and a half after that racism still persisted as one of the country's most vexing and enduring problems. And by 1700 the middle colonies of Pennsylvania, New York, and New Jersey were already emerging as centers of diversity, multiculturalism, commerce, and toleration that would also be a force helping to shape the American character."[163]

The above paragraph is loaded with words and ideas that everyone is supposed to believe are true, absolutely true. Two mottos in early America were 'Order out of Chaos' and 'A New Secular Order.' The wilderness of the land represented chaos. The Indian wars represented chaos. The institution of slavery represented chaos. The religious wars represented chaos. The constant regional conflicts represented chaos. The violent political protests represented chaos. America, having no real currency of its own, represented chaos. [Stores might price items in multiple local or world currencies.] And eventually, some of these forms of chaos led to the American Civil War. The goal of the War was to create a National Unity, i.e. order, where none had existed before. Before the War, America was a nation of multiple powerful independent States. After the War, American power was centered in Washington, D.C. Order, it was believed, had finally been attained, or at least the power was there to force a similar order/law on everyone.

One of the Code Names for the new era becoming a reality in America was The Age of Reason. Reason means not Faith. The Age of Faith represented personal opinion, and every person had a different idea about what constitutes faith. However, Reason is considered scientific and thus beyond debate. America had a history of one conflict after another—even before the Civil War. A system of government was needed that would unite the people of America. All differences must be put aside in order to create a greater good. It is kind of like modern football: the athletes come from different backgrounds; they have different religions views; they are different races; and the have different moral standards. In order to make the players to become a team, a greater goal must be presented to them. If the players unite behind the idea of a national championship, all their differences become minor in comparisons.

---

[163] Young. P. 33.

So what was the great goal that would unite the whole nation? Actually, there were several goals. A different goal was presented to each sub group in the land. To the Blacks, the nation promised to make them all equal to the White race. To the White race, they were promised immense prosperity. To the religious, the promise was that each could operate without any government interference. To the businessman, there was the promise of a global empire which would create a global market for his goods. To each group, promises were made that could only be attained if everyone would conform to the Government's narrative. Every culture needs an absolute god, and the government of the United States became the new god of American Order. All other minor gods must submit to the rule of the central government.

The American Revolution did more than establish America as a separate political entity, it also set up the new United States to change the philosophy of life, i.e. religion. A new nation required a religion that had no connection to the religion of its enemy. The Satanic deception was so great that no one seemed to be aware the Biblical Christianity came to an end, and American generic Christianity was created. [CINO—Christianity in name only.] Shortly before the Revolution, America was invaded by the Enlightenment philosophy. "By midcentury intellectual trends from Europe became the vanguard of a new rational age—the Age of Reason, or the Enlightenment—that sought to explain the phenomena of life scientifically, logically, and rationally rather than as manifestation of God's will. ...it encouraged critical thinking and challenged time honored beliefs and principles. Coterminous with Enlightenment thinking, a decades-long religious revival swept the colonies, the Great Awakening, when scores of clergymen decried the mounting rational secularism that seemed to be turning religion into a cold, emotionless ritual. These ministers sought to reverse this process and to restore emotion and enthusiasm to religious conviction by initiating a serious [series] of spiritual revivals."[164]

This was also the beginning of a new American Church. Some Christians chose abandon the world of reason, the material world, and chose to operate in the invisible realm of reality. This way the church could avoid any conflicts with

---

[164] Young. P. 35.

the enlightened ones who were taking over government, philosophy, and business. The true message of the Bible, it taught, would bring the church into conflict with the ruling powers and the new revolutionary thinking of America. The conflict between reason and faith created a divide in America. "...both, in their own way, stimulated discontent with the existing realities, and helped stir up dissent. Both impulses encouraged ordinary people, as well as the intellectual elite, to question authority and to think for themselves. Moreover, these impulses motivated individuals to examine the meaning of natural rights and personal salvation and whether these principles universally applied to all people."[165] A minority of Christians formed a religious oasis in the midst of social and religious turmoil: it was called Fundamentalism.

The Age of Reason was concurrent with the Scientific Revolution. "Astronomical discoveries by Nicolaus Copernicus, Tycho Brahe, Johannes Kepler, and Galileo Galilei, as well as the advent of Newtonian physics, established that the Earth was not the center of the universe as had been previously assumed; therefore it only stood to reason that humankind was not the center of God's attention. ... The growing emphasis on science and rational thinking raised significant doubts about, and was a potent challenge to, traditional assumptions about politics, religion, social relations, and culture."[166] A disoriented Church surrendered to the trends of the times. Remember, the whole world was excited about the new age and to oppose the excitement of the age would be like opposing the ocean's tide. The goal of Christians was to create a new religion that made Christians acceptable in the eyes of the elites and the masses.

It was during this age that John Locke published his treatises on government. In 1690, he published his *Second Treatise of Government*. He applied the laws of the scientific method to society in order discover the Laws of Nature that could be applied to humans and their government. "The *Second Treatise* states that all men are born equal in a state of nature and possess the natural rights of life, liberty, and property. Locke argues that government becomes necessary in order to preserve and safeguard those rights; and so

---

[165] Young. P. 35.
[166] Young. P. 35.

people enter into a social contract in which they give up a portion of their rights (for example, the right to punish a transgressor) to the government, and in return they gain a higher portion of security. If the government, however, does not protect life, liberty, and property or if it in fact infringes on those rights, then the people have right to rebel—they have the right to overthrow that government because it is violating its part of the social contract—and **set up another government that will protect those rights.**"[167] (Emphasis added.)

Under Christendom, rulers were considered representatives of God and His Laws. The people were accountable to their King, and the King was accountable to God. If a King violated that responsibility, he could be excommunicated which resulted in his no longer having the authority to rule over his people. This eliminated his ability to collect taxes from the people. Any attempt to collect taxes was an illegal act. In those days, people took excommunication seriously. After all, a person's human soul and his salvation depended upon obeying God and His representatives over mere humans: and kings were human. After Locke, rulers got their authority from 'the people.' The government was expected to protect the 'rights' of the people. **Rights were also a new thing. No one could go to God and demand one's rights.**

These new rights were separate from God and His order. Rights gave people the impression that they were gods unto themselves. This became the new American religion. Even men's relationship with God changed. Now, God became one's personal 'genie' to provide the material and psychic benefits a person feels he needs. Some called it the Gospel of Prosperity. Man was considered sovereign over his own destiny. Man had the freedom to accept God or reject him. The evangelist became God's salesman who would attempt to sell God to the potential customers in the audience. Evangelists, whose salary often depended upon his success in converting people, made it easier and easier to become a Christian: raise your hand, say a prayer, and now you have been saved from hell. Nothing could be easier than that. Studies have been done on the people who raised their hand and looked at their life one year later. Only about five per cent had completely changed their lifestyle.

---

[167] Young. P. 35-36.

Locke also introduced another concept that was introduced into the government and its schooling and the Christian Church: everyone was born with a 'blank slate' in their mind. [Each child was born with blank software, so to speak. God provided the hardware, but mankind was responsible for the software installed in each human being.] Of course, no institution is better equipped to write a child's software that the government and its ability to spend a lot of money on 'free' education. Because the government has been charged with protecting the rights of the people, it is only logical that only the government should have the power to craft each child in a way that he will understand his rights and seek to obey the government that protects those rights. If the government allows the parents to write a child's software, there is no guarantee the child will end up as a responsible citizen who understand his responsibility—to his government--in a Democracy.

You see, the church is only concerned with saving souls and teaching the doctrines of some ancient text. There is nothing here to guarantee that the child will develop into a responsible subject who is the god of Democracy. The American church grew to accept Locke's picture of the social world of Democracy. It should be noted that one of the arguments for reparations can be seen in this light. The experience of slavery placed within one's ancestors a false software. This became part of one's genetic heritage and false programming has continued to handicap that person for centuries. For most Americans, it was the culture of work and success in the material world that was written into their software. Of course, this belief resulted in racial wars as those who were slaves or freed slaves, had a different software which resulted in two different cultures, two different ideas about a family, two different ideas about work, and two different ideas about God. What is missing today is that global Corporations brought slaves to America to serve corporations. Slaves were very expensive and that is why only five per cent of the population in the South owned slaves. The slaves were needed to provide the giant Corporate cotton mills of England with a steady supply of cotton. And yet, it is the common people who bear the blame. What is neglected is that even a nation's 'software' has created a narrative that affects everyone whether it is true or not.

It could be easily stated that John Locke created modern America more than the beliefs of the Christians. We are first all followers of Locke, and only secondly followers of the Bible. We all live in a blank slate universe where man is 'free' to write on that slate. Also, the Overlords who control the blank slate can control reality for all those who are under the control of their software. The god of any culture is the one who writes the software. Under Christendom, the Bible wrote the software. After the Reformation, the new nation/states took on the role of writing upon the minds of those under its control. Man's reality has shifted from God's world, created by Him for the glory of glory of God, to a world men can create for the glory of individual and corporate Man. Only when history is viewed from this perspective can a person understand the importance of understanding God's Revelation of true reality.

Proverbs 11:4. By humility *and* the fear of the LORD *are* riches, and honour, and life. **5 Thorns *and* snares *are* in the way of the froward:** he that doth keep his soul shall be far from them. **6 Train up a child in the way he should go**: and when he is old, he will not depart from it. **7 The rich ruleth over** the poor, and **the borrower *is* servant to the lender. 8** He that **soweth iniquity shall** reap vanity: and the rod of his anger shall fail. **9** He that hath a bountiful eye shall be blessed; for **he giveth of his bread to** the poor. **10** Cast out the scorner, and contention shall go out; yea, strife and reproach shall cease. **11** He that loveth pureness of heart, *for* the grace of his lips the king *shall be* his friend. **12** The eyes of the LORD preserve knowledge, and he **overthroweth the words of the transgressor.**

The above the Biblical version of the 'blank slate' theory of John Locke. It is the role of the parents to train the child. It is important to consider the very next verse describes the reality when the State is allowed to train up a child. The rich will end up controlling the masses, i.e. the poor, and the poor will become servants, i.e. slaves, to the rich. The result will be that when people rebel against God's reality, the nation and its culture produce vanity, i.e. Emptiness; want of substance to satisfy desire; uncertainty; inanity.

Proverbs 27:20. Hell and destruction are never full; so **the eyes of man are never satisfied.**

Visitors to the United States, starting in the 19th century, described Americans as constantly on the move, always restless, and never content with the present moment. When America started its own version of Christianity after the Revolution, the people lost the peace that passeth all understanding. The rich ended up ruling over the nation and the poor became slaves to the lenders. This became accepted as normal because, without the Bible, the people lost a frame of reference in which to judge reality. The Bible teaches the type of culture that is the result of following the teachings of the Bible and how a people will act when the Bible is rejected as a cultural foundation:

Galatians 5:18. **19** Now the works of the flesh are manifest, which are *these*; Adultery, fornication, uncleanness, lasciviousness, **20** Idolatry, witchcraft, hatred, variance, emulations, wrath, strife, seditions, heresies, **21** Envyings, murders, drunkenness, revellings, and such like: of the which I tell you before, as I have also told *you* in time past, that they which do such things shall not inherit the kingdom of God. **22** But the fruit of the Spirit is **love, joy, peace, longsuffering, gentleness, goodness, faith, 23 Meekness, temperance**: against such there is no law.

*

Insert: You cannot read an American history textbook without encountering a long section about Southern slavery. In some textbooks, it seems just about every section includes some aspect about slavery and its influence on every aspect of America since the very beginning. American culture, we are told, was not founded by the Puritans, those of the Enlightenment, or by its many wars. The American Way of Life was based upon slavery, either in its overt form, or in its treatment of all minorities who were considered slaves to the White power structure: women, the poor, Indians, Mexicans, Blacks, and non-European immigrants.

However, it is the Black Slaves who dominate the official American cultural narrative. Global slavery is largely ignored, but only Southern slavery. The one area of slavery in the whole world where Biblical Christians owned slaves. And remember, the actual owners of the slaves are the last people in the chain of events that produced American Slavery. I start with the fact that America was basically founded by businessman seeking riches. The Puritans and the Pilgrims are nice little cover stories to direct people's attention away from the fact that America was from the beginning a colony to be exploited by those who controlled the global wealth. North America was blessed with abundant resources which were readily available. Oh, there were a few Indians in the way, but that was no problem. It is interesting that America was a great exporter and one of the most unusual was ice. Workers cut giant blocks of ice out of the lakes in New England in the winter and shipped that ice as far away as the Philippines. [The blocks were packed in sawdust and stored below the water line, so the ice arrived in the Far East largely still intact.]

The giant mills in England that were brought about through the Industrial Revolution caused the small home cotton producers to fail. With the giant factories, staffed largely by children, a great need was created for cotton. The Southern United States was an ideal place for cotton growing. However, there were two problems. A lot of workers were needed and it was really hot in the South in the summer. Blacks proved to be especially tolerant of the heat. They could still work when White Men were looking for shade. Thus, the Global International Trade Cartel set up large Cotton plantations in the South. Some of these were like small cities with slaves performing a whole host of trades to support the population. Every kind of business you would find in any American village was found on these plantations. The movie image of just people picking cotton is not quite real. In fact, cotton picking takes about only six weeks out of the year.

Yes, there were crimes committed on the plantations, some by slaves and some by owners. But you would find similar crimes in most cities in the United States at that time. The bigger cities had districts where you did not want to walk alone. However, any White on Black crime was considered typical of White Men and their ownership of slaves. That was propaganda by taking isolated events and telling everyone that such events were common. The point that is vital to remember is that the slave system in the United States was being used for other purposes than just the production of cotton and it involve the total control of the lives of White workers. This misdirection was used to disguise the results of American abandoning Biblical Law and Christianity. America was being turned

316

into a colony of worker bees. To suppress this knowledge, the workers are told that they are free because they are not Black slaves. That is one reason the issue of Black slavery must never be allowed to die: Blacks are too useful to the total American economy—just be happy you are not a slave; look what it has done to them.

When you study the history of the American worker after the Revolution, you gain a picture of White people being treated much worse than the slaves were treated. That is the story that is not being told. We are only told how difficult it was to pick cotton and those White people had it so easy. This is one of the great deceptions of American history, and what I find amazing is how every history book tells the same story. The reason is to keep the White worker from understanding that he was being exploited more than the slave. The slave was fed and clothed and housed by his master. The White man was given a minimum wage and then he had to cloth and feed his family. On top of that, there was no sick pay, no retirement, and saving for the future was impossible for the White worker. Older and ailing slaves were cared for their entire lives.

The White worker culture was one of survival and little more. The history books cover the condition of the slaves, but rarely mention the urban tenements or the shacks that tenant farmers lived in. They often had just old pieces of canvas for doors. In the 19th center, debtor's prisons were common. You miss a few payments and you were cast into literal dungeons. The goals was to so mistreat these prisoners that their friends and relatives would raise the money to pay their debt. Also, there was little concern for the health and safety of the workers in the factories. In the steel mills, it was common for ten percent of the workers to die on the job every year. It was hot and dangerous work. And the worker received just enough money to live for another day. These men were not slaves, but lived in conditions worse than slavery. According to modern texts, these men were living the American Dream—they were free: they were free to work under horrendous conditions of die. That is what White 'slavery' was like.

The slavery mythology has been so useful in keeping the American White man in subjection to intolerable conditions that that the true nature of slavery must be suppressed. The White man must not be told his history of toil, suffering, and abuse at the hands of the corporate leaders. There were a few slave revolts before the Civil War, but few textbooks cover the multiple, violent strikes by White men against their cruel working conditions. Those stories of worker insurrections are rarely more than briefly mentioned. When White men complain about being exploited until their death, that isn't worth mentioning. **History telling is one of the most subtle forms of propaganda because it is noted for what it does not tell, not by any lies it might tell.**

*

I want to continue with the story of how White men faced continual hardship and civil unrest. Again, this aspect of history is largely neglected in favor of more stories that promote the narrative of rich White men owning Black slaves. The average White man had no supremacy and often led lives of social conflict and despair. Yes, in America. Just as Europe had a large peasant class, attempts were made to convert the American worker into the same status as the poor Europeans. Another example of how the common man actively resisted their subjection occurred in 1719. There was a grain shortage in New England. The problem was that grain merchants could make more money by exporting their grain supply than by selling it locally. Bread became quite expensive. Scores of men broke into one of rich merchant's warehouses looking for grain to loot. When the Lt. Governor tried to intervene, he was shot. This one ended favorably as laws were passed to prevent the exporting of grain during a shortage.

In 1745, wealthy landowners attempted to raise the rents on tenant farmers. Some of the tenant farmers had purchased their land from the Indians and felt any rents were illegal. When three tenant farmers were arrested, the people fought back. As one tenant farmer was being transported to jail, three hundred farmers attacked and freed the prisoner. After that success, the mob proceeded to the jail to free the other two farmers. The sheriff and his men were outnumbered, so they called upon the public to come to their aid. No one did. Eventually, the mob stormed the jail and released the prisoners. This is so typical of early America. Americans were not afraid to use violence to right a wrong.

This event in American history should be headlined in textbooks, but of course, it is not—and for good reason. In 1733, the editor of the *Journal* in New

York, ran a series of articles revealing the corruption of the colony's Governor. "It was public knowledge that [Governor] Colby was bribing legislators and judges, embezzling funds from the colony's treasury, and falsifying election results. The *Journal* argued that freedom of the press was necessary because the press was the only institution that could serve as a watchdog against political corruption and the misuse of power and misuse of power. [The Editor argued] 'If men in power were always men of integrity, we might venture trust them with the direction of the press, and there would be no occasion to plead against the restraint of it.' But men are corruptible, and therefore a free press is essential to keep them in check. **If freedom of the press and freedom of speech were restricted, liberty itself would be snuffed out.**"[168] (Emphasis added.)

This case became pivotal in America's early history. Remember, America was still under British rule. The Governor of New York, had the editor arrested for libel and shut down the newspaper. Under the British law, under libel, it only had to show evil intent in publishing certain facts. The truth of the facts did not matter. "When the court acquitted [the editor], it was a momentous victory for the principle of freedom of press. The acquittal also was pivotal in establishing the precedent that no political official was exempt from public censure."[169] This victory in court set a precedent which made it legal for America's newspapers to criticize British rule in America. As I write, the pendulum has swung the opposite way and the editor would have been charged with publishing fake news and spreading false information. Like before, truth is not a determining factor today in squelching freedom of speech, but merely the intent to harm the government in the carrying out of its intended duties constitutes a violation of the freedom to say and publish something. Speaking the truth is no longer an adequate defense; challenging the official narrative is the crime.

What must be noted about the history of American resistance against those in government and in business was this: these people had something in their mind and in their background that motivated them to resistance. These people had a vision about ethical life and were willing to fight and die for that belief in

---

[168] Young. P. 22-23.
[169] Young. P. 23.

their minds. One of the goals of the American Overlords has been to eliminate that vision of a reality other than the one taught in the media and public schools. Historically, this is one reason the Bible has been banned by so many governments throughout the ages. It is very good at planting images and ideas in a person's mind. One reason it is so successful is that the words of the Bible conform to the nature of one's mind and personality. Biblical Words and human mind are a perfect fit, by design.

Now, every tyrant needs to understand this process. Some have attempted to place new words in the mind that are similar to the Bible. Some have attempted to reward those who play the unreality game. People will pretend to be anything if they are paid enough. There is a more drastic measure and that is to remind everyone that resistance is futile. There is no chance of achieving any type of future envisioned in your mind. This is where the Bible becomes a real problem. It teaches that the vision in a person's mind is real; men are to work toward that vision of reality.   However, ultimately, men will find that dream in only fulfilled in heaven with God. How can you defeat a man if he is destined for a better life even though the present life has been under attack? That is why so many Christians have been 'rewarded' with an early trip to their eternal reward. No tyrant can defeat true reality, only false realities. That is why it is so important to plant false realities into the minds of the young—before they can by chance read the Bible on their own.

*

I regard the American Civil War as the great turning point in American history. The principles of being subjected to a tyrannical way of thinking was forcible implanted into the American mind. The War to free the slaves was a great diversion from the true indoctrination that was the goal of the War. Dramatic new laws were passed that sent the message that men are to live in a new reality: a government reality as opposed to any other reality, including the Biblical one. It was at this time that a false form of Christianity was created and that for about a hundred years became the new State Religion. That is why so many were fooled into thinking that America was a Christian nation. No. After the War the new State religion took on many of the words associated with

Christianity and gave them new meanings. The state and media-approved Church became the standard by which a person worshipped God. The artist Norman Rockwell transformed the new religion into a series of paintings that adored the covers of the highly influential *Saturday Evening Post.* Those covers pictured the ideal Christian family gathered together in church or at dinner with smiles on their faces. Those covers became the image most had in mind of what Christianity was all about. Growing up in a small town in the 1950's, I loved reading that magazine because it reinforced the values of my town and made them the values of the nation. However, the more I read the Bible, the more I realized those covers pictured a secular Christian religious view of the real world. Yes, a picture of a large family all sitting in one pew together seemed sentimentally religious, but that is not what Christianity is about.

The Norman Rockwell world came under attack in the 1960's, and no one rose to dissent in any meaningful way. The Lawrence Welk TV show became a symbol of the 1950's for American adults, and its style of music was hated by the hippies of that era. However, except for Welk, everyone seemed to flow with the times. For around 350 years Americans were a nation of protestors, sometimes violent protesters who had an ideal they were willing to fight to defend. The infamous violent protestors of the 1960's were not defending some ideal in their mine, they were merely destroying the civilization that represented the American ideal in the minds of the adult, disillusioned world. The 1950's was pictured as a way of life that either never existed, or should never have existed. Life was pictured as just too good, and that did not represent reality. When I was required to read the literature of despair in high school, I complained. I was told that I had to learn to accept the real world. I was disillusioned to think that others regarded the 50's as representing an imaginary world and it was about time I grew up and saw the real world for what it was: a struggle to find light in a dark world where light does not exist. The American Civil War and the protests of the 1960's were two great Revolutions that most could not see. The first created the idea of a tyrannical government being able to accomplish great things [end slavery], and the other destroyed the hope of any ideal order outside of a government to impose one upon everyone [equality for everyone]. .

During the Revolutionary era, law and order did not exist on the frontier. That meant, the criminal element took advantage of that situation. Bands of outlaws roamed the countryside taking what they wanted as a single famer could not hold off a gang of criminals. As a result, the famers banded together to form their own army of about five hundred men. "They decided to impose law and order themselves by regulating and punishing outlaws and those who aided and abetted them." The opposite situation occurred in North Carolina where "...there were too many corrupt governmental officials and bureaucrats who were extorting money from backcountry settlers. In 1768, after failing to convince the government to recall the corrupt officials, the regulators [citizens] banded together and vowed not to pay any of the fees and taxes that were being levied on them. Within a few years the regulator protests had escalated to the point where they were kidnapping local officials and committing acts of violence against property and persons, even capturing and whipping Edmund Fanning, the corrupt clerk of the Orange County Super Court who was notorious for extorting fees from the populace. Finally, in May 1771, the governor sent a force of one thousand militiamen to engage a much larger, although ill-equipped regulator army. The regulators were routed, several of their leaders were executed, and the movement fell apart."[170]

The point that is important here is that Americans often demanded good government, and if it was not delivered, did take the law into their own hands to establish some kind of law and order that the government was not providing. This was the spirit that resulted in the Revolutionary War. However, once a Constitutional government was formed, this attitude did not change. That is why after the United States became a nation, there were multiple major riots and civil conflicts against the new government.

In 1783, there was the Pennsylvania mutiny by army against the Congress.

In 1786, there was Shays' Rebellion.

In 1786, there was the paper money riot in New Hampshire.

In 1788, there was the Doctors Mob Riot in New York City.

---

[170] Young. 62-63.

In 1791-1794, there was the Whiskey Rebellion. President Washington personally led the largest army he had ever commanded to crush this rebellion.

In 1799, there was Fries's Rebellion which was a tax revolt by farmers in Pennsylvania.

The above all occurred in the first ten years of the nation's existence. **Americans still retained their right to government themselves when the government became corrupt, or too demanding.** This attitude continued up until the civil war. There were the labor union strikes of the 19th century, but America was gradually being 'tamed' into becoming subjects to governmental orders. I must emphasize that modern rebellions and riots are of a very different order. Riots have been 'weaponized' against the masses. False flag riots have been used to as an excuse to prevent the mases from doing what they had done before the Civil War. Modern riots serve the interest of the Overlords. Even when patriots attempted to protest the 2020 election on January 6, 2021, the protestors were treated as enemy soldiers. The complete overreaction was to assure that Americans would never again resort to their private armies of early America. The Overlords fear the Americans of the 18th and 19th centuries. That is their idea of 'never again.'

As I write, the New World Order is announcing its plans for the future and what people can expect. However, before these new policies can be carried out, the groundwork must be prepared so that people, like in the 18th century, do not form their own armies. The Overlords are preparing to launch a global plantation with everyone [Those that survive the manufactured plagues, food storages, and nuclear wars.] experiencing a new level of slavery, i.e. freedom slavery. People will be confined to limited spaces, with controlled spending, mandatory vaxxxes, and total surveillance. **As long as you understand the rules, you are free to play the game.** People will 'discover' that they did not need all of things people did in the past. With holographic lenses and implanted chips, your brain is free to experience the freedom of total stimulation. **The possessions in your mind will be almost like you owned them in the material world**—maybe better as they cannot get old, get stolen, or require payments. In order for this transition to occur, people must be prepared. The age of rebellion is over. Submit or die.

Chapter Twenty-Seven: Teaching violence to Americans.

While there has been a lot of talk about the educational propaganda of the American school system, few have focused as the school system as the educator of violence and psychical unrest. There is an evil wisdom in the system of American education that has largely gone unnoticed. Our minds operate within some kind of order that must be learned from others. The Human Being has no instincts. Ideally, the parents of a child teach him what the real world is really like. However, modern American elites have been at war with the family and the extended family: they have so structured society so that the family clan becomes separated from each other. Additionally, the mother also has to work to support the family: one workers families have become obsolete by design. Of course, the State steps in to raise your child for you from day care, to pre-school, to kindergarten, and the elementary school. Parents are free to be with their children but only when the state does not have possession of them.

For some reason, parents seem to think that any idiot can raise a child. The government idiots are no better than any other deranged mind. By a deranged mind I mean a mind that does not recognize the reality of God's creation. The secular school teaches an alternative reality to the child that transfers the child's thought processes into a different realm than reality. In a sense, the secular school teaches a false reality and the child grows up to think that this godless reality is the only real world. Most tyrants know that expecting to control a nation through force creates resistance, but if the tyrant can teach the child to behave in an acceptable way, force can be hidden behind the curtain. Brute force masquerades as educating a child into the true world, a world created by the tyrant. People might rebel against a tyrant, but never against a false reality if they have been taught that it is the only reality there is. .

We are taught that cultures just happen naturally. It is like planting a kernel of corn, and up sprouts a giant corn stalk. The idea is that when people find a successful way to grow food and sell it, then a culture naturally grows up around that. However, man cannot live by bread alone, and he cannot by just seeking to survive to eat again form a culture. Men are more than cattle grazing in a field. That is why cultures are born and that is why governments are created to protect a people's culture and way of life. "Societies, cultures, sub-cultures, and all other social groups exist because they share ideas, beliefs, stories, customs, jokes, nicknames and such like. ... Most of the time ... we are simply unaware of the shared ideas and beliefs – they are simply 'the way things are', the 'deep structures' on which other ideas are constructed. Trying to step outside the belief system is alien. Any who appears to have beliefs different to 'the way things are' is ignored, trivialized or demonized."[171] Today, such ideas contrary to popular thinking, are labelled 'misinformation' and are considered disseminating a 'fake' reality.

Despite all of the hoopla about tolerance and acceptance, these ideas are included in a culture and have a narrow band of definition. There is and can be no tolerance of those who propagate a different cultural story. People are free to disagree about minor facts, but no one is allowed to teach a different reality than the one every person must accept. One of the purposes of modern laws is different than traditional laws which punish criminals. Society must be protected against those who would murder, steal, and assault other people. The new laws target those who would challenge the new culture of multi-culturalism under the umbrella of a uni-culture. Every tyrant knows that a government cannot easily control the thinking of its people, it can only control their physical acts. When physical acts are controlled, the people are readily aware that they are being forced to conform to some alien reality. However, if their thinking is controlled, they are basically unaware that they are being forced to act a certain way: they are just doing what comes naturally.

The basic purpose of education and the media is to make sure everyone believes in the same basic building blocks of reality. Just as in the Middle Ages, those who promoted heresies were isolated from the general population, so too today modern cultural heretics are being de-platformed, demonetized, and eliminated from the popular search engines. These heretics are allowed to live—in most cases—but they exist only as invisible people. Even those individuals on the social media who speak without raising their hand and getting permission may find themselves with zero followers. As I write, a new cultural norm is being imposed upon everyone: the Woke Culture. It started out as kind of a joke as a minority insisted upon everyone start using politically correct words and phrases. At first the generic word 'he' was transformed into a sexist word and an attack upon women. The Bible teaches that God created Man, man and female created he them. (Genesis 1:27) For centuries the language of the King James Bible was

---

[171] Simon Danser. The Myths of Reality. Alternative Albion. 2005. P. ix.

considered proper English. Not anymore; new cultures require new definitions. And new Bible versions also.

The tyrant loves to reconstruct reality because it does not require the passage of laws. It merely requires the ability to control the way people think without having to use overt force. Very few people form an army to rebel against the 'real' world. For centuries Western Civilization ruled without people understanding that they were obeying 'unwritten' laws. "Conscious awareness of our cultural conventions is doubly difficult in the west because 'our' worldview has been insidiously promoted as the 'best', most 'evolved' and the dominant worldview by which all others are judged. The western ideology regards reality as essentially unchanging—something that exists independent of the ways of describing it."[172] Growing up in government schools, I was taught that American culture was the standard by which we were to judge all other cultures and nations. American reality was the 'Bible' of understanding the true world.

The modern idea of tolerance is one of the most deceptive ideas imposed upon mankind. When the Bible teaches that man can have no other gods, it is teaching intolerance. For example, insanity cannot be tolerated by the sane. To allow the insane to control education, government, or even health care, is allowing a false reality to be tolerated as just another or an alternative reality. The Bible teaches there is only one reality, and every other one comes from Satan. However, Satan's reality is like an atom bomb: it destroys everything, both the good and the bad. As long as God's world can be destroyed, Satan has no concern about collateral damage. Hell is where Satan's reigns and his goal is to create a preview of hell here on earth. That is the only reality Satan knows and hell reveals his true nature. When we see beauty and love, we are seeing much more than that, we are seeing God's very nature revealed openly to us. Understand, the war upon God by Satan is expressed through the false realities he imposes upon a people through his servants in government, education, and the media.

*

---

[172] Danser. P. 7.

History can be defined as who get to control reality. Plato's famous book, *The Republic,* lays out a plan on how reality can be controlled by installing specially trained philosophers to teach everyone about the real world—the world beyond the shadows. "[Plato] ...viewed the state as one large body, individuals existing only to serve the body. This point of view inevitably leads to slavery and violence because collectivists are forever trying to subdue individual action which they believe will harm the unity of the state. Individuals have to be trained, not to promote their own happiness and worthwhile achievement, but to serve the needs of the state whatever the leaders of the state determine those needs to be. The collectivist's point of view is basic and necessary to tyranny."[173]

Under Western Civilization, children were educated by their parents, their churches, their community, and private schools. "People expected to rise or fall as result of their own ability, industry, and good fortune. ... Individuals were becoming ever more prosperous, ever more responsible. Thousands of educational institutions were being formed. ... To collectivists this was chaos. They hated individual thought and individuals who claimed sovereignty over their own minds. They saw the world, not as a world full of promise, challenges, and opportunities for growth and development, but as a world which frightened and dismayed them. There was no master plan, no individual or group of individuals taking charge of the lives of the masses. They yearned for a return to the slave mentality."[174] Man as created by God is an enemy of every tyrant. God's man has been created in such a way that he resists those who seek to destroy that nature of man through government operations. Tyrants must be understood as servants of Satan or you will be deceived.

*

No society can exist without a god. A nation's gods provide the necessary unity which every culture needs. One of the new gods was introduced to modern man through Auguste Comte (1798-1857). He environed a future order where mankind could be trained to live in a controlled order. He said freedom is very messy and does not always produce desirable results. Men have personal goals,

---

[173] Erica Carle. The Hate Factory: Teaching Children to Hate. Author House. 2008. P. 4.
[174] Carle. P. 5.

and these goals do not always work for the common good. In fact, individuals oppose any restrictions on their personal lives and will fight any entity which seeks to impose any restrictions upon their personal freedoms. The only way to establish a New Order of the Ages would be to gradually wean the masses off the idea of personal individualism. It is this belief in any personal rights that can lead to civil and national wars.

Comte saw progress from the early clans and tribes to nations and then empires. The result of these groupings has always been conflicts, chaos, and wars. The masses must be conditioned to accept one order for the whole world. This is the only way there can be peace upon the earth. The Scientific Revolution that had produced so many new products supported the belief that science could be applied to the social order also: what men could do with the material world they could also with social world. Just as there are laws of science, there are also laws of forming a social order. Allowing the masses to vote on laws and their rulers is ridiculous. The masses know nothing about science and the way people should come together for some common goal. Each person votes only for his own personal interest, not for the interest of the greater good.

Just as there has been evolution upon the physical earth, there must also be evolution in the social world. Comte looked forward to a time when the Christian Religion can merge with other religions to form a religion of humanity. The doctrines of this new religion are becoming mainstream in the 21st century. The doctrine of total equality is the starting point. Society has imposed differences upon people which has led to all types of conflict. Students must be taught to think globally, not in terms of their own locality or even their own interests. It is when men exalt personal freedoms and rights above the rights of humanity that social problems result: some are poor and others are rich; some have nice houses and others live in slums; some have good jobs, and others have no jobs; some areas have good schools and others have totally substandard schools. It is people putting themselves and their family above the common good that has created this world of divisions.

Carle lists the following goals for the new Comtean Order:

1. To develop emotional rather than intellectual responses to what are called 'social problems.'
2. To direct emotions toward collective rather than individual or family relationships.
3. To train students toward self-sacrifice rather than self-respect.
4. To convince students that as individuals they are ineffective—that worthwhile goals must be pursued through group effort or under group control.
5. To idealize distant, long-range and even impossible achievements so people can be bound together in common effort for indefinite periods of time.
6. To alienate children from parental influence and Christian moral teaching.[175]

Obviously, Western and Christian Civilization must be destroyed in order for the above goals to be achieved.

Comte's new science of man was called sociology. "In reality sociology is not a science, not a search for objective truth, but a way of looking at life. It is closer to a religion than a science, but it is a destructive, not a constructive religion. It is a religion of distortion, half-truth, immorality and deception—a religion which does not seek truth, but attempts to manufacture it. It is a religion which seeks to destroy, rather than perfect human nature and individuality. ... To a sociologist there is no such creature as an individual human being who uses his own intelligence and acts on his own initiative. We are all but members of a larger body who have no real existence outside that larger body. The intelligence of the larger body acts on us and controls us. **We react and respond, but have no free will**."[176] (Emphasis added.)

Humanity is seen as a herd of animals. The goal of the social scientist is to understand how the herd can be controlled and directed toward some pre-determined goal as established by Plato's philosopher kings. Satan's new religion is disguised as a science which is sold as being the product of modern man, not some group of ancient men. Those who hold onto the old ways are pictured as resisting social change and destroying progress. America's Civil War was one of

---

[175] Carle. P. 16.
[176] Carle. P. 16-17.

the first battles on the road to a new national religion and a new form of social unity. Local identities came under attack and racial loyalties were also under attack. The post-Civil War era saw the beginning of new loyalties and new identities. The idea of separation in any form must be eliminated. Integration is the new form of salvation. Even religions must be integrated: Christians and Muslims must unite in Chrislam. Unity is in the State, not in any separate forms of loyalty and identity.

One of the foundational beliefs of Sociological education is that the child's true personality and thinking has been corrupted by the family's and church's oppressive measures of control. "In the sociologist's view, which is the one your children learn, their hypothetical person had succumbed to the unrelenting pressures of social conformity. His case was presented as if, after years of discipline and repression, his spirit had finally been broken."[177] Even the teaching of delayed gratification and impulse control is seen as being oppressive of a child's true personality. To deny a child's immediate desire to perform some act of personal expression is deemed harmful to the child's inner psyche. The Christian idea of self-denial, and personal sacrifice are a modern taboo. That is why anti-Christian cultures hate the idea of marriage and till death do us part covenant: people change over time and people must be free to change, along with everything else in their life that is changing.

As Orwell taught in the book *1984,* New Speak is an important part of controlling any group. The language of a people is one of the means of producing unity without a nation. New laws and new forms of control require new words. "Since sociology is supposed to be the study of groups, and since the road to power is through the construction, use, consolidation and control of groups; sociologists attempt to bind students to the idea of groups. Instead of saying 'family,' they say 'primary groups.' Instead of saying 'friends,' they say 'peer groups.' Instead of saying employers, associates, teachers, etc., they say either primary or secondary groups. Those who are outside are deviants or non-conformists."[178] In a sense, Americans are to think of themselves as belonging to

---

[177] Carle. P. 21.
[178] Carle. P. 22.

various forms of non-binding tribes. Any group that implies some kind of commitment, responsibility, or personal expectations are now taboo: such associations expect controls upon a person's free expression.

It is ironic that the same people who attempt to liberate children from forms of relationships found in Western and Christian Civilizations, are quite willing to place the child under modern forms of control.

"The sociological argument of heredity vs environment distracts one from recognizing the existence of such a free will and puts human beings on an animal level as creatures who react and respond, who must be maneuvered into the 'proper' condition. It does not recognize them as thinking individuals capable of conceiving and perceiving intangible moral principles and directing their own lives."[179]

The sociological god of Comte is at war with just about everything the Bible teaches.

"The denial of moral principles and an individual's freedom to choose may be one reason may children fare so badly today. They are told they are under the power of groups—that morality is decreed by groups, --that their personality was formed by groups—that they are made to adhere to the standards of groups. It could make them feel helpless, caged in, pushed by 'Society.' They are left with only two choices: conform or rebel!"[180]

When I used to counsel teenagers, I would hear such things as: 'Who am I?' Teens no longer feel like they belong to a family, community, or church tradition. They feel adrift in a restless mob, all searching for something that says to them that they belong to something more than a crowd or tribe. Such people, with proper propaganda, can easily bond themselves to the personality of a supreme leader who is controlled the by power of the Overlords. In a sense, when God is expelled from a nation, a substitute god will make itself known. This god is not merely a figment of the imagination, but has the power of Satan indwelling within it.

---

[179] Carle. P. 23.
[180] Carle. P. 23,

There is another aspect of modern education and its war upon traditional or Western Civilization: civilization have agreed upon definitions of normal and acceptable. These terms never had to be spelled out in some law, they were just standards absorbed by a child growing up in a community where the people expect certain behaviors in public. The following is a list that used to be considered part of all education whether public or private:

1. Respect property.
2. Be respectful of adults.
3. Say please and thank you at appropriate times.
4. Do not use profane language or bad grammar.
5. Be neat and clean.
6. Do not lie or cheat.[181]

That was never challenged or even thought of being challenged on some legal basis. Today, lawsuits have been filed on the behalf of students who had their own definitions of neat and clean. Some minorities felt that such restrictions reflect White culture and were impositions of some view of racial superiority. Of course, the child was not taught to think this way. The leaders of a society are always working to divide a culture into multiple subgroups. Before WWII, there was even a common music for all ages. Everyone was singing the same melodies and families could even have singalongs around the piano. Singing together is a form of community that also had to be dissolved.

As I write, the basic tenants of Western and Christian Civilization are being dissolved. Multiple code words are used to make the masses feel that they are experiencing a new age of progress toward a One World Order in which all differences can be dissolved into a unity of peace and prosperity. The sinful nature of man which has been with us since the Garden of Eden is ignored as the cause of mankind's constant problem. The blame has been attributed to the divisiveness of the Biblical doctrines which definitely divides people into the saved and the lost. The story of the Tower of Babel was Satan's answer to the division of mankind into those who follow God and those who follow Satan. Satan's teachers have rebranded Satan as the bringer of light into a dark world, Lucifer.

---

[181] Carle. P. 37.

Satan brings people together. He does not teach any Commandments, and he does not judge people. Satan's message is that all are welcome to serve him in any way they desire. That is the story of the 21st century: Satan's Kingdom of sensual delight sounds a whole lot better to the masses than God's restrictive one—those horrific Ten Commandments.

Chapter Twenty-Eight: Truth and the Pavolian Order.

The goal of every tyrant is to discoverer some means of total control. Without control, tyrants are just no better than a taxi driver. The key element in control is to understand man as an evolutionary animal. That is why the government promotes evolution in the schools and in the movies. It is essential to convince men who they really are—or who they are supposed to be. Evolution is not about science, it is about control. Men cannot be allowed to view themselves as higher than the animals, especially so high that they were created in the very image of God. Think of that—actually, do not think about that. That is an order, i.e. sit. The real goal of government education is animal training. It does not matter whether the animal becomes a doctor or a bus driver, both must be trained to respond to the Overlords bells and whistles. That may be why doctors had no problems administering the death jab to everyone during the Covid-19 planned-population reduction exercise. Pavlov rang the bell and the doctors salivated on demand: how much money do I get for each clot shot?

*

It is best to start with a quick overview of the Russian, Ivan Pavlov (1849-1936). In his work with dogs, he discovered by accident that his dogs would salivate when they saw the white lab coat of his assistant who had been feeding the dogs. The dogs learned to associate food with lab coats. That became known as a conditioned response and led to what is called Behavioral Psychology. In time, men discovered that humans could be trained to have conditioned responses just like dogs. While some used this technique to 'cure' some people's desire for cigarettes, others developed other forms of association to sell products or to support some tyrant. The fact that humans could be trained just like circus animals became one of the great stories of the 20th century. Controllers learned that they could bypass the conscious mind of a person and deal directly with the unconscious part of the part and condition that part of a man without his being aware that he is becoming a trained animal. The problem is that dictators and tyrants began using behavioral training upon their subjects. They were especially trained to respond to certain words: racism, sexism, homophobia, supremacism, slavery, genocide, Nazism, nationalism, patriotism, and many others. Each word was designed to bring forth a programmed response. That is why all totalitarian orders must control the media and the school system. All must be conditioned to respond in the politically correct manner. 'Woof, woof'. 'Good boy'.

A partnership developed between Freud's study of the unconscious mind and Pavlov's ability to train the unconscious to influence man's conscious behaviors without men noticing the connection. Men go about living their lives believing they are free, but are actually responding to certain stimuli that someone had planted within their subconscious mind. In times past, dictators would force people to do things by the threat of force. I call that the **visible gun** approach to control. The problem is that the people can see the guns pointed at them. By using psychological techniques upon a person, the tyrant can rule his subjects using **'invisible guns.'** While the new system of Social Credit to control people is becoming more and more common, there is nothing like using the media and school system to train a mind to become an obedient follower to some system of thought. The schools teach that any guy can become a girl: "Yes, cut off my penis to save the planet from overpopulation." If dogs get neutered, why not other animal species, say man. That illustrates how powerful conditioning really is. If the Overlords can convince guys to depart from their 'pride and joy', there is really nothing that they cannot do to the human thought process.

*

One of the goals of conditioning a man's mind is to implant the idea of a 'civilization' inside a person's conception of reality. Those implanted ideas become just like gravity, part of the world no one can change. For most of history, everyone thought that the terms 'male' and 'female' were pretty well established. That is until the war upon the family became a primary means of breaking down Western Civilization. The family was foundation to both Western Civilization and the Kingdom of God. At other times, those who rebelled against their sexual identity were considered to have mental or emotional disturbances: they need some kind of hormone treatment or therapy. The way it works is to take one aspect of a person's personality and isolate it from his overall picture of himself. A lot of kids form close bonds, i.e. blood brothers, with a friend growing up. That is normal. However, now that normal phase has become associated with one's permanent identity. When I was young, it was popular for two friends to take a pin and cause some blood to flow. They would place a drop of each other's blood on a card and carry it with them, i.e. blood brothers. That isolated and transitory event of childhood now becomes a permanent part of one's personality—except other bodily fluids are exchanged. It is all part of the conditioning process.

Association is one the keys to conditioning a person. Normal thoughts and behaviors are associated with some other aspect that is not normally connected. In a sense, just as Pavlov's dogs associate white lab coats to food, so the child is conditioned to associate a normal feeling, i.e. friendship, with some other desired feeling as instructed by the conditioner: blood brothers means you are gay. The role of the conditioner is to supply a connection that the subject would not normally associate without direction. Two unassociated thoughts become associated. When that process is successful, the child has been trained to think in a certain way. In today's news, around twenty per cent of the children in government schools have been trained to think of themselves in what used to be called 'abnormal'. The schools even have psychic rewards for those who 'come out' or declare themselves a new gender. Pavlov would probably be shocked at what trained human dogs can become with a little education.

One of the main purposes of the Bible is no longer recognized: it is an instruction book to reality. Satan, in the Garden of Eden, presented a false reality to Adam and Eve. They really believed that Satan had to power to make them into gods. I mean, who would not want to become a god? Eating of the tree of the Knowledge of Good and Evil was associated with becoming a god, even though there was no known connection. It was Satan who introduced the connection, association, in the minds of Adam and Eve. The process occurs in many other phases in a person's life. Are those association real or are they planted within us as being real? Again, in matters of foundational importance, the Bible gives us the Creator's viewpoint of the real world. If you eat of the Tree of the Knowledge of Good and Evil, you will die—both physically and spiritually. That is the real world and all of us have to deal with the consequences of that act in the Garden of Eden. That has led a few to search out God's remedy for the dilemma of becoming a fallen creature who is in rebellion against God's reality.

*

One of the popular terms of the last few decades has been something called 'politically correct speech.' All of us are taught a language when we were young. Those words on the paper or in speech became 'symbols' of something other than sounds and scratches on a piece of paper. We learned to associate the word 'hamburger' with the real object. Words are vital in the Bible. God created the universe with 'words'. Jesus is described as the living 'word'. In a sense, words are sacred and people can be taught to worship false words. Words describe reality and the Overlords can teach people false words, or what I call, 'Fiat Words.' Just as fiat money that is worthless, people can also be taught false words which have no connection to the created world. Modern words have become idols: symbols of a false reality. Again, all part of a child's training. 'Hamburger' now becomes associated with eating the meat of a cow that is polluting and destroying the earth. A word that used to bring pleasure now brings a feeling of guilt or disgust.

The words given to us are the mediators between us and the real world. It has been observed that if a culture does not have a word for some experience, people will not understand that experience. It is invisible. Man's man cannot 'see' it. That is why when Jesus is the Word, God is giving us a word to describe an experience we would not see without Him giving us a word for it. "Man learns to think in words and in the speech figures given him, and these gradually condition his entire outlook on life and on the world. ...he who dictates and formulates the words and phrase we use, he who is master of the press and radio, is master of the mind."[182] When politically correct language first made its appearance in the last part of the 20th century, it was considered a joke and everybody was laughing at the stupidity of redefining everyday words. However, when people started getting fired for using the wrong words, people started to understand that the mind controllers were quite serious. I regard this time as when Satan started to openly declare war upon Western and Christian Civilizations. The first word change I remember was when homosexual became 'gay'. The 1890's were called the Gay Nineties. The 1990's were the Gay Nineties also, but with a whole different meaning.

Governments and corporations were among the first to understand the nature of association and word control. "In the Pavlovian strategy, terrorizing force can finally be replaced by a new organization of the means of communication. Ready-made opinions can be distributed day by day through

[182] Joost Meerloo. The Rape of the Mind. Martino Publishing. 2015. (1956). P. 46-47.

press, radio, and so on, again and again, till they reach the nerve cell and implant a fixed pattern of though in the brain. ... The Pavlovian strategy in public relations has people conditioned more and more to ask themselves, 'What do other people think?' As a result, a common delusion is created: people are incited to think what other people think, and thus public opinion may mushroom out into a **mass prejudice.** ... Expressed in psychoanalytic terms, through daily propagandistic noise backed up by forceful verbal cues, people can more and more be forced to identify with the powerful noisemaker. Big Brother's voice resounds in all the little brothers."[183] (Emphasis added.) People now feel uneasy when their behavior and ideas separates themselves from the human herd. No one wants to be the only one in his group to not have taken the clot shot.

If you watch students on college campuses, you will notice how they react to certain words and phrases. They have been conditioned. "Political conditioning should not be confused with training or persuasion or even indoctrination. It is more than that. It is taming. It is taking possession of both the simplest and most complicated nervous patterns of man. It is the battle for the possession of the nerve cells. It is coercion and enforced conversion. Instead of conditioning man to an unbiased facing of reality, the seducer conditions him to catchwords, verbal stereotypes, slogans, formulas, symbols. Pavlovian strategy in the totalitarian sense means imprinting prescribed reflexes on a mind that has been broken down."[184] In fact, students who have been conditioned to respond to certain ideas have demanded safe places on campus where they can avoid any stimuli contrary to their training. Peace within themselves can only be found in such safe zones. Meerloo believes that "in order to tame people into the desired pattern, victims must be brought to a point where they have lost their alert consciousness and mental awareness. Freedom of discussion and free intellectual exchange hinder conditioning. Feelings of terror, feelings of fear and hopelessness, of being alone, of standing with one's back to the wall, must be installed."[185] Obviously, American college campuses have banned open discussion and free intellectual exchange. A conservative speaker on campus can lead to all

---

[183] Meerloo. P. 47
[184] Meerloo. P. 49.
[185] Meerloo. P. 49.

kinds of violence. He is a destroyer of the peace. Programmed people have a phobia of people who have not been mentally indoctrinated. Ugly people do not want to see pictures of beautiful people: lookism.

*

The American public became aware of 'brainwashing' after American prisoners of war in North Korea during the Korean War renounced their own nation. Americans have been trained to have an arrogance about their nation and the home of the brave. It was learned that people under threat, tension, and anxiety opens a person's mind to suggestions, i.e. mental viruses. One of the characteristics of those who were best able to resist the Communist mind viruses has been totally underplayed. "Often those with a rigid, simple belief [Fundamentalists] were able to withstand the continual barrage against their minds than were the flexible, sophisticated ones, full of doubt and inner conflicts. The simple man with deep-rooted, freely absorbed religious faith could exert a much greater inner resistance than could the complex, questioning intellectualist. The refined intellectual is much more handicapped by the internal pros and cons."[186] The Bible believer has implanted in his mind absolute words that cannot be manipulated. That is why the American school and college system is at war with all absolutes: strong beliefs prevent the ability of the government to change the masses into zombies in service to their nation and its leader.

When Meerloo wrote his book, he looked upon Communist countries as the center of the new way of thinking about human animals. However, his description sounds very much like 21st century America. "In totalitarian countries, where belief in Pavlovian strategy has assumed grotesque proportions, the self-thinking, subjective man has disappeared. This is an utter rejection of any attempt at persuasion or discussion. Individual self-expression is taboo. Private affection is taboo. Peaceful exchange of thoughts in free conversation will disturb the conditioned reflexes and is therefore taboo. No longer are there any brains, only conditioned patterns and educated muscles. In such a taming system neurotic compulsion is looked upon as a positive asset instead of something pathological. The mental automaton becomes the ideal of education."[187] While

---

[186] Meerloo. P. 50-51.

America was fighting Communism, something strange happened, American schools were taken over by those who wished to transform man into the same kind of animal man as found in Communist nations. That is why in 2023, as the nation adopts Communism, most have been trained to accept such a form of social order as normal.

The goal was to transform man into an obedient servant of a new totalitarian American order, i.e. Marxism. Meerloo cites one psychologists who wrote: "The entire reactionary nature of this approach to man is completely clear. Man is an automaton who can be caused to act as one wills! This is the ideal of capitalism! Behold the dream of capitalism the world over—a working class without consciousness, which cannot think for itself, whose actions can be trained according to the whim of the exploiter! This is the reason why it is in America, the bulwark of present day capitalism, that the theory of man as a robot has been so vigorously developed and so stubbornly held to."[188] The New World Order desires men who will willingly submit to a work/consume culture. That is why American education has been turning out a generation of those who are more concerned with their sexual identities than with the real world of God's creation.

Modern animal man is viewed as a creature that pursues pleasure and avoids pain. These two opposite goals can be used to create a generation quite willing to obey the new world being created by the World Economic Forum. Everyone will become merely a temporary tool to serve the global elites. No one will own anything, but will rent everything. Everyone will work and make rental payments. And when a person dies, he will be replaced by another renter of your possessions. There will be no need for the type of mind as described in the Bible: a being that has a personal relationship with his creator and is designed to reflect the very character and personality of God. Modern America cannot be understood unless you understand the Satanic nature of this war against the special nature of man: he is not an animal and with God, Man is given the power to resist the animal trainer. God does not create zombie, Satan does. Why? That

---

[187] Meerloo. P. 51.
[188] Meerloo. P. 51.

is his nature just being reflected in his followers. A prelude to Hell. "The ideal of the totalitarian psychology, on the other hand, is to tame men, to make them willing tools in the hands of their leaders."[189] These leaders are servants of Satan who are carrying out his mission against God's creation: including their love of war and the killing that it produces.

The last few years there has been an all-out war against opinions contrary to the official narrative. Those who oppose totalitarian rule and publically oppose such rule have been labelled as disseminators of fake or false information. They are considered enemies of the 'people' and even have been considered promotors of treason. "If our ideal is to make conditioned zombies out of people, the current misuse of Pavlovians will serve our purpose. But once we become even vaguely aware that in the totalitarian picture of man the characteristic human note is missing, and when we see that in such a scheme man sacrifices his instinctual desires, his pleasures, his aims, his goals, his creativity, his instinct for freedom, his paradoxically, we immediately turn against this political person of science. Such Pavolian techniques is aimed at only at developing the automaton in man, not his free alert mind that is ware of moral goals in life. Even in laboratory animals we have found that affective goal-directedness can spoil the Pavlovian experiment. When during a bell-food training session, the dog's **beloved master** entered the room, the animal lost all its previous conditioning and began to bark excitedly. **Here is a simple example of an age-old truth: love and laughter break through all rigid conditioning.**"[190] (Emphasis added.)

When the Roman Empire was filled with chaos and on its decline, the Christians triumphed over the despair in the land. The Romans said this of those Christians: 'They sure know how to laugh.' Especially, knowing that **their Master** is in every situation with them.

There are multiple ways in our society that enhances the creation of automatons. People are being separated from each other in many ways. Covid-19 lock downs was more about teaching people to get along without others. People are being trained to associate through the social media and not through

---

[189] Meerloo. P. 52,
[190] Meerloo. P. 53-54.

eye-to-eye contact. As I write, AI chats are available to everyone now. These chats are totally addicting as the computer knows all about you and it changes his interaction to fit the level of comfort for the user. The joy of personal comfort and laugher are disappearing. Previously, people learned their ability to interact joyfully in their family. With families becoming separated through the expanded hours spent at school, and the need for both parents to work to keep up with inflation, children no longer grow up in a cheerful family setting. Tyrants know that zombies and automatons will never revolt against their Overlords. Also, the school as an impersonal factory minimizes the development of powerful ties of friendship. Those with strong, long-lasting personal ties to others are able to resist cultural conditioning. It is better to have one strong friend than the approval of a crowd.

*

One of the first persons to apply Pavlov's techniques to the general society was Edward Bernays. He is considered the Father of modern advertising. The first very successful advertising understood the importance of association in the minds of the targeted customers. Brainwashing became customer washing. However, Bernays did not look upon propaganda as bad, he called it proper-ganda. He felt it could fulfill a proper need of informing the public and in helping businesses sell their product. "He believed in war and peacetime propaganda campaigns that seed the interests of the ruling power classes against the unreliable, undisciplined, but malleable masses."[191] Without guidance, the masses really did not know what they needed or wanted. That is the role of the advertiser, i.e. proper-gandist.

Bernays was so good at his discipline, that he was able to change human behavior and the mass's conception of reality. When he was hired by the American Pork Producers, he was able to make bacon part of the normal breakfast. He hired 'doctors' in white coats to sell the idea of a good breakfast for workers and students. They stated that a good breakfast of bacon and eggs was necessary in today's competitive world. He also was able to change the public's

---

[191] Edward Bernays. The Edward Bernays Reader: From Propaganda to the Engineering of Consent. Ig Publishing. 2021. P. 6.

attitude toward smoking. Before Bernays, it was considered a disgrace for a woman to smoke in public. People associated public smoking by women as something only a prostitute would do. The American Tobacco Company hired Bernays to change that perception in order to increase their cigarette sales: after all, half the population was women.

Remember the power of association. Bernays understood this power and was able to use it to make female public smoking totally acceptable. He hired female models to walk in New York's Easter Parade, all smoking Lucky Strike cigarettes. He hired photographers to take pictures of the beautiful women. Not only did he associate smoking with feminity, he took it a step further and associated public smoking with the women's liberation movement. He called cigarettes, Torches of Freedom. For a woman to smoke in public now became a symbol of her liberation from a male-dominated culture. "The front page of the Monday, April 1, 1929 *New York Times* read: 'Group of Girls Puff at Cigarettes as a Gesture of "Freedom."' The article described the manufactured event…. Within five weeks, freedom-loving female puffers were allowed access to the smoking areas of theaters, just like men."[192] And after that staged event, in cooperation with the media, the world was changed forever.

There is a philosophy behind the above types of advertising. The goal is not just to sell a product, but to change the culture of the product. The aim is not just to sell the product once, but to make the product a part of life. That ensures a repeat customer. For this insight Bernays was a genius and his understanding of civilization changed, not only the selling of products, but the selling of people and ideas. **From then on, those in charge realized that everything in a culture is a product.** Religion is also a product that must be sold in order to become part of a culture. Any religion that is separate from the general culture will be little more than a cult. A successful American religion must also understand the nature of association. Many attempted to associate Christianity with prosperity in order to better sell their product: the respectable person in a community was the regular church attendee.

---

[192] Bernays. P. 9.

This is how Bernays viewed American life: "Public opinion is subject to a variety of influences that develop and alter its views on nearly every phase of life today. Religion, science art, commerce, industry are in a state of motion. The inertia of society and institutions is constantly combated by the activity of individuals with strong convictions and desires. Civilization, however, is limited by inertia. We repeat constantly our beliefs and habits until they become a cumulative retrogressive force. Our attitude toward social intercourse, toward economic, toward national and international politics continues past attitudes and strengthens them **under the force of tradition**."[193] (Emphasis added.) Civilizations by their very nature are conservative. That is their role—to preserve a social order. Without a traditions, every day would require the remaking of our understanding of the world.

However, Civilizations are also the enemy of those who profit from change. The business must sell the idea the 'new and improved' applies to their latest product. The government must sell the idea that change requires new laws. A stable civilization does not need new laws. As you know, the primary product of a government is the making of laws. Just as a business must sell its product, the government must sell its product—new and improved laws. The masses are usually content with a life where everything remains the same. No one likes to change unless they have to change. The goal of advertising is to sell change, and the role of government schools is also to sell change. Even in the 1950's, I remember the teachers telling us in elementary school how much different we were from our parents: our parents were a product of the Great Depression, but we were the product of the generation that won World War II. We were told that by attending a modern school, we were special.

Yes, our parents were captives to the traditions of the past. However, it was the role of the teacher to educate us for a new world that our parents did not understand. Here again, we were being taught association. Our parents were products of the bad times of the 1930's, but we were the product of the glorious 50's. The world was changing and we were told how lucky we were to be living in an exciting and changing world. I remember feeling how privileged we were to be

---

[193] Bernays. P. 17.

young in the 1950's. In a sense, we were being told that the old civilization was dying, and we were the ones who could create a new one. For Bernays, it is public opinion that can change the future:

"Opposing this traditional acceptance of existing ideas is an active public opinion that has been directed consciously into movement against inertia. Public opinion was made or changed formerly by tribal chiefs, by kings, by religious leaders. Today the privilege of attempting to sway public opinion is everyone's. It is one of the manifestations of democracy that anyone may try to convince others and to assume leadership on behalf of his own thesis. ... Looked at from the broadest standpoint, it is the power of the group to sway the large public in its attitude toward ideas. New ideas, new precedents, are continually striving for a place in the scheme of things. Very often these ideas are socially sound and constructive and **put an end to worn-out notions**. Usually they are **minority ideas**, for naturally, but **regrettable majority ideas are most often the old ones**. Public opinion is slow and reactionary and does not easily accept new ideas."[194] (Emphasis Added.)

The above paragraph is one of the most sophisticated attacks upon Western and Christian Civilizations. The new Age of Democracy is the age where minorities are free to change the world and defeat the stagnant ideas of the old majority. The new idol of modern man is PROGRESS. However, as nice sounding as it is, it is really a war against **traditional** Western Civilization and Christian values. The other god is DEMOCRACY which means that people, i.e. the elites, are freed to manipulate the masses to do the bidding of the controllers. Democracy makes the war on civilization sound a like a legitimate war in which the people are in charge of their own destiny. Democracy exalts those who know how to manipulate events so that women will want to smoke cigarettes.

The citations of Bernays that I am citing in this section were written in 1928. Bernays worked with George Creel during WWI to transform a nation that did not want to go war into a 'willing' participate in that bloodbath. He and Creel were pioneers in the new psychology of influencing and controlling the minds of men on a mass scale. In times past, those who sought to influence the masses

---

[194] Bernays. P. 17-18.

would give rational arguments for some proposed actions. Even businesses would attempt to sell their products reasoning with the potential customers. Bernays recognized that the masses do not think with their brains, but with the emotions: control man's emotions, you control his powers of reason. The following is from *Manipulating Public Opinion*:

"The innovator, the leader, the special pleader for new ideas, has through necessity developed a new techniques—the psychology of public persuasion. Through the application of this new psychology he is able to bring about changes in public opinion that **will make for the acceptance of new doctrines, beliefs, and habits.** The manipulation of the public mind [A secular missionary.], which is so marked a characteristic of society today, serves a social purpose. **This manipulation serves to gain acceptance for new ideas.** It is a species of education in that it presents new problems for study and consideration to the public, and leaves it free to approve or reject them. Never before was so broad a section of the general public so subjected to facts on both sides of so many problems of life. Honest education and honest propaganda have much in common. This this dissimilarity: Education attempts to be disinterested, while propaganda is frankly partisan."[195] (Emphasis Added.) Of course, in the 21st century, education and propaganda have become one: both seek to transform the masses into some purpose greater than any past civilization.

Propaganda and Law have also become one. The goal is to unite everyone into one reality and under one power. Those who are unwilling will be either retrained or eliminated according to the laws of the land. The Covid-19 vaxxx, the mandatory jabs for many, and the threat of even more drastic events signify the total reshaping of humanity. The new association is 'LIFE equals OBEDIENCE.'

---

[195] Bernays. P. 18.

Chapter Twenty-Nine: All Laws must be based upon God's Laws.

Laws, God, and Reality are one. One of the goals of Satan is to separate the above three into separate categories. **First**, God becomes a distant observer over life. Man is allowed to be **free** to make his own choices and God will reward each man according to his deeds, for good or for ill. **Second**, God created a material world. This world is to become clay in the hands of man. With the material elements of this universe, man is **free** to use his reasoning powers to create an improved version of earth. **Third**, man is **free** to create the necessary laws in order to perfect the social life of mankind. The God of the Bible grants man a very limited kind of freedom. Even 'Christians' feel that God has created a playing field and within that field, they are free as long as they stay inbounds—keep the basic commandments. That is best illustrated in the Fundamentalist legal view of life. Church is about teaching people the rules of the game so that they can be pleasing to God as they pursue the American Dream and Way of Life.

The first scenario represents the viewpoint of the American Secularist world view. The second viewpoint represents the American Secular Church worldview. The third is the individualist view of reality. Governments are established so the solitary individual can possess and enjoy life, property, and liberty. The battle between the Kingdom of God and the Kingdom of Satan is not included in any of the above worldviews. The battle is fought on another level for those who decide to be combatants in this war. Most Americans are merely content to have as much fun as possible. Man's freedom is the right to decide which form of pleasure that he wants to pursue. Strictly stated, the real battle is viewed as a war between Government Laws and Christian traditional Laws. Those who follow Satan avoid using the language of occultic laws or Satanic anti-laws: that is just too revealing. Satan rarely reveals his true nature. Church people avoid the term Biblical Laws as there are so many laws in the Bible that they find it a bit embarrassing. They tend to focus upon the church operations, and a salvation experience of some kind. This scenario creates secular Christian freedom. Modern Christians are not required to be logical.

To start with, the god of every society is the lawmaker of the society. People debate whether America is or ever was a Christian nation. The question to ask is this: Are or were the laws of the land ever based upon the Bible? Obviously, the answer is no. In a Democracy, the voice of the people is the voice of god. The American Constitution makes this clear when it refused to include any law system in that document or to reference the Biblical God in any way. America is not a Christian Nation. There were Christians in America but they were only free in local communities. These local power centers only existed until the post-Civil War Amendments nationalized all laws. Even Cactus Flats was expected to be an anti-Christian city. That is why the very first Commandment is that a person or a nation can have no other gods before the true God. The other Commandments that follow all depend upon that first Commandment: One God; one law system. Any other law systems do not come from God.

The architecture of a nation is often a subtle way of expressing a nation's beliefs. America's government buildings often reflect Greek temple architecture. "Because for the Greeks mind was one being with the ultimate order of things, man's mind was thus able to discover law (*nomos*) out of its own resources, by penetrating through the maze of accident and matter to the fundamental ideas of being. … Modern humanism, the religion of the state, locates law in the state and thus makes the state, or the people as they find expression in the state, the god of the system."[196] When the Constitution left out the God of Biblical Law, this was a religious revolution. A new god was now the ruler of the nation. What is amazing is that few Christians understood that the nation's religion had changed. Church life went on like nothing had happened. The god of the Enlightenment was the new god. A new god; No problem. Each person was still relatively free to pursue his own private form of pleasure. That is the American Way.

How could the church not notice that there had been a national and cultural coup d'état [Pardon my French.] against Western Civilization and the Bible? That should reveal a lot. The early Roman Christians knew that they were living in a nation that did not worship the true God. Of course, the Caesars made it pretty easy by calling themselves a god. In reality, all the Christians had to do to avoid the lions was to state that the gods of the Roman Empire were equal to the God of the Bible Just take a simply oath stating that they would not allow their service to their God interfere with their duty to the Empire. Just say that 'Caesar is Lord', i.e. Supreme lawgiver, and the Christians could be on their merry way. For many, it was just a meaningless ritual that the State required: kind of like the Pledge of Alliance in the United States. Most Christians maintained that they could serve the State without having to believe in the divinity of the Caesar: just leave us alone and everything will be fine. We are hard-working, honest taxpayers. However, this was where they got into trouble. What true Christians were really saying is this: God's Laws are superior to the Laws of Rome. Where they conflict, the Christian must follow the Laws of the Bible. Oops! And the Roman chorus all sang: The lions are hungry tonight.

Fortunately for the American Church, the people were allowed to serve the State and its Laws without having to take a loyalty oath: it was just assumed that the State's laws superseded the Laws of the God. After all, the American Church lived in a Democracy and citizenship required that a person obey the laws of the land. The Church had no intention of living outside of the law: outlaws. To escape this dilemma, many churches adopted an American theology of Biblical

---

196 Rousas John Rushdoony. The Institutes of Biblical Law. The Craig Press. 1973. P. 5.

Laws. The laws of the Old Testament were considered just for that time and did not apply to those who live under the freedom of the New Testament laws. Others taught that Biblical Laws only applied to the Old Testament nation of Israel and those laws were suspended until the Millennium when God would raise up a renewed nation of Israel. Therefore, the American Church developed a theology where they could serve two gods and feel at harmony with both: the god of the State, and the God of the Church building.

Rushdoony explains: "Since the foundations of law are inescapably religious, no society exists without a religious foundation or without a law-system which codifies the morality of its religion. ...there can be no tolerance in a law system for another religion. Toleration is a device used to introduce a new law-system as a prelude to a **new intolerance.**"[197] (Emphasis added.) As I am writing this morning, a YouTube site showed a clip from the NHL network TV show. The speaker was calling for the firing of the one player in the league who refused to wear a gay pride jersey. Notice how quickly the movement went from just wanting to be tolerated to one totally intolerant toward those who disagree. When a nation abandons the true God, there will also be a new sheriff in town.

As America increasingly falls under the control of a new god, the new morality of that god is at war with all other value systems. "Every law-system must maintain its existence by hostility to every other law-system and to alien religious foundations, or else it commits suicide."[198] That is why when anyone publically denies the new law-system or refuses to obey the new laws, he is forced to make a public apology and confess his 'sins' and appear to be contrite: I will never do that again. The Catholic Church used to enforce public confession, penance, and excommunication when it dominated Christendom. The new American god enforces the same practices today. That is why people who refuse to recant of their sin of political incorrectness are excommunicated from their job or position. This is one way to recognize which god is in charge of a nation: wear that jersey with Pride.

---

[197] Rushdoony. P. 5.
[198] Rushdoony. P. 5-6.

In the Declaration of Independence, Jefferson invoked Nature's God to give credence to his declaration of American faith. Many church people were tricked into thinking this: Because God created Nature, then Nature must reflect the God of the Bible. Therefore, laws derived from Nature are no different than the Laws as taught in the Bible. "For the Bible, there is no law in nature, because nature is fallen and cannot be normative. Moreover, the source of law is not nature but God. There is no law *in* nature but a law *over* nature, God's law. ... Apart from revealed law, man cannot claim to be under God but only in rebellion against God."[199] I find it amazing how even Church people hate the mention of God's Laws. There seems to be some instinctive feeling that if God's Laws are still in effect, then they have a real problem—a problem they would rather avoid.

*

No city, no nation, and no empire can exist without a system of laws. In fact, the same applies to the modern corporation. The modern corporation can be favorably compared to the Vatican of the Middle Ages. The Corporate model, some say, is based upon the corporate model of the Catholic Church. The Pope is the CEO of the Church's organization. And just like the Vatican, CEO's come and go, but the organization is eternal. The Corporation is actually more religious than people realize. As I write, Corporations are promoting the new LGBTQ agenda in the commercials and in their hiring and employment practices. In order to become a member in good standing, a person must either actively or passively adopt the religion of the Corporate faith. A mentioned earlier, Advertisements are a form of religious propaganda as they attempt to plant certain beliefs within the mind of the targeted subject. Corporations use advertisements, not just to sell their product or service, but to reveal their doctrinal beliefs. 'Hello everyone, just to let you know that we here at Corporate X worship the correct god.'

At first, men believed that there were many gods and each god promoted its own particular lifestyle: that is called a multiverse. In a sense, the Corporate world reflects the nature of this belief as there are many Corporate gods, each making the laws of its own domain. When you belong to one corporation, you obey the laws of that corporation. Generally, those laws are considered absolute

---

[199] Rushdoony. P. 10.

as they are necessary for the unity of the workforce and the having a stable working environment. When I worked for one large multi-national corporation, the mention of religion or the wearing of religious symbols was forbidden. Those were divisive to the goals of the corporation. Everyone is to submit to the rules of the CEO and his laws of corporate unity. Once, when a corporation was called out for selling its products to every nation in the world regardless of their religion, political alignment, i.e. Communist, or cultural makeup, the CEO stated that it is not the business of the free market to differentiate between customers. The only common denominator in the market is the ability to pay for what you purchase. Religion or religious laws have no place inside the secular world of Finance Capitalism. Only Corporate Laws and the laws of Finance Capitalism are allowed to exist.

The laws of the Corporate Global Market act as a religious laws operated during the Age of Christendom. However, instead of the Vatican imposing its laws upon everyone, the Corporate CEO's impose their laws upon everyone. There is no such thing as Democracy in such a world: no one votes on the laws of business and finance. It can be said that even the governments of the world are compelled to operate under the laws of Finance Capitalism. Who are the true rulers of this super world of global laws? As I write, the American government is agreeing to operate under the laws of the World Health Organization. Who put WHO in charge of the world? (Okay, I will say it: WHO is now on first.) And the same question can be asked of the World Economic Forum, the Bank of International Settlements, and many others.

This is where the real issues are confronted. If the god of a nation is revealed in its laws, what god is in charge of all of these global centers of power? That is the question that rarely gets asked because the answer is what no one wants to hear. There are only two sources of power and of laws in this world: God and Satan. Those are the only two gods and therefore, the only two sources of law. Also, no one can separate laws and power. There is no such a thing as a law that need not be enforced by power. Civilizations produce customs that everyone accepts as reality, but laws are acts of those in power to force their ideas upon a population. Tyrannical power and dictatorial power can be observed when the laws declare war upon timeless customs—such as the current laws seeking to overthrow six thousand year 'tradition' that people are born either male or female. Such laws that not only go against custom and God's Laws, their enforcement requires total force—and that is actually the goal to pass laws that need the force of a tyrant.

*

A new Corporate Law system is being enforced upon Americans as I write. As Corporations have been transformed into multinationals, the era of a company town are over. I grew up in a company town. The employment in that town depended upon the ups and downs of that business and its cyclical demand. In time, the business diversified into a multi-national with just a core amount of workers kept in its original city. It stabilized local employment at a much lower level, but there was something added to a person's job: diversity training became part of the job. With a global workforce, in a multicultural, multiracial, multi-religious, and multi-identity world, the Corporation must become ecumenical. An ecumenical church can unify the masses around a common faith in God and the Bible. The Corporation copied the Catholic Church and decided to become a new kind of religion. The multi-national Corporation is ecumenical: everyone globally belongs to the same Corporation and devotes their life to the success of the business. Common rules binds everyone to the same social milieu.

CEO's make very poor theologians. When they go about starting a religion they do not have a clue. They only know popular social-media culture and the kind of beliefs promoted by the TV and movies. I believe this is how the corporation adopted the political correctness of the Woke culture. From all that the average businessman knows, that is the future. There is no going back to the days of the small-town farmer and his community. The future is a global culture with a global ethical system. Remember, images are everything in the modern world, and people think in terms of associations. The Corporation's future depended upon aligning itself with the beliefs of the future. All trends point toward a different kind of world than the one we currently are experiencing. The leaders of American Corporations are placing their bets upon globalism and wokeism. To oppose global beliefs is like opposing automation in previous times. Those that did not automate got left behind.

The future of the new Corporation depends upon not offending any minorities. Throughout history, minorities have often the heralds of a new age. They are the ones who are feeling the distress of the current age and are seeking to discover a new life upon the ruins of the old one. Very few look upon traditional Christianity as belonging to the future. The 21st century is an age of transition and those who can hitch their future to the proper movement will prosper. Religious Fundamentalists are noted for holding onto the past and seek to live their life in the memories of ancient times, as revealed in the Bible. The Corporation stays in business by knowing and understanding the future. Many CEO's are betting that Wokeism is the future—however offensive it may be to the older generation. But those people are dying and it is the younger generation that belongs to the future. The bets are on the table and no one is betting on the revival of Western and Christian Civilizations.

*

Wokeism is not confined to Corporations. It is being taught in the government schools and being enforced by American Laws and American Courts. However the motives are different. Education is controlled by those who are in rebellion against God. Sinners always desire to make others into sinners. The government wants to create a one world government: this requires a one world culture. The Corporations understand the importance of having a workforce that can/will be tolerant of differences. Of course, Satan is working through all three, but each is working to form a world according to their own needs. This is vital to understand: every group has global designs. No one wants to preserve the personal life of the community in the small town. Somehow, if mankind can control every person in the whole world, the utopian millennium will arrive.

As I write, the dream of a world of eternal prosperity and bliss is dying. The fantasy that science can produce a miracle cure for every disease has vanished. Science was used to create the deadly vaxxx causing untold suffering and death. Financial prosperity was bled dry in attempt to take down the Russian Federation. Russia was pictured as the last domino to fall preventing a New Order of the Ages.

Russia's rural people were proving more resilient than anticipated. The Russian Orthodox Church appeared to have risen from the dead and to have restored the Russian people to the faith of their ancestors. The down-sized Soviet Union was proving to be a nation on the rise, and a nation that did not buy into the global political correctness. Their promotion of the traditional family and their crackdown on Western sexual liberation infuriated the sexually liberated West.

Ukraine was chosen to be the vehicle to force Russia into a Vietnam like war that would slowly deplete the Russian ability to carry on a long-term conflict. A huge NATO style army of around seven to eight hundred thousand was trained after the United States' takeover of Ukraine in 2014. By 2021 they were ready to attack and kill the Russian residents of eastern Ukraine: a move designed to make Russia retreat from the world stage or to move to protect its own people inside the Donbas region. Finally, the West had their war which they hope would destroy the Christian nation of Russia and bring either secularism or atheism to the entire planet. It appears that the secular West fears Christian Russia more than atheistic China. Servants of Satan sometimes form strange bedfellows. With Satan controlling both the United States and China, for Satan it was a case of heads he wins and tails he wins. Satan could not care if the people of both China and the United States kill each other as Satan glories in the death and destruction of God's personal creations and His earthly beauty. Reality must be seen in this environment of God versus Satan which knows no official boundaries on a map.

Chapter Thirty: God's Kingdom in Christ, and the End of Satan's Kingdom.

As I write, the most quoted book on the internet is the Book of Revelation. The final war between God and Satan appears to be in the offing. One of the reasons is that the followers of Satan are no longer hiding their deviant behavior, but shouting it from the rooftops, i.e. the social media. Government schools and the Mainstream Media are joining in to proclaim their victory over the God and His Commandments. Rebellion against God and His Ethical demands are now labelled liberation, not sin. Huge Gay Pride Parades draw hundreds of thousands in major cities across the United States. These parades can be compared to the huge post WWII parades after Japan and Germany had been defeated. Except now, it is God who appears to have been defeated. This brings us to the Book of Revelation when God will finally say to those who claim victory—

Revelation 11:15. And the seventh angel sounded; and there were great voices in heaven, saying, **The kingdoms of this world are become *the kingdoms* of our Lord, and of his Christ;** and he shall reign for ever and ever. **16** And the four and twenty elders, which sat before God on their seats, fell upon their faces, and worshipped God, **17** Saying, We give thee thanks, O Lord God Almighty, which art, and wast, and art to come; because thou hast taken to thee thy great power, and hast reigned. **18** And **the nations were angry**, and thy wrath is come, and the time of the dead, that they should be judged, and that thou shouldest give reward unto thy servants the prophets, and to the saints, and them that fear thy name, small and great; and **shouldest destroy them which destroy the earth**. **19** And the temple of God was opened in heaven, and there was seen in his temple the ark of his testament: and there were lightnings, and voices, and thunderings, and an earthquake, and great hail.

*

The above is a spoiler alert, but I want to document the nature of the battle which we are apparently engulfed in right now. Most of the world is celebrating the God's defeat. Government schools have transformed football halftime shows into times of celebrating those who have declared their sexual liberation from God. Whether in movies, TV shows, theme parks, and court decisions, the whole world is declaring that man has finally won the victory promised to Man in the Garden of Eden by Satan: Every man can become his own god. This is the foundation of all conflicts upon the earth since Cain killed his brother Abel. In today's world, when Cain is victorious in any way, the world has cause to party. Men think to win a battle against God mans they have won the war. That is why the Book of Revelation is in the Bible. The War is not over.

*

Actually, Jesus announced the beginning of the real war at the start of His ministry. Satanic rulers had conquered almost all of the earth and almost the entire population of the earth had already surrendered to Satan and his national rulers. When Jesus was crucified, it appeared all was lost. The war started by Satan against God's created beings in the Garden of Eden had been won. However, let's start at the beginning:

Mark 1:14. Now after that John was put in prison, Jesus came into Galilee, preaching the gospel of the kingdom of God, **15** And saying, The time is fulfilled, and **the kingdom of God is at hand**: repent ye, and believe the gospel. **16** Now as he walked by the sea of Galilee, he saw Simon and Andrew his brother casting a net into the sea: for they were fishers. **17** And Jesus said unto them, Come ye after me, and I will make you to become fishers of men. **18** And **straightway they forsook their nets**, and followed him. **19** And when he had gone a little further thence, he saw James the *son* of Zebedee, and John his brother, **who also were in the ship mending their nets. 20** And straightway he called them: and **they left their father Zebedee in the ship with the hired servants**, and went after him.

The inauguration of the Kingdom of God is THE major event in history. And yet, you will not find this occurrence in any history text book or other accounts of world history. For modern man there was only one conclusion: The Kingdom of God was only Jesus launching fake history; or for the Christian, it was Satan's strategy was to have his servants completely eliminate any mention of God's action within history. Try to find any mention of the Kingdom of God in any history textbook. I will save you some time: there are not any. History is the story of man versus nature and man versus man. It is not the story of God versus Satan. Biblically, it is the story of God's Kingdom establishing a beachhead during the time of Jesus and then the spreading of God's message throughout the world. As Jesus taught us to pray: 'Thy kingdom come. Thy will be done, as in heaven, so in earth.' **That is God's declaration of war against all earthly kingdoms.**

The Kingdom God is both real and invisible. In Egypt, the Pharaohs built the pyramids and temples to display their power upon the earth. In the Old Testament, the promise of a coming Messiah was interpreted to mean a man who would rule with similar symbols of power, like Nimrod of Babylon, a Pharaoh of Egypt, or a Caesar of Rome. Just as Nimrod built a giant Tower to symbolize his power so the Caesars built giant structures—like the Coliseum--to communicate the power of Rome. In the same way, the Jews of the Old Testament had a magnificent Temple in Jerusalem to give expression to the power of their beliefs. When questioned by Pilate about what symbolized the power of Jesus's Kingdom, He gave this answer which satisfied no one:

John 18:33. Then Pilate entered into the judgment hall again, and called Jesus, and said unto him, **Art thou the King of the Jews? 34** Jesus answered him, Sayest thou this thing of thyself, or did others tell it thee of me? **35** Pilate answered, Am I a Jew? Thine own nation and the chief priests have delivered thee unto me: **what hast thou done? 36** Jesus answered, **My kingdom is not of this world**: if my kingdom were of this world, **then would my servants fight**, that I should not be delivered to the Jews: but now is my kingdom not from hence. **37** Pilate therefore said unto him, **Art thou a king then?** Jesus answered, Thou sayest that I am a king. **To this end was I born**, and for this cause came I into the world, **that I should bear witness unto the truth.** Every one that is of the truth heareth my voice.

Remember, the minds of the people of that day had an image of what it meant to be a king and have a kingdom: A giant and beautiful headquarters; a piece of land claimed to be part of that kingdom; a bureaucracy to administrate that land; and an army to defend that land. The Jews expected Jesus to create a Kingdom like all the other kingdoms upon the earth. Imagine being able to feed a whole army with a few fish and some bread. Generally, rulers in ancient times claimed to be a god and use the powers of a god to create an empire. The Kingdom of God was not like any other Kingdom. And yet, no one could imagine any other kind of kingdom than one that had all of the physical attributes of greatness. That is why Pilate was so confused. If Jesus was truly a King, why did his own people turn Him in for sedition against the reign of Caesar? Why was His army not seeking to rescue Him from the throes of death? Jesus had none of the traditional symbols of power.

The Jewish symbol of power was their Temple. And that symbol of power was going to be destroyed and replaced by Jesus with a heavenly temple, Jesus Himself.

Matthew 26:61.   And said, This *fellow* said, I am able to **destroy the temple** of God, and to **build it in three days**.

Jesus was going to destroy the old Temple, and he would become our priest and God's Temple would REIGN from heaven.

Hebrews 10:1. For the law having a shadow of good things to come, *and* not the very image of the things, can never with those sacrifices which they offered year by year continually make the comers thereunto perfect. **2** For then would they not have ceased to be offered? because that the worshippers once purged should have had no more conscience of sins. **3** But in those *sacrifices there is* a remembrance again *made* of sins every year. **4** For *it is* not possible that the blood of bulls and of goats should take away sins. **5** Wherefore when he cometh into the world, he saith, Sacrifice and offering thou wouldest not, but a body hast thou prepared me: **6** In burnt offerings and *sacrifices* for sin thou hast had no pleasure. **7** Then said I, Lo, I come (in the volume of the book it is written of me,) to do thy will, O God. **8** Above when he said, Sacrifice and offering and burnt offerings and *offering* for sin thou wouldest not, neither hadst pleasure *therein*; which are offered by the law; **9** Then said he, Lo, I come to do thy will, O God. He taketh away the first, that he may establish the second. **10** By the which will we are sanctified through the offering of the body of Jesus Christ once *for all*. **11** And every priest standeth daily ministering and offering oftentimes the same sacrifices, which can never take away sins: **12** But this man, after he had offered one sacrifice for sins for ever, sat down on the right hand of God; **13 From henceforth expecting till his enemies be made his footstool. 14** For by one offering he hath perfected for ever them that are sanctified. **15** *Whereof* the Holy Ghost also is a witness to us: for after that he had said before, **16** This *is* the covenant that I will make with them after those days, saith the Lord, I will put **my laws** into their hearts, and **in their minds** will I write them; **17** And their sins and iniquities will I remember no more. **18** Now where remission of these *is, there is* no more offering for sin. **19** Having therefore, brethren, boldness to enter into the holiest by the blood of Jesus, **20** By a new and living way, which he hath consecrated for us, through the veil, that is to say, his flesh; **21** And *having* an high priest over the house of God; **22** Let us draw near with a true heart in full assurance of faith, having our hearts sprinkled from an evil conscience, and our bodies washed with pure water.

When Jesus rose from the dead, that ended the need for a Temple where animal sacrifices would be offered unto God. God's Temple was in heaven and God's people were to give expression to the reign of God here upon earth. God's army was to operate upon faith and the power of witnessing to the truth of God's Kingdom in full operation with a different kind of conquering army.

Hebrew 11:24.   By faith Moses, when he was come to years, refused to be called the son of Pharaoh's daughter; **25** Choosing rather to suffer affliction with the people of God, than to enjoy the pleasures of sin for a season; **26** Esteeming the reproach of Christ greater riches than the treasures in Egypt: for he had respect unto the recompence of the reward. **27** By faith he forsook Egypt, not fearing the wrath of the king: for he endured, as seeing him who is invisible. **28** Through faith he kept the passover, and the sprinkling of blood, lest he that destroyed the firstborn should touch them. **29** By faith they passed through the Red sea as by dry *land*: which the Egyptians assaying to do were drowned. **30** By faith the walls of Jericho fell down, after they were compassed about seven days. **31** By faith the harlot Rahab perished not with them that believed not, when she had received the spies with peace. **32** And what shall I more say? for the time would fail me to tell of Gedeon, and *of* Barak, and *of* Samson, and *of* Jephthae; *of* David also, and Samuel, and *of* the prophets: **33 Who through faith subdued kingdoms, wrought righteousness, obtained promises, stopped the mouths of lions**, **34** Quenched the violence of fire, escaped the edge of the sword, out of weakness were made strong, waxed valiant in fight, turned to flight the armies of the aliens. **35** Women received their dead raised to life again: and others were tortured, not accepting deliverance; that they might obtain a better resurrection: **36** And others had trial of *cruel* mockings and scourgings, yea, moreover of bonds and imprisonment: **37** They were stoned, they were sawn asunder, were tempted, were slain with the sword: they wandered about in sheepskins and goatskins; being destitute, afflicted, tormented; **38** (Of whom the world was not worthy:) they wandered in deserts, and *in* mountains, and *in* dens and caves of the earth. **39** And these all, having obtained a good report through faith, received not the promise: **40** God having provided some better thing for us, that they without us should not be made perfect.

The above is the Kingdom of God in operation. Some experienced mighty victories and some were persecuted for their witness to the truth of God's Kingdom. Those in Christ are called to be witnesses to God's Kingdom and to live lives that give a physical expression to God's true nature and His Laws. Americans have confused the physical church building and the people that meet therein as the Kingdom of God. No. The Church is where God's people meet to help and encourage others in the pursuit of living lives dedicated to be a witness to the power of God and how His Truth shall be spread throughout the earth. When Christians do that, they establish a Civilization. That is the invisible nature of God's rule. Armies can defend nations and kings, but Civilizations arise out of the hearts and beliefs of a people and can never be preserved by armies and guns. When armies and guns are at the door of a true civilization, that means the vultures are gathering around an already dead and decaying civilization.

*

Jesus announced to the Jews of the Old Testament that their idea of a kingdom was ending. Their physical nation was about to be destroyed—which happened 40 years after the death and resurrection of Jesus Christ.

Matthew 21:43. Therefore say I unto you, **The kingdom of God shall be taken from you**, and **given to a nation bringing forth the fruits** thereof.

Many church people teach that the Kingdom of God is in the future after God's people had been removed from earth into heaven, i.e. the rapture. However, Jesus informed His followers that the Kingdom would arrive quickly after His resurrection.

Luke 22:18. For I say unto you, I will not drink of the fruit of the vine, until the **kingdom of God shall come**.

Daniel spoke of the Kingdom that would be established by God and that this Kingdom would find expression throughout the earth.

Daniel 7:14. And there was given him dominion, and glory, and a kingdom, that all people, nations, and languages, should serve him: his dominion *is* an everlasting dominion, which shall not pass away, and **his kingdom *that* which shall not be destroyed.**

Paul wrote that the people of the New Testament had received God's Kingdom unto themselves.

Hebrews 12:25. See that ye refuse not him that speaketh. For if they escaped not who refused him that spake on earth, much more *shall not* we *escape*, if we turn away from him that *speaketh* from heaven: **26** Whose voice then shook the earth: but now he hath promised, saying, **Yet once more I shake not the earth** only, but also heaven. **27** And this *word*, Yet once more, signifieth the removing of those things that are shaken, as of things that are made, that those things which cannot be shaken may remain. **28** Wherefore **we receiving a kingdom** which cannot be moved, let us have grace, whereby we may serve God acceptably with reverence and godly fear: **29** For our God *is* a consuming fire

God's Kingdom is to operate as an invisible presence within the power structures of this world. The Kingdom of God operates by infiltration and not by force. Those who seek to gain control of the levers of power in order to promote the Kingdom of God are operating contrary to the principles as taught by Jesus in the Gospel narrative.

Luke 13:18.   Then said he, Unto what is the kingdom of God like? and whereunto shall I resemble it? **19** It is like a grain of mustard seed, which a man took, and cast into his garden; and it grew, and waxed a great tree; and the fowls of the air lodged in the branches of it. **20** And again he said, Whereunto shall I liken the kingdom of God? **21** It is like leaven, which a woman took and hid in three measures of meal, till the whole was leavened.

During the end of this age, the nations of the world will once again adopt the Kingdom of Satan and establish rulers who operate on the level of a god, i.e. tyrant. The Bible warns that Christians are to avoid thinking that the world can be saved through political action or protesting. There is coming a time when even the very idea of a Christian or Western Civilization will be considered evil. There is coming a time when even the leaven of the Gospel will be ineffective.

Revelation 18:3.   For all nations have drunk of the wine of the wrath of her fornication, and the kings of the earth have committed fornication with her, and the merchants of the earth are waxed rich through the abundance of her delicacies. **4** And I heard another voice from heaven, saying, **Come out of her, my people,** that ye be not partakers of her sins, and that ye receive not of her plagues. **5** For her sins have reached unto heaven, and God hath remembered her iniquities

Hebrews 13:13. Let us go forth therefore unto him **without the camp**, bearing his reproach. **14** For here have we no continuing city, but we seek one to come.

*

The first thing to remember is that the local Church is not the Kingdom of God. It is really open to all, but those who wish to enter the Kingdom of God, that is another story. There is a big difference between those who only want to be saved and those who want to serve God. Any church that wants to be successful will emphasize the simple Gospel of easy salvation. I remember when I was young and serving in a youth ministry. I got reprimanded because I was not presenting the easy Gospel. The ministry was looking for numbers—that is also how you attract donors who support a youth ministry: 'We had two hundred kids raise their hand to accept Jesus last year." To stay 'in business' a ministry needs to make it as easy as possible to become a Christian. The theory was if we can get kids to start praying, then it is up to God to take them to the next step. The mention of the Kingdom of God was not part of the evangelism ministry. (That is when I gave up the youth ministry as the Biblical message was treated as a vitamin supplement to make up for your poor, fast-food spiritual diet.)

The message of Jesus over and over was about the Kingdom of God. Yet, I grew up in a Fundamentalist Church and I do not ever remember hearing about the Kingdom of God. I believe the reason is this: the Kingdom requires total commitment. "Mark (1:14-15) thus makes its plain that the burden of Jesus' preaching was to announce the Kingdom of God, that was the central thing with which he was concerned. A reading of the teachings of Jesus as they are found in the Gospels only serves to bear this statement out. Everywhere the Kingdom of God is on his lips, and it is always a matter of desperate importance. What is it like? It is like a sower who goes forth to sow; it is like costly pearl; it is like a mustard seed. How does one enter? One sells all that he has and gives to the poor; one becomes as a little child. Is it a matter of importance? Indeed it is! It would be better to mutilate yourself and enter maimed than not to get in at all. So paramount, in fact, was the notion of the Kingdom of God in the mind of Jesus that one can scarcely grasp his meaning at all without some understanding of it.

But for all his repeated mention of the Kingdom of God, Jesus never once paused to define it.[200]

There is a reason Jesus did not define what the Kingdom of God meant. Few would have understood what he meant. Remember, the nations of Judea and Israel in the Old Testament thought in terms of nations and borders. And for good reason: the whole world was divided up by nations who protected their borders. I am sure most would have thought that the Kingdom of God was just another nation except it would be enforcing the laws of God upon the land and the people. Consider what God promised to Abraham:

Genesis 17:1. And when Abram was ninety years old and nine, the LORD appeared to Abram, and said unto him, I *am* the Almighty God; walk before me, and be thou perfect. **2** And I will make my covenant between me and thee, and will multiply thee exceedingly. **3** And Abram fell on his face: and God talked with him, saying, **4** As for me, behold, my covenant *is* with thee, and **thou shalt be a father of many nations**. **5** Neither shall thy name any more be called Abram, but thy name shall be Abraham; for **a father of many nations** have I made thee. **6** And I will make thee exceeding fruitful, and I will make nations of thee, and kings shall come out of thee. **7** And I will establish my covenant between me and thee and thy seed after thee in their generations for an everlasting covenant, to be a God unto thee, and to thy seed after thee. **8 And I will give unto thee, and to thy seed after thee, the land wherein thou art a stranger**, all the land of Canaan, for an everlasting possession; and I will be their God.

God is promising a lot more to Abraham than just the solitary nation of Israel. In a sense, God is promising many nations of Israel to Abraham. Of course, they would go by different names, but they would all be Kingdoms of God. Not only did Jesus proclaim he was taking away the nationhood of the New Testament Israel but that he was giving it to another more deserving people (Matthew 21:43). Jesus is describing the true New World Order that was about to be inaugurated upon the earth and it would encapsulate many nations, but the nation of Israel in Palestine would not be one of them. If those who are

---

[200] John Bright. The Kingdom of God: The Biblical Concept and Its Meaning for the Church. Abingdon-Cokesbury Press. 1953. P. 17.

descendants of Abraham are to form many nations, how can we determined who is a true descendent?

Romans 9:4. Who are Israelites; to whom *pertaineth* the adoption, and the glory, and the covenants, and the giving of the law, and the service *of God*, and the promises; **5** Whose *are* the fathers, and of whom as concerning the flesh Christ *came*, who is over all, God blessed for ever. Amen. **6** Not as though the word of God hath taken none effect. **For they *are* not all Israel, which are of Israel: 7** Neither, because they are the seed of Abraham, *are they* all children: but, In Isaac shall thy seed be called. **8** That is, **They which are the children of the flesh, these *are* not the children of God: but the children of the promise are counted for the seed.**

Those who are or who have become true Israelites by faith, not genetics, are to form many nations in the teachings of Jesus and His Kingdom. The Kingdom of God is not to be one nation and it is a group of nations but not held together by a government or an army, as in an empire. These are concepts that the people of Jesus would have understood. That is why Jesus did not define the Kingdom for his followers. The nature of the Kingdom of God would be revealed in time as the people of God, the true Israelites, went forth and conquered the world with the Word of God. So what happened? After the Fall of the Roman Empire, something called Christendom developed. It lasted for about 1000 years. Christendom was basically a Christian Civilization. After the Reformation, Western Civilization was another civilization built upon the teachings of the Kingdom of God. However, the Kingdom of God was divided between the church kingdom and the government kingdom. No man can serve two masters and neither can two ideological groups share the same kingdom. From Luther and Calvin to today the question has always been this: what is the dividing line between church and state. That war has never ceased, although the State has claimed victory in the 21st century, i.e. total victory.

*

Because history since the time of Jesus has been about the Kingdom of God, it is essential to understand what Jesus said about it. One reason people have a problem with thinking about God's Kingdom is that they still think in terms of the Old Testament idea of a nation. Because of that, some attempt to form a

Christian nation of God rather than working to form a Kingdom of God. This leads to all kinds of problems as those who seek to impose an order by the point of a gun will not succeed. God's Kingdom is built up through the power of the Holy Spirit working within a nation or nations. It is like the yeast (leaven) in the dough of bread. When the Holy Spirit is freed to work within a nation, a Civilization rises up much like the loaf of bread expanding to form a whole loaf. Here is Jesus defining the mysteries of His Kingdom:

Matthew 13:1. The same day went Jesus out of the house, and sat by the sea side. **2** And great multitudes were gathered together unto him, so that he went into a ship, and sat; and the whole multitude stood on the shore. **3** And **he spake many things unto them in parables,** saying, **Behold, a sower went forth** to sow; **4** And when he sowed, some *seeds* fell by the way side, and the fowls came and devoured them up: **5** Some fell upon stony places, where they had not much earth: and forthwith they sprung up, because they had no deepness of earth: **6** And when the sun was up, they were scorched; and because they had no root, they withered away. **7** And some fell among thorns; and the thorns sprung up, and choked them: **8** But other fell into good ground, and brought forth fruit, some an hundredfold, some sixtyfold, some thirtyfold. **9** Who hath ears to hear, let him hear. **10** And the disciples came, and said unto him, Why speakest thou unto them in parables? **11** He answered and said unto them, Because it is given unto you to know the **mysteries of the kingdom of heaven**, [Mystery: no one had ever seen a multi-national kingdom before.] but to them it is not given. **12** For whosoever hath, to him shall be given, and he shall have more abundance: but whosoever hath not, from him shall be taken away even that he hath. **13 Therefore speak I to them in parables: because they seeing see not**; and hearing they hear not, neither do they understand. **14** And in them is fulfilled the prophecy of Esaias, which saith, By hearing ye shall hear, and shall not understand; and seeing ye shall see, and shall not perceive: [Religious people today still promote the Kingdom as something governments and their laws can produce.] **15** For this people's heart is waxed gross, and *their* ears are dull of hearing, and their eyes they have closed; lest at any time they should see with *their* eyes, and hear with *their* ears, and should understand with *their* heart, and should be converted, and I should heal them. **16** But blessed *are* your eyes, for they see: and your ears, for they hear. **17** For verily I say unto you, That many prophets and righteous *men* have desired to see *those things* which ye see, and have not seen *them*; and to hear *those things* which ye hear, and have not heard *them*. [No one understood what the Kingdom of God was because they could think outside the box of their nationalistic thinking.]

18 Hear ye therefore **the parable of the sower. 19** When any one heareth the word of the kingdom, and understandeth *it* not, then cometh the wicked *one*, and catcheth away that which was sown in his heart. This is he which received seed by the way side. **20** But he that received the seed into stony places, the same is he that heareth the word, and anon with joy receiveth it; **21** Yet hath he not root in himself, but dureth for a while: for when tribulation or persecution ariseth because of the word, by and by he is offended. **22** He also that received seed among the thorns is he that heareth the word; and the care of this world, and the deceitfulness of riches, choke the word, and he becometh unfruitful. **23** But he that received seed into the good ground is he that heareth the word, and understandeth *it*; which also beareth fruit, and bringeth forth, some an hundredfold, some sixty, some thirty. [Not everyone understands the Kingdom or gives expression to it on the same level.]

24 Another parable put he forth unto them, saying, The kingdom of heaven is likened unto a man which sowed good seed in his field: **25** But while men slept, his enemy came and **sowed tares among the wheat**, and went his way. **26** But when the blade was sprung up, and brought forth fruit, then appeared the tares also. **27** So the servants of the householder came and said unto him, **Sir, didst not thou sow good seed in thy field? from whence then hath it tares? 28** He said unto them, An enemy hath done this. The servants said unto him, Wilt thou then that we go and gather them up? **29** But he said, Nay; lest while ye gather up the tares, ye root up also the wheat with them. **30 Let both grow together until the harvest: and in the time of harvest I will say to the reapers, Gather ye together first the tares, and bind them in bundles to burn them**: but gather the wheat into my barn. [The Kingdom of God will be inhabited by both good people and bad people. Because it is often difficult to tell them apart at times, there should be no attempt to pass laws to separate the good and the bad religious people. This is not about criminals who must be punished, but those who obey the laws of the Kingdom only to gain the benefits of conforming to a dominate culture.]

31 Another parable put he forth unto them, saying, The kingdom of heaven is like to a grain of mustard seed, which a man took, and sowed in his field: **32** Which indeed is **the least of all seeds: but when it is grown, it is the greatest among herbs, and becometh a tree,** so that the birds of the air come and lodge in the branches thereof. [Preaching and teaching just Words seem so pointless, but those Words if put into practice will totally take over a nation and its culture.]

33 Another parable spake he unto them; The kingdom of heaven is like unto **leaven**, which a woman took, and **hid** in three measures of meal, till the whole was leavened. [The Word of God is often operating within a nation without people being aware of God's hand in the affairs of a nation.] **34** All these things spake Jesus unto the multitude in parables; and without a parable spake he not unto them: **35** That it might be fulfilled which was spoken by the prophet, saying, I will open my mouth in parables; I will utter things which have been kept secret from the foundation of the world. **36** Then Jesus sent the multitude away, and went into the house: and his disciples came unto him, saying, Declare unto us the parable of the tares of the field. **37** He answered and said unto them, He that soweth the good seed is the Son of man; **38** The field is the world; **the good seed are the children of the kingdom**; but the **tares are the children of the wicked one**; **39** The **enemy that sowed them is the devil**; the **harvest is the end of the world;** [Be assured, the evil people in your midst will be punished and they will suffer eternal regret.] and the reapers are the angels. **40** As therefore the tares are gathered and burned in the fire; so shall it be in the end of this world. **41** The Son of man shall send forth his angels, and they shall gather out of his kingdom all things that offend, and them which do iniquity; **42** And shall cast them into a furnace of fire: **there shall be wailing** and gnashing of teeth. **43** **Then** shall the **righteous shine forth** [Christian's time will come—their frustration will come to an end.] as the sun in the kingdom of their Father. Who hath ears to hear, let him hear.

44 Again, the kingdom of heaven is like unto treasure hid in a field; the which when a man hath found, he hideth, and for joy thereof goeth and **selleth all that he hath**, and buyeth that field. [This is why very few preach the Kingdom of God.]

45 Again, the kingdom of heaven is like unto a merchant man, seeking goodly pearls: **46** Who, when he had found one pearl of great price, went and **sold all that he had,** and bought it. [Christians store up their wealth in heaven.]

47 Again, the kingdom of heaven is like unto a net, that was cast into the sea, and gathered of every kind: **48** Which, when it was full, they drew to shore, and sat down, and gathered the good into vessels, but cast the bad away. **49 So shall it be at the end of the world: the angels shall come forth, and sever the wicked from among the just, 50** And shall **cast them into the furnace of fire**: there shall be wailing and gnashing of teeth. **51** Jesus saith unto them, Have ye understood all these things? They say unto him, Yea, Lord. **52** Then said he unto them, Therefore every scribe *which is* instructed unto the kingdom of heaven is like unto a man *that is* an householder, which **bringeth forth out of his treasure *things* new and old.** [The idea of a civilization is new, but the contents of that Civilization are old.]

We live in an age of nationalism/globalism where ruling elites seek to impose by LAWS their goals and force everyone into the Kingdom of Satan.

*

American history, as I have been citing here, is the about the story of the coexistence of the wheat and the tares within the United States. This is the true reality in which people live out their daily lives. The concept of the Kingdom of God started with the Exodus and the formation of a nation unlike any other nation in history. The principles revealed in this founding are meant to teach us about God's rule upon this earth. The Kingdom of God as taught by Jesus was a continuation of God's progressive conquering of the earth. Ever since Satan subverted the mission of Adam and Eve, God has been working to teach and restore man's understanding of the true reality upon the earth. While we are not told everything, we do know that there was a race of 'entities' here before man. They had been completely conquered by Satan when he rebelled and took a third of the angels with him. After that, God sought a way to restore this earth to his control—not through force, Satan's way, but through His act of supreme love.

The Nation of Israel was to learn about the principles of God's rule through the trials and tribulations of the national and religious life. The nation was located in the center hub of the major world trading routes. Caravans of as many as 20,000 camels would pass through their land. People of all lands, cultures, religions, and races would challenge God's people in their different ways and ideas. They really were different. [If nothing else, the circumcision of all males was a mark that others could not avoid noticing. Public baths were common.

That was a ritual which placed God's 'brand' upon his people. Because temple prostitutes were part of pagan worship, circumcision certainly prevented the male from pretending to be one of pagans looking for a little temple 'worship'.] God placed His people at the very center of the commercial world. Today, people do not understand that it has always been difficult to be a follower of God in a secular and pagan world.

The true basis of power in the Nations of Judah and Israel were expressed in the following:

Zechariah 4:5. Then the angel that talked with me answered and said unto me, Knowest thou not what these be? And I said, No, my lord. **6** Then he answered and spake unto me, saying, This *is* the word of the LORD unto Zerubbabel, saying, **Not by might, nor by power, but by my spirit**, saith the LORD of hosts.

This is one of the most difficult principles for anyone who is living within the Kingdom of God. Paul teaches that God's people operate within a different realm than those considered ordinary. Faith in God's Laws and His Word moves mountains:

Hebrew 11:6. But **without faith *it is* impossible** to please *him*: for he that cometh to God must believe that he is, and *that* **he is a rewarder of them that diligently seek him. 7** By faith Noah, being warned of God of things not seen as yet, moved with fear, prepared an ark to the saving of his house; by the which he condemned the world, and became heir of the righteousness which is by faith. **8** By faith Abraham, when he was called to go out into a place which he should after receive for an inheritance, obeyed; and he went out, not knowing whither he went. **9** By faith he sojourned in the land of promise, as *in* a strange country, dwelling in tabernacles with Isaac and Jacob, the heirs with him of the same promise: **10 For he looked for a city which hath foundations, whose builder and maker *is* God.**

The Kingdom of God operates on the same principles as established throughout the Old Testament. Because the Satanic way of thought so dominated the whole world from Adam to the time of Jesus, when Jesus revealed the coming of His Kingdom, most could not understand what it would be. "Jesus, where is your army?" The post-Exodus founding of God's nation began a new history that was designed to over-write other versions of history. "For Israel had begun its history as a nation summoned by God's grace to be his people, to serve him alone and to obey his covenant law. The notion of a people of god, called to live under the rule of God, begun just here, and with it the notion of the Kingdom of God."[201] The nation of Israel was promised a special relationship with the God of History. **However, this relationship was conditional. The calling was unconditional, but the relationship depended upon obedience to God's Laws.**

*

The early days of the nation started out with a very unusual form of existence. "Here we see the clans maintaining a precarious existence, surrounded by foes but without government, central authority, or state organization of any sort. [In times of danger, God would raise up a special leader to repel any foreign invader.] He would rally the surrounding clans and deal with the foe. While his victories no doubt gained him prestige, he was in no sense a king. His authority was neither absolute over all Israel nor permanent; in no case was it hereditary. The battle strength of the judge was the voluntary levy of the clans; he had no standing army, no court, no administrative machinery whatever."[202] This situation is very close to how Jesus expected the Kingdom of God to operate. The early Christians were living within Israel that was under the rule of Rome—Israel contained a large number of people who wanted to be in rebellion against the nation's domination by a pagan empire. When Christians travelled outside of the province of Israel, Christians were confronted with a vast bureaucratic empire. Rome ruled by an iron and brutal fist. The very idea of the Kingdom of God in operation seemed disconnected from reality.

There was another aspect about the founding of the Nation of Israel. Their history started with their escape from Exodus. Then after spending 40 years wandering in the Desert, upon settling in, they became a nation of farmers. Just like the Kingdom of God, the nation of Israel was designed for communities, farmers, and families. It is interesting that Israel attempted to live the type of life that God had ordained for them. "[Israel] did not organize a state or make any move to do so. Specifically, she did not imitate the city-state pattern of Canaan. Nor was this an accident. On the contrary, the idea of monarchy was consciously rejected. This is illustrated in the words with which stout Gideon spurned a

---

[201] Bright. P. 28.
[202] Bright. P. 31.

crown: **"I will not rule over you, and my son will not rule you; the Lord will rule over you"** (Judge. 8:23). It echoes in the fable told by Jotham (Judg. 9:7-21), **which makes it plain that only a worthless bramble of a man, who had no useful employment, would aspire to be a king."**[203] (Emphasis added.)

This ideal of having no standing army or a king was the pattern for the Kingdom of God. God was to be the king of Israel. However, that meant the people would have to serve and obey God. Remember, the nation of Israel was founded at the crossroads of the commercial trade routes. The intention of God was that the nation of Israel was to be a witness to the nature of the true reality. The merchants of the world would be passing through Israel. They did not have to go outside their borders in order to be a witness to the truth: just live the truth and become a beacon of truth. So what happened? Many of the Israelites discovered there was more money to be made from catering to the merchants than farming. Many became rich and rich people worry about one thing: losing their riches. Under the old system of farming, the people vowed to depend upon God to be their protector. That does not work if you decide to serve riches rather than man. So what happened?

The people of Israel decided that they wanted a nation like all the other nations in the world. Depending upon God to preserve His people only on condition of their obedience was just too risky: the price was just too high. The people came to their leader Samuel and the following conversation took place:

I Samuel 8:5. And said unto him, Behold, thou art old, and thy sons walk not in thy ways: **now make us a king to judge us like all the nations. 6** But the thing displeased Samuel, when they said, Give us a king to judge us. And Samuel prayed unto the LORD. **7** And the LORD said unto Samuel, Hearken unto the voice of the people in all that they say unto thee: for they have not rejected thee, but **they have rejected me, that I should not reign over them. 8** According to all the works which they have done since the day that I brought them up out of Egypt even unto this day, wherewith they have forsaken me, and served other gods, so do they also unto thee. **9** Now therefore hearken unto their voice: howbeit yet protest solemnly unto them, and shew them the manner of the king that shall reign over them.

---

[203] Bright. P. 32.

10 And Samuel told all the words of the LORD unto the people that asked of him a king. **11** And he said, **This will be the manner of the king that shall reign over you:** He will take your sons, and appoint *them* for himself, for his chariots, and *to be* his horsemen; and *some* shall run before his chariots. **12** And he will appoint him captains over thousands, and captains over fifties; and *will set them* to ear his ground, and to reap his harvest, and to make his instruments of war, and instruments of his chariots. **13** And he will take your daughters *to be* confectionaries, and *to be* cooks, and *to be* bakers. **14** And he will take your fields, and your vineyards, and your oliveyards, *even* the best *of them*, and give *them* to his servants. **15** And he will take the tenth of your seed, and of your vineyards, and give to his officers, and to his servants. **16** And he will take your menservants, and your maidservants, and your goodliest young men, and your asses, and put *them* to his work. **17** He will take the tenth of your sheep: and ye shall be his servants. [God warned the Nation of Israel that secular governments will end up exploiting the people they are to serve.] **18** And ye shall cry out in that day because of your king which ye shall have chosen you; and the LORD will not hear you in that day.

19 Nevertheless the people refused to obey the voice of Samuel; and they said, Nay; but we will have a king over us; **20** That **we also may be like all the nations**; and that our king may judge us, and **go out before us, and fight our battles**.

The Nation of Israel and the Kingdom of God followed similar patterns of decline. During the thousand years between the fall of Rome and the Protestant Reformation was an era called Christendom, or the Age of Faith. Some have called it the Dark Ages because nothing seemed to happen. People lived contented lives and there were universal laws that brought a new kind of order to the world. Yes, the tares and the wheat were growing together during this time, but the Church did all it could to limit the power of the tares and their influence over mankind. What historians have done is to write history from the 'tares' point of view. The Christian families, communities, and their local parishes do not make for exciting reading: "Let's focus on the corruption inside the Vatican." Now that makes for tabloid style history.

*

Remember, from the very first, Jesus set about teaching about the true nature of God's Kingdom and those that serve Him in that Kingdom.

Matthew 5:1. And seeing the multitudes, he went up into a mountain: and when he was set, his disciples came unto him: **2** And he opened his mouth, and taught them, saying, **3 Blessed** *are* **the poor** in spirit: for theirs is the kingdom of heaven. **4 Blessed** *are* **they that mourn**: for they shall be comforted. **5 Blessed** *are* **the meek**: for they shall inherit the earth. **6 Blessed** *are* **they which do hunger and thirst** after righteousness: for they shall be filled. **7 Blessed** *are* **the merciful:** for they shall obtain mercy. **8 Blessed** *are* **the pure in heart**: for they shall see God. **9 Blessed** *are* **the peacemakers**: for they shall be called the children of God. **10 Blessed** *are* **they which are persecuted** for righteousness' sake: for theirs is the kingdom of heaven. **11 Blessed are ye, when** *men* **shall revile you**, and persecute *you*, and shall say all manner of evil against you falsely, for my sake. **12** Rejoice, and be exceeding glad: for great *is* your reward in heaven: for so persecuted they the prophets which were before you.

13 Ye are the salt of the earth: but if the salt have lost his savour, wherewith shall it be salted? it is thenceforth good for nothing, but to be cast out, and to be trodden under foot of men. **14** Ye are the light of the world. A city that is set on an hill cannot be hid. **15** Neither do men light a candle, and put it under a bushel, but on a candlestick; and it giveth light unto all that are in the house. **16 Let your light so shine before men, that they may see your good works,** and glorify your Father which is in heaven.

Jesus tells everyone what type of person it takes to proclaim the Kingdom of God upon the earth. His people come across as a bunch of outcasts and losers. They are to be like the planned Kingdom of Israel of the Old Testament. They are to live a life that reflects the knowledge of God and His character. But who wants to live the life of a common farmer who finds his joy in serving God and his neighbors? Just as the Nation of Israel wanted to become a great nation, so the Reformation in its revolt against Christendom, made way for the modern Nation States. Christendom survived awhile but with reduced influence under the name of Western Civilization. But the modern Nation/State was on the rise. The Kingdom of God was replaced by the Church and it secular methods of serving God. The Church was content to let a professional class serve God while the church members were freed to purse a life of comfort and riches—much like the people in the time of Samuel who became quite wealthy through Israel's becoming a commercial empire. Yes, we read about David and Solomon and their mighty military victories, but the price was high. Israel was no longer a light unto the nations, but a source of wealth. The riches of Solomon are described as insurmountable: much like America's mega cathedral churches.

The story of the United States is certainly the story of the tares and the wheat uniting together to form a great nation: the American Global Empire created the riches of Babylon. Because Americans have been taught to think of the American Church as the high point of Christianity, I want to return for a bit to the times when the new Nation/States were at war with the remains of Christendom. There is no better example of this than Henry VIII of England. We all know about his many wives, but few know about his war upon the community of saints who still served God as in the days of Christendom. The War upon Christendom does not make the history books. The Nation/State, from Henry VIII and on, writes the official history of secular man and his modern civilization and all of its 'accomplishments.'

So what did Henry VIII do to kill Christendom and the people that lived under the principles of the Kingdom of God? "In the Middle Ages, in addition to the many charitable institutions established and endowed by the Gilds, England was studded with monasteries and religious houses, all centres for the relief of suffering humanity. Much land had been given or bequeathed to them by the rich who were deeply impressed with the social teachings of the Church, viz., that the wealthy did not own their wealth absolutely, but rather held it in trust as the administrators of God who gave it. Over seven hundred and fifty medieval hospitals are known to have existed in England. Moreover, there were many leper-houses; at one time they numbered two hundred.

"There were, in addition, many rest-houses for wayfarers and pilgrims, homes for the aged, feeble and destitute. All these were conducted under the direction of the monasteries or religious. Attached to the monasteries were also the schools. Such was Catholic England down to the time of that royal tyrant, Henry VIII."[204] Under Christendom, Christians, who believed in living the Kingdom of God lifestyle, functioned as a total education and welfare culture. This system operated outside of the Government and without the need for tax money. So, why did the English government destroy such a system? In short, they looted it for its wealth and property. Also, in time, the people came to look to the government and not to the church for aid and comfort. The following is one

---

[204] R. S. Devante. The Failure of Individualism: A Documented Essay. Greenwood Press. 1948. P. 268.

description of the consequences of the pillaging of the Christian welfare organizations:

"In the general scramble of the 'Terror' under Henry the Eighth, and of the *anarchy* in the days of Edward the Sixth ... the monasteries were plundered even to their very pots and pans. The almshouses in which old men and women were fed and clothed were robbed to the last pound, the poor alms folk being turned out in the cold at an hour's warning to beg their bread. The splendid hospitals for the sick and needy, sometimes magnificently provide with nurses and chaplains, whose very *raison d'etre* was that they were to look after and care for those who were past caring for themselves, these were stripped of all their belongings, the inmates sent out to hobble into some convenient dry ditch to lie down and die in, or crawl into some barn of hovel, there to be tended, not without fear of consequences, by some kindly man or woman, who could not bear to see a suffering fellow-creature drop down and die at their own door-posts."[205]

The warning God gave to the people who wanted to be ruled by a King has proved true over and over in history. Governments are to be limited and the last thing any people want for their government is a standing army and the power to tax to support the bureaucracy of the King and his administrators. When people are allowed to govern themselves and take care of their neighbors, the need for a powerful government is eliminated. When a powerful, centralized government is formed, the need for a people to behave in a moral manner, to obey the Laws of God, and the need to be dependent upon the government of God are eliminated.

The Bible describes what happens when the Kingdom of God is in operation. The Bible states this about the coming of Jesus, the Messiah, and His Kingdom:

Isaiah 9:6. For unto us a child is born, unto us a son is given: and **the government** shall be upon his shoulder: and his name shall be called Wonderful, Counsellor, The mighty God, The everlasting Father, The Prince of Peace. **7** Of **the increase of** *his* **government** and peace *there shall be* no end, upon the throne of David, and upon his kingdom, to order it, and to establish it with judgment and with justice from henceforth even for ever. The zeal of the LORD of hosts will perform this.

---

[205] Devane. P. 269.

The following is the section of the Bible Jesus quoted when announcing the start of his ministry.

Isaiah 61:1. The Spirit of the Lord GOD *is* upon me; because the LORD hath anointed me to preach good tidings unto the meek; he hath sent me to bind up the brokenhearted, **to proclaim liberty** to the captives, and the opening of the prison to *them that are* bound; **2** To proclaim the acceptable year of the LORD, and the day of vengeance of our God; to comfort all that mourn; **3** To appoint unto them that mourn in Zion, to give unto them beauty for ashes, the oil of joy for mourning, the garment of praise for the spirit of heaviness; that **they might be called trees of righteousness**, the planting of the LORD, that he might be glorified.

4 And **they shall build the old wastes, they shall raise up the former desolations, and they shall repair the waste cities, the desolations of many generations. 5** And strangers shall stand and feed your flocks, and the sons of the alien *shall be* your plowmen and your vinedressers. **6** But **ye shall be named the Priests of the LORD**: *men* **shall call you the Ministers of our God**: ye shall eat the riches of the Gentiles, and in their glory shall ye boast yourselves.

Those who lived during the Age of Christendom attempted to live under the government of reality established by the Kingdom of God upon this earth. Men were not perfect and there were *tares* [the Vatican] sprinkled amongst the wheat. Historical narratives focus on the 'tares' to discredit the whole era and to support the need for a strong government to keep order. Again, back to the Old Testament, God warned that Satan would operate within any powerful government established in place of God's Kingdom and his principles of rule. Another thing rarely written about is this: Satan is working within history to promote his agenda. Sometimes he leaves his fingerprints. Apparently random events are not as random as thought. Look for who profits from some event. A good example is the Reformation and what led up to that event. I would maintain that there was a Satanic fingerprint in the Black Plague in Europe in the years 1347-1351. Around 75-200 million Europeans died during those years--about one third of the population.

This mass death weakened the Church. God was expected to protect his people. Good people along with bad people died. Many sought some assurance of salvation that was not connected to the Bible and the Church. Also, the leaders of society suffered like everyone else. Plagues of such a size tend to cancel out cultural traditions and new traditions are built up. I believe that when Europe was finally repopulated, there was a political and social blank slate. It was during this time that Martin Luther instigated the Protestant Reformation. This is one of those events that has been so politicized that the real reformation is overlooked. The Catholic Church lost much of its power. The Protestant Church did not seek to take that power to itself. The individual churches were considered the real sources of power. But that power could only be expressed locally. The Churches were incapable of defeating the rising tide of Finance Capitalism, Patriotic Nationalism, and Corporate Statism. All three were powerful movements that could create their own laws and cultures. In a sense, several New World Orders were created to supplant the Age of Christendom. This is important because it reveals that Satan is at War against the Kingdom of God and the Laws of God. Events in history reveal this war. History books are written on the thesis that 'stuff happens.' No. There are powers working behind to create 'stuff' in order to bring in some form of Satanic World Order.

Henry VIII is often regarded as some kind of 'hero' for bringing Protestantism to England. In his constant need for more money, he decimated the poor people in England. Devane cites H. B. Gibbon: "'Before the close of his reign the laboring classes became impoverished, and the tenant framers were ruined with high rents exacted by the new nobility.' With the spoliation of the Church and the amassing of wealth in the hands of supporters of the Reformation there opens up the *era* of Money and Power."[206] Yes, once the elites were freed from the Laws of God and the Laws of Christendom, they set up systems to steal from the middle and lower classes. American Church people have been totally brainwashed when it comes to the Reformation and how Christens are free today because of Martin Luther. The Middle Ages was an egalitarian and rural culture. Work till you drop Capitalism had not yet been invented: Most people could earn enough working just two days a week. The Church and local cultures celebrated around 200 holidays a year.

Every dictator knows, you cannot control contented people. That is why the Reformation and the resulting 'religious' wars were needed to bring

---

[206] Devane. P. 272.

discontent to the lands of Europe. Harold Laski wrote: "It created a solid party in favour of maintaining the new order of things. It facilitated the building up of great estates, and, hence, the progress of the enclosure movement. It stimulated the accumulation of capital, and there by, the numbers of men prepared to risk their surplus wealth in the new commercial adventures. There can be little doubt that the policy represented by the Reformation is, psychologically, the expression of nothing so much as the breakdown of medieval economic order."[207] The above represents one of the things that Satan had in mind when he helped start the Reformation. This is one reason anti-Christians helped Luther—even to the printing of Luther's tracts. Princes helped hide Luther from those who wished him harm. It is important to remember the ultimate effects of the Reformation: "The Reformation, not only in England but in the other Protestant countries, made the rich richer, the poor poorer. Dollinger says that 'The depression, detriment, and spoliation of the lower classes have everywhere followed in the revolutionary change called the Reformation.'"[208]

The equality attained during the Age of Christendom was probably like no other time in history. One reason is that the rich gave their wealth when they died to organizations to help the poor. Unlike today, the money did not go to an expensive bureaucracy where few dollars actually reach the poor. The money went to people who viewed life in the Kingdom of God as one of service, not the attainment of riches. The Reformation brought about more than a change of financial distribution, the Reformation installed a new Civilization upon the Western World. A world where tyrants, capitalists, bankers, and religious hucksters could feel at home. Bad men do not feel at home in a Christian culture. Civilizations are designed to be comfort zones. It works in both ways; true Christians feel comfortable in the Kingdom of God. Civilizations are about building a home that reflects the values of the people who choose to live in that home.

*

I cannot emphasize enough that the Reformation was a lot more than just an internal dispute between the Catholics and the Protestants. That was a cover story to hide the fact that a war of civilizations was underway. Even the political

---

[207] Devane. P. 272-273.
[208] Devane. P. 273.

wars were called 'religious' wars. Religion was another excuse to fight another nation or group: it was only the political powers that profited from such wars. It is the old fight for 'God and Country' scam. That is why so much of written history is sponsored by governments or corporations. Alternative historical writings often have to be self-published. Every elitists group seeks to push their view of reality upon a naïve public. That is why the total control of all education is so vital for every government and every business culture. I once attempted to get a job at a Christian school. I discovered that the state government had first to certify every teacher in the state, regardless of whether it was public or private. Of course, like everything, it is against 'the law' to have unauthorized teachers relating any knowledge to any student.

The Reformation imposed a new Civilization upon England, and it was not Christendom. "The squires, twenty years after Henry's death, had come to possess, through the ruin of religion, some like *half* of the land of England. With the rapidity of a fungus growth the new wealth spread over the desolation of the land. The newly enriched captured both the Universities, all the Courts of Justice, most of the public schools. They won their great civil war against the Crown. In little more than a century after Henry's folly they had established themselves in the place of what had once been the Monarchy and central government of England. The impoverished Crown resisted in vain; they killed one embarrassed King—Charles—and they set up his son Charles II, as an insufficiently salaried puppet. Since their victory over the Crown they and the capitalists who had sprung from their avarice and their philosophy, and largely from their very loins, have been completely masters of England."[209] [Hilaire Belloc, *Europe and the Faith.*]

The England that emerged was actually the Kingdom of Satan wearing an Anglican State Church mask. England's philosophers, its writers, its political leaders, its educators, its bankers, its generals, and its armies were not Christian. There were Christians in the lower classes and ironically, England did export Christianity to the rest of the world through its massive army of missionaries. They operated under the protection of England's global army and navy. Many of these missionaries were quite successful in bringing the Gospel and English Civilization to the rest of the world. The large number of Bible Translators not

---

[209] Devane. P. 274.

only translated the Bible into multiple languages, but these translators often had to create alphabets so they could translate the Biblical texts. The Bible they brought to the people was more important than their British traditions that were part of their message. However, Western Capitalism became part of the Gospel message. That is one reason the British military supported the missionaries. The Gospel message made it easier to control the native populations.

*

Growing up in an American Fundamentalist Church, we celebrated Reformation Sunday every year. Besides the usual celebration of Easter, Thanksgiving, and Christmas, the patriotic holidays were also important. America was said to be the greatest Christian nation in the history of the world: we celebrated that. We thanked God for all of the material benefits that had resulted when a nation 'serves' God. The blessings of God had come to mean materialism in most people's eyes. However, the Bible reveals a different reality:

Psalm 106:15. And he [God] **gave them their request**; but **sent leanness into their soul.**

While the bad Popes make the news and the movies, there are Popes who had the wisdom a Pope should have. Pope Leo XIII [Served 1878-1903] said the following:

"Public institutions and the very laws have set aside the ancient religion. Hence, by degrees it has come to pass that working men have been surrendered isolated and helpless to the hard-heartedness of employers and the greed of unchecked competition. This mischief has been increased by rapacious usury, which, although more once condemned by the Church, is nevertheless, under a different guise, but with the injustice, still practiced by covetous and grasping men. To this must be added that the hiring of labour and all manner of trade are concentrated in the hands of the comparatively few; so that a small number of very rich men has been able to lay upon the teeming masses of the laboring poor a yoke little better than slavery itself."[210] This form of White slavery has been almost totally erased from the textbooks.

---

[210] Devane. P. 275-276.

Pope Leo XIII served during that time between the American Civil War and WWI. This was the age when the Scientific/Financial/Corporate world attained supremacy over the manufacture of a new form of Civilization. A culture of individualism and business came to dominate the thinking of everyone. Every person growing up was expected to have some career in mind or at least one he could tell others who asked. The Work/Consume environment was the nature of everyone's life: you work during the day and come home to consume some product or some form of entertainment. This is important because the American Church had to adjust its doctrines so that the members could feel religious both as a worker and a consumer. The Christian no longer thought in terms of the Kingdom of God and seeking ways to serve others with his given talents, but in terms of finding a niche in life where a person could enjoy the American Way of Life and still feel like a real Christian.

While people still hoped that there was a heaven above, the goals of life for most were to develop some form of heaven on this earth. It was called by some, the Age of Scientific Progress. Progress previously had been associated with Evolution: some failed and some succeeded, i.e. some became poor and some became rich. That is just how Evolution worked. However, Americans during this age wanted to takeover Evolution and apply their knowledge to the creating a more perfect Union and lifestyle. The poor and failures were consoled with the fact that a better world was coming in which everyone could share the spoils of global exploitation. Political and Corporate Empires could so manipulate the laws of Nature and Politics that everyone could enjoy the blessings of personal enjoyment in a world of plenty. There was no longer a need for anyone to even think about serving others as a new form of government was in the process of creating where everyone, even the poorest, could feel that life was good.

Of course, the Laws of the Bible were pictured as being totally opposed to the Modern World. There were parts of the Bible that could be applied to one's personal and private life, but such laws should be kept in one's personal closet. After all, there are so many options and laws in life, it is best if everyone have both an acceptable public and a private life of their choice. In private, a Christian could practice his Biblical beliefs, but when in public and when on the job, a person was expected to behave in a way that is acceptable to everyone. Every Corporation is founded upon certain ethical concerns, and a successful business requires that everyone adopt those principle when on the job. In the

Corporation, everyone is to become as one, serving the same goals. [Just like those living under Nimrod and His Tower of Babel.]

The famous economic historian, R. H. Tawney, wrote: "Capitalism in the sense of great individual undertakings, involving the control of large financial resources, and yielding riches to their masters as a result of speculation, money-lending, commercial enterprise, buccaneering, and war, is as old as history. Capitalism, as an economic system, resting on the organization of legally free wage-earners, for the purpose of pecuniary profit, by the owner of capital or this agents, and **setting its stamp on every aspect of society, is a modern phenomenon.**"[211] (Emphasis added.) Yes, Capitalism does leave 'its stamp on every aspect of society' used to be thought of as a religion. A nation's beliefs about their 'god' permeates into every aspect of daily and political life. And when beliefs become interwoven with a perceived reality, then everyone in that order comes to believe that their life is part of the natural world, and that it is also the best of all possible worlds. Not perfect, just the best. The critics of that order are perceived as those who did not get their fair share and are attacking the hand that did not feed them what they deserved—at least in their own eyes.

The political writer, Harold Laski, by no means a Biblicist scholar, wrote the following about what really happened because of the Reformation:

"Broadly, we may say that the contribution of the sixteenth century is the destruction of ecclesiastical authority in the economic sphere. This enables property relations to develop unhampered by theological considerations. There emerged from this a secular State which sought, and found, its mission upon the basis that it replace the Church as the guardian of social and well-being. It builds its own morality, based upon utility, to suit its new prestige."[212] [*The Rise of European* Liberalism] R.H. Tawney added this insight: "As a result of the Reformation the relations previously existing between the Church and the State had been almost exactly reversed. In the Middle Ages the former had been at least in theory, the ultimate authority on questions of public and private morality, while the latter was the police-officer which enforced its decrees. **In the sixteenth century, the Church became the ecclesiastical department of the State, and religion was used to lend a moral sanction to secular social policy.**"[213] [Forward. *The Protestant Ethic and the Spirit of Capitalism.*] (Emphasis added.)

---

[211] Devane. P. 276.
[212] Devane. P. 277.
[213] Devane. P. 277-278.

One minister of this age recognized the new reality in which the Protestant Church was forced to accept. The Rev. W. Cunningham stated that the new rules of business were based upon expediency. Efficiency became the standard by which the actions could be evaluated. "...Christian moralists were no longer able to give positive teaching as to what was right or wrong; they were contented to appeal to sentiments which practical men regarded as merely fanciful."[214] [*The Growth of English Industry During the Early and Middle Ages.*] During the Reformation era, there was some famous preachers such as Zwingli and Calvin. Commercial morality was viewed as more in touch with the real world. Christian ideals of business morality were seen as only applicable to ancient times. Dr. Cunningham stated, "...when the leaders of the Calvinist and Zwinglian parties explained away the scriptural prohibitions no firm ground was available for reproving any usurious practices that were permitted by civil or municipal law...."[215]

The Reformers recognized that the world was heading in a direction over which they had no control. If the leaders of the Reformation opposed the new Nation/States and the business order that they were promoting, the Church would fall by the wayside. The Reformation would be consigned to where all defeated nations go to die. With the rise of Finance Capitalism, the goals of life changed from attaining a good life of service under Biblical principles to the accumulation of wealth. The Church either supported this new Statist/Commercial order or faced the total the end of Biblical Christianity.

*

The following debate took place in Moscow in the midst of the Cold War. Nixon felt constrained to defend the American Way of Life as being superior to Communism. It is important to understand that America believed its greatness was based upon its technology. Some have called it the Great Kitchen Debate.

The Kitchen Debate - transcript 24 July 1959 Vice President Richard Nixon and Soviet Premier Nikita Khrushchev U.S. Embassy, Moscow, Soviet Union [Both men enter kitchen in the American exhibit.]

---

[214] Devane. P. 278.
[215] Devane. P. 279.

Nixon: **I want to show you this kitchen.** It is like those of our houses in California. [Nixon points to dishwasher.]

Khrushchev: We have such things.

Nixon: This is our newest model. This is the kind which is built in thousands of units for direct installations in the houses. In America, we like to make life easier for women...

Khrushchev: Your capitalistic attitude toward women does not occur under Communism.

Nixon: I think that this attitude towards women is universal. What we want to do, is make life more easy for our housewives.....

Nixon: This house can be bought for $14,000, and most American [veterans from World War II] can buy a home in the bracket of $10,000 to $15,000. Let me give you an example that you can appreciate. Our steel workers as you know, are now on strike. But any steel worker could buy this house. They earn $3 an hour. This house costs about $100 a month to buy on a contract running 25 to 30 years.

Khrushchev: We have steel workers and peasants who can afford to spend $14,000 for a house. Your American houses are built to last only 20 years so builders could sell new houses at the end. We build firmly. We build for our children and grandchildren.

Nixon: American houses last for more than 20 years, but, even so, after twenty years, many Americans want a new house or a new kitchen. Their kitchen is obsolete by that time....**The American system is designed to take advantage of new inventions and new techniques.**

Khrushchev: This theory does not hold water. Some things never get out of date-- houses, for instance, and furniture, furnishings--perhaps--but not houses. I have read much about America and American houses, and I do not think that this is exhibit and what you say is strictly accurate. Nixon: Well, um... Khrushchev: I hope I have not insulted you.

Nixon: I have been insulted by experts. Everything we say [on the other hand] is in good humor. Always speak frankly.

Khrushchev: The Americans have created their own image of the Soviet man. But he is not as you think. You think the Russian people will be dumbfounded to see these things, but the fact is that newly built Russian houses have all this equipment right now.

Nixon: Yes, but...

Khrushchev: In Russia, all you have to do to get a house is to be born in the Soviet Union. You are entitled to housing...In America, if you don't have a dollar you have a right to choose between sleeping in a house or on the pavement. Yet you say we are the slave to Communism.

Nixon: I appreciate that you are very articulate and energetic...

Khrushchev: Energetic is not the same thing as wise.

Nixon: If you were in the Senate, we would call you a filibusterer! You--[Khrushchev interrupts]--do all the talking and don't let anyone else talk. This exhibit was not designed to astound but to interest. Diversity, the right to choose, the fact that we have 1,000 builders building 1,000 different houses is the most important thing. We don't have one decision made at the top by one government official. This is the difference.

Khrushchev: On politics, we will never agree with you. For instance, Mikoyan likes very peppery soup. I do not. But this does not mean that we do not get along.

Nixon: You can learn from us, and we can learn from you. There must be a free exchange. Let the people choose the kind of house, the kind of soup, the kind of ideas that they want. [Translation lost as both men enter the television recording studio.]

Khrushchev: [In jest] You look very angry, as if you want to fight me. Are you still angry?

Nixon: [in jest] That's right!

Khrushchev:...and Nixon was once a lawyer? Now he's nervous.

Nixon: Oh yes, [Nixon chuckling] he still is [a lawyer].

Other Russian speaker: Tell us, please, what are your general impressions of the exhibit?

Khrushchev: It's clear to me that the construction workers didn't manage to finish their work and the exhibit still is not put in order...This is what America is capable of, and how long has she existed? 300 years? 150 years of independence and this is her level. We haven't quite reached 42 years, and in another 7 years, we'll be at the level of America, and after that we'll go farther. As we pass you by, we'll wave "hi" to you, and then if you want, we'll stop and say, "please come along behind us." ...If you want to live under capitalism, go ahead, that's your question, an internal matter, it doesn't concern us. We can feel sorry for you, but really, you wouldn't understand. We've already seen how you understand things.

Other U.S speaker: Mr. Vice President, from what you have seen of our exhibition, how do you think it's going to impress the people of the Soviet Union?

Nixon: It's a very effective exhibit, and it's one that will cause a great deal of interest. I might say that this morning I, very early in the morning, went down to visit a market, where the farmers from various outskirts of the city bring in their items to sell. I can only say that there was a great deal of interest among these people, who were workers and farmers, etc... I would imagine that the exhibition from that standpoint would, therefore, be a considerable success. As far as Mr Khrushchev's comments just now, they are in the tradition we learned to expect from him of speaking extemporaneously and frankly whenever he has an opportunity. I can only say that if this competition which you have described so effectively, in which you plan to outstrip us, particularly **in the production of consumer goods**...If this competition is to do the best for both of our peoples and for people everywhere, there must be a free exchange of ideas. There are some instances where you may be ahead of us--for example in the development of the thrust of your rockets for the investigation of outer space. There may be some instances, for example, color television, where we're ahead of you. But in order for both of us benefit...

Khrushchev: [interrupting] No, in rockets we've passed you by, and in the technology...

Nixon: [continuing to talk] You see, you never concede anything.

Khrushchev: We always knew that Americans were smart people. Stupid people could not have risen to the economic level that they've reached. But as you know, "we don't beat flies with our nostrils!" In 42 years we've made progress.

Nixon: You must not be afraid of ideas.

Khrushchev: We're saying it is you who must not be afraid of ideas. We're not afraid of anything....

Nixon: Well, then, let's have more exchange of them. We all agree on that, right? Khrushchev: Good. [Khrushchev turns to translator and asks:] Now, what did I agree on?

Nixon: [interrupts] Now, let's go look at our pictures.

Khrushchev: Yes, I agree. But first I want to clarify what I'm agreeing on. Don't I have that right? I know that I'm dealing with a very good lawyer. Therefore, I want to be unwavering in my miner's girth, so our miners will say, "He's ours and he doesn't give in!"

Nixon: No question about that.

Khrushchev: You're a lawyer of Capitalism, I'm a lawyer for Communism. Let's kiss.

Nixon: All that I can say, from the way you talk and the way you dominate the conversation, you would have made a good lawyer yourself. What I mean is this: Here you can see the type of tape which will transmit this very conversation immediately, and this indicates the possibilities of increasing communication. And this increase in communication, will teach us some things, and you some things, too. Because, after all, you don't know everything.

Khrushchev: If I don't know everything, then you know absolutely nothing about Communism, except for fear! But now the dispute will be on an unequal basis. The apparatus is yours, and you speak English, while I speak Russian. Your words are taped and will be shown and heard. What I say to you about science won't be translated, and so your people won't hear it. These aren't equal conditions.

Nixon: There isn't a day that goes by in the United States when we can't read everything that you say in the Soviet Union...And, I can assure you, never make a statement here that you don't think we read in the United States.

Khrushchev: If that's the way it is, I'm holding you to it. Give me your word...I want you, the Vice President, to give me your word that my speech will also be taped in English. Will it be?

Nixon: Certainly it will be. And by the same token, everything that I say will be recorded and translated and will be carried all over the Soviet Union. That's a fair bargain. [Both men shake hands and walk off stage, still talking.][216]

This debate happened when I was a young teen. I read it through the eyes of a youth who had been educated in government schools. The fact that the United States could produce a better kitchen with modern appliances was seen as America being superior to the Russians. There was no mention of Atheistic Communism versus a form 'Christianity' in the United States. American was great because it could produce more consumer goods and modern kitchens available to everyone. The production of time-saving consumer goods was touted as the goal of a good government. In fact, from the very beginning, the pursuit of happiness in the United States has meant the accumulation of wealth and the **consumption** of **consumer** goods. To justify America's material consumption, 'things' were labelled Blessings from God. Consumption of God's 'gifts' replaced the using of one's God-given talents to serve Him and other people. This bait and switch is why America is called a 'Christian Nation.'

The American Church teaches the doctrines of materialism and individual fulfillment as the real Kingdom of God. That is why the church is incapable of opposing the evils of this age. As a result, in 2023, evil prospers and God is nowhere to be seen.

Soli Deo Gloria

---

[216] https://www.cia.gov/readingroom/docs/1959-07-24.pdf